THE REIGN OF
WONDER

THE REIGN OF WONDER

NAIVETY AND REALITY IN AMERICAN LITERATURE

BY

TONY TANNER

Fellow of King's College, Cambridge

CAMBRIDGE
AT THE UNIVERSITY PRESS
1965

PUBLISHED BY

THE SYNDICS OF THE CAMBRIDGE UNIVERSITY PRESS

Bentley House, 200 Euston Road, London, N.W.1
American Branch: 32 East 57th Street, New York, N.Y. 10022
West African Office: P.O. Box 33, Ibadan, Nigeria

CAMBRIDGE UNIVERSITY PRESS

1965

Library of Congress Catalogue Card Number: 65-15304

*Printed in Great Britain by Spottiswoode, Ballantyne & Co. Ltd.,
London and Colchester*

To

THOM GUNN

And as the moon rose higher the inessential houses began to melt away until gradually I became aware of the old island that flowered once for Dutch sailors' eyes—a fresh, green breast of the new world . . . for a transitory enchanted moment man must have held his breath in the presence of this continent, compelled into an aesthetic contemplation he neither understood nor desired, face to face for the last time in history with something commensurate to his capacity for wonder.

F. SCOTT FITZGERALD, *The Great Gatsby*

CONTENTS

ACKNOWLEDGEMENTS

I would like to take this opportunity to express my gratitude to the Commonwealth Fund for awarding me a Harkness Fellowship which enabled me to commence my American studies, and to the American Council of Learned Studies for awarding me a grant to return to America and complete this work. In addition I would like to acknowledge here my inestimable debt to two of my teachers at Cambridge—the late A. P. Rossiter and Professor Philip Brockbank. I would also like to express my thanks to Professor David Daiches and Professor Richard Blackmur who read various parts of the manuscript and offered most helpful suggestions and corrective comments. I also profited from many conversations with Professor Richard Bridgman and my colleague Dr John Broadbent, and certain suggestions about re-organizing my material offered by Professor Douglas Grant. I am also most grateful to the Mark Twain Estate for allowing me to quote from hitherto unpublished material, and I am much in the debt of Mr Frederick Anderson who proved such a constant, valuable and willing aid in his capacity as librarian of the Mark Twain papers in Berkeley. Above all I must express a great debt to Professor Henry Nash Smith who, by his own work, his advice, and his example, both aided the inception of this work and encouraged its completion. Finally I wish to thank Marcia Albright for reading the proofs with an intelligence and care which were invaluable. The errors in this book are, of course, my own; but if it contains any material of interest much of the credit must go to these people and I would consider myself well rewarded if they would be willing to acknowledge the fact.

Chapter 16 was previously printed in a slightly different form in *Essays and Studies 1963*, published by John Murray Limited for the English Association. The poems by William Carlos Williams on pages 89–91 are reprinted from his *Collected Earlier Poems* by permission of New Directions and MacGibbon & Kee Limited. The extracts from Sherwood Anderson are © B. W. Huebsch, Inc., renewed 1951 by Eleanor Copenhaver Anderson. The extracts from Ernest Hemingway are reprinted by permission of the executors of the Ernest Hemingway estate, Jonathan Cape Limited and Charles Scribner's Sons (renewal copyright © Ernest Hemingway).

Cambridge, December 1964   T. T.

INTRODUCTION: THE SLEEP OF REASON

. . . could I then take part
In aught but admiration, or be pleased
With anything but humbleness and love;
I felt, and nothing else; I did not judge,
I never thought of judging, with the gift
Of all this glory fill'd and satisfi'd.

WORDSWORTH, *The Prelude*, Book XI

. . . to him, judgment is second to wonder.

SAUL BELLOW, *The Dangling Man*

ROUSSEAU's detailed instructions for the enlightened education of the child Emile were a major influence on the romantic writers who emerged into prominence in the early years of the nineteenth century. The idea that the child enjoys a special point of view and enjoys a special relationship and intimacy with nature was one which was eagerly adopted and developed. But it is worth reminding ourselves briefly of what Rousseau's scheme of education was so that we can then take note of what the romantics took, and what they rejected. For the sum of these rejections affords us a key insight into the romantic point of view.

'Childhood has its own ways of seeing, thinking, and feeling; nothing is more foolish than to try and substitute our ways;'[1] this insistence on the uniqueness, the difference of childish vision is stressed and summed up most tellingly in the following passage.

What would you think of a man who refused to sleep lest he should waste part of his life? You would say, 'He is mad; he is not enjoying life, he is robbing himself of part of it; to avoid sleep he is hastening death.' Remember that these two cases are alike, and that childhood is the sleep of reason.[2]

An age suffering from an excess of 'reason' might well wish to return to that sleep—Rousseau here offers them the perfect prescription. By implication, but not by intention. For the whole burden of Rousseau's work is that childish modes of perception must give way to more complex and sophisticated modes. His main concern is to avoid any of the mischievous effects of trying to force a child into reasoning too prematurely. Let the sleep be slept out to the full, *in order that* the waking may be more healthy and vigorous. This emphasis the romantics forgot. Yet Rousseau is very clear on this point. For mainly he stresses the limitations of children's vision, even as he demands reverence for 'the sacred innocence in their ever brightening glance'.[3] Thus: 'His [i.e. Emile's] ideas, if indeed he has any ideas at all, have neither order nor connection'[4] and 'The child sees the objects themselves, but does not perceive their relations, and cannot hear their harmony'.[5] The child is limited to separate sensations, is passive in face of nature. But looking further we read: 'He who sees relations as they are has an exact mind . . . he who does not perceive any relations at all is an imbecile'.[6] And there is a faculty more important yet than the perception of relations. 'In the sensation the judgment is purely passive . . . in the percept or idea the judgment is active; it connects, compares, it discriminates between relations not perceived by the senses.'[7] To perceive relations is precisely what the child cannot do. It is limited to sensations 'but having no power to place them side by side it can never compare them, it can never form a judgment with regard to them'.[8] The major aim of Rousseau's education is to produce sure and accurate judgement; the ultimate aim is to ensure that Emile 'may judge rightly of good and evil in human society'.[9] Uncorrupted by early abuse the reason may awaken and attain the highest dignity of true moral judgement. And that is Rousseau's ambition. The child's passivity to detail, its inability to generalize and judge which the romantics were to elevate into positive virtues were, for Rousseau, states which were to be respected and taken into account: but states from which the child must emerge.

When Rousseau writes: 'Youth should never deal with the general, all its teaching should deal with individual instances',[10] this is far from being an anticipation of Blake. Rather it is a means of avoiding error and erroneous habits of mind. 'I care not if he knows nothing provided he is not mistaken . . . reason and judgment come slowly.'[11] In nothing is Rousseau more a child of the Enlightenment that in this loathing of error. The child should limit himself to details and particulars, so that in time he may arrive at a true perception and complex understanding of 'the whole'. Consider this passage from *The Confessions*. It concerns his delight in studying plants. 'Others, at the sight of these treasures of nature, feel nothing more than a stupid and monotonous admiration. They see nothing in detail because they know not for what they look, nor do they perceive the whole, having no idea of the chain of connection and combinations which overwhelms with its wonders the mind of the observer.'[12] For Rousseau an apprehension of 'the whole' was essential if one was to appreciate the parts. The parts themselves would not lead you to the whole. He goes so far as to say that children can feel no rapture in face of nature because they are simply the passive recipients of sensations. Rapture, for Rousseau, depends on the interpreting mind. Nature was not glorious in its details but in its plan: 'as soon as we attempt to give details, that greatest wonder of all, the concord and harmony of the whole, escapes us.'[13] A harmony, note, discerned and appreciated by the working mind and not intuited through a mystic vision. This is still the nature of the divine watchmaker and Rousseau is happy enough to use the very phrase. Emile's education aims at developing the reasoning and judging faculties (which were identical for Rousseau) to the point where he can comprehend the general design of that nature and assess the conduct of men. Rousseau's child is indeed 'innocent' but he enjoys no superior mode of cognition nor does he catch glimpses of visionary gleams. Rather, he is likely to err and confuse things in a manner which would be prejudicial to the proper development of the characteristic human qualities of mind—which are to analyse, to generalize, to judge. Rousseau's education is as much protective as instructive. It seeks to fend off and exclude anything which might impair the faculty of true judgement. But it never aims at retarding the child, at resisting the growth of mind. After all, 'man is not meant to remain a child'.[14] The eighteenth-century tone is unmistakable. It will readily be seen how far from anything we associate with romanticism Rousseau's attitudes and allegiances are.

If we turn to Wordsworth a basic difference is immediately apparent:

> Thou best Philosopher, who yet dost keep
> Thy heritage, thou Eye among the blind[15]

—thus he addresses the child. Rousseau aimed at producing the Philosopher out of the child by slow and careful supervision. For Wordsworth the child already *is* the philosopher. Any mental progress is a retreat from true knowledge. Clearly a very different sort of wisdom and knowledge are here in question. For Wordsworth warns against that very reason Rousseau was at such pains to develop. Wordsworth is distrustful of any perceptual activity which proceeds 'by logic and minute analysis'.[16] He prefers a passive 'beholding' to all 'analytic industry'. For Wordsworth 'the infant Babe' is 'bless'd' because his mind

> Is prompt and watchful, eager to combine
> In one appearance, all the elements
> And parts of the same object, else detach'd
> And loth to coalesce.[17]

Now Rousseau was also desirous of attaining a vision of the unity and inter-relatedness of all things; he also disliked any view of the world which made of nature a mere scattering of discrete particulars. Yet how different is Wordsworth's sense of unity:

> A Child, I held unconscious intercourse
> With eternal Beauty.[18]

Rousseau's child was condemned to separate sensations. The difference is that for Rousseau a sense of 'the whole' could only be gained by an active effort of understanding—analysis and reconstruction. For Wordsworth it was a matter of retaining 'a feeling of the whole'.[19] Feeling rather than understanding—the former neglecting analysis, the latter dependent on it. That is why Wordsworth looks back to his childhood as a state of superior insight:

> ... could I then take part
> In aught but admiration, or be pleased
> With anything but humbleness and love;
> I felt, and nothing else; I did not judge,
> I never thought of judging, with the gift
> Of all this glory fill'd and satisfi'd.[20]

Admiration (wondering at) rather than judging: that is one of the crucial romantic preferences. The very passivity of the child, his inability and disinclination to interfere with nature by mental inquiry, his reliance on a sheer feeling of 'glory', is a condition of his visionary privilege. Rousseau's properly educated man could understand the working harmony of the universe; Wordsworth's uneducated child is blessed with a feeling of its organic wholeness. Childhood thus becomes a visionary state to which man should attempt to return. Rousseau's ideal of progress is thus reversed. Wonder is substituted for judgement. Man seeks to re-enjoy the sleep of reason for in that sleep nature may acquire:

> The glory and freshness of a dream.[21]

The grown man now seeks to learn from Emile, though it is an Emile that Rousseau would never have recognized.

That a suspicion of analysis was a major trait of much romantic writing need not here be argued. It is enough to remind ourselves of the example of John Stuart Mill, described so graphically in his *Autobiography*. He records his sudden realization 'that the habit of analysis has a tendency to wear away the feelings'.[22] He goes on to describe the ill effects and 'the dissolving influence of analysis' and how he arrived at the conviction that 'the passive susceptibilities needed to be cultivated as well as the active capacities'.[23] It is exactly as though Rousseau's Emile had been converted in middle-age by reading Wordsworth. But the man most responsible for developing the idea of passive 'wonder' and making of it a philosophical position was undoubtedly Carlyle. We need not here discuss his varied debts to German thinkers. It will be sufficient to quote certain key passages from *Sartor Resartus*. It will be recalled that he is supposedly transcribing the thoughts of a German thinker called Professor Teufelsdröckh.

For the rest, as is natural to a man of this kind, he deals much in the feeling of Wonder; insists on the necessity and high worth of universal Wonder; which he holds to be the only reasonable temper for the denizen of so singular a Planet as ours. 'Wonder,' says he, 'is the basis of Worship: the reign of wonder is perennial, indestructible in Man; only at certain stages (as the present), it is, for some short season, a reign *in partibus infidelium.*' That progress of Science, which is to destroy Wonder, and in its stead substitute Mensuration and Numeration, finds small favour with Teufelsdröckh, much as he otherwise venerates these two latter processes.[24]

The indictment and lament that 'the reign of wonder is done, and God's world all disembellished and prosaic'[25] recurs throughout. One more example:

The man who cannot wonder, who does not habitually wonder (and worship), were he the President of innumerable Royal Societies, and carried the whole *Mécanique Céleste* and Hegel's *Philosophy*, and the epitome of all Laboratories and Observatories with their results in his single head—is but a Pair of Spectacles behind which there is no Eye.[26]

The most venomous dislike is reserved for 'logic-choppers' and other 'Professed Enemies to Wonder'.[27] Wonder has now become a definite mode of philosophic understanding to be set up against analysis. The truly philosophic Eye is the wondering Eye, for that alone is capable of seeing Nature not as an 'aggregate' but as 'a Whole'. For the universe has now changed from being the fine intricate mechanism of a divine watchmaker and become 'one vast Symbol of God'.[28] It is no longer a question of understanding the harmonious plan which explains the inter-

6

relatedness of all particular phenomena. Rather: 'Rightly viewed no meanest object is insignificant; all objects are as windows, through which the philosophic eye looks into Infinitude itself'.[29] Any single object can afford the wondering eye an intimation of 'the Whole'. There is no need for that perception of relations which for Rousseau was such a crucial step to arriving at true judgement. There is no mention of the value of 'wonder' in Rousseau, just as there is nothing but scorn for 'analysis' in Carlyle. Carlyle indeed wanted to abandon the two basic categories or concepts which men employ in understanding their world—those of Time and Space: 'Deepest of all illusory Appearances, for hiding Wonder, as for many other ends, are your two fundamental world-enveloping Appearances, SPACE and TIME'. They 'blind us to the wonder everywhere lying close on us'. And he continues in words which were to have a far reaching effect on a distant reader: 'with God as it is a universal HERE, so it is an everlasting NOW'.[30] Just by considering these quotations from Wordsworth, Mill and Carlyle we can see why the child held such special interest for the romantic writer. Not only because of his putatively innocent heart, not only because he seems free of all the besetting doubts and distress of adult life, but also because of his point of view, his visual relationship with reality. The distrust of judgement and analysis, the conviction of the need for a renewed sense of wonder and admiration, a new stress on 'the passive susceptibilities', a longing to feel the wholeness of the universe rather than merely understand it—almost inevitably writers who embraced this cluster of ideas fastened on the child's relationship with nature as a symbol of their own aspirations. The child's wondering eye offered the romantic writer an avenue back to a reality from which he fast felt himself becoming alienated. By recapturing a naive vision he might once again enjoy an untrammelled intimacy with nature. There would be a new reverence, a new quietude, a new sense of total glory.

Thus we find the myth of the 'innocent eye' recurring throughout the century. That it is a myth, more recent studies by gestalt

7

psychologists and educational theorists seem positively to demonstrate. The myth maintains that the child stands passively watching nature, seeing each detail with dazzling freshness and vivid clarity, richly appreciative of the wonder of creation and not at all prompted to embark on any disruptive intellectual inquiry. The sleep of reason, if we may alter Goya's famous phrase for a moment, was thought to breed miracles. Miracles of insight and response, at least; miracles of passive appreciation. Salvation lay in the child's wondering eye. Thus the myth: in fact it would seem that William James's words—'the buzzing, booming chaos which is the child's world'—are far nearer the truth. But this is not here important. The point is that the myth was operative. The naive or innocent eye was deliberately cultivated as an artistic strategy by many varied artists. The very phrase, 'innocence of the eye',[31] seems first to occur in Ruskin, and he cites the child as an example of that pious receptivity in the face of nature which we need to cultivate. 'Childhood often holds a truth with its feeble fingers, which the grasp of manhood cannot retain, which it is the pride of utmost age to recover.'[32] That 'truth' is an undiscriminating awe for nature's most random trifles: a reverent patience in face of a mysterious plenitude. To take an example from the continent we find Baudelaire writing: 'L'enfant voit tout en nouveauté; il est toujours ivre. Rien ne ressemble plus à ce qu'on appelle l'inspiration, que la joie avec laquelle l'enfant absorbe la forme et la couleur . . . le génie n'est que *l'enfance retrouvée* à volontè.' Man's most memorable and valuable hours are those in which he suddenly sloughs off the dullness of his everyday habits of perception and becomes 'un homme-enfant', thus 'possèdant à chaque minute le génie de l'enfance, c'est à dire un génie pour lequel aucun aspect de la vie n'est *émoussé*'.[33] The child starts the century with a visionary instinct which made him a philosopher and by the end of the century he has a capacity for rapture which makes him the very image of genius. Rousseau would not have understood at all. But we can see that the recurring references to the superior vision of the child testify to a tremendous hunger to discover a new access to reality, a new habit of wonder. This aspect of romantic aspiration can perhaps best be summarized by a phrase from Proust: 'the return to the unanalysed'.

Perhaps the most avid reader of Carlyle's work was Emerson. Even before he knew Carlyle's identity he referred to him as 'my Germanick new-light writer'[34] on the strength of an anonymous piece in the *Edinburgh Review*. Later he referred to him in terms of almost unbounded praise: thus he could speak of him as having 'an imagination such as never rejoiced before the face of God, since Shakespeare'.[35] And when he drew up a list of 'My men' in his journal, the very first entry was—Thomas Carlyle.[36] It was Emerson who first gathered the *Sartor Resartus* papers together into a book and had them published in the United States. More, he wrote an introduction to the book—exactly at the time when he was composing his first really important essay, 'Nature'. Even allowing for Emerson's eclectic reading and borrowing there seems little doubt that he derived a great deal of his 'Germanick' thought from Carlyle's work. It is certainly permissible to suggest that three of Emerson's key ideas received tremendous impetus from Carlyle's work. First, the need for a new attitude of 'wonder' towards nature; second, the conviction that any object, no matter how trivial, was a 'symbol' of God and could serve as a 'window' to 'infinitude' if viewed aright; third, the rejection of history in favour of 'the everlasting NOW'. More than that he admired the 'sinew and vivacity' of Carlyle's style and praised his paragraphs as being 'a sort of splendid conversation'.[37] It is indisputable that Carlyle was a major influence on Emerson. And yet how different a writer Emerson is from Carlyle. The latter was aware of this and in writing to Emerson about his essay 'Nature' he made a shrewd comment which has relevance for a good deal of American literature. 'We find you a Speaker indeed, but as it were a *Soliloquizer* on the eternal mountain-tops only, in vast solitudes where men and their affairs all lie hushed in a very dim remoteness; and only *the man* and the stars and the earth are visible.'[38] Carlyle's philosophical advocacy of 'wonder' did not prevent him from stressing the need for duty and discipline; he was pugnaciously involved in the society of his time. Whereas Emerson stressed the entire independence of man, leaving him without history, location or society, suspended in front of sheer nature. Nothing must interrupt the wonder. What was for Carlyle more of a polemical philosophic concept became for Emerson a completely assimilated disposition, almost a way of life.

In this book I shall try and demonstrate the peculiar importance of 'wonder' in American literature by examining a number of key writers from Emerson up to the present day. As I have very briefly indicated there was a continuous interest in 'wonder' and the naive vision in European and English literature throughout the nineteenth century: I am not trying to suggest that American writers' interest in and use of these ideas was in any sense unique and without parallel. But two things do seem to me to be true. From the start 'wonder' was put to much more far-ranging uses in American writing than in any other literature. The American writer faced different problems and had different needs, and 'wonder' became a key strategy where in Europe it tended to remain one idea among others. For analysis was never really abandoned in nineteenth-century European writing; rather it was put to different use. Compare Whitman and Baudelaire, respectively the greatest poets of their countries; it is the former who really does eschew analysis, the latter deploys it to transmit a new vision. Or think of Flaubert and Mark Twain. The former writes in his letters 'I am at home only in analysis'; the latter is hostile to analysis, and himself perfects the naive vision as a novel strategy. A major problem facing American writers was simply, overwhelmingly, the need to recognize and contain a new continent. The wondering vision was adopted as a prime method of inclusion and assimilation. The second consideration is this. The stance of wonder has *remained* a preferred way of dealing with experience and confronting existence among American writers. When Bronson Alcott wrote 'A wonderless age is godless'[39] in 1840 he was not saying anything that might not have been said in another country. But the two following quotations from contemporary novels could, I maintain, only be American. The first is from a recent novel called *The Moviegoer* by Walker Percy. The alienated narrator is describing his life in Gentilly, New Orleans:

... and there I have lived ever since, solitary and in wonder, wondering day and night, never a moment without wonder. Now and then my friends stop by, all gotten up as young eccentrics with their beards and bicycles, and down they go into the Quarter to hear some music and find some whores and still I wish them well. As for me, I stay home with Mrs Schexnaydre and turn on TV. Not that I like TV so much, but it doesn't distract me from the wonder. That is why I can't go to the trouble they go to. It is distracting, and not for five minutes will I be distracted from the wonder.[40]

And more succinctly, the narrator of Saul Bellow's first novel, *Dangling Man*: 'to him, judgment is second to wonder'.[41] Whatever other attitudes the modern European writer has taken up in front of reality, they do not include 'wonder'.

With these two considerations in mind it seems to me legitimate to study the recurring use of wonder and the naive vision in American literature as something related, indeed, to a general European phenomenon, but more importantly as a phenomenon unique in itself. This is not to stress the 'American-ness' of American literature but only to suggest that certain problems and certain solutions are observably present in many American writers and that these may be profitably approached by considering their predilection for the strategy of the naive vision, that deliberate attempt to regard reality with minimum reference to previous familiarity and interpretative knowledge, that enduring preference for wonder over analysis.

This book attempts to show that many American writers worked to develop a new point of view, a new way of appropriating reality, a new angle of vision. Desire for a new naivety of response involved them in a renewed and lasting interest in the child. Not only as an uncomprehending focus of pathos (as was usually the case in English writing of the nineteenth century), but as a superior witness of the world. When Sherwood Anderson, for instance, writes: 'A man, if he is any good, never gets over being a boy'[42] or when Saul Bellow asserts 'It's hard in our time to be as naive as one would like',[43] the accent and emphasis is distinctly American and does not involve an idealization of mere immaturity but rather a feeling for some valuable unencumbered simplicity of response. That American writers have often been drawn to the figure of the child is scarcely a new observation; but I should stress that in this book I am mainly concerned with their adoption of the child's point of view: what insights it made possible, what limitations it involved. It is, after all, in American literature that we find the first incarnation of the fully plausible child narrator. But this is not primarily a book about the child in American literature. It is about the search for a new vision.

A new vision clearly requires a new style to transmit it. For language, as Eric Auerbach so brilliantly demonstrated in his book *Mimesis*, reflects a particular attitude towards reality, a certain way of world-watching: style *is* vision. It concentrates on certain aspects of reality and omits, ignores and neglects others. It determines focus and distributes emphases. 'The limits of my language are the limits of my world', as Wittgenstein put it. Thus this book also attempts to document some of the effects of the new point of view on American style, not only on tone and vocabulary but more importantly on syntax. For syntax reveals the way a man chooses to order his perceptions and thus offers us important insights into his angle of vision. (In this connection I shall be making use of two rather ugly but useful words: *Paratactic*, the syntax which puts things next to each other without trying to relate them, and *hypotactic*, the syntax which organizes and relates things by means of a variety of subordinate clauses. Auerbach has shown how useful these terms can be in analysing literature and as I can think of no shorter way of conveying these rather crucial characteristics I have made use of the words quite often. This should be regarded as economy rather than display.)

In discussing the need for a new point of view and a new language American writers often cited the superior virtues of the vernacular. This is understandable. They 'craved a sense of reality'[44] and thus they also wished for words which would register the circumpressure of the experienced world, words full of the shape of things, heavy with the weight of things. Of course Wordsworth exemplified the romantic interest in the vernacular when he spoke of his ideal of 'a selection of the language really spoken by men'. But, once again, this stock romantic interest was developed and taken much further in America. One reason for this was that the 'mandarin' style of the official culture of New England was not only a classical style, it was heavily freighted with the European past: it carried a built-in European point of view. For an American writer properly to discover the reality all about him it was essential that he broke to some extent with this style and its accompanying lofty, literary attitudes. Thus it is more than a primitivistic gesture when we find writers from Emerson onwards citing the superior wisdom and language of the vernacular figure. His words, like his hands, had a firm grasp on a palpable proximate reality. And that they envied him; that they sought to emulate. It is for this reason that we shall be involved in discussing the vernacular type almost as often as we have to refer to the image of the child.

One more general point should be made here, and once again it involves taking note of an attitude that was voiced by European romantics but enthusiastically embraced by American writers. We noted that Carlyle wrote of getting out of time 'into an ever-lasting NOW'. Emerson returned to this point time and time again. He called himself 'an endless seeker with no Past at my back'.[45] He insisted on the supreme value of 'the Here and the Now'; he staked everything on 'the pot-luck of the day';[46] he sought to 'come to the quality of the moment, and drop duration altogether'.[47] He insisted on the need to 'set up the strong present tense'.[48] Once again there were practical reasons for this insistence. Emerson wanted to see the birth of a truly national literature and as long as America was devoted to the Past, just so long would it remain in mental thrall to Europe. 'We are idolaters of the old. . . . The voice of the Almighty saith, "Up and onward for evermore!" We cannot stay amid the ruins.'[49] History is the domain of the dead. Only the present moment is alive, real, and veridical. As with the strategy of the innocent eye (which, after all, is an eye uninformed by time, free from the deposits of history), and the vernacular, the devotion to the immediate present was all part of the attempt to establish contact with the real, living, flowing world; the attempt, in Emerson's words, to 'make friends with matter'.[50]

This attempt to renunciate and exclude the past from present perception and awareness has one very important stylistic implication to which it will be wise to alert ourselves from the outset. For it involves an attempt to abandon all associationist modes of writing: nothing from the past was to be allowed to be brought to bear on the awareness of the present moment. Gertrude Stein sums up this intention as neatly as anyone:

Ordinarily the novels of the Nineteenth Century live by association; they are wont to call up other pictures than the one they present to you. I didn't want, when I said 'water', to have you think of running water. Therefore I began by limiting my vocabulary, because *I wanted to get rid of anything except the picture within the frame.* While I was writing I didn't want, when I used one word, to make it carry with it too many associations. I wanted as far as possible to make it exact, as exact as mathematics; that is to say, for example, if one and one make two I wanted to get words to have as much exactness as that. [my italics][51]

The italicized sentence summarizes as well as one sentence can one of the major stylistic intentions of many American writers. It also points back to the three basic interests which I have briefly mentioned above: the interest in the naive eye with its unselective wonder; the interest in the vernacular with its immediacy and concrete directness; and the effort to slough off the Past and concentrate exclusively on the present moment. Together, these interests and intentions could be said to comprise an effort to 'get rid of anything except the picture within the frame'. This book attempts to document that effort.

This dedicated concentration on the present has enabled American writers to make discoveries denied to those who prefer to see the present through the eyes—the styles—of the past. On the other hand there could be risks and disadvantages involved in this refusal of the instructive debate between past and present. As Leibniz put it, the present moment is always duplex: it is 'chargé du passé' as well as 'gros de l'avenir'. The picture within the frame may sometimes be better appreciated and comprehended by consulting material which lies outside the frame. To attempt to excise the past is to risk neglecting a great aid to understanding. Such an act of total renunciation is one which the European mind is somewhat wary of making. The past can cripple, blind and suffocate, certainly: but it can also illuminate, just as it can sometimes offer aids to stability and tokens for necessary tenacities. American writers, it seems to me, have demonstrated both the advantages and drawbacks involved in America's brave and exhilarating apostasy from history.

But we do well to suppress hasty value-judgements, particularly when approaching a new literature. If we can agree with the Proustian notion that 'the only true voyage of discovery . . . would be not to visit strange lands but to possess other eyes, to behold the universe through the eyes of another', and feel, as he did, that art alone makes such voyages possible, then we shall find something inestimably refreshing, instructive and exciting in trying to understand, even to experience, the new vision which many American writers seem to have been working to perfect. It is perfectly possible to disagree with a certain writer's ideas, beliefs and intentions and still to profit greatly from having suspended personal conviction and prejudice and looked at the world through his eyes. The reward for this temporary act of trust and submission is not a new philosophy but simply a new breadth of mind and a widened range of sympathy. These are not qualities with which the world is conspicuously over-endowed, yet they are qualities which all serious art will conspire to nourish in us if we allow it the proper chance.

PART I

THE TRANSCENDENTALISTS

. . . embosomed in beauty and wonder as we are . . . .
EMERSON, *Essays*, 'New England Reformers'

We see, as in the universe of the material Kosmos, after meteoro-logical, vegetable, and animal cycles, man at last arises, born through them, to prove them, concentrate them, to turn upon them with wonder and love.
WALT WHITMAN, *Democratic Vistas*

CHAPTER I

SAINTS BEHOLD: THE TRANSCENDENTALIST POINT OF VIEW

A HOSTILE American reviewer of Wordsworth noted that 'he tries to look on nature as if she had never been looked on before' and he bemoaned that fact that the poet seemed to be attracting an 'ever increasing school of devoted disciples'[1] in America. Now, what he blames Wordsworth for accurately sums up the ambition of many of the Transcendentalists. There is no need here to disentangle the indigenous emotional drive from the imported European ideas in Transcendentalist thought.[2] But it is important to stress how eager the Transcendentalists were to develop a new attitude towards nature, a new point of view. Picking up the Wordsworthian hint they developed it for their own purposes. Thus Theodore Parker echoes Wordsworth in describing the correct way to respond to the world. He is discussing terrestial beauty.

Now to many men, who have but once felt this; when heaven lay about them, in their infancy, before the world was too much with them, and they laid waste their powers, getting and spending, when they look back upon it across the dreary gulf, where Honor, Virtue, Religion have made shipwreck and perished with their youth, it seems visionary, a shadow, dream-like, unreal. They count it a phantom of their experience; the vision of a child's fancy, raw and unused to the world. Now they are wiser. They cease to believe in inspiration. They can only credit the saying of the priests, that long ago there were inspired men; but none now; that you and I must bow our faces to the dust, groping like the Blind-worm and the Beetle; nor turn our eyes to the broad, free heaven; that we cannot walk by the great central and celestial light that God made to guide all that come into the world, but only by the farthing-candle of tradition. . . . Alas for us if this be all.[3]

An awareness of the divine beauty of the world should not be made

THE TRANSCENDENTALISTS

dependent on 'tradition', nor on any inherited and institution-
alized modes of thought or belief. It would be apprehended
directly by any one who could maintain the requisite reverence
of attitude and recapture a personal conviction that the world was
'instinct with the Divine Spirit'.[4] 'When this day comes, man
will look on Nature with the same eye, as when in the Eden of
primitive innocence and joy.'[5] It was the privilege of unmediated
admiration and response which the Transcendentalists were
determined to secure for their age. It was for this reason they
took issue with the Unitarians with their Lockean materialism
and passionless contention that only through the biblical miracles
was God revealed to man. Such an attitude seemed to impoverish
the present world.

It is negative, cold, lifeless, and all advanced minds among Unitarians
are dissatisfied with it, and are craving something higher, better, more
living and lifegiving. . . . Society as it is, is a lie, a sham, a charnel-
house, a valley of dry bones. O that the Spirit of God would once
more pass by, and say unto these dry bones, 'Live!' So I felt, and
so felt others.[6]

Thus Orestes Brownson described the original thrust behind the
movement. The Transcendentalists refused to see the world as
'a mute and dead mass of material forms': rather, it was 'a
living image, speaking forth the glory of God'.[7] At least, it was
that if it was looked at properly. The eye which was 'purified of
the notes of tradition'[8] would see God in all things. Here. Now.
That thralldom to old and cramping ways of thought, which
inhibited and policed the individual response, would be broken.
It was such a release from tradition that the Transcendentalists
sought to achieve so that they might indulge a proper admiration
for a present America neither subservient nor inferior to Europe.
And the most forceful concept with which to challenge the traditional eye was clearly the innocent eye.

Innocent, the soul is quick with instincts of unerring aim; then she
knows by intuition what lapsed reason defines by laborious inference;
her appetites and affections are direct and trustworthy. . . . By reasoning the soul strives to recover her lost intuitions; groping amidst the

obscure darkness of sense, by means of the fingers of logic, for treasures present always and available to the eye of conscience. Sinners
must needs reason: saints behold.[9]

So Bronson Alcott summed up the extremity of his position.
For him 'thought disintegrates and breaks'[10] the unity of soul a
child enjoys with the world. The prescribed cure was obvious:
unlearn reason and behold the world with child-like passive
admiration. The word recurred in much Transcendentalist
writing. 'Wisdom does not inspect but behold'[11] wrote Thoreau;
while Emerson recommended for the 'habitual posture of the
mind—beholding'.[12] Saints behold, and so do children. The
way back into a divine nature was through the innocent eye.
Alcott himself was an educational experimenter of some audacity
and he took his beliefs to their logical conclusion. He held
conversations with children on the gospels and made their
response a test of the validity of Christianity. 'If these *testimonies
of children,* confirm the views of adults—that *Christianity is
grounded in the essential Nature of Man*—than shall I add to its
claim upon our faith.'[13] It is hard to imagine Wordsworth
making so literal an application of his poetic assertion that the
child was a prophet and philosopher. There was much more
interest in the child's point of view in America than in Europe
at the time. It was revered to an unusual degree. Thus Miss
Peabody, who worked in Alcott's experimental school, could
observe:

It was very striking to see how much nearer the kingdom of heaven
. . . were the little children, than those who had begun to pride themselves on knowing something. We could not but often remark to each
other, how unworthy the name of knowledge was that superficial
acquirement, which has nothing to do with self-knowledge; and how
much more susceptible to the impressions of genius, as well as how
much more apprehensive of general truths, were those who had not
been hackneyed by a false education.[14]

There is knowing and knowing. The knowledge which is a
mere accumulation of data will tend to support the *tabula rasa*
theories of the psychological sensationalists and make man the

sport of matter. But the knowledge which seems to deliver itself as unharassed intuition, which seems to be the result of a generous impressionability and an out-reaching sense of spiritual qualities shared by perceiver and perceived, this knowledge will justify the Transcendentalists in their assertions. 'The mind must grow, not from external accretion, but from an internal principle',[15] in the words of Sampson Reed. Given this emphasis on the 'internal principle', the process of true knowing, and the diminished concentration on the thing known, then clearly the child's mind can be expected to attract novel focus. The interest, that is to say, is in a cognitive stance, a stance of reverent response and assimilation. There is far less interest in the end results of analysis and prolonged inquiry, such as finished doctrine, intricate theology, or logical demonstration. For the Transcendentalists the central question was: how should a man look at the world to recover and retain a sense of its 'actual glory'? And for many of them the answer was—behold it with wonder, like a child.

Just as the child was used as a positive image to set up against the claims of tradition, so the claims and rights of the uneducated vernacular type were pushed against the aristocratic hegemony of Europe over American thought. 'We are now the literary vassals of England, and continue to do homage to the mother country. Our literature is tame and servile, wanting in freshness, freedom, and originality. We write as Englishmen, not as Americans. . . . Moreover, excellent as is the English literature, it is not exactly the literature for young republicans. England is the most aristocratic country in the world.'[16] Orestes Brownson continuously stressed the democratic implications of transcendentalist thought. He insisted that 'the light which shines out from God's throne, shines into the heart of every man'.[17] The relevance of this for the writer was brought out by George Ripley: 'The most sublime contemplations of the philosopher can be translated into the language of the market.'[18] So he instructs the American writer: 'He is never to stand aloof from the concerns of the people; he is never to view them in the pride of superior culture or station as belonging to a distinct order from himself.'[19] Clearly a totally new perspective, disregardful of the past and the accumulated precedents of culture, was being sought and required. The call was for the point of view of the uninstructed: the eye of the child, the language of the market. The optimism involved in this idealization of the untutored need not be underlined. But there is one further implication of Transcendentalist thought which should be brought out. Many of the Transcendentalists were Unitarians who became dissatisfied with the mere observance of orthodox and seemly forms. They were more interested in sentiment than institutions and there was current enmity between them. So Brownson wrote: 'The sentiment now breaks away from that form, which, if one may so speak, has become petrified.'[20] Perhaps this attitude was most significantly dramatized by Emerson's resignation from the Unitarian ministry in 1832. 'I am not engaged to Christianity by decent forms' he explained later, 'what I revere and obey in it is its reality, its boundless charity, its deep interior life. . . . Its institutions should be as flexible as the wants of man. That form from which the life and suitableness have departed should be as worthless in its eyes as the dead leaves that are falling around us.'[21] I think one may take this as a more general apostasy from all formalism—in art as well as in religion. Because if all nature is good and the unmediated inner impulse of man reliable, then there is no need for life to be transmuted and reworked into art: art must rather emulate nature; flow with it, grow like it. Such an art—it is characteristic of much American writing—can display an almost unique breadth of hospitality, a spontaneous generosity of inclusion, a free-ranging wonder and compassionate attention which more than justify its daring neglect of accredited forms. For indeed there are forms which the instinct of health will cry out to scatter and demolish; forms which condone mental sloth, which perpetuate habitual responses, which flatter old complacencies, which smother all emerging novelty. But if we may adapt Emerson's words a little and say that the Transcendentalist felt that form could afford to be, indeed ought to be, as flexible as sentiment, then we could fairly point out that this

23

might involve them in problems of organization. The vivifying enthusiasm and stimulus of the Transcendentalists provided the essential impetus for the development of a genuine American literature. But their own well-warranted animus against forms has often, for subsequent writers, changed into the real and often arresting problem of how to assemble and contain their material. An excess of flexibility may well let everything in, but at the cost of not being able to hold very much together.

The Transcendentalists themselves could hold everything together by mystical generalizations. They disliked Unitarianism because 'it cannot pass from the Particular to the General'.[22] Transcendentalism could do exactly this, with effortless confidence. But it should here be pointed out that the Transcendentalist, by relying so much for his poise and faith on fervent but vague feelings and generalizations, does expose himself to the risk of a shockingly abrupt disillusion, a very sudden sense of blighting deprivation, an impotent gloom which is the residue of an evaporated enthusiasm. And indeed the Transcendentalists at times revealed the precariousness of their position. Consider these two quotations from George Ripley.

The creation in itself, without reference to the Almighty Spirit from which it sprung, is formless and without order—a mass of chaotic objects, of whose uses we are ignorant, and whose destiny we cannot imagine. It is only when its visible glory leads our minds to its unseen Author, and we regard it as a manifestation of Divine Wisdom, that we can truly comprehend its character and designs. To the eye of sense, what does the external creation present? Much less than we are generally apt to suppose. . . . Merely the different arrangements of matter, the various degrees and directions in which the light falls on the object admired, and the change of position with regard to space. This is all that is seen. The rest is felt. The forms are addressed to the eye, but the perception of beauty is in the soul. And the highest degree of this is perceived, when the outward creation suggests the wisdom of the Creator. Without that, it is comparatively blank and cold and lifeless.[23]

Without that—everything depends on religious conviction. There are no compromise assurances, no working rules, no limited certainties, no veracities attainable by the senses alone. It is all or nothing. Again:

Without religion, we are buried in this world as in a living tomb. Mystery—Darkness—Death—Despair—these are the inscriptions which are born on the portals of our gloomy prison-house. Doomed and unhappy orphans, we know not whence we came, why we are here, nor whither we go. . . . All is blank, and desolate, and lifeless, for to our darkened eye no God is present there. And God, my friends, is necessary to man.[24]

Some of these images have a prophetic air. The lost child becomes a frequent figure in American literature, and images of confinement and imprisonment obtrude themselves in the works of writers as remote as Poe and Sherwood Anderson. The journey of which the path and destination are no longer sure becomes a common theme (it is in Melville and Mark Twain), and the material world as chaos instead of God's order is the insistent tenor of the work of Henry Adams. One could say that Pragmatism was a necessary solution to the dangerous extremism of response countenanced by Transcendentalist thought.

Perhaps the simplest definition of what Transcendentalism meant to those who embraced it is given by Ripley: 'It thirsts after the primitive, absolute, all pervading Truth. It is not contented with the knowledge of barren insulated facts.'[25] They believed you could take a single discrete fact and infer from it some absolute truth: hence the continual shift from particularization to generalization in their writing. But take away that all-maintaining confidence in God, and man is left surrounded by 'barren insulated facts' with only the 'eye of sense' to help him. The Transcendentalists asserted that a man who could not see God everywhere was blind. The blind men of a later age duly had to return to a braille-like reading of the world.

CHAPTER 2

EMERSON: THE UNCONQUERED EYE AND THE ENCHANTED CIRCLE

EMERSON unquestionably played a key role in the shaping of the American imagination, and yet he seems to have had some trouble in defining his own role in his own times. Once he ceased to be a minister he did not start to become an artist; his work has neither the intense passion or still serenity of the true mystic nor the intellectual rigour of the philosopher. He experimented with various characters or projections of parts of his own uncommitted imagination—the Scholar, the Seer, the Man of Genius, the Contemplative Man, the Student, the Transcendentalist, even the Reformer and the Hero. Professor Henry Nash Smith is surely correct in referring to these as 'a collection of embryos' and in going on to suggest that we should understand the essays and addresses in which Emerson deploys these characters as 'rudimentary narratives rather than as structures of discursive reasoning'.[1] In his work, therefore, it is wiser to seek the suggestive drift of the whole than to attempt to establish a consistently developed system of thought. In his many characters he canvassed many problems, but recurringly, insistently, he returned to the discussion of the relationship between man and nature, 'the marriage of thought and things'. He saw no basic hostilities in nature and no radical evil in man. When he does turn his attention to the problem of pain and suffering his tone remains suspiciously bland.[2] It is hard to feel that he has deeply registered some of the more rigorous paradoxes of existence; hard to feel that he ever experienced the chaos within. Evil was neither lasting nor real to Emerson. Thus the problem he addresses himself to is not how to restrain what is dark in man, but rather how to maintain a sense of the enveloping, involving divinity of the world. 'What is life but the angle of vision'[3] he

26

asserts, and much of his work is occupied with attempts to define the appropriate angle of vision. He felt that one of America's deepest needs was a 'general education of the eye'[4] and it was just such an education that many of his essays and addresses attempted to give. I want to suggest that in the course of his 'education' he procured special prestige for the angle of vision of the child.

In his diagnosis of what was wrong with contemporary attitudes towards the world, Emerson insisted that the fault was not in the world itself so much as in man's manner of regarding it. 'The ruin or the blank that we see when we look at nature, is in our own eye. The axis of vision is not coincident with the axis of things, and so they appear not transparent but opaque. The reason why the world lacks unity, and lies broken and in heaps, is because man is disunited with himself.'[5] If things appeared to lack unity that was because of some disorder in the eye: a new eye would unify the world in a new way—salvation is visual. Emerson shifts attention from environment to spectator. In one way he was merely continuing the tradition of neo-platonic thought among the romantics. When he writes: 'Not in nature but in man is all the beauty and worth he sees'[6] we hear echoes of Blake and Goethe, and Coleridge. But in emphasizing the responsibilities and creative powers of 'the eye of the beholder' he had a motive which the European romantics could not have had. For, as long as the interest of a locale was considered to be inherent in the place rather than the viewer, then Americans would be forever looking to Europe. By denying a hierarchy of significance among external objects he not only eliminated the special prestige of Europe (since everywhere is equally significant), he confronts the eye with an enormous, if exciting, task.

In the introduction to his earliest work he had written: 'Why should not we also enjoy an original relation to the universe?'[7] and he had started out with the resolution: 'Let us interrogate the great apparition that shines so peacefully around us.'[8] Emerson wanted the eye to see the world from scratch, wanted to inculcate 'the habit of fronting the fact, and not dealing with it at second hand, through the perceptions of somebody else'.[9] But from the start we should alert ourselves to a doubleness which is inherent in almost everything Emerson says about man's visual relationship with nature. Briefly this doubleness consists of an emphasis which points both to the importance of particulars *and* the unmistakable presence of general truths. The world is full of isolated details which should command our equal attention and reverence, and yet ultimately it is all one vast simple truth: the world is both a mosaic *and* a unified picture which admits of no fragmentation. To pick up his own words the world is both opaque and transparent—it both resists and invites visual penetration. His complaint is that 'as the high ends of being fade out of sight, man becomes near-sighted, and can only attend to what addresses the senses'.[10] The senses bring us indispensable particulars but to limit knowledge to the 'sensuous fact' is to be a Materialist: the Idealist, by a deliberate 'retirement from the senses',[11] will discern truths of which material things are mere representations, truths of 'the high ends of being'.

We live in succession, in division, in parts, in particles. Meantime within man is the soul of the whole; the wise silence, the universal beauty, to which every part and particle is equally related; the eternal ONE. . . . We see the world piece by piece, as the sun, the moon, the animal, the tree; but the whole, of which these are the shining parts, is the soul.[12]

Man must see all the shining parts of the world anew, as for the first time with his own uninstructed eye: but this is merely the prelude to his discerning 'the ONE'. Emerson's work would seem to prescribe an ascent from materialism to idealism and thence to mysticism—a passionate scrutiny of the minute particulars of a world which suddenly turns transparent and gives us an insight into 'the background of being', 'the Over-Soul', 'the ONE'. This duality of vision Emerson himself recognized, noting in his journal: ' Our little circles absorb us and occupy us as fully as the heavens; we can minimize as infinitely as maximize, and the only way out of it is (to use a country phrase) to kick the pail over, and accept the horizon instead of the pail, with celestial attractions and influences, instead of worms and mud pies.'[13] Emerson is not consistent in his advice for he is quite as likely to recommend that a man should scrutinize the pail rather than kick it over. But the passage describes very graphically one of his own habitual practices; for both visually and stylistically he moves from the pail (the discrete detail) to the horizon (the embracing generalization). Sherman Paul, who has written so well on Emerson, shrewdly adopts an idea from the work of Ortega y Gasset, and makes a similar point about Emerson. 'The eye brought him two perceptions of nature—nature ensphered and nature atomized—which corresponded to the distant and proximate visual powers of the eye.'[14] Emerson, seeking a sense of the unity and inter-involvement of all things, felt there was a great value in focusing the eye on 'an unbroken horizon':[15] not only because the unbroken horizon offers an image of an unbroken circle, not only because at the horizon different elements meet and marry, but also because when the eye pitches its focus thus far, all things between it and the horizon fall into what Paul calls 'a blur of relatedness'.[16] Seen thus, individual things seem not to be discrete and unrelated but rather a part of one vast unifying process. The world appears as a concave container. On the other hand, when the eye fastens on to one single detail the rest of the world falls away and one is only conscious of the separateness and isolation of the thing: there is no hazy unity but only the encroaching fragment. The world becomes convex, thrusting out its differentiated particulars. The dangers of the close scrutinizing vision were clear to Emerson: 'If you bury the natural eye too exclusively on minute objects it gradually loses its powers of distant vision.'[17] The paradox is, I think, that Emerson himself effectively, if unintentionally, stressed the value of the close scrutinizing vision. In his case, of course, the detail seldom failed to reveal the divine spirit which rolls through all things. But Thoreau developed a habit of close scrutiny, a reverence for details, which occupied itself with 'minute objects' to a degree never intended by Emerson. Thoreau was convinced that every fact, no matter how small, would flower into a truth, conveying to him a sense of the whole, the unity which maintained the details. Yet he seems to bear out Emerson's warning in a late melancholy complaint: 'I see details, not wholes nor the shadow of the whole.'[18] In such a phrase he seems to anticipate what could, and I think did, happen to subsequent writers. For many of them the eye got stuck at the surface, it was arrested among particulars. The mosaic stayed illegible with no overall, or underall, pattern discernible. Emerson himself gives intimations of such a possibility. 'Nature hates peeping'[19] and, more forcefully, 'Nature will not be a Buddhist: she resents generalizing, and insults the philosopher in every moment with a million of fresh particulars'.[20] One of Emerson's natures is one divine unbroken process wherein all the teeming, tumbling details are seen as part of a flowing Unity, a Unity not described so much as felt, passionately, ubiquitously, empathetically. This is the nature that Whitman was to celebrate. But the other nature described by Emerson is a mass of discrete, clearly defined objects, a recession of endless amazing particulars—particulars which seem to quiver with hidden meanings but which never afford us the revealing transparency. This nature of clear contours and suggestive details is the nature of Anderson, Stein, Hemingway and many others.

As we noticed, the threat to the Transcendentalist lay precisely in the extreme generality of his assertions, his reliance on the all-explaining presence. For without a final mystical concept of nature Emerson confesses that he is left 'in the splendid labyrinth of my perceptions, to wander without end'.[21] Without the affirmed presence of the Over-Soul the world becomes a labyrinthine maze of perceptions which do not add up. The only way out of the maze was to look at it in a different way: this is why Emerson continually raises the question of how man should look at the world.

'Make the aged eye sun-clear'[22]—so Emerson appeals to Spring in one of his poems: it is an appeal which follows logically from his constant complaint that 'we are immersed in beauty, but our eyes have no clear vision'.[23] The age of an eye is pre-

sumably its sum of acquired habits, its interpretative predispositions, its chosen filter through which it sieves the world even while
regarding it. Emerson thought that a person could become fixed
in his ways of looking just as we talk of people getting fixed in
their ways of thinking. Consequently he wants the eye to be
washed clear of those selective and interpretative schemata which
prevent us from 'an original relation to the universe'. As we
now think, without these acquired schemata vision would be
impossible: we have to learn to see and a 'washed' eye would be
an eye blinded by undifferentiated confusion. But the important
thing is not that Emerson did not understand the mechanics of
sight but that he thought it possible and desirable to start looking
at the world as though one had never seen or heard of it before.
What Emerson wanted from man was a renewed faculty of
wonder. 'All around us what powers are wrapped up under the
coarse mattings of custom, and all wonder prevented . . . the wise
man wonders at the usual.'[24] 'The invariable mark of wisdom
is to see the miraculous in the common.'[25] In this kind of visual
relationship between the eye and the world, the eye stands completely passive and unselective while the surrounding world
flows unbroken into it. Something like this was envisaged by
Emerson when he described himself in the following way:

Standing on the bare ground—my head bathed by the blithe air and
uplifted into infinite space—all mean egotism vanishes. I am become
a transparent eyeball; I am nothing; I see all; the currents of the
Universal Being circulate through me; I am part or parcel of God.[26]

The notable aspect of this visual stance is its complete passivity,
its mood of pious receptivity. Unfocusing, unselecting, the eye
is porous to the 'currents of the Universal Being'. Rather similar
is Emerson's description of the delight he receives from a fine day
which 'draws the cords of will out of my thought and leaves me
nothing but perpetual observation, perpetual acquiescence, and
perpetual thankfulness'.[27] Thus relieved of the active will and
conscious thought, Emerson could feel himself reabsorbed into
the flowing continuum of unselfconscious nature.

Of course it was because of his optimistic mysticism that Emerson endorsed this mode of seeing, for he was convinced that if man could reattain a primitive simplicity of vision the ubiquitous divinity of the world would suddenly become clear to him. The wonder he advises is a form of visual piety: to see naively is to see religiously. This explains his interest in the animal eye and the child's eye—neither of which have been overlaid with the dust and dirt of custom and second-hand perception, both of which are free from the myopic interference of reason. The child sees better than the man. 'To speak truly, few adult persons can see nature. Most persons do not see the sun. At least they have a very superficial seeing. The sun illuminates only the eye of the man, but shines into the eye and the heart of the child.'[28]

The desired point of view is one which allows nature unhindered, uninterrupted access to the eye, thence to the heart. Because for Emerson this meant capitulation to a superior source of virtue. 'Man is fallen; nature is erect'[29] and 'all things are moral'.[30] It follows we must not try and impose our will on nature but rather 'suffer nature to intrance us'[31] for our own good. Man's fall is not into knowledge of evil—but into consciousness: for Emerson, as Yeats noted, has no 'vision of evil' and maintains, rather incredibly, that what we call evil would disappear if we acquired a new way of looking at things: 'the evils of the world are such only to the evil eye.' How such evil finds its way into an intrinsically benign and moral universe is not clear —but the extremity of Emerson's position is. To be conscious is the curse, for to be conscious is to be alienated from our original home or womb (and Emerson often uses words like 'cradle' and 'nestle' and 'embosomed' to describe the proper quasi-infantile relationship with nature), it is to have lost the comfort of our primary ties. The unselfconsciousness of animals is enviable. 'The squirrel hoards nuts and the bee gathers honey, without knowing what they do, and they are thus provided for without selfishness or disgrace.'[32] Man's dilemma is based solely on his consciousness. 'Man owns the dignity of the life which throbs around him, in chemistry, and tree, and animal, and in the involuntary functions of his own body; yet he is balked when he tries to fling himself into this enchanted circle, where all is done without degradation.'[33] Only the *involuntary* actions of man have any dignity: we hear nothing of 'the dignity of judgment' in James's phrase, nothing of the enlightened will, of considered intent, of the disciplined pursuit of noble ends. Consciousness is seen only as an inhibitor—for what Emerson really wants is to get back into the enchanted circle, to regain what he calls 'the forfeit paradise'.

> And so, perchance, in Adam's race,
> Of Eden's bower some dream-like trace
> Survived the Flight and swam the Flood,
> And wakes the wish in youngest blood
> To tread the forfeit Paradise,
> And feed once more the exile's eyes:[34]

And he makes the point as strongly in prose: 'Infancy is the perpetual Messiah, which comes into the arms of fallen men, and pleads with them to return to paradise.'[35] Not a change of heart but a change of eye, a new mode of access into nature, is the burden of Emerson's lay sermons. As exemplars he cites 'children, babes, and even brutes' because 'their mind being whole, their eye is as yet unconquered; and when we look in their faces we are disconcerted'.[36] Man's eye has been conquered—that was the fall: man has been 'clapped into jail by his consciousness'.[37] This is why the child sees the sun properly and the adult does not. 'Infancy, youth, receptive, aspiring, with religious eye looking upward, counts itself nothing and abandons itself to the instruction flowing from all sides.'[38] This is the child's genius: the openness to sensations, the visual abandon he is capable of. We are at our best when we too can 'gaze like children'.[39] 'It is very unhappy, but too late to be helped, the discovery we have made that we exist. That discovery is called the Fall of Man. Ever afterwards we suspect our instruments. . . . Once we lived in what we saw; now the rapaciousness of this new power, which threatens to absorb all things, engages us.'[40] 'We suspect our instruments'—Emerson diagnoses a crisis of vision: we see, but we are not sure what we see and how correct is our seeing. There is perhaps something greedy and predatory about the conscious eye, which scans the panorama of creation with utilitarian intention, every glance of which is an act of visual spoliation. But the eye which seeks passively and humbly for true connection and orientation lacks confidence. However the child and the animal still seem to live in what they see with no subject–object dichotomy to haunt them, with none of the sense of severance which assaults the conscious eye. If the adult eye is glazed and dull and blind to the lessons of nature, still the naive eye—idiot, Indian, infant—seems to pay the most profitable kind of attention to things, to enjoy a lost intimacy with the world, to have the freshest, clearest perceptions. Thus Emerson seems to have seen the problem and located the salvation.

Whether or not Emerson felt he had any medical and anthropological evidence for his description of the naive eye of the child and native is not important: for ultimately he was using the notion as a metaphor. His conception of the naive eye is not scientific so much as religious. It was a prelude to worship rather than a preparation for action. It is in this light that such curious passages as the following should be read:

The child with his sweet pranks, the fool of his senses, commanded by every sight and sound, without any power to compare and rank his sensations, abandoned to a whistle or a painted chip, to a lead dragoon or a ginger-bread dog, *individualising everything, generalising nothing*, delighted with every new thing, lies down at night overpowered by the fatigue which this day of continual pretty madness has incurred. *But nature has answered her purpose with the curly dimpled lunatic.* . . . This glitter, this opaline lustre plays around the top of every toy to his eye to insure his fidelity, and he is deceived to his good. *We are made alive and kept alive by the same arts.*[41] [my italics]

It is the intellectual (not the mystical) generalization, so detrimental to a proper habit of awe, which Emerson is writing against; it is a new sort of naive wondering individualizing he is anxious to inculcate. And although he indulgently calls the child a 'dimpled lunatic' he elsewhere talks more seriously of 'the wisdom of children'.[42] Although he sometimes asserts a superior mode of vision which sees through all particulars to the Over-Soul, although he sometimes warns against the rapt attention to detail with which he credited the child, the savage and the animal; nevertheless he often returns to the superiority of the naive eye precisely because of the generous attentive wonder it displays in front of nature's multiple particulars.

Perhaps the child was ultimately Emerson's image for his own best intentions. 'The first questions are always to be asked, and the wisest doctor is gravelled by the inquisitiveness of the child.'[43] Adult maturity is no real maturity since we have lost the right approach to nature, the knack of correct penetration: in fact we no longer ask the right questions. The child in his unencrusted innocence does. There is a dangerous form of extremism here: Emerson's rejection of the past includes not only a denial of the accumulated wisdom of the race but also the lessons of experience. The inquiry ideally should commence afresh each day. Nothing accrues, everything is always to be asked: such is the extreme implication of the Emersonian stance. And certainly since his time the habit of renewed wonder, the ever-novel interrogation of experience has become a recurring theme in American literature, a temperamental predisposition and a literary strategy. Naivety has become an important form of wisdom.

*   *   *

If we cannot make voluntary and conscious steps in the admirable science of universals, let us see the parts wisely, and infer the genius of nature from the best particulars with a becoming charity.[44]

(Emerson)

I have already suggested that although Emerson's vision alternated between detail and generalization, the 'mud pies' and the 'celestial influences', the overall effect of his work is to secure a new respect for close vision. What I want to point out in this section is how Emerson, despite his own preference for 'the admirable science of universals', focused unusual and exciting attention on 'the best particulars'. More remarkably he often equated the best particulars with low and commonplace objects and continually suggested that the need for 'a language of facts'[45] could best be answered by turning to the vernacular. These emphases alone make him a major figure in American literature and they merit special attention here. Only rarely does Emerson give the impression that it might be disconcerting if one could not make the pieces of the mosaic add up to one flowing, binding picture. We just have some hints. 'But all is sour if seen as experience. Details are melancholy; the plan is seemly and noble.'[46] Having lost all sense of the 'seemly and noble' plan Henry Adams, for one, found the remaining heaps of particulars not only sour and melancholy but terrifying. Emerson, to whom mystical generalizations came all too easily, could tie up the world in a sentence. 'Our globe seen by God is a transparent law, not a mass of facts.'[47] Facts on their own were indeed 'heavy, prosaic' and 'dull strange despised things': but Emerson maintained that simply by wondering at them man would find 'that the day of facts is a rock of diamonds; that a fact is an epiphany of God'.[48] With such experience open to him Emerson could well afford to stress the value of a close regard for facts.

If you believe that the universe is *basically* such a perfect continuous whole then certain things follow. For a start every detail will be equally significant. 'A leaf, a drop, a crystal, a moment of time, is related to the whole, and partakes of the perfection of the whole. Each particle is a microcosm, and faithfully renders the likeness of the world.'[49] 'There is no fact in nature which does not carry the whole sense of nature.'[50] 'The world globes itself in a drop of dew. The microscope cannot find the animalcule which is less perfect for being little.'[51]

Now the interesting aspect of this belief that 'the universe is represented in every one of its particles'[52] is that it can easily lead, not to the mystical generalization, but to an extreme of particularization, a devoted preoccupation with the minutiae of existence. It can encourage a prose devoted to ensnaring the crystalline fragments of momentary experience. Emerson works against his own intentions here by giving a tremendous prestige to the smallest details of the material world: his mystical enthusiasm is, as it were, diffused among all the details he sees. There is no hierarchy of value or significance operative: *all* details are worthy of the most reverent attention because all are equally perfect and equally meaningful. If Thoreau, as Emerson said, was 'equally interested in every natural fact',[53] then he was only putting into practice an Emersonian prescription. The implications of this attitude are worth pondering. If every fact is equally interesting where does one find a criteria of exclusion, a principle of abridgement without which art cannot start to be art for it cannot leave off being nature? Emerson is endorsing an eye which refuses to distinguish and classify, which denies priorities of importance and significance, which refuses to admit of any sort of difference in import and value. From one point of view one could call this the egalitarian eye: an eye which affirms the equality of all facts. All facts are born equal and have an equal claim on man's attention. Yet in most art there is what we might call an aristocratic tendency: a claimed prerogative to exercise a lordly right of selection, omission, evaluation, and rearrangement. The aristocratic eye tyrannizes its facts: the egalitarian eye is tyrannized by them. This is not to say that the egalitarian or naive eye cannot discover things to which the aristocratic eye remains blind: it can, for it has that humility which makes new insights possible. It needed the naive eye as described by Emerson and adopted by Thoreau and Whitman, for America to be seen at all in its own right. But it is worth pointing out at this stage that there are distinct problems of organization and evaluation inherent in Emerson's concept of vision. What is completely absent is any sense of a scale of relative complexity, any feeling that small clusters of selected facts can yield a restricted amount of wisdom, any notion of a gradual increase of intelligence, any awareness of various modes of classification, any reference to the accumulating density of experience. There is the leaf—and there are the hidden laws of the universe: and

37

nothing in between. Certainly not society, the notable omission in Emerson. For Emerson is a man talking metaphysics with his eye glued to the microscope, and plenty of American writers have taken their turn at the microscope after Emerson and his disciple Thoreau. This notion of Emerson's had far-reaching repercussions. For if the meaning of the world is to be found in a drop of dew, then the meaning of a given situation may be contained in the contingent objects which surround the participants. The lesson could be drawn from Emerson's thought that if the writer looks after the details the significances will look after themselves. A writer might construe his task to be a scrupulous itemizing of particulars, from the smallest to the largest with no accompanying distribution of significance, no perspective with its recession of priorities, no 'comparison and ranking of sensations'. Indeed he gives a clear warrant for such an attitude. Thus: 'the truth-speaker may dismiss all solicitude as to the proportion and congruency of the aggregate of his thoughts, so long as he is a faithful reporter of particular impressions.'[54] This means that a work of art depends for its form on the individual notation; no larger unit of meaning need be constructed. As he very revealingly wrote—'ask the fact for the form':[55] an attitude far removed from that which relies on the form to assign meaning to the fact. Although Emerson talked of the importance of the 'Intellect Constructive', the major emphasis of his work falls on the 'Intellect Receptive'.[56]

Emerson's belief that the part contained the whole—by implication, or in shorthand as it were—leads quite naturally to his mystique of facts. We remember his instructions to 'see the miraculous in the common': he goes on to arraign our blindness to the worth and significance of small everyday facts. 'To the wise, therefore, a fact is true poetry, and the most beautiful of fables.'[57] Facts contain their own story if we will simply look at them afresh. 'Pleads for itself the fact'[58] he says in one of his poems and he means just that: things will 'sing themselves'[59] if we learn to listen in the right way. Again we note that the prescribed attitude is passive. We do not impose a meaning on facts, rather we try and make 'facts yield their secret sense'.[60] 'Every moment instructs and every object; for wisdom is infused into every form.'[61] Genius, then, will consist of 'the habit of fronting the fact';[62] the intellect is ravished 'by coming nearer to the fact'.[63]

Emerson's emphasis was most important for American writers of the time: because among other things he was continually dragging eyes back to the worth and status of American facts. He scorned artists who could only discern beauty through the conventions of the old 'sublime'. 'They reject life as prosaic, and create a death which they call poetic.'[64] Emerson was constantly canvassing for an artistic acceptance of prosaic every-day life. It is the instinct of genius, he affirmed,

to find beauty and holiness in new and necessary facts, in the field and road-side, in the shop and mill. Proceeding from a religious heart it will raise to a divine use the railroad, the insurance office, the joint-stock company; our law, our primary assemblies, our commerce, the galvanic battery, the electric jar, the prism, and the chemist's retort; in which we seek now only an economical use. . . . The boat at St Petersburg which plies along the Lena by magnetism, needs little to make it sublime.[65]

We can hear prophetic echoes of Whitman's enthusiastic listing of things here. It may sound naive to us but at the time this opinion of Emerson's rendered American literature a real service: his influence helped to make available whole areas of contemporary American life which had hitherto been considered all but ineligible for serious treatment. It was Emerson's insistence on 'the worth of the vulgar' which made Whitman's work possible. He himself chooses the simplest of objects as carriers of sublime revelations. His prose often seems to create a still-life of separately attended-to particulars. It conveys a sense of the radiance of things seen. Emerson succeeded in vivifying the 'common, the familiar, the low':[66] he dignified the details of 'the earnest experience of the common day'.[67] He invokes a new respect for contingent, mundane particulars.

But in order to see details properly man has to separate one thing from another. So although Emerson believes that there are no walls or separating barriers in the flowing tide of nature he yet talks of 'the cool disengaged air of natural objects'[68] and affirms that 'things are not huddled and lumped, but sundered and individual'.[69] Emerson the mystic talked on and on about the fluid inter-relatedness of all things, the transparency of nature to the ONE: but the Emerson whose influence is most marked in American literature was the man who asserted that 'the virtue of art lies in detachment, in sequestering one object from the embarrassing variety',[70] who approved 'the power to fix the momentary eminency of an object'.[71] And if it be asked what connection this particular virtue has with the naive eye we should recall that Emerson said: 'To the young mind everything is individual, stands by itself'.[72] The naive eye, as he depicted it, was likely above all others to be alert to the unique significance of the isolated random details of the material world.

In encouraging a new way of 'seeing' Emerson also made some comments on 'saying', on 'the language of facts' which we must now examine.

First, the indictment: 'The corruption of man is followed by the corruption of language . . . new imagery ceases to be created, and old words are perverted to stand for things which are not; a paper currency is employed, when there is no bullion in the vaults . . . But wise men pierce this rotten diction and fasten words again to visible things.'[73] Secondly, the precedent from which we should learn. 'Children and savages use only nouns or names of things, which they convert into verbs, and apply to analogous acts.'[74] As well as the child and the savage, Emerson cites the 'strong-natured farmer or backwoodsman'[75] as exemplifying the proper use of language. This equating of the child, the savage, and the vernacular type is questionable if a serious attempt to analyse speech-habits is being offered. But they occur more as exemplars in a sermon. Emerson wants to communicate the notion of some sort of verbal intimacy with the stuff of nature, a state in which words and things are at their closest. We should see like children: we should also speak like children and vernacular types, or at least with the simple, specifying concreteness that Emerson imputes to them. Just as Emerson wanted the eye to concentrate on concrete facts, so he wishes language to be full of concrete factualness, and for the same reasons: a new or renewed intimacy with these facts affords us our quickest means of contact with the unifying sublime presence which runs through all things. So the concentration is always on the simplest forms of speech, on the speech which arises from physical involvement with nature rather than the subtle refined concepts used by those who meditate on life through the mind's eye. 'Life lies behind us as the quarry from whence we get tiles and copestones for the masonry of to-day. This is the way to learn grammar. Colleges and books only copy the language which the field and work-yard made.'[76]

An important by-product of this contention of Emerson's is his complete rejection of the classification of facts, things, and words into 'high' and 'low', a classification based on the dualism of spirit and body which was then still a major influence on New England thought. 'The vocabulary of an omniscient man would embrace words and images excluded from polite conversation. What would be base, or even obscêne, to the obscene, becomes illustrious, spoken in a new connection of thought.'[77] The effect of this enlightened passage is to offer a card of eligibility to a whole range of experience and vocabulary which had hitherto been considered inherently unfit for literature.

More central to Emerson's theory of language is his assertion that 'It does not need that a poem should be long. Every word was once a poem', and the related idea that 'bare lists of words are found suggestive to an imaginative and excited mind'.[78] Every word was once a poem because every word was once a thing, or at least a 'brilliant picture' of a thing. ('Language is fossil poetry'[79] wrote Emerson, thus anticipating Fenellosa's notion of language as a pyramid with an apex of generality and a base composed of 'stunned' things.) Since every thing equally displays or hints at the divine plan of the universe, a list of words becomes a list of revelations, each noted fact an encountered epiphany. The influence of this belief on Emerson's own style can be discerned. His style, most characteristically, is composed of an effortless shifting from the suggestive list of facts and things to what he revealingly calls 'casual'[80] abstraction and generalization. In his own words: 'There is the bucket of cold water from the spring, the wood-fire to which the chilled traveller rushes for safety—and there is the sublime moral of autumn and noon.'[81] The philosophy is revealed in the style: he ascends direct from 'a crystal' to the 'Universal Spirit'.[82] Clusters of unrelated facts occur continually, embedded in his discursive sentences, pegging them to the ground. Examples can be proliferated. 'There is nothing but is related to us, nothing that does not interest us—kingdom, college, tree, horse, or iron shoe—the roots of all things are in man.'[83] His prose asserts but never analyses these relationships. We could recall the famous passage on the 'worth of the vulgar' which employs a similar method of assembling 'things', but things left separate and static: 'The meal in the firkin; the milk in the pan; the ballad in the street; the news of the boat; the glance of the eye; the form and gait of the body;'[84]—details which reveal not any one man's world but God's world. Such passages in Emerson serve as the springboards for his sublime leaps: and obviously even as he is enumerating these 'things', telling his beads of facts as we might say, they seem to reveal universal laws to him. As in Whitman, they 'sing' to him. The more successful passages in Emerson are weighed down with concrete facts, laced with particulars which alert the mental eye. What has gone from his writing is almost all purposive complexity of syntax: his style is extremely paratactic and his sentences often start with an unintroduced enumeration of things, things held up for our beholding in the belief that they will 'plead for themselves'. One final example must suffice:

The fall of snowflakes in a still air, preserving to each crystal its perfect form; the blowing of sleet over a wide sheet of water, and over plains; the waving rye field; the mimic waving of acres of houstonia, whose innumerable florets whiten and ripple before the eye; the reflections

42

of trees and flowers in glassy lakes; the musical, steaming, odorous
south wind, which converts all trees to wind-harps; the crackling and
spurting of hemlock in the flames, or of pine logs, which yield glory
to the walls and faces in the sitting-room—these are the music and
pictures of the most ancient religion.[85]

This is writing of considerable visual sensitivity but which has
no sense whatever of the relation and inter-relation of things
and things, things and people, people and other people. It is a
prose that stops before society and the problems of human
behaviour start. His idea that 'bare lists of words are suggestive'
is crucial here. They are suggestive if the words are what he
thought words should be—concrete facts, pictures of things—
but even so such bare lists help us not at all in the problems of
living among those facts and things. Emerson's prose feels its
way over the surfaces and round the contours of parts of the
empirical world but has no means of discussing the problems of
action and interruption in that world. By way of meaning he
can only produce the mystical generalization, but as faith in such
generalizations has diminished it is the former aspect of his prose,
the respect for details, which seems to have had most influence in
American literature.

Of the duality of his own vision he writes very clearly. 'We
are amphibious creatures, weaponed for two elements, having
two sets of faculties, the particular and the catholic. We adjust
our instruments for general observation, and sweep the heavens
as easily as we pick out a single figure in the terrestrial landscape.'[86]
Emerson found it easy to 'sweep the heavens' but subsequent
writers have found it less so. The heavens have changed for one
thing—or rather man's relationship with them has. They now
seem to mock, whereas to Emerson they seemed to smile on, the
'casual' all-explaining generalization. But there remains the
'faculty' for particulars, and the ability to isolate 'single figures
in the terrestrial landscape' and this faculty has perhaps been cultivated as the other faculty has increasingly come under suspicion
—though it has by no means disappeared (see the Afterword).
Not surprisingly Emerson admired Plato above all others, and in

43

his essay on him he manages to tell us a good deal about himself. This is Emerson's Plato: 'If he made transcendental distinctions, he fortified himself by drawing all his illustrations from sources disdained by orators and polite conversers; from mares and puppies; from pitchers and soup-ladles; from cooks and criers; the shops of potters, horse-doctors, butchers and fishmongers.'[87] Plato, that is, obeyed Emerson and 'embraced the common, explored and sat at the feet of the familiar, the low'. Perhaps the most revealing thing that Emerson says about Plato is this: 'Plato keeps the two vases, one of ether and one of pigment, at his side, and invariably uses both.'[88] The pigment of low concrete facts and the ether of mystical generalization—they are both to be found in Emerson. And it is worth repeating that for him peculiar prestige attaches itself to the 'low' in language and in facts and in people. 'The poor and the low have their way of expressing the last facts of philosophy as well as you.'[89] As well as, and by veiled implication, perhaps better. There is actually a preference for those minds which 'have not been subdued by the drill of school education'.[90] 'Do you think the porter and the cook have no anecdotes, no experiences, no wonders for you? Everybody knows as much as the savant. The walls of crude minds are scrawled over with facts, with thoughts.'[91] This is an attitude which could endorse the vernacular as a literary mode; which could encourage the belief in the superior wisdom of the backwoodsman, the rural inhabitant, the person living outside any urban-civilized field of force. It is difficult to assess the influence of one writer. Emerson is perhaps as much symptom as cause. The point is that certain novel attitudes and predilections which recur in many American writers seem to emerge articulated in Emerson's work for the first time. Some of these might be summed up as follows: the emphasis on 'seeing' things freshly; the prescription for the innocent non-generalizing eye; the concomitant preference for simple people and simple speech, whether that of the uneducated labourer, the savage or the child; the exhortation to accept *all* facts, the vulgar trivia of the world, as being potential harbingers of meaning; the celebration of the details of the concrete world and the (more than intended, perhaps) prestige accorded to the particularizing faculty, that faculty which develops the closest relationships between man and the natural world. 'We penetrate bodily this incredible beauty; we dip our hands in this painted element; our eyes are bathed in these lights and forms.'[92] Mysticism, yes: but a mysticism which encouraged a scrupulous yet wondering rediscovery of material appearances, which attached maximum importance to a new intimacy with the basic undistorted 'pigment' of 'this painted element', the world. In encouraging men to 'wonder at the usual' Emerson bestowed perhaps his greatest benefit on American literature.

CHAPTER 3

THOREAU AND THE SAUNTERING EYE

March, 8. 9 a.m.—Up Assabet

I meet Goodwin paddling up the still, dark river on his first voyage to Fair Haven for the season, looking for muskrats and from time to time picking driftwood—logs and boards, etc.—out of the water and laying it up to dry on the bank, to eke out his wood pile with. He says that the frost is not out so that he can lay wall, and so he thought he'd go and see what there was at Fair Haven. Says that when you hear a woodpecker's rat-tat-tat-tat-tat on a dead tree it is a sign of rain. While Emerson sits writing in his study this still, overcast, moist day, Goodwin is paddling up the still, dark river.[1]

THOREAU, *Journal* 1857

THAT almost offhand comparison between the philosopher Emerson and the muskrat-hunter Goodwin—made with no additional comment—gives us a clue to Thoreau's own difference from his master. Where Emerson prescribed, Thoreau ventured forth and made a real effort to insert himself into the physical world, to become its intimate undemanding acquaintance. Goodwin, saturated with that kind of lore and wisdom which a man acquires by osmosis after long immersion in a particular element or set of surroundings, seemed to Thoreau somehow superior to the speculator-philosopher who stayed within doors and kept his feet dry. In Emerson we noted a curious doubleness of emphasis which alternately elevated the particular and the general: in Thoreau the emphasis falls more consistently on the details of a physical universe located in time and space. There is something theoretic even in Emerson's interest in the particular; where he would write of 'the weed at the water side' Thoreau is more likely to write: 'Feb. 19. . . . Saw an otter-track near Walden.'[2] The first is a generic particular, as it were; the second a unique detail with an identity of time and place. The difference is perhaps most easily shown by a comparison of the titles the two men gave to their work. Whereas Emerson's essays are general —'Nature', 'The Over-Soul', 'The Poet'—Thoreau restricts himself to actual places—'Walden', 'A Week on the Concord and Merrimack Rivers', 'Cape Cod', etc. The similarities between the two are of course very marked and Thoreau's debt to Emerson was great, but the shift from philosopher to practitioner is important and Thoreau does more than merely reiterate Emerson's ideas about the innocent eye and the significant fact.

If anything Thoreau is even more insistent in his stress on the importance of 'seeing'. 'How much virtue there is in simply seeing! We may almost say that the hero has striven in vain for his pre-eminency, if the student oversees him. The woman who sits in the house and *sees* is a match for a stirring captain. . . . We are as much as we see.'³

But for Thoreau the only valuable kind of 'seeing' is one divorced from knowledge, understanding, and philosophy. These seemed to him to hinder one's perfection of 'the discipline of looking always at what is to be seen',⁴ a discipline which he devoted his life to mastering. He speaks very confidently of the 'advantages of ignorance',⁵ going on to affirm that 'a man's ignorance is sometimes not only useful but beautiful, while his knowledge is oftentimes worse than useless, besides being ugly'.⁶ Understanding is an inhibiting not an enabling power. 'We shall see but little way if we require to understand what we see. How few things can a man measure with the tape of his understanding! How many greater things might he be seeing in the meanwhile!'⁷ Measurement precludes true appreciation; the desire on the part of the intellect to reduce the seen world to number and length and category obstructs the proper business of the eye: which is to see, to see without knowing, to see without understanding, in fact 'to see without looking'. This seeming paradox means something specific and crucial in Thoreau's work.

I must walk more with free senses. It is as bad to *study* stars and clouds as flowers and stones. I must let my senses wander as my thoughts,

47

my eyes see without looking. Carlyle said that how to observe was to look, but I say that it is rather to see, and the more you look the less you will observe. I have the habit of attention to such excess that my senses get no rest, but suffer from a constant strain. Be not preoccupied with looking. Go not to the object; let it come to you.[8]

Emerson's advice was to cultivate 'indolent vision', a sort of visual 'wise passiveness'—a similar point is made by that last sentence. It is not for the eye to address itself to the world, rather it should let the world address it in any way it chooses. Thus Thoreau's prescribed method follows logically: 'What I need is not to look at all, but a true sauntering of the eye.'[8] The effort, clearly, is to escape from all mental domination and intellectual motivation. Even the programmatic observation which he himself embraced is dangerous. 'If you would make acquaintance with the ferns you must forget your botany. You must get rid of what is commonly called *knowledge* of them.'[9] Like other Transcendentalist writers, Thoreau insisted on a distinction between kinds of knowledge: false knowledge was the mere amassed result of cold analysis whereas true knowledge was the unsought-for reward of attentive susceptibility. He thus describes how nature affords us her teaching and influence in terms at an extreme remove from the Baconian ideal of putting nature on the rack. Thoreau's nature 'must steal upon us when we expect it not, and its works be all done ere we are aware of it. If we make advances, it is shy; if, when we feel its presence, we presume to pry into its free-masonry, it vanishes and leave us alone in our folly.'[10] The eye should meander, passively absorbing impressions from the external world. 'Sauntering' is a key idea in Thoreau both as a way of living and a mode of thinking and seeing, and indeed of writing. Analysis is always to be avoided. 'We should not endeavour coolly to analyse our thoughts. . . . Impulse is, after all, the best linguist . . . .'[11] And clearly there is a close relation between his two ideas that man should 'obey the spur of the moment'[12] and that 'it is a great art to saunter'.[13] Now this ideal of the sauntering eye has clear stylistic implications as I hope to show later. Here I want to draw out some of the philosophical implications. Thoreau's ideal of 'natural piety'[14] and his insistence on an effortless docility of eye follow from a belief that nature is everywhere and always good, that it is 'sound',[15] that it forever 'preserves her integrity'.[16] Just as Emerson endorsed a visual capitulation to the tyranny of the world because he believed that the tyrant was moral and benign. Both men saw nature as the perfect instructor rather than a threat or a challenge. The same idea is to be found in Whitman when he writes that all things are 'unspeakable miracles all referring to all and each distinct and in its place'[17] and a later disciple, Henry Miller, has stated the basic conviction they all share with admirable succinctness. For him 'the world *is* order incarnate'.[18] There is no need to impose order *on*, or elicit order *from*, the world, nor to make any moral discriminations or qualitative differentiations: all things are in their proper place and all things are good. One can detect an echo of this idea in Wallace Stevens:

> Perhaps there are times of inherent excellence,
> As when the cock crows on the left and all
> Is well, incalculable balances,
> At which a kind of Swiss perfection comes
> And a familiar music of the machine
> Sets up its Schwarmerei, not balances
> That we achieve but balances that happen. . . .[19]

Compare this extract from Thoreau's journal—1851:

One afternoon in the fall, November 21st, I saw Fair Haven Pond with its island and meadow; between the island and the shore, a strip of perfectly smooth water in the lee of the island; and two hawks sailing over it; and something more I saw which cannot easily be described, which made me say to myself that the landscape could not be improved. I did not see how it could be improved. Yet I do not know what these things can be; I begin to see such objects only when I leave off understanding them. . . .[20]

Thoreau was particularly aware of 'times of inherent excellence' and was continually responding to 'balances that happen', as indeed should be the case for anyone who believes that the world as it is, undisturbed by man's mind, is 'order incarnate'.

Stevens has not the same kind of conviction, his whole statement is prefaced by a tentative 'perhaps', and much of his work is devoted to 'achieving' balances that do not 'happen'. But for Emerson, Thoreau and Whitman the 'inherent excellence' of the world was a constant fact if only we could regain the eye to see it as such. Hence the distrust of the interfering mind; hence the deprecation of conscious 'art' since it seeks to improve on a world that by definition cannot be bettered; hence, therefore, 'the advantages of ignorance'.

Thoreau's famous habit of scrutiny exemplified in such notes as: 'I could have afforded to spend a whole fall observing the changing tints of the foliage'[21] is not only that of the dedicated naturalist; for though he did annotate all the wild life he saw and kept a meticulous account of it in his journals; though, in every sense, he did 'number the streaks of the tulip', he had an anterior motive. Noting how many birds seem to be at home in a winter landscape he makes the following entry in his journal:

'I saw this familiar—too *familiar*—fact at a different angle, and I was charmed and haunted by it. . . . Only what we have touched and worn is trivial—our scurf, repetition, tradition, conformity. To perceive freshly, with fresh senses is to be inspired.'[22] It is not the detached objective scientific eye but the fresh, the innocent eye that Thoreau sought. But that word 'inspired' points to another aspect of Thoreau's thought, the mysticism which he shared with Emerson, the feeling that nature was not merely the sum of visible objects but the manifestation of some divine power. Though he is pre-eminently a man who looked *at* nature he stresses the need to 'look through and beyond her'.[23] This ambiguity will be more clear when we examine his attitude towards 'facts' but we must note it here in order to realize that there is a mystical impulse informing his theory of vision. The impulse is weaker than in Emerson because Thoreau is more preoccupied with actual visible concretions. His advice 'be not long absent from the ground',[24] his avidity for 'a nature which I cannot put my foot through',[25] and his conviction that 'Heaven is under our feet as well as over our

THOREAU AND THE SAUNTERING EYE

heads'[26] give evidence of a downward tug in his writing which anchors him more firmly in the palpable physical world than Emerson. Whereas Emerson does quite often kick over the pail and accept the horizon, Thoreau admits that his genius and predilections make him value proximate vision more than distant vision. He explained that his eye 'is educated to discover anything on the ground, as chestnuts, etc.' and he goes on to assert, 'It is probably wholesomer to look at the ground much than at the heavens'.[27] Nevertheless the fact that he considered himself as something more than a botanist can be traced to the mystical vein in his writing, and it is this latent mysticism which leads him to elevate the innocent eye above the scientific eye, which makes him prefer 'the keen joy and discrimination of the child who has just seen a flower for the first time' to 'modern botanical descriptions (which) approach ever nearer to the dryness of an algebraic formula'.[28]

Thoreau's primitivism is well documented but the connection he makes between the correct response to the world ('seeing without looking') and the child needs to be emphasized. When he writes in *Walden* that 'I have always been regretting that I was not as wise as the day I was born' he merely goes on to say that 'The intellect is a cleaver; it discerns and rifts its way into the secret of things'[29] without going on to suggest that the wisdom of the child consists precisely in his inability or disinclination to 'cleave' the world intellectually, in his habit of rapt undifferentiating attention. The implication is clearer in his journals.

I think that no experience which I have today comes up to, or is comparable with, the experience of my boyhood. . . . Formerly, methought, nature developed as I developed, and grew up with me. My life was ecstasy. In youth, before I lost any of my senses, I can remember that I was all alive, and inhabited my body with inexpressible satisfaction; both its weariness and its refreshment were sweet to me. This earth was the most glorious musical instrument, and I was audience to its strains. To have such sweet impressions made on us, such ecstasies begotten of the breezes![30]

51

This pre-intellectual rapport with his environment he feels he has in some measure lost so it is not surprising to find him writing of his attempts to 'recover the lost child that I am'.[31]

More remarkably he writes in his journal:

I think that we should treat our minds as innocent and ingenuous children whose guardians we are,—be careful what objects and what subjects we thrust on their attention. Even the facts of science may dust the mind by their dryness, unless they are in a sense effaced each morning, or rather rendered fertile by the dews of fresh and living truth. Every thought that passes through the mind helps to wear and tear it, and to deepen the ruts, which, as in the streets of Pompeii, evince how much it has been used. How many things there are concerning which we might well deliberate whether we had better know them! Routine, conventionality, manners, etc., etc.,—how insensibly an undue attention to these dissipates and impoverishes the mind, robs it of its simplicity and strength, emasculates it![32]

If one cannot return to childhood one can at least preserve a child-like mind, a mind not furrowed by an excess of thought nor cluttered and stultified with useless information and knowledge. Notice that acquired information should be effaced each morning, or at least refreshed and revivified—as it were rethought; for this clearly desiderates a mind forever fresh and sensitive to 'the incessant influx of novelty'[33] which each new day provides. 'To the common eye a dust has settled on the universe':[34] the common eye is the average adult eye and the dust is simply its own dulled habits of vision. Healthier by far, thought Thoreau, to try and recapture 'the open eyes of children'.[35] Hence such trenchant, seemingly paradoxical statements as: 'It is only when we forget all our learning that we begin to know.'[36] All his emphasis falls on the need for the new point of view. He reveals this very clearly in one of his complaints about his fellow-men: 'I take my neighbour, an intellectual man, out into the woods and invite him to take *a new and absolute view of things*, to empty clean out of his thoughts all institutions of men and start again; but he can't do it, he sticks to his traditions and his crotchets'[37]

[my italics]. For Thoreau no accretions of precedent or formulated intentions or conceptualizations should intrude on the sacred
intimacy of the innocent senses and the unfallen world: the violat-
ing cleaving mind is above all to be avoided. For to master 'the
discipline of looking always at what is to be seen' we must learn
to 'see without looking', and for that the innocent eye is the
perfect organ. Emerson continually stressed the importance of
'wonder' in man's relation with the world and for Thoreau
similarly the only knowledge worth being in possession of is
'a novel and grand surprise . . . an indefinite sense of the grandeur
and glory of the universe'.[38] For both men knowledge was a
state of the senses rather than a cerebral hoard, a capacity for
delight rather than a disposition to dissect.

In Emerson a concomitant of the interest in a new eye was the
stress on 'facts' and his praise of Thoreau was 'he was equally
interested in every natural fact'. And again whereas Emerson
prescribes an attitude Thoreau seems to embody it. For when
Thoreau writes about 'facts' or 'reality' there is a muscular
urgency and confident physical mastery in his prose which
Emerson could not emulate. Thus in the classic statement from
Walden:

I went to the woods because I wished to live deliberately, to front
only the essential facts of life, and see if I could not learn what it had to
teach, and not, when I came to die, discover that I had not lived. . . .
I wanted to live deep and suck out all the marrow of life, to live so
sturdily and Spartan-like as to put to rout all that was not life, to cut
a broad swath and shave close, to drive life into a corner, and reduce
it to its lowest terms, and, if it proved to be mean, why then to get
the whole and genuine meanness of it, and publish its meanness to
the world; or if it were sublime, to know it by experience, and be able
to give a true account of it in my next excursion.[39]

This hunger to establish contact with something veridical and
concrete stimulates Thoreau to a much more transitive, effortful,
militant attitude than the meditative excursions of Emerson.
Thoreau is much more aware of a solid, angular, three dimen-
sional world outside of himself. Emerson's nature, although

53

densely populated with things and facts drawn from the ground and the lowliest conditions of man, nevertheless seems always about to become transparent: as one recalls it, it seems oddly floating and translucent, apparitional and pliant; no recalcitrant objects obstruct, no unavoidable litter impedes: realistic in detail it seems, in sum, a mirage. Thoreau indeed also asks for a nature he can see through, but he is far more intent on a nature you cannot put your foot through, and it is that nature which he brings so keenly home to us.

Let us settle ourselves, and work and wedge our feet downward through the mud and slush of opinion, and prejudice, and tradition, and delusion, and appearance, that alluvion which covers the globe . . . till we come to a hard bottom and rocks in place, which we can call *reality*, and say, This is, and no mistake. . . . If you stand right fronting and face to face to a fact, you will see the sun glimmer on both its surfaces, as if it were a cimeter, and feel its sweet edge dividing you through the heart and marrow, and so you will happily conclude your mortal career. Be it life or death, we crave only reality. If we are really dying, let us hear the rattle in our throats and feel cold in the extremities; if we are alive, let us go about our business.[40]

Thoreau wanted the challenge of a piercing accuracy and it is the sense of challenge and his resolution to meet it that give his prose a tenseness where Emerson's is sometimes slack and facile for want of a sense of effort. Emerson's prose does not meet with any obstacles as it were: Thoreau's words move through a physical world. Because he maintained that 'In sane moments we regard only the facts, the case that is';[41] because he tried to 'say what that thing really is before a true gaze';[42] he waged war with whatever came between him and reality so that the ground between him and the fact would be cleared and he could learn to see 'what is to be seen'.

One could sum up this attitude of Thoreau's by quoting from his journals this typical statement: 'We admire any closeness to the physical fact'; but we should have to finish the sentence which continues: 'which in all language is the symbol of the spiritual'.[43] That sounds distinctly Emersonian and here we must try and make clear how far Thoreau moved away from his master. He can indeed seem to contradict himself as when he writes in his journals: 'I find the actual to be far less real to me than the imagined'[44] and 'when my task is done . . . I devote myself to the infinite again'.[45] But for all the recurring presence in his vocabulary of such transcendentalist words as *spiritual*, *infinite*, etc., he uses them decreasingly and by the time of *Walden* he almost never uses the word God. Emerson saw nature as a revelatory symbol of some ubiquitous divinity, a nature which still offered hints of some contained and containing deity: he also saw it as a metaphor for man's mind since the same deity dwelt there also. For Thoreau nature came to be final; not merely a manifestation of God, an allegory of the divine presence. Hence this important speculation mid-way through his work. 'May we not *see* God? Are we to be put off and amused in this life, as it were with a mere allegory? Is not nature, rightly read, that of which she is commonly taken to be the symbol merely?'[46] For Thoreau there was only nature; but of course it was still a nature divine and benign: more than that it still offered him symbols for his own internal life, it still conveyed to him intimations of things spiritual and powers infinite. He seems to have had less and less notion of transcending nature and more and more ambition to be like the finest product of nature: he did not wish to be merged with the Over-Soul but rather to become as fine as the hawk. For Thoreau had definite ideas of organic progress, of nature perfecting herself. 'You pass from the lumpish grub in the earth to the airy and fluttering butterfly. The very globe continually transcends and translates itself, and becomes winged in orbit.'[47] Nature transcends herself—by drawing the butterfly out of the grub, the hawk out of the reptile. Thoreau saw winged things as the final result of a process which started in the slime. The hawk flies and soars so freely because it has 'earned this power by faithfully creeping on the ground as reptile in a former state of existence'.[48] But the hawk and the butterfly are still in nature, even if they are at the top of a hierarchy. Here it

55

must be noted that Thoreau does seem at times to envisage some form of ultimate release from earth-boundness: as Sherman Paul noted, for Thoreau 'evolution from excrementitious to aerial forms was a process of purification'.[49] Yet he is finally the man who sought out the smallest and lowest of natural things, who trained the mouse to eat from his hand, who studied ants for hours through a magnifying glass, who exhibits an almost religious devotion to the factuality of the proximate world. He is of course in many ways still a Transcendentalist, but instead of indicating a fact and then asserting the generalized divinity which flowed through it, he preferred to try and state facts so that they took on a lambent mythic glow. 'I would so state facts that they shall be significant, shall be myths or mythologic.'[50] If one may risk so crude a distinction, one could say that Thoreau wanted a poetry, rather than a theology, of facts.

His intention is apparent in the relative crudity of *A Week on the Concord and Merrimack Rivers*, for there a scrupulous scrutiny of the seen world alternates with thrust-in fragments of poetry, other writers' and his own. In doing this he discovered that what he had thought separable had to be merged. 'I have a common-place book for facts', he wrote in his journal a few years after writing about his river trip and shortly prior to finishing *Walden*, 'and another for poetry, but I find it difficult always to preserve the vague distinctions which I had in my mind, for the most interesting and beautiful facts are so much the more poetry and that is their success.'[51] This realization, that the writer need not surround native local facts with established 'poetry' but can entice fresh and relevant poetry from the facts themselves, *simply by stating those facts*, has had a profound influence on American writing. Emerson gave the idea its most important impetus, but Thoreau is even more specific in his insistence on the lyrical qualities of plain unadorned facts of the most unpretentious kind. Thus, on his river trip, 'We had recourse, from time to time, to the Gazetteer, which was our Navigator, and from its bald natural facts extracted the pleasure of poetry'.[52] The poetry to be extracted from bald facts has attracted American writers as various as Whitman and Hemingway, and—this is the point—it is a poetry best discerned by the naive eye, audible only to the innocent uncorrupted senses. (It is a poetry, for instance, which Huck Finn can pick up.) Thoreau's impulse to mythologize the real is in evidence whenever he describes any of the simple earth-bound characters he meets in the woods or by the river. 'Who should come to my lodge this morning but a true Homeric or Paphlagonian man. . . .':[53] 'You shall see rude and sturdy, experienced and wise men, keeping their castles, or teaming up their summer's wood, or chopping alone in the woods, men fuller of talk and rare adventure in the sun and wind and rain, than a chestnut is of meat . . . greater men than Homer, or Chaucer, or Shakespeare. . . .'[54] In his descriptions of local characters like Goodwin or Minott he describes their movements, their appearance in a landscape, their talk, their varying activities with a kind of meticulous reverence which gives them tremendous presence and contour as well as a dimension of mystery as they loom up from time to time and then drop out of his writing. This is an example of Thoreau's method of stating—not explaining or commenting on—a fact, so that it shall have a mythologic air. It is the logical way of writing for a man who believed that 'if men would steadily observe realities only' they would discover that 'reality is fabulous'.[55]

The sauntering innocent eye, the eye that sees without looking, the eye that can discern 'the case that is', the eye that fronts the facts, and yet also extracts the poetry from the facts, the eye that mythologizes the facts in the act of beholding them—what sort of style will this result in? Thoreau himself made many comments on the sort of style he desired and esteemed. He arraigns De Quincey, for instance, because he expresses himself 'with too great fullness and detail'. His sentences 'are not concentrated and nutty . . . his style is nowhere kinked and knotted up into something hard and significant, which you could swallow like a diamond, without digesting'.[56] What Thoreau wants is 'sentences which suggest far more than they say, which have an atmosphere about them, which do not merely report an old, but make a new, impression . . . which lie like boulders on the page . . .'[57] and elsewhere he expresses rather strikingly a preference for 'sentences uttered with your back to the wall'.[58] Writing approvingly of Sir Walter Raleigh and his contemporaries he says that when you come across a sentence by one of them in modern books 'it is as if a green bough were laid across the page'. This fertility image is carried on: 'The sentences are verdurous and blooming as evergreen and flowers, because they are rooted in fact and experience'.[59]

Nut, diamond, boulder, bough, evergreen, flower—the images are interestingly mixed. The first three suggest something hard, solid, finished, inert, heavily-contoured, enduring, three-dimensional, multi-faceted and with a distinctive surface texture. The last three enlist the notions of growth and fecundity, of something well-rooted and flowering. (They remind us of Emerson's dual view which saw the things of the world both 'in a flood and fixed as adamant'.)[60] What all the images suggest is a kind of writing which is corporeal, substantial, and has material identity of its own. It excludes all abstract referential and notional writing and leans heavily on an incarnational view of language. Emerson shared this view of language. Of the vernacular of truckmen and teamsters he wrote in his journal: 'Cut these words and they would bleed; they are vascular and alive; they walk and run.'[61] Thoreau, too, sees a close connection between manual labour, contact with things, and a forceful alive style. 'I find incessant labour with the hands . . . the best method to remove palaver out of one's style'[62] and not unexpectedly he insists, rather in the way Emerson had done, that 'the roots of *letters* are *things*'.[63] But there is another quality he is after which is perhaps best intimated by his image of the diamond, that quality in words which empower them 'to suggest far more than they say', to radiate an atmosphere which is not swallowed up in the literal meaning. 'The volatile truth of our words should continually betray the inadequacy of the residual statement.'[64] He wants a halo of unstated undiminishing significance round his 'bald facts'. Thoreau's method of invoking this aura can be deduced from what we have quoted from him so far. The botanist's analytic scrutiny of facts robs them of their inner resonance and life: it is the innocent sauntering eye which will see them in the right way, from the correct angle, with the appropriate response— that reverence which celebrates without cleaving, that porousness to nature's stealthy influence. This will result in a prose which attempts to emulate the shape and organization of nature, which seeks to disturb as little as possible the structure of the world. What he writes in his journals about proper conversation with friends applies equally to his ideal of writing, namely, that it should 'vary exactly with the scene and events and the contour of the ground'.[65] Sauntering is the ideal procedure because this allows nature to claim your attention in the order which she chooses, it is the way to escape from programmatic systematic intellectual inquiry. One can see evidence of this sauntering throughout his journals. For instance in the report of his visit to Philadelphia: 'Looked from the cupola of the Statehouse, where the Declaration of Independence was declared. The best view of the city I got. Was interested in the squirrels, gray and black, in Independence and Washington Squares.'[66] Surrounded by the history of his country his attention is claimed by the squirrels: he moves as easily from one to the other, with no sense of disparity of significance. As Emerson said, he was equally interested in every natural fact. The prose moves as the eye moves and the eye refuses to consult any hierarchy of importance in its dealings with the world.

Another entry (complete): 'The song sparrow and blackbird heard today. The snow going off. The ice in the pond one foot thick.'[67] The absence of verbs is really the result of a refusal to interrupt or intrude on the world. The eye allows certain facts of jewel-like separateness and brightness to catch its attention: these facts are translated into words with a minimum of tampering and embellishment. Not, of course, that this is Thoreau's style at its best; nor would he himself have maintained that those entries exemplified his own ideal of style—but they are symptomatic. The journal is really Thoreau's perfect genre since it

59

allows him to set down his impressions in random order; it caters generously for the impulse of the moment.

Similarly his best essays are in every sense 'excursions'. This is not to say that Thoreau never interested himself in the formal organization of his material. *Walden* meanders as myths can afford to do, because its organizing pattern lies deep and is not over-scrupulous in assessing the relevance of detail, confident that its meaning will emerge from the accumulating power and direction of its metaphors and a certain grand simplicity of progression in its parts. It starts with a man leaving a society where men are 'smothered and crushed'[68] or turned into machines (and how many subsequent American books have made a similar start!): it ends with the famous parable of the bug which hatched out in a table, bursting out of its imprisoning matter into freedom and flight. It reminds us of 'the beautiful and winged life' which may yet and always emerge from 'the dead dry life of society';[69] it sums up Thoreau's story of a life renewed and released. Thus the seasons of the year around which *Walden* organizes itself provide Thoreau with metaphors of his own metamorphosis: as Sherman Paul has noted the important image clusters are ice–thaw–flux, seed–flower–fruit, grub–chrysalis–butterfly. Unlike *A Week on the Concord and Merrimack Rivers*, where Thoreau found no satisfactory way of integrating his facts and poetry, *Walden* reveals a man with a higher degree of organizing tact: the outward facts follow the curve of the year (ending of course in Spring, not Winter); the inward events avail themselves of that shape to trace out their own arc—the two are interdependent but not confused. The result is a work which had a form which is vague, suggestive, memorable, like the simplest and most basic of myths. But if it has form in the whole, it has very little form in the parts. Individual paragraphs read like entries in his journals and for the same reasons. Analysing a passage will bring this out.

As I sit at my window this summer afternoon, hawks are circling about my clearing; the tantivy of wild pigeons, flying by twos and threes athwart my view, or perching restless on the white pine boughs behind my house, gives a voice to the air; a fish hawk dimples the glassy surface of the pond and brings up a fish; a mink steals out of the marsh before my door and seizes a frog by the shore; the sedge is bending under the weight of the reed-birds flitting hither and thither; and for the last half-hour I have heard the rattle of railroad cars, now dying and then reviving like the beat of a partridge, conveying travellers from Boston to the country.[70]

First of all it is written from the point of view of the first person singular; the passage would not be written without Thoreau sitting at his window and looking, or rather 'seeing'. It is worth emphasizing this as it is really with the Transcendentalist writers that the first-person singular achieved its pre-eminence as a literary strategy in American literature, a pre-eminence which it has retained. The writers of the time were aware of its significance. Emerson predicted that novels would give way to diaries and autobiographies, while Thoreau starts *Walden* by boasting that he will retain the '*I*, or first person'[71] in his work as there is nobody else he knows so well. And of course the first draft of Whitman's poems starts challengingly with the assertion: 'I celebrate myself'. Prestige has gravitated towards the experiencing ego, the seeing individual eye.

To return to the passage under discussion. Syntactically the most striking feature is the number of semi-colons; grammatically the dominant feature is the number of present participles and verbs in the present tense—*circling, flying, perching, bending, flitting*, etc., and *sit, dimples, steals*, etc. Everything between each pair of semi-colons constitutes a separate and entire impression, there is no overlapping or interpenetration. This is the discipline of 'looking at what is to be seen' in action, the syntax follows the movements of the sauntering eye; it is in fact sauntering syntax. There is no imagery, no metaphorical panache—only one simile at the end which serves to translate a man-made noise into a part of the diapason of nature. We are given literally stated 'bald facts', as separate and entire as boulders, as excludingly contoured as jewels, and their paratactic isolation in the sentence gives an impression not of scientific accuracy but naive

61

wonder. There is no sophisticated summarizing or blurred generalizing, but rather an equal amount of reverent attention for each and every discernible fact and particular of the here and now. Hence the present tense and participles: the eye is involved in world of movement and present process, and no attempt is made to disrupt, amend, or categorize the varying activities. It is a case of allowing maximum concessions to nature, it is the piety of the submissive innocent eye. Yet—and this is one of the curious features of his prose—this isolating reverence for each separate visual incident actually has an arresting effect, it enforces a *stasis* when it is aimed at establishing a sense of organic movement. He exemplifies Emerson's ideal of 'sequestering one object from the embarrassing variety' yet sequestering has the effect of immobilizing. We noted the mixture of metaphors Thoreau employed to describe his ideal style, and we can say that the diamond effect is more marked than the flowering air. In this his prose offers pre-echoes of the Imagists, Anderson, Hemingway, and Stein, and I maintain that it is one of the results of attempting to re-establish an innocent visual relationship with nature.

Finally we must say something about Thoreau's vocabulary. Sometimes he is capable of a very trenchant economic Saxon speech—'What is man but a mass of thawing clay'[72] for example: then again he often falls into the vernacular, a vernacular which sometimes hovers uneasily on slang. He can speak of people who have 'lost their subscription ticket to morning time in this world'[73] and can say of a pond that 'it took a short siesta at noon'.[74] But over against this he often attempts to utter what he calls 'big thoughts in big words'.[75] For example:

As every season seems best to us in its turn, so the coming in of spring is like the creation of Cosmos out of Chaos and the realization of the Golden Age—

'Eurus ad Auroram Nabathacaque regna recessit,
Persidaque, et radiis juga subdita matutinis.'[76]

This two-way pull in his writing between the Saxon-vernacular and the Latin-elevated styles corresponds to his habit of keeping one notebook for facts and one for poetry, it is an extension of his split intention to 'front only the essential facts' and to 'devote myself to the infinite', an echo of Emerson's shift from the pail to the horizon. As we noted, his prime allegiance is to the earth, the substantial, the incarnate, and undoubtedly his preference was, as he himself put it, for 'fresh English words' over 'conventional Latinisms'.[77] But he is not in complete control of his prose, he oscillates between the portentous and the plain, the florid and the vernacular. What was needed, as he himself noted, was a successful merging of the factual and the poetic; the poetry should radiate from the fact and not be superinduced by the surrounding prose. Thoreau came nearest to achieving this 'merging' in *Walden* where he relies almost exclusively on a direct vernacular mode of address, yet the effect is hardly sustained. And in his later essays he finds it increasingly difficult to merge his facts with his poetry, with his ideas, his truths. As Leo Marx has noted of his late work: 'he could handle either facts or ideas, but he could no longer fuse them.'[78] The innocent eye with its sauntering reverence for 'the case that is', and the simple earth-rooted vernacular, were undoubtedly the strategies best calculated to achieve this effect of facts poetically perceived. But something else was needed.

What of course is missing in all Thoreau's nature is human nature. As he revealingly says: 'It would be sweet to deal with men more, I can imagine, but where dwell they? Not in fields which I traverse.'[79] (Juxtapose with that confession Keats's remark 'Nature is fine, but human nature is finer'—and you have one of the major differences between American and English romanticism thrown into sharp relief.) Consequently Thoreau is not really interested in the moral possibilities of the innocent eye. This is true of Emerson, of course, and of Whitman too, for he was only interested in people in the mass and not in their dramatic interinvolvement: it is only with Twain that we find the innocent eye promoted to the function of moral assessment and evaluation. Nevertheless Thoreau's work does convey a sense of the sheer reality which surrounds a man, and which a man may rediscover by taking 'a new and absolute view of things'.

63

CHAPTER 4

WALT WHITMAN'S ECSTATIC FIRST STEP

No shuttered room or school can commune with me,
But roughs and little children better than they.[1]

WHITMAN, Leaves of Grass

IN attempting to describe the most desirable relationship with the visible world, Emerson often cited menial and manual workers as having maintained the correct rapport with their surroundings, but where his reference was general Thoreau pointed more specifically to known local acquaintances, Minott or Goodwin. In one important sense Whitman took the utilization of the vernacular uneducated figure a stage further, for in effect he let him write his first cycle of poems. This needs some clarification. When the first edition of *Leaves of Grass* was published in 1855 the name of the author was omitted from the title page. But on the opposite page there is a daguerreotype of a bearded workman, dressed only in a shirt and rough trousers and a hat tilted at a rakish angle to the back of his head. One hand is in his pocket and the other rests insouciantly on his hip. There is no writing under the portrait and in the absence of any other evidence he would seem to be the author of the poems that follow. Malcolm Cowley has pointed out[2] that whereas on the copyright page there is written: 'Entered according to Act of Congress in the year 1855, by Walter Whitman', half-way through the first long poem we are introduced to: 'Walt Whitman, an American, one of the roughs, a Kosmos.'[3] Even on such slight evidence I think we are entitled to say that Walter is the concealed author, in fact a printer and journalist, while Walt is a persona adopted for the purposes of what he wants to say. The author, that is, has concealed himself behind a vernacular narrator in the interests of vocabulary and point-of-view.

Why did Whitman adopt this persona? Broadly, in the interests of a new response, what kind of response we can start to understand by considering some of his own statements. In his very first poem in that irresistibly familiar tone which was so new in American literature he told his readers:

> You shall no longer take things at second or third hand . . .
> nor look through the eyes of the dead . . . nor feed on the
> spectres in books,
> You shall not look through my eyes either, nor take things
> from me,
> You shall listen to all sides and filter them for yourself.[4]

and later:

> Long enough have you dreamed your contemptible dreams,
> Now I wash the gum from your eyes,
> You must habit yourself to the dazzle of the light and of
> every moment of your life.[5]

and in a poem written later he has these key lines expressing his intentions:

> To be absolv'd from previous ties and conventions, I from
> mine and you from yours!
> To find a new unthought-of nonchalance with the best of
> Nature!
> To have the gag remov'd from one's mouth![6]

All implies a removal of previously erected barriers and filters which in his view inhibited a proper engagement between man and his world. He wishes to abandon the formality of sensory intercourse enforced by old schemata, to dismiss literary conventions, to wipe the eye clean of old accretions. The eye was of crucial importance to Whitman; it even takes precedence over his sense of touch. He wrote in the introduction to the first edition:

Who knows the curious mystery of the eyesight? The other senses corroborate themselves, but this is removed from any proof but its own and foreruns the identities of the spiritual world. A single glance of it mocks all the investigations of man and all the instruments and books of the earth and all reasoning. What is marvellous? What is unlikely? What is impossible or baseless or vague? After you have once just opened the space of a peachpit and given audience to far and near and to the sunset and had all things enter with electric swiftness softly and duly without confusion or jostling or jam.[7]

We shall have occasion to comment on the importance of eyesight in examining his first long poem but as a single example of this belief in the importance of eyesight we could note his later poem 'Salut Au Monde'[8] in which the key line is 'What do you see Walt Whitman?' and in which the phrase 'I see . . .' is repeated eighty-three times. And there is no hierarchy of admission: the hospitality is as indiscriminate as it is wide ('nothing too close, nothing too far off'),[9] because—and this has major formal implications—since 'the palpable is in its place and the impalpable is in its place'[10] there can be no confusion of apprehension. The order in which objects swarm to the eye, the sequence in which the eye feels the urgent tug of one thing, the subtle allurement of another, this is an order which cannot be improved on. Indeed the important thing is not to disturb it. The uninstructed vagaries of the eye are a symptom of health; it is the classifying, categorizing, analytic eye of the educated man which is diseased. Hence the unlettered vernacular persona. For in Whitman's belief: 'There is that indescribable freshness and unconsciousness about an illiterate person that humbles and mocks the power of the noblest expressive genius.'[11] The adoption of the vernacular persona in the interests of freshness, and a healthy reverent informal unselfconsciousness (for its naivety as opposed to the myopia of the learned) is a clear continuation of Emerson's tentative preference for those minds which 'have not been subdued by the drill of school education'. Just as it echoes Thoreau's deprecation of the tape-measure of understanding and his expressed desire for 'free senses' as opposed to study. Walt Whitman, the writer of the poems, is a man who will 'see without looking'. Thoreau would have agreed with Whitman

66

that 'to glance with an eye . . . confounds the learning of all times'; the glance being an act of unpremeditated attention and assimilation, as opposed to the calculated scrutiny of the scientific inquirer.

But the syndrome of virtues possessed by the vernacular narrator extends beyond the naive open eye. We can best assemble these virtues by turning to the very important introduction written for the first edition of *Leaves of Grass* before seeing them in operation in the poems. It starts with an exaltation of America—'The United States themselves are essentially the greatest poem'[12]—and in particular of the kind of people it is breeding. 'Here are the roughs and beards and space and ruggedness and nonchalance that the soul loves.'[13] Even this is a calculated act of indecorum since the New England of the time, which was the source of all important literature so far written in America, tended to extol a cultivated dignity of demeanour and a social formality which had no place in it for rough nonchalance. Whitman continues his praise of these types—for their 'freshness and candor', the 'picturesque looseness of their carriage', 'the fluency of their speech', stating his preference for the mechanic or farmer gifted with 'firm eyes and a candid and generous heart' over the 'bound booby and rogue in office at a high salary'.[14] So when he writes that the bard is to be 'commensurate with the people'[15] we can see clearly which section of the population he had in mind. His intention is to create a form of writing which will be infused with the qualities of the vernacular type: the freshness, candour, the fluency and the looseness, and the generosity of heart. The looseness of carriage will become a looseness of verse form, the candour and fluency will be demonstrated in the diction, and the generosity of heart will become a warm hospitality of the senses. And what is the overall aim? Similar to Emerson's and Thoreau's: a new unobstructed perspective on the world, a new way of indicating and annotating reality. The poet, he says, 'shall go directly to creation':[16] not via any literary precedents. Ornaments and embellishments of style are to be eschewed: 'I will not have in my writing any elegance or effect or originality to hang in the way, not the richest curtains. What I tell I tell for precisely what it is.[17] Any selfconscious tricks of style that obtrude themselves between man and 'the perfect facts of the open air'[18] are to be eliminated. He once formulated his intention to write in 'a perfectly transparent, plate-glassy style, artless, with no ornaments, or attempts at ornaments, for their own sake'[19] and to this end avail himself of 'common idioms and phrases—Yankeeisms and vulgarisms'[20] so that the achieved effect would be one of 'clearness, simplicity, no twistified or foggy sentences, at all'.[21] The curtains of established stylistic convention were to be drawn back as far as possible. He might have echoed the cry from the Indian Sacred Book which Yeats quotes in his essay on Modern Poetry: 'They have put a golden stopper into the neck of the bottle; pull it! Let out reality!'[22] Or again we might say he fulfilled Lawrence's prescribed function for the poet: 'Man fixes some wonderful erection of his own between himself and the wild chaos, and gradually goes bleached and stifled under his parasol. Then comes a poet, enemy of convention, and makes a slit in the umbrella; and lo! the glimpse of chaos is a vision, a window to the sun.'[23] Except of course that where other people saw chaos, Whitman affirmed the presence of 'form and union and plan.'[24] His quarrel with existing conventions was that they did not allow enough of America into literature. Against the more traditional formulae of selection, exclusion, and rearranging he set up an ideal of absorption. The poet will absorb his country, he must 'incarnate its geography and natural life and rivers and lakes.'[25] The real world must not be made to queue up deferentially outside the poet's haughty sensibility; rather it must be let in with a rush. Hence the recurrence of tidal imagery in his writing. The poet must 'flood himself with the immediate age as with the vast oceanic tides'.[26] The relationship between this avowed aim and his use of the naive eye is explicitly revealed in one of the short poems in the first edition called 'There was a Child went forth'.[27] It is a fine example of Whitman working at his simplest, though not making particular use of the vernacular mask.

> There was a child went forth every day,
> And the first object he looked upon and received with
> wonder or pity or love or dread, that object he became,
> And that object became part of him for the day or a certain
> part of the day . . . or for many years or stretching cycles
> of years.[28]

The rest of the poem comprises five sentences which are simply
enumerations of the things that become part of the child—for
example:

> And the appletrees covered with blossoms, and the fruit
> afterward . . . and woodberries . . . and the commonest
> weeds by the road;
> And the old drunkard staggering home from the outhouse
> of the tavern whence he had lately risen.[29]

The countryside, the home—'all the changes of city and country
wherever he went',[30] they all become part of the child whose
naivety acts as a sort of sponge to the teeming fragments of the
real world. At moments Whitman manages to invest this uncritical assimilation with a real lyricism, the lines themselves seem
to approximate the eye's wondering and delighted ranging over
the near and far of the seen world:

> The village on the highland seen from afar at sunset . . . the
> river between,
> Shadows . . . aureola and mist . . . light falling on roofs and
> gables of white or brown, three miles off,
> The schooner near by sleepily dropping down the tide . . .
> the little boat slacktowed astern,
> The hurrying tumbling waves and quickbroken crests and
> slapping;
> The strata of coloured clouds . . . the long bar of maroontint
> away solitary by itself . . . the spread of purity it lies
> motionless in,
> The horizon's edge, the flying seacrow, the fragrance of
> saltmarsh and shoremud;
> These became part of that child who went forth every day,
> and who now goes forth and will always go forth every
> day,
> And these become of him or her that peruses them now.[31]

We should note that despite the apparently random and undiscriminating progress of the eye, the admitted details do in fact compose a scene. Often in Whitman's verse there is a cunning sense of selection at work in the almost artless grouping of details: what is important is that his verse should retain the air of unpremeditation and unselectiveness. And for this effect the naive eye was indispensable. It is the naive eye that will let the world in unquestioningly: that is the point. We saw in Emerson and Thoreau a desire to look at the world as though for the very first time; Whitman seems to have approached that state. He writes in a later poem very significantly on this:

> Beginning my studies the first step pleas'd me so much,
> The mere fact consciousness, these forms, the power of
>   motion,
> The least insect or animal, the senses, eyesight, love,
> *The first step I say awed me and pleas'd me so much,*
> *I have hardly gone and hardly wish'd to go any farther,*
> But stop and loiter all the time and sing it in ecstatic songs.[32]
> [my italics]

Not to be blasé, not to receive the world sieved through classes and genres and types; rather to note each item as a small miracle, to regard the diversity of particulars with a lucid awe, to let the eye travel from apple-blossom to a drunkard with no diminution of wonder and no access of moral judgement; this is the required facility. And Whitman thought that the child and the uneducated vernacular figure were gifted with this facility. To some extent so did Emerson and Thoreau but where Whitman advances on them is in trying to formulate a style mimetic of this response to the world. There is a minimum of active verbs—though, as in Thoreau's writing, there are many participles (as people or animals are discerned in an act but not watched through a complete action): to match Emerson's numerous semi-colons there are the series of dots, indicative of the time taken for the eye to move from one object to the other but with no attempt to relate the various parts to each other and subsume them into a complex whole. ('They are but parts . . . any thing is but a part.')[33]

Things are allowed to lie separate and undisturbed: no plan is imposed, no deductions are made, no nets of theory draw them together in compound sentences. This would be a falsification, just as to tighten the poem into a regular rhyme scheme would be a falsification, since that would disturb the holy order in which the world entered the eye and interpose the meddlings and severings of the mind between the eye and the circumpressure of reality. Whitman practises what Emerson and Thoreau preached: visual capitulation to the benign tyranny of the material world.

But this reverence and respect for the corporeality and plenitude of the material world is not an end in itself. Just as Emerson found the details of the real world emblematic of the Over-Soul, and just as Thoreau felt that reality was literally fabulous and mythic, so Whitman affirmed 'a moral purpose, a visible or invisible intention, certainly underlying all'.[34]   At the end of his life he wrote bitterly against what he called 'the growing excess and arrogance of realism'.[35]   Indeed in *Democratic Vistas*, written after the war to a different America and in a more mordant frame of mind, Whitman seems at times to become an apostate from his own religion of the real. One paragraph fairly sums up this later attitude, though it is an attitude latent in his earliest work:

The elevating and etherealizing ideas of the unknown and of unreality must be brought forward with authority. . . . To the cry, now victorious—the cry of sense, science, flesh, incomes, farms, merchandise, logic, intellect, demonstrations, solid perpetuities, buildings of brick and iron, or even the facts of the shows of trees, earth, rocks, etc., fear not, my brethren, my sisters, to sound out with equally determin'd voice, that conviction brooding within the recesses of every envision'd soul—illusions! apparitions! figments all! True, we must not condemn the show, neither absolutely deny it, for the indispensability of its meanings; but how clearly we see that, migrate in soul to what we can already conceive of superior and spiritual points of view, and, palpable as it seems under present relations, it all and several might, nay certainly would, fall apart and vanish.[36]

It was never mere enumeration that Whitman was after—despite Emerson's complaint that he had written the country's inventories

—for in his first preface he says that in the work of a proper poet 'as they emit themselves facts are showered over with light'[37] and that when the poet 'breathes into any thing that was before thought small it dilates with the grandeur and life of the universe':[38] he wanted not mere annotation but the 'vivification' of facts without which 'reality would seem incomplete'.[39] From the start the intention is religious, even mystical. The world is admitted en masse and no questions asked, but only to be etherealized, to be related to 'the central divine idea of All'.[40] The underlying aim is clearly expressed in a poem added later called 'Starting from Paumanok':[41]

> I will make the poems of materials, for I think they are to be the most spiritual poems . . .[42]

and later:

> I will not make poems with reference to parts,
> But I will make poems, songs, thoughts, with reference to ensemble,
> And I will not sing with reference to a day, but with reference to all days,
> And I will not make a poem nor the least part of a poem but has reference to the soul,
> Because having look'd at the objects of the universe, I find there is no one nor any particle of one but has reference to the soul.[43]

The material *is* the spiritual, if seen in the right way: and though he had said 'any thing is but a part' we find cocooned within that assertion a belief that the parts in their scattered disarray actually form a secret ensemble, again only visible to the devout yet uninquiring eye. Whitman's universe is not atomistic to himself as poet: if it seems so to us then, so he would argue, that is because we have lost the all important sense of ensemble. It is perhaps the sense that all mystics are trying to convey, the sense which Whitman is continually trying to recapture and recreate. For to lose this sense is the mystic's nightmare or dark night of the soul. Whitman in later life had such moments.

72

Yet, yet, ye downcast hours, I know ye also,
Weights of lead, how ye clog and cling at my ankles,
Earth to a chamber of mourning turns—I hear the o'er-
weening, mocking voice,
*Matter is conqueror—matter, triumphant only, continues
onward.*[44]

If reality is not spiritual, then what of pain and death? Without
the sense of ensemble and belief in spirit the optimistic mystic
will simply cave in when confronted with what Yeats called 'the
brutality, the ill-breeding, the barbarism of truth'[45] and Whitman
had the honesty to record such moments. One for instance when
he suddenly found himself thinking of the endless murderousness
of the sea and its indifferent swallowing of human life. He
imagines a ship foundering and the moment when some helpless
women await death:

'A huge sob—a few bubbles—the white foam spirting up
—and then the women gone,
Sinking there while the passionless wet flows on—and I
now pondering, are those women indeed gone?
Are souls drown'd and destroy'd so?
Is only matter triumphant?'[46]

And sometimes the sheer extent of human cruelty and misery
quieted his euphoric confidence:

'I sit and look out upon all the sorrows of the world . . .'[47]

so the poem starts, and after a list of these sorrows ends:

'All these—all the meanness and agony without end I
sitting look out upon,
See, hear, and am silent.'[48]

But such moments are rare: usually Whitman is aware only of
'form, union and plan'. Whitman's moments of doubt were too
fleeting to take the edge off his initial optimism, even though the
later poems are often flat and assertive, and marked by the pulpit-
pounding of a man who has lost the brio and élan of his original
vision. But just from these moments of doubt and worried

73

silence we can extract a hint of the possible dangers and limitations of the naive vision: i.e. its inability to assimilate discordant facts, its vulnerability to the harsher textures of existence, the likelihood of its being irrecoverably bruised and stunned by the darker side of human life whenever it should happen to stumble upon it. But we must return to Whitman's first and perhaps greatest poem for here he was writing under the tremendous influence of what must have amounted to a mystical experience, and here it is that he is most alive to the material world, most alert to its dazzling variety of content, most sensitive to its inexhaustible plenitude, most able to assimilate 'the common, the familiar, the low' with a nonchalant generosity and warmth which are among the cardinal virtues of the naive eye.

Before discussing the morphology of the poem I want to draw attention to the uses to which Whitman puts his adoption of the vernacular persona and the naive eye. His 'poet' is pre-eminently a susceptible spectator. He 'watches and wonders', he sees, he looks and views, he peers and peruses, he gazes and beholds: 'I have no mockings or arguments . . . I witness and wait.'[49] The words recur and often appear in unobtrusive yet telling sequence, for example in section eight:

> 'The little one sleeps in its cradle,
> I lift the gauze and look a long time, and silently brush
>   away flies with my hand.
> The youngster and the redfaced girl turn aside up the
>   bushy hill,
> I peeringly view them from the top.
> The suicide sprawls on the bloody floor of the bedroom,
> It is so . . . I witnessed the corpse . . . there the pistol had
>   fallen.'[50]

Birth, love, death: the sequence of glances is not unpremeditated, just as the three visual attitudes change subtly from meditative reverence, to a sort of excited voyeurism, on to an almost cold shocked detachment. Whitman is in some ways the 'mirror carried through the street, ready to render an image of every created thing'[51] which Emerson said the great poet should be, but it would be unwise to ignore the order in which he lets his glance be attracted by things. And after all it is the man carrying or containing the mirror who decides which way it is to turn, where next to offer its reflective surface. The key thing is the stance, the perspective, the angle of vision: Whitman, as Emerson had done, stressed the importance of *'point of view'*(his italics) and later in life he recalled how he decided that it was time to see and 'chant' America from the point of view and with the 'utterance' of 'the born child of the New World'.[52] This is where Whitman's vernacular persona proves itself indispensable.

> 'I lean and loafe at my ease ... observing a spear of summer grass.'[53]
> 'I am satisfied ... I see, dance, laugh, sing;'[54]
> 'Apart from the pulling and hauling stands what I am,
> Stands amused, complacent, compassionating, idle, unitary,
> Looks down, is erect, bends an arm on an impalpable certain rest,
> Looks with its sidecurved head curious what will come next,
> Both in and out of the game, and watching and wondering at it.'[55]

The idle nonchalance of 'one of the roughs' proves to be a fruitful strategy of absorption. Not being immersed myopically in any one activity, nor concerned to argue, justify or account for ('to elaborate is no avail'),[56] this poet can lean back and 'indicate reality'.[57] But this is no Addisonian spectator seeing most of the game; there is no note of patronizing savoir faire, of contemptuous withdrawnness in this voice. This poet watches everything in order to wonder at it ('the wise man wonders at the usual'—it is the Emersonian prescription) and the amusement and complacency are of a kind felt by a man of infinite sympathy, a man who can 'compassionate'.[58] It is typical that Whitman should revive that old usage and allow it to be an activity in its own right ('Whoever walks a furlong without sympathy walks to his own funeral, dressed in his shroud').[59] It is worth stressing these two qualities since two of Huckleberry Finn's great virtues are his capacity for wonder and natural reverence, and the endless spontaneity of his sympathy. This is not to force a genealogy but rather to indicate a family likeness, since Huck also is the adopted naive vernacular mask of his creator.

Wonder and sympathy effectively produce empathy: it is as though by leaning idly back *out* of the game Whitman's poet more easily loses himself *in* the various aspects of it as they pass before his eye, or his mind's eye. One of the things that happens in the poem is that the poet increases his range of vision and depth of penetration. Vision becomes visionary without—and this is the remarkable thing—losing any of its meticulous specificity. He manages to become a spectator of the country's activity without having recourse to a ruinously vague generality.

Here we must raise the question of the over-all form of the first 'Song of Myself'. Whitman's poetry has often attracted the accusation of utter formlessness and not without good reason; and yet there is a direction, a shape, a significant commencement and conclusion to the poem, and some of the sections which at first seem so abandoned and random, on subsequent readings reveal a purposive energy in their progress, an irresistible sense of sequence. Despite apparent lacunae in the developing intent, despite many moments of too private febrile associationism, a sense of some basic unity does loom up through the poem. A unity which we can perhaps borrow some words of Proust's to describe (though he used them of a very different writer): 'a unity that has been unaware of itself, therefore vital and not logical, that has not banned variety, chilled execution.' An ordered perspective is something the wondering poet Walt Whitman cannot afford to appear to have: yet some sense of dominant and sustaining purpose is something no work of art can afford to be without. The question really is this: what sort of organizing form the strategy of naive wonder and empathy can provide for its local responses. Clearly it will be a form which is loose, permissive, tending more to omnivorousness than parsimony; a form not like a containing shell but like a hidden spine which controls and yet facilitates a maximum of movement. The difficulty for Whitman of course is that since all things are perfect and in their proper place and since 'I believe a leaf of grass is no less than the journey work of the stars' he has no criteria of exclusion or preference, no reason to emphasize or concentrate on one detail more than another, no cause to leave anything out at all (and yet all art depends to a large extent on what is left out). Hence indeed the pace, the giddiness, the gulping desperate inclusiveness of some of the sections.

> To me the converging objects of the universe perpetually flow

and

> I help myself to material and immaterial,
> No guard can shut me off, no law can prevent me.[60]

The excitement and to some extent the unique quality of the poem are due to the way in which it seems to catch the teeming encroachment of the world, and the effect whereby nature's processes seem always about to take over from art's laws, the occasional sense that control has passed from man to matter. The art of this particular poem is an art perpetually on the point of ecstatic surrender to nature (a surrender, let it be said, sometimes made— to the detriment of the poem). And yet finally there is an envisioning form and at the end of the poem the poet's voice has conveyed more than nature's muteness. There has been an access of meaning.

In asserting that the poem does have a definite direction one must at once concede that its logic is vague and not always sufficient to organize the included material. Put simply the poem moves in the following direction. The poet experiences all the joys of the physical world through sight and touch, then he finds he has to suffer all the agonies of the world and confront the atrocities of nature and man ('agonies are one of my changes of garments'):[61] then he throws off that 'fit' and is resurrected beyond lamentation, beyond doubt, beyond any one specific type of belief, beyond self, into an ultimate calm which seems to discern the deepest rhythms of nature and accepts death as the

77

source of life. Whereas his empathy with the miseries of the world bring him to the ground as a shamefaced beggar (see line 952), he thereafter 'rises . . . with the true gravitation'.[62] There are recurrent images of rising and the risen to develop his theme: words like mount, the 'eleves', stand up, dilate, buoy up, expanding; and lines like—

> Old age superbly rising! Ineffable grace of dying days![63]

All these prepare us for the final import of the poem by bringing forward the notion that the descent towards earth is in fact an ascent into some sublime mystery of life, by hinting of the fecundity of darkness and death.

The poet 'tramps a perpetual journey'[64] which is more than geographic; he entices us onto 'a plain public road'[65] which is the thoroughfare of the whole continent; and at the end when he tells us 'I stop some where waiting for you'[66] he is still Walt Whitman, the nonchalant vernacular wonderer, yet at the same time he has become air, water and earth. In anticipation, in imagination he has returned to the elements. So we have such striking lines as:

> I depart as air. . . . I shake my white locks at the runaway sun
> I effuse my flesh in eddies, and drift it in lacy jags.
> I bequeath myself to the dirt to grow from the grass I love
> If you want me again look for me under your bootsoles[67]

And we should remember that in the early part of the poem where he is celebrating life, growth and physical contact, the grass first appears as the soft bed of pure sensual love ('Loafe with me on the grass')[68] and then, in a remarkable line, the symbol of the fertility of death: 'And now it seems to me the beautiful uncut hair of graves'.[69] The grass is thus the loveliness of life which, if it tends inevitably to death also emerges endlessly from it. (It is around such hints and echoes and accumulations of significance that the poem to some extent organizes itself.) And it is thus with perfect rightness that the poem moves towards evening; the dusk of the day, the twilight of the individual life. In fact it is the declining light, the poet tells us, which 'coaxes me to vapor and dusk'.[70] It ends on a note of sunset and death which is yet a note of calm ecstasy. For the poet has seen in death not an end but the secret of all beginnings: with perfect rightness the last line is in the present tense, and (in the first edition) it rightly refuses the finality of a full-stop. Thus the man, the journey, the road, and the day, which provide, as it were, the primary form of the poem, transform themselves, generalize themselves as the poet proceeds through his religious experience and is resurrected into the serene far-sightedness of prophecy.

Whether such a vague, though impressive formal direction is enough to bind together all that Whitman wants to include is still a debatable point. In his desire to vivify the common facts of life, to illuminate them with a new kind of reverence, to bathe them in wonder, he sometimes lets the naive eye move from one thing to another so fast and so unrestrictedly that the excess of particulars starts to blur and we lose the sense of any logic as his ecstatic gaze sweeps on. When he is 'afoot with my vision'[71] he can be hard to keep up with. Of course his whole strategy of enumeration is related to Emerson's idea that things sing themselves and Thoreau's contention that the clearly stated fact will appear fabulous. Such theories on their own provide no hints for the ordering of the fabulous facts, for the orchestration of the singing things. As Walt Whitman extends his wondering gaze to include the whole continent it is not always clear why one thing follows another: there is often no sense of rigorous connection though there can be a powerful flow of unstated association. However, we can at least say this: we are seldom prompted to complain of the incongruity of Whitman's juxtapositions and to have made them too clearly congruous would have constituted for him an excessive intrusion on the passive idle gaze, the nonchalantly empathizing wonder which he valued as the correct 'point of view'. But in addition to the sense of order and direction which derive from the onward urgings of the poet's 'journey' over America and towards death, Whitman does have a sense of local composition and specific sequence. The whole poem is indeed conceived paratactically and there is often little syntactical relating of part to part: but the parts usually coalesce within themselves. They do hold together although Whitman often contents himself with seemingly straight listing of things unexplored by metaphor, unpenetrated by thought, unexplained by comment. Let us take an example from Section Ten. There his empathy makes him a hunter, a clam-digger, a guest at a trapper's wedding, the helper of a runaway slave. His capacity to identify with various moods and situations gives the various passages a fine immediacy. It is so unhindered, so easily done, so unselfconsciously achieved. It seems like a valuable instinct and not a literary manoeuvre. He does not simply *see*—he tries to *become* what he sees.

> I am the hounded slave . . . I wince at the bite of dogs[72]
> I do not ask the wounded person how he feels. . . . I myself
>   become the wounded person[73]

Similarly as hunter ('amazed at my own lightness and glee')[74] and clam-digger ('I tucked my trouser-ends in my boots and went and had a good time')[75] there is a sense of absolute freshness of participation. On the other hand it is hard to feel any particular necessity in the sequence of different rôles and experiences. If the over-all momentum and thrust of the poem flags then the parts will tend to fall away from each other, revealing their inherent unrelatedness and separateness. But usually the parts themselves are finely composed. For example the trapper's wedding which he witnesses:

> I saw the marriage of the trapper in the open air in the far-
>   west . . . the bride was a red girl,
> Her father and his friends sat near by crosslegged and
>   dumbly smoking . . . they had moccasins to their feet and
>   large thick blankets hanging from their shoulders;
> On a bank lounged the trapper . . . he was dressed mostly in
>   skins . . . his luxuriant beard and curls protected his neck,
> One hand rested on his rifle . . . the other hand held firmly
>   the wrist of the red girl,

She had long eyelashes . . . her head was bare . . . her coarse
straight locks descended upon her voluptuous limbs and
reached to her feet.[76]

That is the whole section—the dots are Whitman's own. His
eye moves hungrily from detail to detail and the effect is to fix
an instant in time, immobilizing it in its vividness, translating it
into a tableau, perhaps even turning it into a carnival of gods,
unnamed but statuesque.

Where Whitman seems to take the biggest risks is in the breathless catalogues, most notably in Sections Fifteen and Thirty-three.
Section Fifteen, for example, is sixty-nine lines long and most of
those lines comprise one sentence, each line beginning with the
itemization of a person or thing and ending with a comma or
semi-colon. It is paratactical to an extreme degree. And yet as
he introduces type after type, person after person, there is a
cumulative effect of combination in variety, the 'indescribable
crowd'[77] of city and country which is yet one nation, the singu-
larity of individuals which yet adds up to a unity of race. The
juxtapositions are not unconsidered or irresponsible, though we
are obviously intended to feel, rather than ponder or comprehend,
the relevance of the contiguities, the similarities in the differences.
For example:

> The President holds a cabinet council, he is surrounded by
> the great secretaries,
> On the piazza walk five friendly matrons with twined arms;[78]

where we should momentarily half-feel, half-visualize these two
very different yet almost elementally important groups: the
fathers of a new nation, the mothers of its necessary men. On the
other hand it may be the contrast of things in proximity which we
are to feel:

> The bride unrumples her white dress, the minutehand of the
> clock moves slowly,
> The opium eater reclines with rigid head and just-opened
> lips,[79]

time has slowed down for both of them: the bride in anticipation of life, the addict in exhaustion with it.

Then again it may be simply the range of various activities which the new continent calls forth: plougher, pikefisher, flat-boatmen, coon-seekers, hunters and trappers—these types create a sort of section within the section. The overall unity cannot be stated, perhaps just as the unity of America, as it was then, with its centrifugal movements and its incoming variety, could hardly be grasped or demonstrated but only felt. Whitman wants to convey his sense that somehow the teeming differing crowd is basically a sort of family, and if we can respond to his vision then many of his so-called catalogues come alive and knit themselves together.

Section Thirty-three has similar hidden organization; or perhaps it is better to say tendencies towards organization, towards significant grouping, since in no sense is the organiza-tion rigorous and fully worked out. One might call it a sort of deliberately inchoate form which nudges things together rather than autocratically regimenting them to reveal finished form and total lucidity of arrangement. Here the poet 'travels and sails'.[80] We are shown some of the lonely pursuits of men in the unclaimed part of the continent—trailing, prospecting, gold-digging: this leads on to a filling in of the menacing wildness of the natural background—panther, rattlesnake, alligator, black-bear, etc. Then the poet takes us back to the frontier where the domesti-cation of nature has set in, and we travel over the roughness and wild beauty of nature until we are actually inside a farmhouse:

> Where the cheese-cloth hangs in the kitchen, and irons straddle the hearth slab, and cobwebs fall in festoons from the rafters:[81]

Then he opens into a more general survey, bringing together the palpitating energy both of the human heart and the 'triphammers', putting the steamship next to the shark's fin, suggesting the vigour and movement alive in a new continent, in the air, on land, at sea. A sequence of festivals and almost saturnalian celebrations leads

quite naturally into a wide variety of matings, nestings and roost-
ings. A sudden and ominous, yet natural reminder of 'burial
coaches' and 'winter wolves'[82] prepares us for the gradual move
towards all the cruelties, the sufferings and deaths, which the
poet's empathy is going to have to absorb before his 'travelling'
is through. And so on. The whole section requires the closest
attention to see what hidden currents manipulate the surface
drift; to discover the relentless purpose in the random air. Of
course the poet must not appear to have a sequence in mind; all
must occur as discovery, all must be noticed as for the first time.
You cannot adopt the naive wondering eye and at the same time
appear to know what you expect to find. Whitman's poem *has*
to appear unpremeditated, unpredictable, formless and amazed
just as Whitman the poet must eliminate the distance between
himself and his subject matter. This 'caresser of life'[83] does not
wish to withdraw out of arm's reach of anything. He stands so
close to the details that he feels no temptation to relapse into
summaries or general comment: he leaves the particulars to speak
for themselves, content to move from one to another and give
them clarity and immediacy. (In a narrative context this can be
very effective: it has the concealed power of controlled understatement—as for instance in these lines from his account of the
fall of Alamo in Section Thirty-four:

> The second Sunday morning they were brought out in
>   squads and massacred . . . it was a beautiful early summer,
> The work commenced about five o'clock and was over by
>   eight.[84]

This is far more effective and shocking than any plangent invoca-
tion to outrage could be—it is a method which Hemingway was
at some pains to perfect. It is a prose which confronts only the
essential facts. Thoreau's prescription for coming to grips with
nature revealed a whole new range of effects when it was adopted
for the description of human actions and incidents.) But despite
Whitman's commitment to proximate vision in the parts, the
poem as a whole is organized by the long vision of the mystic.

This cannot provide very much order—perhaps it does not provide enough for modern tastes: then again, sheer enthusiasm must always run the risk of amorphousness just as excessive punctiliousness of craft endangers the existence of feeling. Where the mystic fervour simply asserts unity it does very little to help the poem: the order it does provide is a matter of an infectious movement on multiple levels which keeps the geographic and metaphysical journeys easily allied for most of the time. More than that it provides significant contexts which manage to draw in and hold together the unmarshalled fragments of the continent. And this was order enough for a man who craved the whole American reality and who wanted to caress it verbally in its seething sum and not merely relish a few select parts.

Perhaps now his strategy becomes clear. He wanted his poem to let in a maximum of reality; a sort of hospitable passive nonchalance and unselfconsciously empathizing naivety provided the point of view, the attitude that was needed. These are however strategies. Behind the nonchalance there is a mystic with a definite end in view; the naive eye which sees and absorbs the world as for the first time was the instrument of a visionary who felt he had seen deep into the secrets of nature. It was the vernacular persona which provided him with both the nonchalance and the naivety. Revealingly enough the poet puts himself on a level with 'roughs and little children' thus showing how much he felt their attitudes to the world had in common. The vernacular stance also allowed Whitman to use an unconventional 'unliterary' style which enabled him to place himself on almost insolently familiar terms with the world:

> Earth! you seem to look for something at my hands,
> Say old topknot! what do you want?[85]

(Emerson had said 'we cannot bandy words with nature'[86] but Walt Whitman did just that.) It also enabled him to avoid stylized modes of praise, it allowed him to communicate that freshness of appraisal which was the essence of his intent; for example, the mocking bird 'trills pretty well to me'.[87] The vernacular character uses a fact-rooted speech not attuned to generalizing or forming abstractions. The man who sees with the naive eye must speak a form of vernacular if he is to transmit what he sees in all its freshness; established poetic tropes are merely false encrustations on reality, while philosophic or scientific terminology presents the results of prolonged meditation on and measuring of reality. Both miss the raw uniqueness, the quality of novelty of the stuff itself. This Whitman was out to catch. When he tries to incorporate odd French words or operatic terms or biblical echoes or scraps of pretentious rhetoric into his verse, as in the later work he often does, he damages the quality which makes his first poem so fine: the conveyed excitement, the delight and awe, the pain and ecstasy, of a simple person really seeing the new world for the first time. For Whitman is really best at 'wonders': 'the wonders that fill each minute of time forever and each acre of surface and space forever',[88] particularly the wonders of 'the usual routine'[89] and 'everyday objects':[90] when the solemn bard takes over from the naive nonchalant Yankee some of the wonder starts to leak out, the everyday objects lose the miraculous dazzle they have in his first poems. His later scheme for a vast calendrical plan with poems for each day of the year seems to me less successful as an organizing principle than the unflagging push of his first poem. Whitman did not have a genius for consciously contrived form: he cannot give us a made world to explain, evaluate and ordain the real world. Nor did he wish to. But the wonder of a thing-packed, humanly-populated world, the feeling for the vast range of energies and types at work in a country which was making itself, the flow of the world's plenitude to the eye, the potentially mythopoeic resonance of the minutest particular: these he conveys as no American writer before him had attempted to do. In Whitman's early work the naive vision really demonstrates some of its peculiar virtues for the first time.

> Walt Whitman, an American, one of the roughs, a kosmos,
> Disorderly fleshy and sensual . . . eating drinking and
> breeding,

No sentimentalist . . . no stander above men and women or
apart from them . . . no more modest than immodest.[91]

This was the character—as much persona as person—who tried
to see what America was by looking around him as though for the
first time. Effectively he brought a continent to life. We have
perhaps lost some of the sense of the audacity of that undertaking
and yet his first poem makes a gesture which is in fact one of
the perennial gestures of art: a gesture of passionate attention
towards vast stretches of ignored reality. He is, as he confesses,
not the explorer of life; neither is he the arranger, the describer,
the analyser of life; nor is he the improver of life: he is 'the
reminder of life'[92] and the strange but persistently true thing is
how often humanity needs such reminders, such reminding.

CHAPTER 5

TRANSCENDENTALISM AND IMAGISM

WE can see how the visionary exercise of the Transcendentalists became a consciously adopted strategy for later writers if we turn our attention briefly to certain significant similarities and differences between the Transcendentalists and the Imagists. The Imagists emerged out of the symbolist movement. Now the symbolists described the perceived world with great finesse and sensitivity, but not merely for its own sake. They imbued the external thing with subtle spiritual and symbolic meanings even if they were meanings which only the poet could personally detect and apprehend. Gentle and persistent sculptors, they worked at external reality until they created visible analogues for an internal mood. This is a sort of transcendentalism without faith: they found in matter, not God, but some fugitive echo and response to something inside man. Imagism was not symbolism: it was in fact less ambitious, much narrower in its aims, but it took over from the French movement a belief in the intense suggestiveness of separately perceived objects, a feeling that an object properly regarded will release an aura which has a more effective meaning content than abstract predication. The Transcendentalists also believed in the careful scrutiny of particulars. Thoreau, for instance, maintained that 'the universe is not rough-hewn, but perfect in its details; she invites us to lay our eye level with the smallest leaf, and take an insect view of its plain'.[1] Sampson Reed insisted that man should 'respect the smallest blade that grows'.[2] The belief that God was ubiquitous in the world naturally encouraged a scrutiny of 'the minutest of its parts'.[3] The Imagists did not share the belief yet they adopted a similar habit of scrutiny. Both movements, I am suggesting, encouraged the incorporation of carefully contoured, objectively observed particulars into literature. That is to say, quite simply,

87

that the Imagist and the Transcendentalist took up a similar visual stance in front of the external world.

When the Imagists started to publish their work they were often greeted with extremely derisive and adverse criticism; and some of the terms of abuse are very significant. They were derided for preoccupying themselves with the 'little minutiae of life' and refusing to weave them 'into a larger picture or situation'. They were reproached for their 'passivity' of attitude in face of the 'incumbent universe'. Often their 'naïveté', the 'naïveté of infancy' was singled out for scorn. Their poems were contemptuously referred to as being 'full of the simple wonder of a child'; they themselves as being 'content merely to look at things'.[4] Now clearly many of these phrases will apply to the Transcendentalists. They stressed the need for passivity, they ascribed maximum importance to 'simply seeing'; and as for 'the naïveté of infancy', 'the simple wonder of a child'—these were terms of praise as far as they were concerned. They deliberately did not relate varied sense impressions 'into a larger picture' but instead placed them reverently side by side. Yet whereas the naive vision was a genuine mode of access to the divine for them, for the Imagists it was a strategy consciously adopted. Let us consider one comparison. First a piece of prose by a minor Transcendentalist, Theodore Parker, from an essay entitled 'A Discourse of Matters Pertaining to Religion' (1842). He is stressing the immanence of God in matter. 'The influence of God in Nature, in its mechanical, vital, or instinctive actions, is beautiful. The shapely trees; the leaves that clothe them in loveliness; the corn and the cattle; the dew and the flowers; the bird, the insect, moss and stone, fire and water, and earth and air; the clear blue sky that folds the world in its soft embrace . . .': the inventory continues at some length and is concluded by this final assertion: 'all these are noble and beautiful; they admonish while they delight us, these silent counsellors and sovereign aids.' He immediately continues by saying that too many men only feel this once: 'when heaven lay about them in their infancy'.[5] So he is advocating a return to that state which the hostile critics of the Imagists deplored, and saw evidenced in Imagist writing. Note the syntax concomitant with this view; a syntax which avoids all periodic complexity, which leaves the world untouched, which moves from object to object with no attempt to scale the pyramid of abstraction. With this in mind consider these poems by William Carlos Williams.

The Flowers Alone[6]

I should have to be
Chaucer to describe
them—
        Loss keeps
me from such a
catalogue—
But!
        —low, the
violet, scentless as
it is here! higher,
the peartree in full
bloom through which
a light falls as
rain—

And that is gone—

Only, there remains—

Now!
        the cherry trees
white in all black
yards—

        And bare as
they are, the coral
peach trees melting
the harsh air—
                excellence
priceless beyond
all later

                fruit!

And now, driven, I
go, forced to
another day—

Whose yellow quilt
flapping in the
stupendous light—

Forsythia, quince
blossoms—

             and all
the living hybrids

and:

Sea–Trout and Butterfish[7]

The contours and the shine
hold the eye—caught and lying

orange-finned and the two
half its size, pout-mouthed

beside it on the white dish—
Silver scales, the weight

quick tails
whipping the streams aslant

The eye comes down eagerly
unravelled of the sea

separates this from that
and the fine fins' sharp spines

and a more famous poem:

The Red Wheelbarrow[8]

so much depends
upon

a red wheel
barrow

glazed with rain
water

beside the white
chickens

Apart from dashes and a few exclamation marks the poems are
empty of all punctuation; the last poem does not even have
recourse to capital letters. The first poem is a deliberately frag-
mented catalogue, but employed to capture a mood rather than
God. Yet the strategy is not so far removed from that of the
Transcendentalist prose. The eye roams—though making full
use of what Thoreau would call the discipline of selection. The
long pauses serve to convey either a sense of loss or a sense of
wonder. It does not seem excessive to me to call this an example
of the naive vision at work as a consciously adopted strategy.
The second poem discusses that strategy. 'The contours and the
shine hold the eye'—that is the reason for commencing the poem.
Later we hear of the eye coming down eagerly, coming down to
'separate this from that', i.e. to unravel a complex experience and
reduce it to its component parts. The last poem is content to
clear away everything between the eye and the wheelbarrow and
the chickens. The poet does nothing except 'indicate reality'.
What depends on the wheelbarrow? We are not told. There is
no attempt to elucidate, to extrapolate a lesson, to legislate about
life or speculate about the universe. For Williams 'emotions
gather around small things': his task is a meticulous notation
which will then attract a comparable accuracy of emotion which
he need not state. Hence the clearing away, the exclusion of
things which might blur, the enforcing of reverent concentration.
It is naive in a technical sense. To a man with a certain view of the
world it might seem symptomatic of chaos (as Imagism did to
some critics). More likely it is a symptom of disorientation. In
a world of melting beliefs, of disintegrating systems, a universe

which seemed recalcitrant to one harmonious integrating explanation, the bewildered poet might take refuge in examining only
the palpable fragment. Substituting momentary awe for systematic theology, he might well think that only by paying
attention to particulars will he be able to gain for himself any
orientation and stability in the world. That such a shift has taken
place between the Transcendentalists and the Imagists seems to
me undeniable. The scattered objects of the world no longer
form God's palimpsest, but are available for anchoring and
delineating the poet's mood.

One final example will bring out the difference and similarities
between the two groups of writers. One critic scorned Imagist
poetry because it is 'full of the simple wonder of a child picking
up pebbles on the beach'.[9] Interestingly enough Margaret Fuller,
the leading female Transcendentalist, wrote: 'Are the stars too
distant, pick up that pebble that lies at thy foot, and from it learn
the ALL.'[10] A conclusive contrast is provided by the ending of
Sherwood Anderson's *Poor White* in which Hugh McVey, an
alienated figure, picks up some pebbles from the beach at Sandusky. In the train as he passes through the depressing industrial
towns, he plays with the stones. 'There was relief for his mind
in the stones. The light continually played about them, and their
colours shifted and changed. One could look at the stones and
get relief from thoughts.'[11]

Relief, not 'the ALL'. The pebble here instead of being a vehicle
of revelation has become a source of consolation. (To complete
this parable of the pebbles we should recall that Ford Madox
Ford compared Hemingway's prose to pebbles seen through
absolutely clear water.) Anderson himself was a man with
Transcendentalist emotions and aspirations; but although he is
willing to bow the knee, the upcast eye sees no God. He describes
his desire to 'abase myself before something not human' in *A
Story Teller's Story*. 'There was no God in the sky, no God in
myself, no conviction in myself that I had the power to believe
in a God, and so I merely knelt in the dust in the silence and no
words came to my lips. Did I worship merely the dust under my

feet?'[12]   The emotion which should fly upward in the form of assured belief flows instead into his attention to the tangible world about him. Dubious of God he dedicates himself to 'dust'. His eye becomes religious in its awe. He looks *at* the pebbles with wonder, not *through* them with conviction.

We could say that later writers took half of Margaret Fuller's advice. They picked up the pebble but instead of learning from it 'the ALL', they discovered that it was all they could be sure of. They staked everything, as it were, on the single clear perception—and formed a pebble-like style. Hemingway's famous rejection of abstractions in favour of local specificity is as relevant to Imagist poetry as it is to his own fiction: 'There were many words that you could not stand to hear and finally only the names of places had dignity. Certain numbers were the same way and certain dates and these with the names of the places were all you could say and have them mean anything Abstract words such as glory, honour, courage, or hallow were obscene beside the concrete names of villages, the number of roads, the names of rivers, the numbers of regiments and the dates.'[13] Just so, William Carlos Williams, opened the Preface to his long poem *Paterson* with the lines:

> To make a start,
> Out of particulars [14]

and elsewhere more succinctly stated—'no ideas but in things'.

PART II
MARK TWAIN

*I can call it all back and make it as real as it ever was, and as
blessed.*

MARK TWAIN, Autobiography

CHAPTER 6

THE DOCTORS OF THE WILDERNESS

Look to yourselves, ye polished gentlemen!
No city airs or arts pass current here.
Your rank is all reversed; let men of cloth
Bow to the stalwart churl in overalls:
They are the doctors of the wilderness,
And we the low-prized laymen.

EMERSON, *The Adirondacks*[1]

THE Transcendentalists commonly cited the superiority of the uneducated vernacular figure and the child to the well-educated socialized man, primarily on account of the visual relationship they seemed to enjoy with nature. But apart from Whitman's tentative though significant experiment with the vernacular figure as putative author of his first book, the Transcendentalists contented themselves with general statements of creed or prescriptions. They never really tried to adopt the point of view prescribed, not did they make any serious efforts to work according to the ethics of vision which they advocated. Even Whitman's poetry departs at all points from the plausible habits or vision of the simple vernacular figure.

Now this theoretical point of view, that the untutored person is superior to the 'polished gentleman', may properly be called pastoral. This genre habitually professes to admire the superior virtue of the uneducated figure, yet the tendency is always for the pastoral writer to appeal to an educated audience who join with him in looking down at the primitive figures. The 'reversal of rank' experienced by the urban man when venturing into rural areas is a temporary imaginative indulgence and does not indicate any profound realignment of values. The 'doctors of the wilderness' remain 'churls'. Emerson may indeed extol the virtues of the vernacular figure and the child; but his writing instinctively appeals to other well-educated New England intellectuals. But among the south-western humorists a very real 'reversal of rank' was taking place. For in their work the simple-vernacular figure turns the tables on the superior writer and his audience until that comfortable and patronizing nexus is broken by a point of view and an informing set of values which render contempt impossible. Instead of the educated writer inviting an educated audience to share his admiration and contempt for the vernacular figure, that figure displaces the confident writer and confronts the reader directly with an unaccustomed perspective and a challenging set of alien presuppositions and values. In his book *Mark Twain and South-Western Humour*, Kenneth Lynn has very convincingly described the gradual emergence of the vernacular figure in the humorists prior to Mark Twain. He points out that there was a political motive in the work of many of the humorists. Appalled by the growth of violent Jacksonian democracy with all that it implied of the unrestrained savagery of the mob, they had recourse to the classical pastoral genre which enabled them to treat the crude Jacksonian opposition in a tone of amused contempt which effectively nullified its challenging energies. That was the intention, at least. Yet it is remarkable to note how the narrator gradually has to give way to the vernacular figure. The pastoral situation is inverted. There is no need to recapitulate Lynn's general thesis, but a few points need to be made. In A. B. Longstreet's *Georgia Scenes* (1835) the genteel narrator of the rural scenes knows his convention and politically, perhaps, is sure of his ground. But linguistically he is less confident. His chosen perspective is one dominated by literary convention, but all too often his exaggeratedly decorous rhetoric is shattered by fragments of vernacular which are distinguished by a self-authenticating pungency. He maintains the correct moral perspective on what he sees, but it is a perspective which increasingly seems unable to hold its materials in steady focus. The narrator is nudged out by the people he has chosen to exhibit and comment on; because their language has a telling mobility and vitality which his own laboured and static style cannot compete with. His style is generalized, literary, and elevated: their's, is specific, vernacular and low. But his style is quite unable to bring the reader into a fruitful proximity with the subject matter. His style creates a tapestry setting: their voices tear through the weave. To rob Marianne Moore of a good line we can say that Longstreet gives us 'imaginary gardens with real toads in them'. Continually we witness Longstreet's style demonstrating its own disability to establish living contact with the author's chosen materials. And the general linguistic unease noticeable throughout the book is a reflection of a deeper uncertainty about his attitude to the rural-vernacular world.

In *Simon Suggs' Adventures* (1845) by Johnson J. Hooper, we can see an increase in that uncertainty. The construction of the book is straight-forward pastoral. The patronizing, detached, even-toned Hooper holds up the crude vernacular Suggs (a caricature for Jackson) for display. But the emotional emphases are not distributed according to classic pastoral prescription. Hooper's distancing, deprecating rhetoric still keeps the rough vernacular fairly safely caged, but while the narrator has all the good taste, Suggs has all the energy. And in competing with the narrator's educated attitudes he reveals a superior weapon—a brutal candour. This energy and candour have a disruptive effect on the unruffled poise of the narrator. The controlled admiration now turns into a sort of unwilling awe, while the contempt starts to take on the colour of fear and repugnance. And just as the narrator's poise is shaken, so is his rhetoric internally disturbed. His style flounders; it is on edge, ill at ease with itself. While Suggs's anti-intellectual sneering has great confidence and sustaining insouciant energy: 'Human natur' and the human family is *my* books, and I've never seed many but what I could hold my own with. . . . As old Jed'diah used to say, book-larnin spiles a man ef he's got mother-wit, and ef he aint got that, it don't do him no good.'[2] Morally, Suggs is a foul old rogue. He casts a cold eye on life and takes it as he finds it. But he does have a quick, itemizing eye for the empiric facts at hand which enlists our interest, if not our sympathy, more easily than does the remote perspective of the educated narrator. In both senses of the word Suggs is in his element and this intimacy with what he is talking about gives his speech a specificity and vividness that the author—who is a good deal out of his element—cannot match. Suggs's cold eye is at least a clear eye and this clarity of eye is in itself a virtue since it enables him to see more, and more closely than the narrator. We are brought nearer to the brute stuff of the world.

By the time we reach George Harris's *Sut Lovingood* (1867) the pastoral situation is vestigial. The elegant educated narrator is all but banished from the book by the extraordinary vernacular hero—Sut. On one of the rare occasions when the narrator starts to tell a story, Sut turns on him with full vernacular derision for his inflated plangent rhetoric insisting that what needs saying can be said, and said better, without the obscuring posturings of a well-manicured rhetoric. The narrator becomes a ghostly presence, still going through the motions of playing patronizingly with the simple vernacular figure: but in fact all the vivid speech, all the energy, and indeed all the judgements, come from the mouth of Sut. His assessment of what he sees is not 'placed' by the narrator's superior ethics; his limited vision is not supplemented by the longer perspective of the author. The man of cloth bows to the stalwart churl in good earnest. The narrator's sole function is that credited to him in the subtitle of the book: 'yarns by a nat'ral birn durn'd fool, warped and wove for public wear by George W. Harris.' But in fact Harris had deployed all his energies in recapturing Sut's vernacular: so far from being 'warped and wove', his language is left as coarse and rough-spun as possible. The narrator never consults his education for some superior verdict on the world or some superior style by which to hold it together. He cedes the initiative to the uneducated Sut who is more patronizing than patronized. And Sut, it is important to note, is a youth. He is also a complete anarchist bringing disorder and destruction wherever he goes. But although he is cruel, lazy, sickly, anti-idealistic, he enlists some of our sympathies and all of our attention because he is the sharpest judge of the general sordidness in which he moves and because he permits us to look into the awful pessimism in his own heart.

I'se a goner I 'speck, an' I jis don't keer a durn. I'm no count, no how. Jis' look at me! Did yu ever see sich a sampil ove a human afore? I feels like I'd be glad *tu be* dead, only I'se feard ove the dyin. I don't keer fur hearearter, fur its onpossibil fur me tu hev ara soul. Who ever seed a soul in jis' sich a rack heap ove bones an' rags es this?[3]

Here the vernacular figure has acquired a new inwardness, an involving confessional candour. Sut tells himself no lies and we come to rely on his mordant, desolate honesty. In a world of hypocrites he emerges as the only reliable guide.

But, more than that, Sut has a new way of visualizing and a new manner of describing his response to what he sees which transcend Harris's political motives and suggest possibilities for the vernacular beyond the limited aims of excoriating a rotten society. This, for example, is how he describes a storm:

I'se hearn in the mountains a fust rate fourth proof smash ove thunder cum onexpected, an' shake the yeath, bringin along a string ove litenin es long es a quarter track, an' es bright as a weldin heat, a-racin down a big pine tree, tarin hit intu broom-slits, an' toof pickers, an'a raisin a cloud ove dus', an' bar, an' a army ove lim's wif a smell sorter like the devil wer about, an' the long darnin needil leaves fallin roun wif a tif-tif-quiet sorter soun, an' then a quiverin on the yeath as littil snake die, an I felt quar in my in'ards, sorter ha'f cumfurt, wif a littil glad an' rite smart ove sorry mix'd wif hit.[4]

This is more than just grammarless violence: the long, rambling sentence which moves from sensation to sensation with unpretentious fidelity, which improvises new similes, which offers tentative approximations of the speaker's response and state of mind, which gives us the experience at the moment of its taking place; which, in effect, secures a novel intimacy with an external and internal reality—this sentence is an early example of the naive vision doing positive work.

More impressive is Sut's description of one of his rare moments
of admiration and content—a woman preparing an evening meal:

Wirt's wife got yearly supper, a rale suckit-rider's supper, whar the
'oman ove the hous' wer a rich b'lever. Thar wer chickens cut up, an'
fried in butter, brown, white, flakey, light, hot biskit, made wif cream,
scrambil'd aigs, yaller butter, fried ham, in slices es big as yure han,
pickil'd beets, an' cowcumbers, roas'in ears, shaved down an' fried,
sweet taters, baked, a stack ove buckwheat cakes, as full ove holes es a
sifter, an' a bowl of strained honey, tu fill the holes. . . . I gets dorg
hongry every time I sees Wirt's wife, ur evan her side-saddil, ur her
frocks a-hangin on the closeline. Es we sot down, the las' glimmers
ove the sun crep thru the histed winder, an' flutter'd on the white
tabil-cloth and play'd a silver shine on her smoof black har, es she sot
at the head ove the tabil, a-pourin out the coffee, wif her sleeves
push'd tight back on her white roun' arm, her full throbbin neck wer
bar to the swell ove her shoulders, an' the steam ove the coffee made
a movin vail afore her face, es she slowly brush'd hit away wif her lef
han', a-smilin an' a flashin her talkin eyes lovingly at her hansum
husbun. I thot if I wer a picter-maker, I cud jis' take that ar supper an'
that ar 'oman down on clean white paper, an' make more men hongry,
an' hot tu marry, a-lookin at hit in one week, nor ever ole Whitfield
convarted in his hole life; back-sliders, hippercrits, an' all, I don't keer
a durn.[5]

F. O. Matthiessen called this a hymn to fertility, and Kenneth
Lynn has pointed to the wistful note of a sense of exclusion
lurking in the style. What is certain is that the introduction of a
naive perspective into the vernacular has immeasurably extended
the value of the style. Such a piece could hardly have come from
the lips of Simon Suggs: he is too world-worn to be capable of
such authentic freshness, such plausible wondering. For in these
passages Sut *is* 'a picter-maker', a visualizer of a high order.
Looking down from above in the classic pastoral stance Longstreet could not establish any vital contact with his materials, but
looking up from below Sut vivifies what he sees. He transmits it
undisturbed, in all its resonant particularity. No literary allusions
intrude their opacity between seer and the things seen. Sut's eye
and Sut's style are translucent; the unmarshalled fragments of

the scene teem into life in front of us. The fleeting gesture, the fugitive quality of the instant, the unique configuration of the unrepeatable moment—these things this style can handle with humble deftness.

The naive-vernacular character, when allowed to speak from his own point of view, with an economic and blunt vocabulary and an unsupervised, unrevised syntax, reveals himself as a new way of getting the living world into words, as a new possible strategy of intimacy and inclusion. That it is the style of an abandoned self-deprecating youth who hasn't joined society, who doesn't subscribe to its values, is immensely significant since it shows that the naive-vernacular style was related, at its outset, to the alienated outsider; and we shall have occasion to ask, as we examine Clemens's perfection of the style and its later adoption by other writers, whether, in fact, it can ever be employed for any but an anti- or pre-social point of view. Emerson, Thoreau and Whitman were all, in their differing ways, against society, or quiet non-conformers on the inside: and their interest in the innocent eye was all part of a larger dissatisfaction with the modes of sight and thought enforced by social living. The organization and complexity of society are reflected in the complexity of its conceptual framework, its need for generality, and the arranging and relating power of the syntax of its language. To cultivate a naive point of view—as so many American writers have found expedient—would seem to entail to some degree the abandonment of the framework of civilization which is concurrently operative. The naive hero will always tend to make 'a separate peace'. That such an apostasy may have its own validity we will see when we come to *Huckleberry Finn*.

CHAPTER 7

A SYSTEM OF REDUCTION

The little book is charmingly written, & it interested me. But it flies too high for me. Its concretest things are filmy abstractions to me, & when I lay my grip on one of them & open my hand, I feel as embarrassed as I used to feel when I thought I had caught a fly.[1]

Mark Twain to William Dean Howells, 1891—on Swedenborg's *Heaven and Hell*

If I might put in my jaw at this point, I should say, stick to actual fact and character in the thing, and give things in detail. . . . *Don't write* at *any supposed Atlantic audience, but yarn it off as if into my sympathetic ear.*[2]

Howells to Twain, concerning his series 'Old Times on the Mississippi'

IN 1867 Samuel Clemens, in the capacity of a newspaper reporter, accompanied a group of earnest 'pilgrims' on their tour of Europe and Asia Minor on the Steamship *Quaker City*. The following year he reworked his newspaper material into a travel book and included in it a description of the Sphinx which was much admired at the time. Here are some representative sentences:

There was a dignity not of earth in its mien, and in its countenance a benignity such as never anything human wore. . . . It was gazing out over the ocean of Time—over lines of century-waves which, further and further receding, closed nearer and nearer together, and blended at last into one unbroken tide, away toward the horizon of remote antiquity. . . . It was MEMORY—RETROSPECTION—wrought into visible, tangible form.[3]

In 1896 in a story called *Tom Sawyer Abroad* Huck Finn, who is telling the story, talks about the Sphinx in the following way:

Awful, yes, so it was, but not dreadful any more, because you could see it was a noble face, and kind of sad, and not thinking about you,

104

but about other things and larger. It was stone, reddish stone, and its nose and ears battered, and that give it an abused look, and you felt sorrier for it for that.[4]

The first passage is deliberately couched in the generalized clichés of the grand manner. It is a typical piece of nineteenth-century tourist eulogy: a stock response, sublime, moralizing, and composed of 'filmy abstractions' which scarcely allow the perceived object to come into focus. Huck's description is translated down into particulars and emptied of all that fulsome awe which makes the first passage ring false. His attitude is nonchalant, unpretentious, sensitive and familiar. Huck 'yarns it off' with the result that we see the object in a new proximity and have a sense of authentic personal response which the first piece lacked. Between the two pieces a stylistic rebellion of the first importance for American literature has taken place. To analyse this rebellion we must examine Clemens's gradual and arduous development of the potentialities of the vernacular; his experiments with a variety of picaresque and irreverent personae which finally produced that novel narrator, Huck Finn; and the significance of his lifelong preoccupation with the child, its diction and its point of view. For it was Clemens who finally and completely inverted the pastoral situation and perfected the vernacular-child-narrator with a fruitfully naive perspective on life and a manner of speaking which was an adequate vehicle for the new point of view.

In any society prestige tends to gravitate towards and cluster around certain educated standards of taste: this we may call the official culture of the time. The official culture in America in the second half of the nineteenth century was one which regulated itself by self-consciously adopted and imitated principles: it was dominated by ideals of propriety, elegance, and refinement, and it prescribed certain literary models (many of them English) and certain model, literary feelings. It was nourished and supported by the waning official religion of the day, and embraced by the mandarin, genteel class of which the apotheosis was Brahmin New England. The gift of such a culture is its 'tone of the centre': its danger is increasing inflexibility. By the time Clemens came to regard himself as a writer it was a culture of forms, frozen on the surface, hollow within; prohibitive rather than enabling; a series of habits adhered to by the imaginatively somnolent. Clemens, as we shall see, oscillated between a desire to emulate the official standards (the elevated attitude, the endorsed perspective, the sublime rhetoric), and a felt need to find a new point of view and a new language to transmit his insights and formulate his feelings. The span of his work offers the interesting spectacle of a gifted man, a conscious artist quite capable of writing in the style prescribed by the official culture, choosing to adopt the narrative mask, first of a buffoon, then of an uncivilized child, and finally deciding to write a complete book in the current sub-social vernacular. Clemens owes the significance of his position in American literature to this paradoxical fact: that he found himself unable to speak to his own satisfaction until he had rid himself of the decorous volubility enjoined by the official culture of his age.

From the start of his writing career, Clemens reveals a preoccupation with language problems. Even in his short articles for the 'Territorial Enterprise' written between 1862–4 in which, among other things, he covered the sessions of the Territorial Legislature and the Constitutional Convention of 1863 in Carson, he spends more time puncturing or parodying empty or vicious rhetoric than analysing politics and current affairs. The first tact that the crude young reporter, Mark Twain, reveals is an unerring sense of the abuse of words, a quick ear for that kind of oratory which was 'all show and pretence, a big washing and a small hang out'.[5] An early letter to the paper, for instance, starts by mocking a legal jargon which is incomprehensible to the common auditor. 'I present the following item giving it in the language in which I received it for fear of making mistakes—for its terms are darkly, mysteriously legal, and I have not the most distant conception of what they mean, or what they are intended to have reference to.'[6] A later letter offers a glorious parody of a politician's harangue. 'Mr. President, I am opposed, I am hostile, I am uncompromisingly against this proposition to tax the mines.

I will go further, sir. I will openly assert, sir, that I am not in favour of this proposition.'[7] The close of the speech with its welter of mixed quotations reveals the insincerity of the speaker.

Heed the prayers of the people and be merciful! Ah, sir, the quality of mercy is not strained, so to speak (as has been aptly suggested heretofore), but droppeth like the gentle dew from heaven, as it were. The gentleman from Douglas has said this law would be unconstitutional, and I cordially agree with him. Therefore let its corse to the ramparts be hurried—let the flames that shook the battle's wreck, shine round it o'er the dead—let it go hence to that undiscovered country from whose bourne no traveller returns (as hath been remarked by the gentleman from Washoe Mr. Stamp), and in thus guarding and protecting the poor miner, let us endeavour to do unto others as we would that others should do unto us (as was very justly and properly observed by Jesus Christ upon a former occasion).[8]

Throughout, the mingling of sanctimonious moralizing and rhetorical attitudinizing are pointed up.

Nevada seems to have been a fertile breeding ground for burlesque at the time. There was, for instance, an institution called The Third House which was a group that met informally to burlesque the processes and results of popular legislation in the official assembly. Reporting the proceedings of The Third House Mark Twain, using the figure of the President, makes a romping attack on 'oratorical eccentricities'.[9] Here is a typical exchange:

Mr. Sterns: . . . in a word, sir, I coincide with him in the opinion that it would be equivalent to taxing the hopes of the poor miner—his aspirations—the dear yearnings of his—
The President: Yearnings of his grandmother! I'll slam this mallet at the next man that attempts to impose that tiresome old speech on this body. . . .[10]

The attack on 'rehashed platitudes'[11] is spirited and unflagging and Twain shows himself well acquainted with all the rhetorical tricks for generating false excitement and spurious sentiment—as he reveals in a long parody of one of those 'noble human sodabottles, so to speak, effervescing with the holy gas of pure

107

MARK TWAIN

unselfish patriotism'.¹² We could use a remark he makes concerning a girl at the opera to cover his reaction to speech wherever
he went. 'When she does forget herself and make use of her own
natural voice and drop her borrowed one, it is the pleasantest
thing in life to see her play.'¹³ Sometimes he uses both voices
himself to effect a sort of rhetorical breakdown—thus: 'The air
was soft and balmy—the sky was cloudless and serene—the odor
of flowers floated upon the idle breeze—the glory of the sun
descended like a benediction upon mountains and meadow and
plain—the wind blew like the very devil, and the day was generally disagreeable.'¹⁴ Arousing conventional anticipation, lulling
the reader into inattention, and then roughly flouting that very
convention by rudely disappointing customary expectation—
this is one of Twain's early crude strategies. But it shows that,
this early, he was acutely aware of a crucial distinction between
borrowed accents and a natural voice, and even these ephemeral
scraps of journalism show an inchoate determination to separate
the one from the other. When he boasts of choosing to 'use the
language of the vulgar, the low-flung, the sinful and such as will
shock the ears of the highly civilized'¹⁵ we may suspect a measure
of playful defiance, but when he asserts moderately but confidently—'My language may be unrefined, but it has the virtue
of being uncommonly strong'¹⁶ we realize that he was aware of a
very real conflict inside the language of the day.

That this conflict was hard to resolve is clear in *Innocents
Abroad*, for throughout that book, as he finally prepared it for
publication, there persist a strain of bad rhetoric, a type of vapid,
stereotyped lyricism which in certain moods he would be the
first to mock. That he feels uneasy with some of the passages of
description, guiltily aware of his own rhetorical legerdemain, is
clear from some of the paranthetic mockery he adds to his set
pieces. 'A more elegant term does not occur to me just now'¹⁷
he will say offhandedly, and he often inserts such self-depre-
catory deflations as '(copyright secured according to law)'.¹⁸ On
the other hand there are many such passages offered in all seriousness and with no subsequent pin-prick waiting in ambush for

108

the pretentious flourish: when he jokingly decides to 'put on a solemnity'[19] to suit the scene, he is only describing what his writing does seriously time and time again. An insidious impulse to gravitate towards the sublime, generalized, or poetic phrase is everywhere in evidence. Examples could be proliferated: 'Many a strange clime'[20]—'domed by the bending heavens'[21]— 'summits swathed in clouds'[22]—'dancing wavelets'[23]—'crested mountains of water'[24]—'It was the aurora borealis of the frozen pole exiled to a Summer land'[25]—'clothed in purple gloom'[26]— 'Finny armies'[27]: or one could consult the dramatic gesturing over Damascus, or the pompous plangency of the description of the hermits, or the Sphinx: all these are examples of the debilitated rhetorical phrase-clusters which stray unchecked into his work. This tendency to lapse into the very mannerisms which he elsewhere denounces is unconscious and symptomatic. He had not yet hammered out his own way of discerning and depicting things. Compare, for instance, his critical comment on a piece of picturesque writing he quotes from a writer called W. C. Grimes, with his own description of Lake Tahoe. The comment on Grimes reads: 'It is an ingeniously written description and well calculated to deceive. But if the paint and the ribbons and the flowers be stripped from it a skeleton will be found underneath.'[28] The description of Tahoe runs:

a sea in the clouds; a sea that has character, and asserts it in solemn calms, at times, at times in savage storms; a sea, whose royal seclusion is guarded by a cordon of sentinel peaks that lift their frosty fronts nine thousand feet above the level world; a sea whose every aspect is impressive, whose belongings are all beautiful, whose lonely majesty types the Deity.[29]

Here are the very 'paint, ribbons, and flowers' he deplores in the writings of others. His own work is still heavy with the ballast of an older style: and to disburden himself of it was no easy task. Yet side by side with this enfeebled rhetoric we can note a very different kind of writing existing and flourishing on its own. Continually he inserts personal humorous anecdotes into the panoramic descriptions which it is his 'official' task to provide. And usually the joke is at his own expense. Such passages take up a much more colloquial, unpretentious, even disrespectful tone, and this tone goes far to making the alternating passages of high-flown description sound hollow in our ears. This oscillation of attitude reveals Clemens's literary unease. One half of him goes through the motions of conventional awe, respect and reverence and adopts the 'high' point of view. The other half found greater comfort and sincerity by playing the fool and maintaining a 'low' view. When Mark Twain tells how he tried his excruciating French on ladies who spoke perfect English, or how he was flattered into buying gloves far too small for him, or of his sufferings in the barber's chair, he achieves an anecdotal intimacy which distances irretrievably the stiff and laboured formality of his high rhetorical passages. And it was through the Mark Twain who called down derision on himself, who showed himself for a gull, who naively confessed his inadequacies of response, that Clemens found the greatest release. For this Mark Twain talks, 'yarns it off',—uninhibitedly, naively, and honestly. This Mark Twain refuses to join the conspiracy of prevailing taste. He knows that he ought to 'tell the customary pleasant lie, and say I tore myself reluctantly away from every noted place in Palestine'[30] but he rejects 'the neat thing' and insists on 'the true thing'.[31] His last comment on the journey to the Dead Sea, Jordan, and Bethlehem is the following simple expostulation: 'And *such* fatigue!'[32] The abandonment of literary etiquette, an engaging familiarity, a refusal to keep up appearances by maintaining a rigid reserve— this is what Clemens contrived to achieve through Mark Twain; the Mark Twain who preferred to be the honest fool in preference to the attitudinizing pilgrim.

This leads us to a consideration of that aspect of the book which is now considered immature. I mean the deliberate irreverence, the almost stubborn impudence, the perverse refusal to be impressed. This syndrome of attitudes exists in a state of hostile intimacy with the aspirations to sublimity. Milan Cathedral, for instance, is 'a fairy delusion of frostwork', 'an anthem sung in stone, a poem wrought in marble'[33] and yet the same eye when it is turned on some fragmentary cathedral statues can only note that they did not have 'any noses left to blow'.[34] The natural voice of disrespect does battle with the borrowed accents of approval, the same man fluctuates wildly in his point of view. Yet the lapse into naive irreverence also betokens a relaxation into the colloquial, and whatever is lost by way of proper respect there is an important gain in authenticity of response. The naive narrator will not try and impose false emotions on us. Of all the possible responses to the rock in the Mosque of Omar, Mark Twain gives us the one which is at once the most naive and the most honest. 'This rock, large as it is, is suspended in the air. It does not touch anything at all. The guide said so. This is very wonderful. In the place on it where Mahomet stood, he left his footprints in solid stone. I should judge that he wore about eighteens!'[35] And here the strategy of a naive response reveals one of his key values: it refuses to be deceived by the world's false accounts. It is wary of hypocrisy. It says nothing rather than tell lies. So when Twain is shown the supposed birth place of Christ he convinces us by his very lack of response. 'I touch, with reverent finger, the actual spot where the infant Jesus lay, but I think—nothing.'[36] Through Twain, Clemens is trying out a new point of view, he wants to see how far towards a new honesty of response a nonchalant naivety will take him. Will Mark Twain's attitude work better than the customary one of the pilgrims, will it grope and stumble its way to the truth, however clumsily: will it be valid as a mode of appraisal? These are the sort of questions that Clemens is toying with in this book. In general his attitude to the past and its stories is: 'splendid legend—splendid lie'[37] and where other travellers had recorded sentiments of sublime intoxication, Twain often confesses to a repugnance at the 'dirt, degradation and savagery'[38] of the Middle East. He often quotes from popular travelogues and then insists on describing the realities of the scene as they appear 'to one's actual vision'.[39] He brings the low fact and the high fiction into an opposition which is always damaging to the latter. He sets about what he calls 'a system of reduction'[40] and especially seeks to undermine the pilgrims who 'have brought *their* verdicts with them'.[41] He makes it his ambition to 'disentangle the woof of glittering sentences'[42] of the guide books and 'strip for inspection the thing itself'.[43] The irreverence, the impudence, the naive undervaluing of the past, the seemingly inapposite intrusion of low sentiments —these are not Clemens's last word on Europe. Rather they are an effort to shatter set patterns of audience response, to break away from traditional perspectives, to inhibit a 'literary' viewing of the world and reacquire a fresh intimacy with its component parts. Scattered throughout the book there are constant pleas for honesty and clear sight—no matter how uncouth the sentiments or how unlovely the scene. He says in his preface that he is not going to show anyone how they 'ought to look at objects of interest beyond the sea' and his one claim is to have written 'at least honestly whether wisely or not'.[44] In this book we can see Clemens trying to find an attitude, a satisfactory point of view. As Henry Nash Smith demonstrates in his authoritative book on Mark Twain, in this work Mark Twain wanders uncertainly between the ranks of the pilgrims and 'the boys', setting the starchy saints off against the slangy 'sinners'. His greatest discontent in this book is not with Europe but with a certain kind of high-pitched rhetoric which was not only the distinguishing mark of the insincere pilgrims, but which seemed to be an ineradicable part of his own style. It was this that he wished to 'reduce' though, as yet, he has no definite idea of what might replace it.

In *Roughing It* Clemens takes the young Mark Twain out to the West and further explores the possible lessons to be learned from a sustained naivety of attitude. And here again there is evidence that he has not solved his language problem. His ideal virtues are 'compactness, simplicity, and vigor of expression',[45] but these virtues are not always practised. Mountains, for instance, seem to precipitate an unhindered flow of clichés of the old style.

We sat . . . contemplating the first splendor of the rising sun as it swept down the long array of mountain peaks flushing and gilding crag after crag and summit after summit, as if the invisible Creator reviewed the grey veterans and they saluted with a smile.[46]

Elsewhere they become 'Sultans of the fastnesses . . . turbaned with tumbled volumes of cloud':[47] the Missouri is spoken of as going on 'a long and troubled pilgrimage':[48] too often there is a touch of this portentous anthropomorphization in his descriptions. The quarrel with such rhetoric is that it deflects attention away from the object to be described and draws attention to its own prowess: it is ingrown and stultifying. Clemens shows himself clearly aware of the problem. He is continually engaged in skirmishes with his own rhetoric. For instance when he tries to find words adequate to describe his discomfort in an alkali desert, he scans the dictionary and awkwardly announces that to try to give the reader an idea of how thirsty they were would be to 'gild refined gold or paint the lily'.[49] Then with a deflating shrug he adds : 'Somehow now that it is there, the quotation does not seem to fit—but no matter, let it stay, anyhow. I think it is a graceful and attractive thing, and therefore have tried time and time again to work it in where it *would* fit, but could not succeed.'[50] 'Leaving it in,' he says, 'will afford at least a temporary respite from the wear and tear of trying to "lead up" to this really apt and beautiful quotation.'[51] The inaptness of the phrase is, of course, its notable feature, and the humour contains a sting of sincere intent: having found no organic use—no radical aptness, no expressive release—in this flower of rhetoric he allows it to stay on sufferance. It is as useless and inert in its context as the dictionary itself was in the desert. In the humour there is a recognition of a divorce between words and things of which Clemens was becoming increasingly aware. Yet the tendency to adopt picturesque formulae recurs: 'Mountain domes, clothed with forests, scarred with landslides, cloven by cañons and valleys, and helmeted with glittering snow, fitly framed and finished the noble picture.'[52] The clothing and the helmeting are stock habits of embellishment which Clemens, as yet, does not know how to replace. The problem can be more clearly seen in a description of the view from Virginia City.

Over your head Mount Davidson lifts its grey dome, and before and below you a rugged cañon clove the battlemented hills, making a somber gateway through which a soft tinted desert was glimpsed, with the silver thread of a river winding through it, bordered with trees which many miles of distance diminished to a delicate fringe. . . . Look from your window where you would, there was fascination in the picture. At rare intervals—but very rare—there were clouds in our skies, and then the setting sun would gild flush and glorify this mighty expanse of scenery with a bewildering pomp of color that held the eye like a spell and moved the spirit like music.[53]

There is a tendency to impersonalize the response, to detach it from the actual viewer and accord it some extra-personal existence. The style is more important than the scenery and the result is a highly pictorial gloss which goes a long way to obscuring the actual qualities of the response by universalizing it. Always the general ideal presence—'you'; never the local, limited response. Similarly the individual beauties of the scene are lost in a generalizing literary haze. The local particularities cannot be seen through the conventional literary schemata. And Mark Twain—the irreverent Mark Twain!—in formulating a response can only produce the stock proof of 'sensibility', that it moved the spirit like music. Sut Lovingood could do better than that, could produce a more vital scene and transmit a more individual response. Clemens had to learn to exclude a certain sort of rhetorical habit of response and appreciation. And his trip West proved to be a great educator in this respect. For whereas in *Innocents Abroad* the naive Mark Twain learned to reassess the conventionally honoured but found nothing to put in its place, in *Roughing It* the naive narrator is not only disabused of his romantic expectations but he discovers a set of positive values in the West which he set about incorporating into his writing. A paradigm for the structure of the book is provided by the charming anecdote of the encounter between the town-bred dog who has 'a good opinion of himself' and who 'thinks he knows something about speed',[54] and a wild native coyote. In the chase the dog's superiority is shaken: the coyote outwits him at every turn for the coyote is truly wild and exhibits powers which the urban patronizing visitor cannot match. Mark Twain plays the part of the dog in this book and the indigenous coyotes continually contrive to make him look and feel ridiculous, until at last he is initiated into the western community and can understand its attitudes and language from the inside. As he travels west he submits what he sees to the same 'system of reduction' that he had employed in Europe. For instance, as they enter the Sahara—an alkali desert—all Twain's naive romanticism asserts itself. 'This was fine—novel—romantic—dramatically adventurous—*this*, indeed, was worth living for, worth travelling for. We would write home all about it.'[55] But this 'gushing' seems absurd after an hour.

The poetry was all in the anticipation—there was none in the reality. Imagine a vast waveless ocean striken dead and turned to ashes; imagine this solemn waste tufted with ash-dusted sage-brushes; imagine the lifeless silence and solitude that belong to such a place; imagine a coach, creeping like a bug through the midst of this shoreless level, and sending up tumbled volumes of dust as if it were a bug that went by steam; imagine this aching monotony of toiling and plowing kept up hour after hour, and the shore still as far away as ever, apparently; imagine team, driver, coach, and passengers so deeply coated with ashes that they are all one colorless color; imagine ash drifts roosting above moustaches and eyebrows like snow accumulations on boughs and bushes. This is the reality of it.[56]

The hard pungent, almost arid accumulation of hard facts, the relentless insistence on the stale unalleviated reality, the touch of grim stoical humour—all this is in some way a departure from prescribed modes of viewing things. It testifies to a new effort of focusing on Clemens's part, a disciplined abandonment of literary recipes. But more positively he found the current vernacular not only amusing, or frighteningly coarse, or even picturesque, but as offering a new linguistic approach to his material. For as the narrator—now older and wiser—recalls: it was on this trip that 'I first encountered the vigorous new vernacular of the occidental plains and mountains'.[57] What he found in the West that he did not find in Europe was 'the attractive indifference to formality of the pioneer'.[58] One of the ways to describe Clemens's achievement is to say that he discovered and utilized the latent possibilities of this informality of speech, this non-chalance of attitude (a nonchalance related to Thoreau's 'saunt-ering' and Whitman's 'loafing'). There are passages in the book where an informal vernacular simplicity of imagery, phrase, syntax and cadence is used not merely to deflate or offset an obvious piece of pedantic rhetoric, but for its own virtues: because it is the most comfortable and unselfconscious way for Twain to express himself. Consider this very simple description of Carson City:

It was a 'wooden' town; its population two thousand souls. The main street consisted of four or five blocks of little white frame stores which were too high to sit down on, but not too high for various other pur-poses; in fact hardly high enough. They were packed close together, side by side, as if room were scarce on that mighty plain. The sidewalk was of boards that were more or less inclined to rattle when walked upon. In the middle of the town, opposite the stores, was the 'plaza', which is native to all towns beyond the Rocky Mountains—a large, unfenced, level vacancy, with a liberty pole in it, and very useful as a place for public auctions, horse trades, and mass meetings, and like-wise for teamsters to camp in. The other sides of the plaza were faced by stores, offices, and stables. The rest of Carson City was pretty scattering.[59]

There is no change of tone or pace throughout: the eye wanders at its leisure over the scene and with an almost dead-pan evenness articulates occasional details. Syntactically the passage is nude, for, apart from one or two relative clauses, the whole piece is written in a paratactic sequence with no compound sentences, no complex attempt to bind the whole picture to-gether. A stark enumeration of details seen from very short perspective is pursued: the passage reads almost like an inventory, or a travelogue of the naive eye. It is colloquial and unpretentious and permits no false embellishments, no moralizing, and no enhancing speculations. It hugs the facts. On one occasion in the book Twain is very attracted by the translucent quality of the water in Lake Tahoe. 'All objects seen through it had a bright strong vividness, not only of outline but of every minute detail, which they would not have had when seen through the same depth of atmosphere.'[60] Official rhetoric seemed like a coloured mist deliberately interposed between viewer and object. Clemens, because among other things he had lived for a long time in 'the domain of fact',[61] wanted to find a mode of writing like the Tahoe water; a medium that offered minimum intervention between reader and object, that would push things up into sharp focus, giving a clarity of detail, and a sort of over-all super lucidity. He wanted a manner of writing which would keep the particulars legible. And for this the strategy of a naive, uninstructed narrator who is forced to put aside convention and see things as though for the first time proved to be most successful. For the truly naive are too innocent to perpetrate sophisticated aesthetic falsehoods. If the Emperor is naked they say so.

Clemens had not solved his language-problem by the time he wrote *A Tramp Abroad*. Once again the naive, colloquial honesty of the wandering, ignorant 'tramp', Mark Twain is exploited, sometimes to good effect, more often for puerile ends. Once again it is in the descriptive passages that Clemens reveals his instability of diction. The huge ruin of Heidelberg Castle, 'deserted, discrowned, beaten by the storms, but royal still, and beautiful', is 'the Lear of inanimate nature'.[62] The vocabulary of painting and literature are consulted for effects. The Rhine plain 'which stretches away, softly and richly tinted, grows gradually indistinct and finally melts imperceptibly into the remote horizon'[63] has all the deliquescence of a bad landscape painting. German forests are haloed with literary reminiscences. 'The great deeps of a boundless forest have a beguiling and impressive charm in any country but German legends and fairy tales have given these an added charm.'[64] 'Charm' is the key word. The tendency in the eighteenth and nineteenth centuries to see landscapes as paintings and to inject an added richness by the deliberate exploitation of literary associations is responsible for that tepid aestheticizing of nature best summed up by that equivocal word—'charm'. Landscapes could always be made charming if certain facts were omitted and certain other allusions superadded. But in arresting, framing, and embellishing nature in this way, literature lost all contact with the local contours and concrete distinctions of pre-formalized nature—nature in process, nature unrefracted through art. Clemens could still see nature as being 'hung with His masterpieces'[65] and could easily allow himself to be led off into such meaningless generalities as 'one seemed to meet the immutable, the indestructible, the eternal, face to face'.[66] Sometimes he manages to take a vernacular view of things as when St Mark's is likened to 'a vast warty bug'[67] or when old gabled houses are colloquially described as 'leaning far over toward each other in a friendly gossiping way'[68] and when he sustains this informal mode he can convey far more detailed specifically located scenes.

> In the front rooms of dwellings girls and women were cooking or spinning, and ducks and chickens were waddling in and out, over the threshold, picking up chance crumbs and holding pleasant converse; a very old and wrinkled man sat asleep before his door with his chin upon his breast and his extinguished pipe in his lap; soiled children were playing in dirt everywhere along the lane, unmindful of the sun.[69]

The sparse phrase-by-phrase description which forces us right into the scene is more apposite than the vague transmuting generalities exemplified above. But such passages could not be said to constitute a new style: they are still modifications within the old. But in this book Clemens affords us a new insight into his dilemma as he conceived it. He praises the sunset at Mont Blanc and adds: 'I could have found out the cause of this awe-compelling miracle by inquiring . . . but I do not wish to know. We have not the reverent feeling for the rainbow that a savage has, because we know how it is made. We have lost as much as we have gained by prying into that matter.'[70]

Clemens has a deep desire to transmit a genuine reverence and wonder in the face of nature and his excursions into literary rhetoric are made with this sincere ambition in mind. Sometimes he is uneasy with his products as we have seen, but as yet he knows of no other way of writing about nature which will convey his awe and do nature justice. So a genuine response is continually being deflected into stereotyped channels. His problem then is to find a new vehicle of wonder. The problem recurred to him with renewed force when he revisited the south and worked his articles for the 'Atlantic Monthly' up into a book called *Life on the Mississippi.* In it he recalls his feelings when he had completed his apprenticeship as a riverboat pilot.

Now when I had mastered the language of this water, and had come to know every trifling feature that bordered the great river as familiarly as I knew the letters of the alphabet, I had made a valuable acquisition. But I had lost something, too. I had lost something which could never be restored to me while I lived. All the grace, the beauty, the poetry, had gone out of the majestic river. I still kept in mind a certain wonderful sunset which I witnessed when steamboating was new to me. A broad expanse of the river was turned to blood; in the middle distance the red hue brightened into gold, through which a solitary log came floating, black and conspicuous; in one place a long, slanting mark lay sparkling upon the water; in another the surface was broken by boiling, tumbling rings, that were as many-tinted as opal; where the ruddy flush was faintest, was a smooth spot that was covered with graceful circles and radiating lines, ever so delicately traced; the shore on our left was densely wooded, and the somber shadow that fell from this forest was broken in one place by a long, ruffled trail that shone like silver; and high above the forest wall a clean-stemmed dead tree waved a single leafy bough that glowed like a flame in the unobstructed splendor that was flowing from the sun. There were graceful curves, reflected images, woody heights, soft distances; and over the whole scene, far and near, the dissolving lights drifted steadily, enriching it every passing moment with new marvels of coloring. . . . No, the romance and beauty were all gone from the river. All the value any feature of it had for me now was the amount of usefulness it could furnish toward compassing the safe piloting of a steamboat.[71]

Pragmatic intimacy precludes reverence. Or does it? This passage is peculiarly fascinating because Clemens gives himself a curious kind of lie. He maintains that he cannot see the river poetically, and then proceeds to embark on a long poetic description. He has not lost the ability to see and write that way—the evidence is in front of us. What he did lose was a belief that this sort of poetic treatment could actually *contain* the empirical realities of the river. He becomes aware with new intensity of the discrepancies between rhetorical treatment and the stuff treated. So much so that later in the book he siphons off his 'poetic' and rhetorical responses to the river and puts them into the mouth of a posturing passenger from whose 'lurid eloquence' Mark Twain can detach himself. Some of the speeches made by this passenger could easily have come from Clemens's earlier work.

What grander river scenery can be conceived, as we gaze upon this enchanting landscape, from the uppermost point of these bluffs upon the valleys below? The primeval wildness and awful loneliness of these sublime creations of nature and nature's God, excite feelings of unbounded admiration, and the recollection of which can never be effaced from the memory, as we view them in any direction.[72]

This is still Clemens writing, it is important to remember: he is still a master of the literary response and can turn it on at will. But in this book he seems to realize with a new clarity the extent of his problem as a writer. By distancing the rhetoric and putting it into another character's mouth he manages to draw back and inspect it with a new rigour of reassessment. It is a moment of truth for him, because it seems that only in writing this book does he become fully aware that the high official rhetoric is of no positive use to him as a writer. The river brought this home to him as Europe and the West never completely managed to. There is a reason for this, for what he says about Bixby's memory of the river applies equally to Clemens. 'The most trivial details remained as distinct and luminous in his head, after they had lain there for years, as the most memorable events.'[73]

The official rhetoric was too abstract, too generalized, too heavy and opaque with literary allusion to allow the detailed realities of the river through. Clemens now had to formulate a way of writing which would take note of the 'distinct and luminous' details, the concrete local particulars, and at the same time transmit the requisite sense of wonder which he did not want to lose. He wants a style which will preserve 'the color, snap, surprise' of his first response to the river. He wants to give us that dawn on the river without dissipating its peculiar configuration of qualities in a vague de-particularizing rhetoric. The alternatives of the pragmatist and the literary exhibitionist both precluded that 'savage reverence' which seemed to him the only proper response to nature. To see the rainbow as a scientist, to see the river as a professional boatman—to do this was to incur a loss. Knowledge inhibits the eye. Yet there could be no return to the 'paint and tinsel' style of rhetoric which had now demonstrated its own inadequacies so irremediably. Clemens's solution was not to divest himself of his acquired knowledge but rather to adopt an alternative mode of response, a pre-adult eye which was too candid to blink at empirical reality and yet which was not too cold to wonder at it: he also decided to stake everything on the vernacular which had always shown itself hostile to rhetorical falsifications and impervious to literary allusions. Huck Finn gave Clemens back his marvellous dawn, every detail distinct and luminous, and the whole passage is saturated with a self-authenticating unpretentious reverence which was new in American literature.

Not a sound anywheres—perfectly still—just like the whole world was asleep, only sometimes the bullfrogs a-cluttering, maybe. The first thing to see, looking away over the water, was a kind of dull line —that was the woods on t'other side; you couldn't make nothing else out; then a pale place in the sky; then more paleness spreading around; then the river softened up away off, and warn't black any more, but gray; you could see little dark spots drifting along ever so far away —trading scows, and such things; and long black streaks—rafts; sometimes you could hear a sweep creaking; or jumbled-up voices, it was so still, the sounds come so far; and by and by you could see a streak on the water which you know by the look of the streak that there's a snag there in the swift current which breaks on it and makes that streak look that way; and you see the mist curl up off of the water, and the east reddens up, and the river, and you make out a log cabin in the edge of the woods, away on the bank on t'other side of the river, being a wood-yard, likely, and piled by them cheats so you can throw a dog through it anywheres; then the nice breeze springs up, and comes fanning you from over there, so cool and fresh and sweet to smell on account of the woods and the flowers; but sometimes not that way, because they've left dead fish laying around, gars and such, and they do get pretty rank; and next you've got the full day, and everything smiling in the sun, and the song-birds just going it![74]

That Clemens could never have achieved such a vibrant, alive, and luminously rendered verbal reincarnation of the seen-world without looking through Huck's eye is easily proved if one seeks in *Tom Sawyer* for anything comparable. It is a book about youth, but not a book by a youth. And Clemens can't hit the note he wants. Here is another dawn.

It was the cool gray dawn, and there was a sense of repose and peace in the deep pervading calm and silence of the woods. Not a leaf stirred; not a sound obtruded upon great Nature's meditation. Bedded dew-drops stood upon the leave and grasses. . . . Now, far away in the woods a bird called; another answered; presently the hammering of a woodpecker was heard. Gradually the cool dim gray of the morning whitened, and as gradually sounds multiplied and life manifested itself. The marvel of Nature shaking off sleep and going to work unfolded itself to the musing boy.[75]

Clemens is too far away: there is none of that sense of immediate visual involvement with the impinging minutiae of the day that Huck conveys. It is an inert exercise, a stock literary evocation of 'dawn': nothing comes to life in the shadow of such portentous phrases as 'great Nature's meditation'. Clemens, in all the books we have so far mentioned, continually manifests an uncertainty of tone, a stilted manner; as though at times he was, as Howells advised him not to, addressing an imagined respectable literary audience. Through Mark Twain he achieves moments of colloquial simplicity: but it is only when Huck 'yarns it off' that full imaginative release is achieved.[76]

The obvious joy in the writing of *Huckleberry Finn* is the joy of a man who for the first time feels he is saying exactly what he wants to. Only with the perfection of the vernacular did Clemens make good his escape from the imprisoning clichés of the official rhetoric. Huck's way of speaking is a triumph of exclusion as much as anything else. Consider, for instance, the stock attitudes apparent in Longfellow's 'Hymn to the Night':

> I heard the trailing garments of the Night
> Sweep through her marble halls!
> I saw her sable skirts all fringed with light
> From the celestial walls!
>
> I felt her presence, by its spell of might,
> Stoop o'er me from above;
> The calm, majestic presence of the Night,
> As of the one I love.[77]

and set by the side of the poem Huck's apparently feeble attempts to transmit his feelings at a comparable time of day:

The river looked miles and miles across. The moon was so bright I could 'a' counted the drift logs that went a-slipping along, black and still, hundreds of yards out from shore. Everything was dead quiet and it looked late and *smelt* late. You know what I mean—I don't, know the words to put it in.[78]

Longfellow's majestic skirted being is a literary creation; his poem gives us nothing of the night and nothing of his unique feelings of the moment. Set against Longfellow's confident vocabulary, Huck's protesting inadequacy, his humble approximations, his almost painful sincerity give us the sense of an experiencing being and an experienced instant of time. Longfellow is suave and undisturbed; Huck fights for words, yet in saying little he says most. That there is something insidious in this style may be immediately admitted: the growing tendency to equate inarticulateness with sincerity and to make sheer naivety the gauge of depth of feeling, which can be traced in American literature, easily lead to simplesse, sentimentality, and anti-intellectualism.

But in *Huckleberry Finn* the style is uniquely successful. Huck's simple phrases have an elemental potency stirring in them, a quality which owes its presence to his almost primitive, reverent response to nature in all her moods: its moments of calm—'The sky looks ever so deep when you lay down on your back in the moonshine; I never knowed it before':[79] and its sudden violences—

It would get so dark that it looked all blue-black outside and lovely; and the rain would thrash along by so thick that the trees off a little ways looked dim and spider-webby . . . and now you'd hear the thunder let go with an awful crash, and then go rumbling, grumbling, tumbling down the sky towards the under-side of the world, like rolling empty barrels down-stairs—where it's long stairs and they bounce a good deal, you know.[80]

That last 'low' indecorous image and the homely intimacy of tone reveal the strong 'democratic' undertow in the vernacular style, its presupposition that all men will repond to its imagery and accents: yet they intensify rather than detract from the sense of savage sensitivity in Huck's speech. But there is a more important aspect of this style to note. Since Huck, unlike Longfellow for instance, is out for no special planned effect, nothing misses his attention: having no eye for the portentous or the traditionally significant, the child seems to include all details in his accounts, for, to him, they all contribute something to the strange wonder of the whole situation. Huck has a sauntering eye: as near as possible he 'sees without looking'. Rather as though he had just taken Whitman's 'first step' Huck absorbs the totality of things unsieved. This unprejudiced scrutiny of unanalysed, unfiltered details has an important effect on American literature—both beneficient and adverse—but whatever its later less fortunate results (in naturalism and realism) there is a true joy in the wide-ranging observation of Huck Finn: the joy, for Clemens, of rediscovering a lost world, lost for previous lack of a proper angle of vision and a fitting language. Objects swarm to Huck's gaze and we re-learn an almost primitive delight in the multiplicity of particulars and pay attention to their scattered significance.

For instance, after a steam boat has passed Huck still finds what happens next worth the telling: 'and by and by her waves would get to us, a long time after she was gone, and joggle the raft a bit, and after that you wouldn't hear nothing for you couldn't tell how long, except maybe frogs or something.'[81] Huck traces every experience to its last dying echoes: there is no lurid concentration on sensational 'sublime' moments. 'All around us what powers are wrapped up under the coarse mattings of custom, and all wonder prevented ... the wise man wonders at the usual.' Again Emerson's words are relevant—and yet it is only with Huck that this wisdom is transmuted into a viable literary style. Huck articulates that recovered wonder which Emerson prescribed and Clemens mourned for in *Life on the Mississippi*: he wonders at the usual and in so doing makes the usual wonderful.

Next you'd see a raft sliding by, away off yonder, and maybe a galoot on it chopping, because they're most always doing it on a raft; you'd see the ax flash and come down—you don't hear nothing; you see that ax go up again, and by the time it's above the man's head then you hear the *k'chunk*—it had took all that time to come over the water.[82]

Huck's seemingly gratuitous details never weary us, as Whitman's sometimes do. This of course is due to the fact that Huck engages us as a palpable character confronting specific problems and with an individual destiny: he is not the vehicle for the author's random inclusiveness. In Huck's verbal wanderings Clemens keeps cunningly to the point. But there is another reason. It is because Huck gives us a world uncut by the utilitarian knife and unclouded by the rhetorician's pyrotechnics, a world not arrested as Thoreau curiously managed to freeze his facts, but a world in motion. Through Huck, Clemens re-established a profoundly simple contact with a nature whole and in process in all of its parts: the naive vernacular child narrator provided him with a language which could establish an effortless yet reverent rapport with the empirical details of the seen flowing world, the world as seen for the first time, that is. For if we allow that verbal formulations of the world are never exhaustive but always tentative and partial then we must allow that Huck's vernacular is as much an artistic 'style' as any other. If Longfellow's 'style' has been abandoned by writers and Clemens's perfection of the vernacular has been adopted and used continually ever since, that is because it proved to be a style which procured maximum access to reality, *as later writers experienced it*. And the way writers like Anderson and Hemingway experienced the world was as though they were seeing it for the first time. This is why Huck's style has been such a formative influence, has provided such a congenial precedent: it is why his style, with its syntactical informality, its unorthodox grammar, its almost primitive simplicity, its emphasis on isolated particulars, and its colloquial approximating tone elicited from T. S. Eliot his tribute to Clemens as 'one of those writers, of whom there are not a great many in literature, who have discovered a new way of writing, valid not only for themselves, but for others. I should place him, in this respect, even with Dryden and Swift, as one of those rare writers who have brought their language up to date, and, in so doing, "purified the language of the tribe".'[83] When Huck 'yarns it off' Clemens manages to exorcize the rhetorical abstractions which had intruded themselves into all his earlier work. Huck involves us in a completely concrete world and in doing so Clemens manages to avoid that uneasy oscillation between the particular and the general which had been at once the boast and the weakness of the Transcendentalists.

CHAPTER 8

THE VOICE OF THE OUTLAW

All the picaresque *part—the tramps, outlaws, etc. are incomparable.*[1]

W. D. HOWELLS on *The Prince and the Pauper,* 1880

Written things are not for speech; their form is literary; they are stiff, inflexible and will not lend themselves to happy and effective delivery with the tongue . . . they have to be limbered up, broken up, colloquialized and turned into the common forms of unpremeditated talk—otherwise they will bore the house, not entertain.[2]

The Autobiography of MARK TWAIN, on lecturing

HAVING examined the way in which the vernacular supplanted the official rhetoric in Clemens's writing, we must now examine some of the details of this important stylistic shift. As Howells noted, Clemens writes best when he seems to be 'yarning it off', when he seems to be talking, perhaps 'chatting' is the best word as it avoids any idea of the prepared address. In this connection it is instructive to consider Clemens's own account of the joy he took in dictating his autobiography. This in a letter to Howells in 1904:

You will never know how much enjoyment you have lost until you get to dictating your autobiography . . . you will be astonished (& charmed) to see how like *talk* it is, & how real it sounds, & how well & compactly & sequentially it constructs itself, & what a dewy & breezy & woodsy freshness it has, & what a darling & worshipful absence of the signs of starch, & flatiron, & labor & fuss & other artificialities. . . . There are little slips here & there, little inexactnesses, & many desertions of a thought before the end of it has been reached, but these are not blemishes, they are merits, their removal would take away the naturalness of the flow & banish the very thing—the nameless something—which differentiates real narrative from artificial narrative & makes the one so vastly better than the other.[3]

127

The virtues, that nameless something, which Clemens defends here are precisely the qualities and effects that he spent much of his life as writer trying to ensnare in written words. As a writer, no less than as a stage performer, his happiest effects are gained when he 'colloquializes' his material, when he turns it into 'the common forms of unpremeditated talk'. Of course, to maintain the air of seeming unpreparedness and improvisation was the result of careful art, and in this connection it is revealing to examine some of his own statements about the care with which he calculated his stage effects. Here is a passage which he omitted from *A Tramp Abroad* concerning a comic speech in German which he had planned: in describing his difficulties he gives us a clear summary of his aims. 'The difficulty had not been to memorize the words, but the pauses, the pretended embarrassments, the hesitations, the taking compulsory refuge in English occasionally,—in a word, the various & sundry tricks of manner & utterance which give to a set speech the struggling, diffident, & confused look of a lame impromptu performance.'[4] Struggling, diffident, confused, impromptu—these words serve admirably to describe some of the novel qualities of Huck's manner of speaking. Again, consider this advice Clemens gave to Howells when the latter was about to do some stage reading:

I learned a trick in Vienna—by accident—which I wish I had learned years ago. I meant to *read* from a Tauchnitz, because I knew I hadn't well memorised the pieces; & I came on with the book & read a few sentences, then remembered that the sketch needed a few words of explanatory introduction; & so, lowering the book & now & then unconsciously using it to gesture with, I talked the introduction, & it happened to carry me into the sketch *itself*, & then I went on, pretending that I was merely talking extraneous matter & would come to the sketch *presently*. It was a beautiful success. I knew the substance of the sketch & the *telling* phrases of it; & so, the throwing of the rest of it into informal talk as I went along limbered it up & gave it the snap & go & freshness of an impromptu.[5]

Similarly in his autobiography he describes the colloquializing process, explaining that first he memorized his pieces, then 'in

delivering them from the platform they soon transformed themselves into flexible talk, with all their obstructing precisenesses
and formalities gone out of them for good'.[6] What Clemens was
after was the very reverse of oratory: he worked to exclude every
rhetorical effect, every symptom of confident declaration. If his
material seemed to have any Ciceronian orderliness about it, he
deliberately confused it; instead of the contrived crescendo he
sought for the lame impromptu; any evidence of precisely planned
or formal qualities he ground down by relaxed or diffident random
talking. Clemens's appearances as Mark Twain—on stage, in
books—reveal the most artful artlessness: it is more than art
concealing art, it is rather art *destroying* art. He does not wish to
appear easily sure of himself, but instead rather confused—more
bewildered than insouciant, more naive than masterful. The
planned artlessness of Mark Twain's stage talk is the essential
step in Clemens's art towards Huck's own speech in which naive
artlessness ('I don't know the words') reaches, perhaps for the
only time in Clemens's work, the level of great art.

Clearly this desire to invert all established canons of oratory
is involved in the inversion of the pastoral situation: the low
uneducated figure is in fact wiser than the educated tourist, and
he speaks more tellingly. Clemens escaped from a dead sophisticated way of writing by evolving an alive, naive way of talking,
the very virtue of which was that it never seemed to know what
it was going to say next. Yet such a style cannot be detached
from a certain kind of speaker: Clemens throughout his early
work can be detected searching for the right mouth. Mark Twain
himself is of course a life-long persona used on stage, in books
and to a curious extent in Clemens's private life; but as we have
seen the mere mask of Mark Twain was not enough to solve
Clemens's language problem. Something, or rather some figure,
more extreme, more clearly defined in his opposition to official
standards, was required if Clemens was to make a clean break
with the values of the official culture of his day. And since ways
of speaking are inextricably involved with ways of living, it is not
surprising that in searching for an anti-conventional, anti-formal

mode of speech, Clemens started making use of characters whose manner of life had no respect for the conventions and forms of society. More or less anti-social figures appear in his work from the start and just as important as their freedom of action is their freedom of speech. (He once planned to introduce a vernacular rebel into *Hamlet* who would make free with Shakespeare.) Clemens was after a speech not sanctioned or legalized by the official culture; inevitably he found himself dealing with 'outlaws'. Their voices can be heard long before the most profound outlaw of them all—Huck Finn—made his appearance. It is worth examining some of these outlaws to see how Clemens finally came to evolve the figure of Huck Finn and all he stands for, and stands against.

In his articles written for the 'Territorial Enterprise' in 1862–4 Clemens introduces a figure called The Unreliable, and in his travel letters to the 'Alta California' in 1865–7 he makes use of a figure called Mr Brown. What these, and all subsequent vernacular outlaws have in common, is their function as Clemens's own partial surrogate: they are distanced, irresponsible spokesmen for all the vulgarity, impudence, uninhibitedness and genuine protest active in a part of his own mind. The Unreliable's very appearance reveals him as a man anarchically at odds with all conventions.

I never saw such an awkward, ungainly lout in my life. He had on a pair of Jack Wilde's pantaloons, and a swallow-tail coat belonging to Lytle ('Schermerhorn's Boy') and they fitted him as neatly as an elephant's hide would fit a poodle dog. I would be ashamed to appear in any parlor in such a costume. It never enters his head to be ashamed of anything, though.[7]

The last sentence indicates a sort of strength and independence of opinion which Clemens was after. Admittedly these two figures for the most part exhibit a crude irreverence: they conspicuously do the thing not done—The Unreliable will gate-crash a wedding and get uproariously drunk, Mr Brown will ride a donkey into a mosque. But their unrefractory actions are accompanied by an unrefractory way of speaking. These men talk with a serene unconscious confidence in the ability of the vernacular to say what needs saying with point, economy, and unanswerable force and directness. And in one of his early pieces for the 'Territorial Enterprise' Mark Twain records a significant encounter between himself (as aspirant to respectability) and The Unreliable.

I meant to say something glowing and poetical about the weather, but The Unreliable has come in and driven away refined emotion from my breast. He says: 'Say it's bully, you tallow brained idiot! that's enough; anybody can understand that: don't write any of those infernal sick platitudes about sweet flowers, and joyous butterflies, and worms and things for people to read before breakfast. You make a fool of yourself that way; everybody gets disgusted with you; stuff! be a man or a mouse, can't you?'[8]

The vernacular outlaw, sufficiently robust to withstand the thralls of any convention, is invariably an implicit or explicit apologist for a new manner of speaking. Mr Brown speaks with a similar explosive forthrightness in the travel letters which were mainly intended for the West, but when Clemens made these letters into a book—*Innocents Abroad*—he eliminated Mr Brown and increased the rhetorical passages such as we noted in the first section. This is significant for the book was intended to sell primarily in the Eastern States, the stronghold of the official culture, and the crude vernacular irreverence had to be cut out or muffled if tastes were not to be completely alienated. Clemens was not yet possessed of the means of making a confident attack: nevertheless, he still has his fun. The pilgrims who made the trip to Europe and Asia Minor were very much the solemn, pompous kind of people who held the citadel of the official culture. Mr Brown was not at hand to deflate their genteel attitudinizing but, in the zoological gardens at Marseilles, Clemens noticed a bird who served his purpose in a subtler way.

This fellow stood up with his eyes shut and his shoulders stooped forward a little, and looked as if he had his hands under his coat-tails. Such tranquil stupidity, such supernatural gravity, such self-righteous-ness, and such ineffable self-complacency as were in the countenance and attitude of that gray-bodied, dark-winged, bald-headed, and preposterously uncomely bird! He was so ungainly, so pimply about the head, so scaly about the legs; yet so serene, so unspeakably satisfied. . . . We stirred him up occasionally but he only unclosed an eye and slowly closed it again, abating no jot of his stately piety of demeanour or his tremendous seriousness. He only seemed to say, 'Defile not Heaven's anointed with unsanctified hands.' We did not know his name, and so we called him 'The Pilgrim'.[9]

Apart from ridiculing the self-satisfied, sanctimonious pilgrims the passage has a further significance. Through Mark Twain and various vernacular outlaws, Clemens 'stirred up' the official culture occasionally: but he had, as yet, found no way of formulating any more radical criticism. As the naive Mark Twain he could pretend not to understand the official values: through the vernacular outlaws he could cock a snook at them: but the citadel stood firm, the 'pilgrim' bird scarcely deigned to blink. Perhaps a rephrasing of this central problem will clarify Clemens's difficulty, and a perceptive aside of Santayana's can help us here. 'Has there been, we may ask, any successful effort to escape from the genteel tradition, and to express something worth expressing behind its back? . . . I might mention the Humorists. . . . The Humorists, however, only half escape the genteel tradition for they have nothing solid to put in its place.'[10] If Clemens was to find firm ground from which to attack the official culture he would have to offer, and artistically exemplify, a more desirable alternative. Before he could make of the low vernacular attitude something more than a medium of burlesque and slapstick irreverence he had to have a finer vision of the values for which it might be made to stand.

Some 'outlaw' figures appear in *Innocents Abroad* as the sinners and the boys, even though the coarse voice of Mr Brown has been suppressed; but in *Roughing It* as Mark Twain records his initiation into the West they reappear more assertively than before. At an early stage in the journey west a woman gets into the carriage and administers a shock to decorous expectations with her 'dislocated grammar' and 'decomposed pronunciation'[11] yet the forthrightness of her candid refusal to stand on ceremony ('I reckon I'm a pretty sociable heifer after all')[12] reveals to the narrator the existence of a whole new range of social standards and practices. In the strange hierarchy of the West unexpected figures acquire an unusual prestige—the stage drivers, the pony-express rider, even that 'outlaw among outlaws'[13] Jack Slade himself. At the time the West was an ambiguous moral territory: 'There was absolutely no semblance of law there. Violence was the rule. Force was the only recognized authority.'[14] In such an atmosphere virtues not recognized by the official culture were seen emerging. There is Captain John, for instance, a typical frontiersman whose virtues include rare conversational powers, 'a singular "handiness" about doing anything and everything'[15] and a spirit of general camaraderie which Mark Twain comes to admire and emulate. Symptomatic of Twain's assimilation of western values is his change in dress. 'I had grown well accustomed to wearing a damaged slouched hat, blue woolen shirt, and pants crammed into boot-tops, and gloried in the absence of coat, vest and braces. I felt rowdyish and "bully" . . . it seemed to me that nothing could be so fine and romantic.'[16] Of course he is still making fun of his own romantic gloss on a harsh reality: but before the end of the book he has been properly initiated into the 'easy and nonchalant brotherhood of the West':[17] he has learned to understand the 'outlaw's' informality of attitudes and informality of speech from the inside.

However, having been initiated, the narrator seems unable to hold on to his new identity, just as he is unable properly to express the values he feels he has gained from the initiation. When he gives up mining to become a reporter in Virginia City the narrator gradually ceases to be the semi-fictional novitiate and lapses back into Mark Twain himself, the improvising opportunistic journalist scratching his memory for material. The hint for organization and projected character which the theme of initiation has provided are now lost. As Henry Nash Smith comments: 'Henceforth his attitudes are quite unstable. On one page he is a spokesman for the official culture, on the next he veers back toward a burlesque of it. On a third he resorts to straightforward, neutral exposition of such matters as the operation of a stamping mill or the technique of pocket mining.'[18] One of the outlaw figures he produces later in the book is regarded with an oddly equivocal air. This is Scotty Briggs. When Buck Fanshaw, a 'distinguished tough' from 'the vast bottom stratum of society'[19] dies, his friend Scotty Briggs calls on the local minister who is a fragile genteel pendant from an Eastern theological seminary. Scotty's mission is to request a proper funeral for his friend—and of course, the minister's pedantic rhetoric is forced into an embarrassing propinquity with the tough's slangy colloquialism for humorous effects. But the narrator at this point seems to find *both* extremes rather amusing: he does not align himself with Scotty Briggs, and the latter's slang in no way foreshadows Huck's vernacular. Here Mark Twain has really sentimentalized the outlaw into the rogue with the heart of gold. He has not truly sympathized with him to try and seek out the roots of new and different values: he has distanced him into fond caricature. Scotty Briggs points towards Bret Harte and not Clemens's own solution of his problem. This is the problem which Henry Nash Smith accurately points to when he says that Mark Twain 'searched his memory for images which could embody the affirmations implicit in a vernacular system of values'.[20] It was a problem, too, of finding exactly the right language to reanimate and dramatize those images, and the right form and fable to provoke the images and language to release their full potential.

Ever since writing 'The Jumping Frog of Calaveras County' Clemens had been a master of getting the oral humorous story on to paper with a minimum loss of 'presence' and vocal effects. But in 1874 he wrote a story for the 'Atlantic Monthly' which was a serious step forward in his progress towards the perfection of *Huckleberry Finn*. He called it 'A True Story' and much later —in 1895—when he was preparing an introduction for the story he wrote in his notebook: 'I tell it because I think it is a curiously strong piece of literary work to come unpremeditated from lips untrained in the literary art. (The untrained tongue is usually wandering, wordy & vague; but this is clear, compact, & coherent—yes, & vivid also, & perfectly simple & unconscious.)'[21] His interest in 'the untrained tongue' was not new, as we have seen, but in this story the cadences of vernacular dialect were not exploited for their comic effects as with The Unreliable— or Scotty Briggs—but for their note of sincere and authentic protest. For this story, this true story, is told by an outlaw of a very special kind, an ex-slave called Aunt Rachel. There is a shadowy introducer of the story, but it is the towering presence of Aunt Rachel and her untrained, unpremeditated speech that commands all our attention. Here is a part of her story:

Aunt Rachel had gradually risen, while she warmed to her subject, and now she towered above us, black against the stars.

'Dey put chains on us an' put us on a stan' as high as dis po'ch— twenty foot high—an' all de people stood aroun', crowds an' crowds. An' dey'd come up dah an' look at us all roun', an' squeeze our arm, an' make us git up an' walk, an' den say, "Dis one too ole," or "Dis one lame," or "Dis one don't 'mount to much." An' dey sole my ole man, an' took him away, an' dey begin to sell my chil'en an' take *dem* away, an' I begin to cry; an' de man say, "Shet up yo' damn blubberin'," an' hit me on de mouf wid his han'. An' when de las' one was gone but my little Henry, I grab' *him* clost up to my breas' so, an' I ris up an' says, "You sha'n't take him away," I says; "I'll kill de man dat tetches him!" I says. But my little Henry whisper an' say, "I gwyne to run away, an' den I work an' buy yo' freedom." Oh bless de chile, he always so good! But they got him—dey got him, de men did; but I took and tear de clo'es mos' off em an' beat 'em over de head wid my chain; an' *dey* give it to *me* too, but I didn't mine dat.'[22]

In this story the accents of the outlaw reveal a new dimension of moral potential, a new ability to articulate serious human emotions. In the story the narrator is a slightly fatuous figure who thinks that Aunt Rachel has never had any trouble, but the monumental dignified sadness of the negress reduces him to a ghostly presence and banishes him from the stage. Again it is a reversal of the pastoral situation: but this time on a more serious level. When Scotty Briggs shows the priest up for a pedant this constitutes no radical attack on society, but the voice of Aunt Rachel not only offers a rebuff to the narrator, it is a reproach to civilization. And here we must pause to emphasize Clemens's art. So well has he managed to simulate and re-create the speech of the negress that, just as he intended, we feel that the story is actually her work. But whatever he heard the woman say, the task and triumph of getting it on to paper belong exclusively to Clemens, as does the inherently indecorous idea of letting an ex-slave tell her own story in her own way. We can get some hint of the work he put into the story from a letter he wrote to Howells at the time. 'All right, my boy, send proof sheets *here*. I amend dialect stuff by talking & talking & *talking* it till it sounds right.'[23] Talking and talking and talking until he— Samuel Clemens, the highly conscious artist—had acquired a completely inward sympathy with the unconscious artlessness of 'lips untrained in the literary art'. By such discipline did he acquire a new moral and aesthetic perspective on the world. Clemens always wrote at his best when portraying the picaresque outlaw elements from 'the vast bottom stratum of society'—as Howells noted—and two years later he hit upon an even more sympathetic outlaw narrator than Aunt Rachel. But before studying the emergence of Huck Finn I want to point to two more vernacular outlaw figures who turn up in *A Tramp Abroad*. This is a far less successful book about Europe than *Innocents Abroad*—the exuberance has diminished and the comic imagination often flags. But when Clemens allows himself to reminisce about various vernacular characters from his past his work catches fire and there is a notable influx of vitality into the writing, which serves to make the European wanderings remote by comparison. And one of these extra-social characters, Jim Baker, has a significant humorous story to tell which yet again reveals Clemens's abiding preoccupation with the linguistic dichotomy he himself was trying to solve.

He was a middle-aged, simple-hearted miner who had lived in a lonely corner of California, among the woods and mountains, a good many years, and had studied the ways of his neighbors, the beasts and the birds, until he believed he could accurately translate any remark which they made. This was Jim Baker. According to Jim Baker, some animals have only a limited education, and use only very simple words, and scarcely ever a comparison or a flowery figure; whereas certain other animals have a large vocabulary, a fine command of language and a ready and fluent delivery; consequently these latter talk a great deal; they like it; they are conscious of their talent, and they enjoy 'showing off'. Baker said, that after long and careful observation, he had come to the conclusion that the bluejays were the best talkers he had found among birds and beasts. Said he 'There's more *to* a bluejay than any other creature. He has got more moods, and more different kinds of feelings than other creatures; and, mind you, whatever a bluejay feels, he can put into language. And no mere commonplace language either, but rattling, out-and-out book talk— and bristling with metaphor, too—just bristling. . . . You may call a jay a bird. Well, so he is, in a measure—because he's got feathers on him, and don't belong to no church, perhaps; but otherwise he is just as much a human as you be. And I'll tell you for why. A jay's gifts, and instincts, and feelings, and interests, cover the whole ground. A jay hasn't got any more principle than a Congressman. A jay will lie, a jay will steal, a jay will deceive, a jay will betray; and four times out of five a jay will go back on his solemnest promise.'[24]

The equation of every sort of duplicity and hypocrisy with florid 'out-and-out book talk' is a sly joke which Clemens did not intend to go unobserved, for his interest was in those 'animals' who 'have only a limited education, and use only very simple words, and scarcely ever a comparison or a flowery figure': animals like Aunt Rachel and Huck Finn, animals whose language never lied.

The other notable appearance in the book is that of Nicodemus Dodge who, with his indifference, his laconic composure, his tattered clothes and careless gestures is pre-eminently a subsocial vernacular type. 'When I was a boy in a printing-office in Missouri, a loose-jointed, long-legged, tow-headed, jeans-clad, countrified cub of about sixteen lounged in one day, and without removing his hands from the depth of his trousers pockets or taking off his faded ruin of a slouch hat, whose broken rim hung limp and ragged about his eyes and ears like a bug-eaten cabbage leaf, stared indifferently around, then leaned his hip against the editor's table, crossed his mighty brogans, aimed at a distant fly from a crevice in his upper teeth, laid him low, and said with composure: "Whar's the boss?"'[25]

Dodge seems vulnerable and gullible—'a butt to play jokes on. It was easy to see that he was inconceivably green and confiding'[26] —yet he outsmarts his mockers with a sort of insouciant resourcefulness which seems more instinctive than acquired. Beneath the shabby clothes there is a touch of Huck Finn's resilience and independence. More seriously he is made the spokesman for a cluster of values which Clemens increasingly came to feel existed among the 'outlaw' figures beneath or outside of society, values rather different from those inculcated and countenanced by the religion of the day. Clemens was to subsume these innate attributes under the generic title of 'the sound heart' and set them against the 'deformed conscience' which was the set of introjected values of a corrupt civilization. He used these terms when describing *Huckleberry Finn* as 'a book of mine where a sound heart & a deformed conscience come into collision & conscience suffers defeat'.[27] As Nicodemus Dodge states his 'religion' to the boss the unresolved conflict between conscience and heart is minor and comic:

Well, boss, you've kind o' got me, thar—and yit you hain't got me so mighty much, nuther. I think't if a feller he'ps another feller when he's in trouble and don't cuss, and don't do mean things, nur noth'n' he ain' no business to do, and don't spell the Saviour's name with a little g, he ain't runnin' no resks—he's about as saift as if he b'longed to a church.[28]

That last vestige of Sunday school catechism consorts rather oddly with the broad humanitarianism of his other values. At a much profounder level this is to be the source of Huck's moral dilemma. Nicodemus Dodge, in the innocence of his youth is a distant relation, but a relation none the less.

Clemens's outlaws were all recognizable for their tatty informality of dress, from The Unreliable right up to Nicodemus Dodge.

In 1875 he had completed a nostalgic book about childhood and into the safe and respectable world of Tom Sawyer's St Petersburg he had introduced another of his outlaw figures, a 'juvenile pariah' called Huck Finn:

Huckleberry was always dressed in the castoff clothes of full-grown men, and they were in perennial bloom and fluttering with rags. His hat was a vast ruin with a wide crescent lopped out of its brim; his coat, when he wore one, hung nearly to his heels and had the rearward buttons far down the back; but one suspender supported his trousers; the seat of the trousers bagged low and contained nothing; the fringed legs dragged in the dirt when not rolled up. Huckleberry came and went, at his own free will. He slept on doorsteps in fine weather and in empty hogsheads in wet; he did not have to go to school or to church, or call any being master or obey anybody; he could go fishing or swimming when and where he chose, and stay as long as it suited him; nobody forbade him to fight; he could sit up as late as he pleased; he was always the first boy that went barefoot in the spring and the last to resume leather in the fall; he never had to wash, nor put on clean clothes; he could swear wonderfully. In a word, everything that goes to make life precious that boy had. So thought every harrassed, hampered, respectable boy in St Petersburg.[29]

In *Tom Sawyer* where Clemens is recreating in idyllic form his own childhood, the latent challenging rebelliousness of Huck is allowed little scope. Writing rather whimsically and indulgently from an adult third-person point of view, Clemens allows the idealized cosiness of his childhood village and the safe pranks and naughtiness of Tom, who is basically a respectable youth, to dominate the tone of the book. Here, in fact, the pastoral situation is maintained. The outlaw does not break the idyllic configuration of images: rather, Huck's basic humanitarian anarchy is muted and made to serve Tom's instinct for that sort of mischief which the respectable village condones and even smiles upon. But there are moments when the voice of the outlaw strikes a note not quite in key with the rest of the book: a note which starts to activate emotions which, if fully developed, would turn against the idealized version of Tom's village. Two of these moments worth quoting reveal Huck's instinctive sympathy

139

with other and, in the eyes of the village, much worse pariahs: the town drunkard accused of murder, and an old negro slave. Tom asks Huck whether he feels sorry for Muff Potter, the drunkard accused of murder.

Most always—most always. He ain't no account; but then he hain't ever done anything to hurt anybody. Just fishes a little, to get money to get drunk on—and loafs around considerable; but, Lord, we all do that—leastways most of us—preachers and suchlike. But he's kind of good—he give me half a fish once, when there warn't enough for two; and lots of times he's kind of stood by me when I was out of luck.[30]

Tom, it is true, helps to clear Muff Potter of the murder, but he tends to see the man as an opportunity for schoolboy heroics: a stylized figure who provides the occasion for a romantic escapade quite in keeping with the idyllic atmosphere. Huck on the other hand is aware of Potter as a living suffering human being, weak but generous and worthy of true sympathy. As usual Huck has a clear humble alert vision of the reality of the external world while Tom's eyes are stuffed with romance. Tom's point of view maintains the idyll: Huck challenges it.

Huck's sympathy with the 'niggerman, Uncle Jake' is more serious and moving as he reveals here the seeds of what is to be his crucial moral problem in *Huckleberry Finn*:

I tote water for Uncle Jake whenever he wants me to, and any time I ask him he gives me a little something to eat if he can spare it. That's a mighty good nigger, Tom. He likes me, becuz I don't ever act as if I was above him. Sometimes I've set right down and eat *with* him. But you needn't tell that. A body's got to do things when he's awful hungry he wouldn't want to do as a steady thing.[31]

His shame at following the humane instincts of his heart illuminates very tellingly the corrupt mores with which society has surrounded him. Conscience is society; and Huck's 'deformed conscience' provides an unconscious indictment of a whole culture. Tom on the other hand never gets so far out of line with society. He flirts with rebellion, but significantly 'he did not care to have Huck's company in public places'.[32] At the end he reveals his true allegiances when trying to persuade Huck to allow himself to be civilized by the Widow Douglas. 'But, Huck, we can't let you into the gang if you ain't respectable, you know.'[33] Tom not only likes to run with the hares and hunt with the hounds, he wants to turn the hares into hounds. Huck's protests against 'cussed smothery houses'[34] and all they stand for in the way of restriction and regularity are deflected into childish prattle by Tom. Indeed one could say that Tom's most important exploit in the book is his preservation of the idyll: as long as he is at hand the voice of the outlaw can be muffled or emasculated.

And Clemens knew something was wrong. He wrote to Howells as soon as he had finished the book:

I have finished the story & didn't take the chap beyond boyhood. I believe it would be fatal to do it in any shape but autobiographically—like Gil Blas. I perhaps made a mistake in not writing it in the first person.... By & by I shall take a boy of twelve & run him on through life (in the first person) but not Tom Sawyer—he would not be a good character for it.[35]

These casual remarks merit a close scrutiny since they contain a decision which was to have a lasting influence on American literature. In fact there are two decisions. The first is to bring the outlaw vernacular Huck forward and banish the respectable Tom (destined in the eyes of the village to become a great lawyer or soldier—a defender and upholder of society): the second is to write it in the first person—i.e. completely from the vernacular point of view. As we have seen Clemens had been experimenting with points of view all his writing life. The grave naive mask of Mark Twain served him when he visited strange territories East and West, and he continually sought to incorporate the irreverence of vernacular outlaws in his work. Yet he still had not found a completely satisfying point of view from which to write: he had not found the voice which really allowed him to get at what he wanted to say. Let us posit a solution to his dilemma. The strategy of a naive narrator who is honest and unpretentious is useful for gaining audience sympathy: should the narrator also subsume the characteristics of the vernacular outlaw, his freedom from all aspirations to gentility, his attractive code of non-social values, his unpremeditated non-chalance of speech, then a powerful figure would emerge—a rebel in command of our sympathies. But since it is imperative not to alienate the audience by repetitious vulgarity, tedious unintelligence and predictable irreverence, the use of an adult vernacular narrator is beset with difficulties. Imagine a whole book by Scotty Briggs: it might be amusing but it could never be—in a word—serious. We might laugh at the audacity and blasphemy and so on but an essential nexus of sympathy would be lacking. But take a child in whom the irreverence and inability to identify with society is spontaneous, unwitting and sincere; let the child address us with an honest naivety and our sympathies will be held. Whatever he says he knows no better: skilful oratory may always lie, but the fumbling apologetic attempts at articulating by a child must be efforts at the truth. As Clemens once noted 'children and fools *always* speak truth':[36] he had already perfected the mask of the fool, in Mark Twain, but his real salvation lay in turning to the child. The decision to let Huck Finn tell his own story was a leap of genius by which Clemens solved his problems as a writer. Vernacular outlaw and narrator merge, and they merge in the figure of a child. And just as Huck's point of view and language solved Clemens's stylistic problem, so his attitudes and values provided him with a standpoint from which to offer a serious criticism of life based on a code not endorsed by the official culture. It is worth remembering that when *Huckleberry Finn* was published at least one New England library banned it. The naive vision of life challenged the supremacy of society—indeed in one sense it threatened the very idea of civilization. Sut Lovingood was an anarchist, but was sufficiently hateful to remain fundamentally alienated from our sympathies. Huck engages us completely, and to be thus affiliated is at the same time to be disengaged from all literary and social decorum. In *Huckleberry Finn* the voice of the outlaw speaks with exclusive authority: the reversal of the pastoral situation is complete, and with a complete seriousness which was beyond the grasp and vision of all the earlier humorists.

CHAPTER 9

THE POND OF YOUTH

But our wiser years still run back to the despised recollections of childhood, and always we are fishing up some wonderful article out of that pond.[1]

EMERSON, *Essays*, 'Intellect'

Jean's spirits are good; Clara's are rising. They have youth—the only thing that was worth giving to the race.[2]

Clemens in a letter to Howells after the death of his daughter Susy

THE older Clemens became the more obsessed with youth he was: indeed his first important works show a chronologically regressive curve. Mark Twain in Europe is followed by Mark Twain in the West who in turn is followed by Mark Twain as a cub-pilot on the Mississippi: the reverse order to the actual sequence of Clemens's own life. By the time of *Huckleberry Finn* he has chosen to write as a child. As we have seen there were stylistic and moral reasons for this chosen point of view, but the strategy of the child-narrator would not have occurred to Clemens had he not felt an increasing tug backwards into the past, his own and America's. And from it he fished up his most wonderful articles. The sense of release, the unhindered flow of his autobiography when he returns to his childhood, gives evidence of a very special sort of 'feel' for the past which cannot be explained by normal wistfulness.

As I have said, I spent some part of every year at the farm until I was twelve or thirteen years old. The life which I led there with my cousins was full of charm, and so is the memory of it yet. I can call back the solemn twilight and mystery of the deep woods, the earthy smells, the faint odors of the wild flowers, the sheen of rain-washed foliage, the rattling clatter of drops when the wind shook the trees, the far-off hammering of woodpeckers and the muffled drumming of

143

wood pheasants in the remoteness of the forest, the snapshot glimpses of disturbed wild creatures scurrying through the grass—I can call it all back and make it as real as it ever was, and as blessed.[3]

This particular passage continues for some pages, effortless and unflagging in its detailed sensory recreation of the minutiae of his life as a child. 'The first step' was the most vivid for Clemens and no subsequent experience obliterated or blurred his early sense impressions which up to his death he could recount with a matchless relaxed verve. And indeed shortly before his death he showed his preference for youth by forming an imaginary organization called the Aquarium which was composed of young schoolgirls with whom he talked and corresponded. As he grew older, references to 'the old old times when we laughed'[4] and 'the reviving wine of the past, the pathetic past, the beautiful past, the dear and lamented past'[5] proliferated in his letters and notebooks. He came to regard the following snatch of poetry

> The day when we went gipsying
> A long time ago

as one of the 'two most pathetic, moving things in the English tongue'[6] and Henry Nash Smith is surely right to say that the line had 'powerful incantatory and talismanic values'[7] for Clemens. His second 'most pathetic moving thing' was simply the phrase 'Departed this life'[8] and it reveals the inevitable hatred of old age and death which is inextricably associated with the idealization of youth. As he reminisces about his boyhood friends in his autobiography he finds himself writing the same sad refrain over and over again. '*He died*. It is what I have to say about so many of those boys and girls.'[9] When he recounts meetings with old friends in later life he reveals how he always looked for evidence of the ghost of youth imprisoned in the ageing body. 'I saw Tom Nash approaching me across a vacant space and I walked toward him, for I recognized him at once. He was old and white-headed, but the boy of fifteen was still visible in him.'[10] '. . . the boy to whom I had told the cat story when we were callow juveniles was still present in that cheerful little old man . . .'[11]

Age is only ever a terrible decline, a cruel and inexplicable process of deprivation. 'It is a pity that we cannot escape from life when we are young',[12] he wrote with complete sincerity. And when his beloved daughter Susy died he stated the sentiment even more revealingly: 'Susy died at the right time, the fortunate time of life, the happy age—twenty four years. At twenty four, such a girl has seen the best of life—life as a happy dream. After that age the risks begin: responsibility comes, and with it the cares, the sorrows, and the inevitable tragedy.'[13] Clemens could only envisage youth and age as existing in a state of almost grotesque oppugnancy. For instance, in his notebooks he records a plan to write a sketch in which two sets of people—one young, one old—visit a house which is transformed into a fairy palace during the night. They are subjected to a sort of vice-versa in which they keep their respective faces and for the rest acquire opposite characteristics. The young faces have old bodies and are full of incomprehensible sorrow: the old faces are joined to delightedly young bodies and only vaguely remember a sort of nightmare in which they were once old people. The spell is dissolved in the morning, leaving the proper young to match up with each other, and the old begging the chief fairy to restore their lost youth. Being refused they march off to a solemn chant.[14] Age appears as a terrible remorseless sentence: a punishment, a blight, an end of joy which is visited on the human race for no apparent reason. This is surely something different from the usual syndrome of emotions which attend upon old age. By way of compensation it was this loathing for old age which seems to have given Clemens's writing about youth its fantastic vividness. When he saw the world innocently, when he viewed it naively, when the senses were discovering the colour and texture of reality as for the first time—when he responded to things as Huck does; then that was life, the best the world had to offer.

Clemens's preoccupation with 'youth' would require a book in itself to probe properly but we can suggest the important relationship between Clemens the man and Huck his youthful creation by noting his response to one of Howells's novels.

MARK TWAIN

Two years after Clemens had finished *Huckleberry Finn* Howells published *Indian Summer*. This is the story of Theodore Colville who, at forty-one, is depressed by the onset of middle-age and seeks temporarily to regain his youth by attaching himself to the youthful, beautiful Imogene Graham. The theme is very simply developed. When Colville watches Imogene at a dance we read: 'Her *abandon* interested Colville, and then awed him; the spectacle of that young unjaded capacity for pleasure touched him with a profound sense of loss.'[15] When out walking with Imogene in Florence he asks about the Cascine:

'Do they keep the fountain of youth turned on here during the winter still?'
'I've never seen it,' said Imogene gaily.
'Of course not. You never looked for it. Neither did I when I was here before. But it wouldn't escape me now.'[16]

Occasionally Howells gives up flirting with symbolism (he makes some heavy points out of the contrast between Spring and Winter) and states his theme outright:

'Perhaps you'll find out after a while that I'm not an old fellow either, but only a "Lost Youth".'[17]

After a few remarks in this vein Imogene decides that it is her mission to restore his youth:

'I want you to feel that *I* am your youth—the youth you were robbed of—given back to you.'[18]

It becomes increasingly obvious that he is *not* young, that they are hopelessly unsuited: a convenient accident with a bolting horse puts Colville out of his senses but restores Imogene to hers. She suddenly realizes that she has no love for him and in one of those tired happy endings which Howells borrowed from the sentimental tradition, Colville marries Mrs Bower who, being in the flower of middle-age, is ideal for him. In a conversation between them Howells reiterates his theme. They have just heard some singing in the street.

146

'I heard just such singing before I fell asleep the night after that party at Madame Uccelli's, and it filled me with fury.'

'Why should it do that?'

'I don't know. It seemed like voices from our youth—Lina.'

She had no resentment of his use of her name in the tone with which she asked: 'Did you hate that so much?'

'No; the loss of it.'

They both fetched a deep breath.[19]

The mere mention of Youth seems to have made an extraordinary number of Howells's contemporaries fetch a deep breath. Excursions into childhood were common—Howells's own *Boy's Town* and Aldrich's *Story of a Bad Boy* are two examples—and quite apart from the normal regrets associated with growing old there is a special cultural factor involved: namely the fact that people who, like Clemens and Howells, were middle-aged in the 1880's had spent their childhood in the Eden of pre-Civil-War America. Dismay with the harsh reality of post-war corruption and the spoliation of the continent thrust them back to the psychic reality of their youth. That they were acutely aware of the break the war caused is hinted at in Howells's novel. During his first conversation with Imogene, Colville mentions an old song which she doesn't recognize.

'Ah, I see,' said Colville, peering at her under his thoughtfully knitted brows, 'you do belong to another era. You don't remember the old negro minstrel song.'

'No,' said Miss Graham. 'I can only remember the end of the war.'

'How divinely young!' said Colville.[20]

We might recall that it was Howells who gave James the seed of his novel *The Ambassadors* which emerged in Strether's important speech to little Bilham: 'All the same, don't forget that you're young—blessedly young; be glad of it, on the contrary, and live up to it. Live all you can—it's a mistake not to.'[21] And James himself very succinctly describes the difference that

147

the Civil War made to those Americans who knew both the previous and subsequent Americas:

The subsidence of that great convulsion had left a different tone from the tone it found, and one may say that the Civil War marks an era in the history of the American mind. It introduced into the national consciousness a certain sense of proportion and relation, of the world being a more complicated place than it had hitherto seemed, the future more treacherous, success more difficult . . . the good American, in days to come, will be a more critical person than his complacent and confident grandfather. He has eaten of the tree of knowledge.[22]

The Civil War was a fall—*the* fall for those who experienced it, and consequently youth, for those who had spent it before the war, took on a paradisaical, mythical glow. Conversely to grow old in post-war America—an America 'rotten, as far as the dollar is concerned'[23] in Clemens's own words—was to experience age as a doubly ugly thing. Bearing all this in mind, consider Clemens's reaction when he had read *Indian Summer*. He wrote immediately and heartfeltly to Howells:

It is a beautiful story, & makes a body laugh all the time, & cry inside, & feel so old & so forlorn; & gives him gracious glimpses of his lost youth that fill him with a measureless regret, & build up in him a cloudy sense of his having been a prince, once, in some enchanted far off land, & of being in exile now, & desolate—& lord, no chance ever to get back there again! That is the thing that hurts.[24]

What is interesting is not only the general sentiment of the piece but the tone—which is in fact very different from the rest of the letter: it is different for this very simple reason, that Clemens has started to talk like Huck Finn. He would not have let Huck say 'measureless regret' or 'cloudy sense' perhaps, but the syntax, the air of spontaneity, the feeling of almost breathless sincerity— these are Huck's. It is a classic example of how the mere mention of youth could bring out the Huck Finn in Clemens, as though only through that lad could Clemens articulate his most important feelings. Small wonder that his wife nicknamed him 'Youth'. According to Jung, in times of stress, deprivation or frustration, it is possible for a person unconsciously to reactivate earlier forms

of adaptation to life, and without wishing to attempt any superficial psycho-analysis of Clemens it can fairly be said that the
more he felt old age and post-war America to constitute a double
state of exile, the happier he felt when he could recover, if only
through writing, his innocent youthful intimacy with a lost past.

An important extension of Clemens's preoccupation with
youth was his lifelong interest in youthful modes of thought and
expression. And it is important to remember that what gives
Huck Finn's speech much of its lyric and moral force is not ✓
simply that he speaks in the vernacular but that he also speaks
and thinks as a child. It would be a mistake to suggest that
Clemens found a nourishing precedent for his own work in the
writing of children, but if we say in general that, as a writer, he
was after an habitual economy of sincere simplicity to oppose
to the inflated rhetoric and attitudinizing endorsed by the official
culture, then we may also say that a childish artlessness could be
as much to his purpose as vernacular irreverence. And as early
as 1864 while he was still a reporter for the 'Territorial Enterprise'
we find evidence of an interest in childish modes of expression.
In one of his letters to that paper he gives a humorous account
of a visit to the local school during which the children read their
compositions:

The 'compositions' read to-day were as exactly like the compositions
I used to hear read in our school as one baby's nose is exactly like all
other babies' noses. I mean the old principal ear-marks were all there:
the cutting to the bone of the subject with the very first gash, without
any preliminary foolishness in the way of a gorgeous introductory: the
inevitable and persevering tautology; the brief, monosyllabic sentences (beginning, as a very general thing, with the pronoun 'I');
the penchant for presenting rigid, uncompromising facts for the consideration of the hearer, rather than ornamental fancies; the depending
for success of the composition upon its general merits, without tacking
artificial aides to the end of it, in the shape of deductions or conclusions,
or clap-trap climaxes, albeit their absence sometimes imparts to these
essays the semblance of having come to an end before they were
finished—of arriving at full speed at a jumping-off place and going
suddenly overboard, as it were, leaving a sensation such as one feels

when he stumbles without warning upon that infernal 'To be Continued' in the midst of a thrilling magazine story. I know there are other styles of school composition, but these are the characteristics of the style which I have in my eye at present. I do not know why this one has particularly suggested itself to my mind, unless the literary effort of one of the boys there to-day left me with an unusually vivid impression. It ran something in this wise:

COMPOSITION

'I like horses. Where we lived before we came here, we used to have a cutter and horses. We used to ride in it. I like Winter. I like snow. I used to have a pony all to myself, where I used to live before I came here. Once it drifted a good deal—very deep—and when it stopped I went out and got in it.'

That was all. There was no climax to it, except the spasmodic bow which the tautological little student jerked at the school as he closed his labours.[25]

Along with this piece I want to consider an extract from an essay called 'A Complaint about Correspondents' which he wrote soon after. He is complaining about the mannerisms of letter writers in the East and goes on to say:

The most useful and interesting letters we get here from home are from children seven or eight years old. This is petrified truth. Happily they have got nothing to talk about but home, and neighbors, and family—things their betters think unworthy of transmission thousands of miles. They write simply and naturally, and without straining for effect. They tell all they know, and then stop. They seldom deal in abstractions or moral homilies. Consequently their epistles are brief; but, treating as they do of familiar scenes and persons, always entertaining. Now, therefore, if you would learn the art of letter-writing, let a child teach you.[26]

And after quoting from a letter from a child which is extremely naive and marked by a random honesty, he comments: 'This child treads on my toes, in every other sentence, with a perfect looseness, but in the simplicity of her time of life she doesn't know it.'[27] One might immediately point out that in the simpli-

city of his time of life Huck was to tread on the moral toes of a
civilization, and it was his very unconsciousness of doing so that
gave it such force. But more interesting are the virtues which
Clemens, thus early, ascribes to children's writing. 'Rigid
uncompromising facts . . . rather than ornamental fancies',
'cutting to the bone of the subject with the very first gash', the
abrupt endings which flaunt the tradition of contrived climax,
the absence of straining for effect, the reverence of familiar details,
the suspicion of abstractions, the avoidance of moral uplift—
these, I submit, are all qualities which Clemens himself sought
for, and which many subsequent American writers have incor-
porated into their writing. With little modification comparable
terms occur in any discussion of writers like Hemingway (who
himself said 'it is years since I added the wow to the end of a
story'), Anderson, Stein, McCullers. Direct influence is of course
not being argued, but that a cultivated naivety of speech and
vision is evident in Clemens and such later writers seems to me
irrefutable. What Clemens, half smilingly, noticed children
doing unconsciously he found analogous to his own ideals as
writer. The evidence that this was so is recurrent. Here for
instance is an extract from a letter he wrote to a young boy
named Wattie Bowser while he was engaged in writing *Huckleberry Finn*. Bowser had sent him a composition on why he
would like to be Mark Twain: the great man answered at length
and included this praise:

I have read your composition, and I think it is a very creditable performance. I notice that you use plain, simple language, short words,
and brief sentences. That is the way to write English—it is the modern
way, and the best way. Stick to it; don't let fluff and flowers and
verbosity creep in. When you catch an adjective, kill it. No, I don't
mean that utterly, but kill the most of them then the rest will be
valuable. They weaken when they are close together, they give
strength when they are far apart. An adjective-habit, or a wordy,
diffuse, or flowery habit once fastened upon a person, is as hard to
get rid of as any other vice.[28]

Much that is bad in nineteenth-century romantic writing—

English and American—can be put down to the plague of unemployed epithets which settled on literature and robbed it of much of its ability to pay any clear-eyed, simple, trenchant attention to the empirical facts of the world. The simple sense units of children's writing, so ignorant of current literary conventions, so refreshingly off-hand and to the point, clearly occurred to Clemens as one way of avoiding the worst vices of the grand manner. Both the anti-social speech of the outlaw and the pre-social speech of the child suggested modes of escape to him. Just as he once planned to introduce a vernacular rebel into *Hamlet* to mock Shakespeare[29] so he also suggested to Howells an article based on 'A Boy's Comments Upon Homer'.[30] In both cases the revered literary object was to be deflated by a low, a naive, non-literary point of view. Two other instances of his interest in children's writing are worth quoting in order to substantiate the claim that Clemens evinced a life-long interest in it which was more than just humorous. In 1887 a school teacher, Miss Caroline B. LeRow, sent Clemens a collection of amusing linguistic errors by her pupils which she had collected during her teaching, asking him if she should publish them. He said she should and also wrote a review of the book in *The Century* called 'English as She is Taught'. For Clemens, the mistakes that the children made prove two things. First, that education is conducted in a most unenlightened way: 'All through this little book one detects the signs of a certain probable fact—that a large part of the pupil's "instruction" consists in cramming him with obscure and wordy "rules" which he does not understand and has not time to understand.'[31] He calls the culture which produces such a method of education 'a brickbat culture'.[32] Secondly he maintained that the mistakes demonstrated the spontaneous simplicity of a child's mind, and its essential inaptness for rigid coercive rules. As we have seen he himself worked to perfect a loose, permissive, flexible formless way of writing and to see children trained out of these virtues which they enjoyed by instinct annoyed him. One of the mistakes quoted in the book pleased him so much that he sent it to Howells repeating the comment he made in his review: 'It is full of naïveté, brutal truth, and unembarrassed directness, and is the funniest (genuine) boy's composition I think I have ever seen.'[33] His interest may be merely comic here, but 'naïveté, brutal truth, and unembarrassed directness' are no bad terms for stressing some of the qualities of Huck's own speech.

Finally it would not do to forget Clemens's delight in his daughter Susy's biography of himself. He quotes from it continually throughout his autobiography. Of course there is the normal parental attachment to the engagingly naive production of his adored child, but his comment on her way of writing has a broader significance. Thus in his autobiography:

I cannot bring myself to change any line or word in Susy's sketch of me, but will introduce passages from it now and then just as they come in—their quaint simplicity out of her honest heart, which was the beautiful heart of a child. What comes from that source has a charm and grace of its own which may transgress all the recognised laws of literature, if it choose, and yet be literature still, and worthy of hospitality.[34]

He also refuses to correct her spelling on the by-now recognizable grounds that 'it would take from it its freedom and flexibility and make it stiff and formal'.[35] Clemens seems to have been one of the first American writers to feel that the whole prescribed cultural orthodoxy of the official genteel culture was altogether too 'stiff and formal' and that what was needed was more 'freedom and flexibility', something more simple and natural—something, in a sense, more child-like. And many of his scattered critical judgements echo his terms of praise for children's writing that we have so far examined. For instance he praises a minor writer called Sage on the grounds of 'an artlessness, an absence of self-consciousness, ditto of striving after effect'[36] and he admired Howe's *Story of a Country Town* because it was 'so simple, sincere, direct and at the same time so clear and strong'.[37] On similar grounds he vigorously defended General Grant's style against the rather precious and pedantic criticisms of Matthew Arnold.

What most significantly emerges from all these comments on children's writing is an undertow of primitivism—'the beautiful heart of the child' always expresses itself well no matter how formlessly, until it is circumscribed and crippled by social and literary rules. In abandoning high rhetoric for the low vernacular, in supplanting the social conformist by the anti-social outlaw, in moving back from age to youth and preferring untutored naivety to formally educated maturity, Clemens effected a triple rebellion of major importance for American literature: and it is worth noting that in every case the rebellion involves a renunciation of established society and the accepted achievements of civilization. The young vernacular rebel is alone with his wonder, his candour, his sound heart.

CHAPTER 10

HUCK FINN AND THE REFLECTIONS OF A SAPHEAD

'You don't ever reflect, Huck Finn, and I reckon you really haven't got anything to reflect with.'

Tom Sawyer in *Tom Sawyer Abroad*[1]

'Shucks, it ain't no use to talk to you, Huck Finn. You don't seem to know anything, somehow—perfect sap-head.'

Tom Sawyer in *Huckleberry Finn*[2]

'Huck, you don't ever seem to want to do anything that's regular; you want to be starting something fresh all the time.'

Tom Sawyer in *Huckleberry Finn*[3]

TOM SAWYER stands for 'style'.[4] He always consults 'the books',[5] he believes in 'the rules'.[6] He does not believe that anyone can improve on the' romantic precedents of the past. He prefers fantasticating 'enchantment'[7] to a crisp assessment of the unadorned facts. No matter what his adventures he is more interested in the scope they offer for 'fancy touches'[8] than the salvation of the innocent or the redressing of an injustice. He scorns Huck's simple and humanely based plan for helping Jim to escape, and substitutes for it a complicated and 'romantical'[9] insane parody of romantic adventure. As he himself boasts, he 'invents *all* the difficulties'.[10] To make Jim's confinement seem like a prison such as 'the books' prescribe he plans to introduce rats and rattlesnakes to torment the bewildered slave. And it is the simple Jim who raises the one consideration beyond Tom's mental scope—'what kine er time is Jim havin'?'[11] He takes his stand on the rules—'I wouldn't stand by and see the rules broke'[12] —and justifies his tissue of idiocies by maintaining that they provide him with 'intellectural'[13] fun.

The manner in which Tom reappears at the end of *Huckleberry*

155

Finn and so changes the whole tone of the book has stimulated a variety of critical explanations.[14] Some defend it by saying that Clemens cleverly reasserts the 'boy's story' atmosphere, others explain it by saying that Clemens found himself with a more serious theme on his hands than he could manage—i.e. what happens to Jim and Huck's search for freedom—and reverted to the style of *Tom Sawyer* as a sort of subconscious evasion of the implications of the issues he had half wittingly roused. That Clemens did not know how to finish *Huckleberry Finn* is more clearly suggested by the fact that he did not know what to do with Huck after he had created him, as we shall see. It remains undoubtedly an unsatisfactory ending, yet an ending rich in innuendos and occasional significance. For it demonstrates at length the perverse folly of Tom's ideal of 'style'. Against those who would suggest that Clemens only intended us to read Tom's plans for Jim's escape as an extended prank I would put up this one fact. That the meanest action of the book is when the Duke and the King having used and abused Huck and Tom for their own selfish ends finally sell Jim—'for forty dirty dollars'.[15] Huck himself, antipathetic to the whole cash-nexus of society (he gets rid of the money he and Tom find), too sensitive to human suffering to be affected by profit motives, always sees straight to the core of human need in any situation. But Tom? For the sake of his conception of 'style' and 'romance' he subjects Jim to a series of indignities and dangers (even to the point of a lynching), and then announces that Jim was free all the time (Jim's freedom was the only thing Huck could think of —in his ignorance of 'the books'). But he offers some recompense to Jim for his prolonged misery—he offers him forty dollars. That the sums are meant to echo each other seems to me certain; perhaps there is even a hint of the Judas betrayal. Tom's sense of the human has been utterly corrupted by his addiction to 'the gaudy',[16] his devotion to style, the books, the rules. I am convinced that Clemens was uncertain of his intentions and tone at the end of *Huckleberry Finn*, but Tom's treatment of Jim can easily be seen as a clumsily emerging comment on the South's treatment of the negro. In his classic study, *The Mind of the South*, W. J. Cash has a good deal to say about the contribution made by romantic illusions to the 'tragic descent into unreality'[17] which he diagnoses as one of the root troubles with Southern society, and Clemens himself held Walter Scott responsible for the Civil War because he provided a hegemony of romantic images in which the South could posture and with which it could delude itself. We have examined his struggle to escape the aesthetic falsehoods condoned and encouraged by romantic rhetoric: in this book we can see him probing the ethical mendacity lurking in everything that 'style' meant to society. For it is important to remember that Tom Sawyer is basically a social conformist: the style, romance and book-rules he believes in, in no way threaten society—in fact they consort with it. And the implications of 'style' are not restricted to Tom's hypertrophied imagination and its consequences for Jim. For instance when Huck stays at the Grangerford household he naively admires the style of the place. 'I hadn't seen no house out in the country before that was so nice and had so much style.'[18] Yet in his naivety he reveals the element of sham involved in the Grangerford style:

On a table in the middle of the room was a kind of a lovely crockery basket that had apples and oranges and peaches and grapes piled up in it which was much redder and yellower and prettier than real ones is, but they warn't real because you could see where pieces had got chipped off and showed the white chalk, or whatever it was, underneath.[19]

Huck's naive eye unconsciously, and unerringly, finds the truthful flaw in the stylistic flamboyance and offers us a quick and telling glimpse of a society both gaudy and chipped. How fatally flawed emerges, of course, in the folly of the feud, the logic of which Huck is at a loss to understand but, we may be sure, Tom would have readily taken to. Buck, defending the romantic idea of feuding, reveals a comparable corruption by romantic notions. After Buck has taken a shot at one of the Shepherdsons Huck questions him.

'Did you want to kill him, Buck?'
'Well, I bet I did.'
'What did he do to you?'
'Him? He never done nothing to me.'
'Well, then, what did you want to kill him for?'
'Why nothing—only it's on account of the feud.'
'What's a feud?'
'Why, where was you raised? Don't you know what a feud is?'
'Never heard of it before—tell me about it.'[20]

Huck was raised somewhere where ideas of 'style' had no currency: his naive standards of humanity are unapt for romantic distortion. And his naive admiration of the 'quality'[21]—who bring their guns to church to listen to a sermon on brotherly love —only underlines his own inability to fully comprehend the extent of the folly of the society in which he finds himself. And interestingly enough when he is forced to play the part of an English valet in the Duke and King's plot to rob Mary Jane and her sisters, and the girls ask him to outline English social customs, he has desperate recourse to the word 'style'[22] to explain the society of idle parsons and ill-treated servants which his imagination provides him with. It is the word which seems to explain the nonsense in Tom's head and the illogicalities and pointless cruelties in society at large. Style meant the paint over the chalk fruit, the romance of feuding over the madness of murder, the myth of feudalism over the cruelty of slavery. Style was how society dressed up its conscience. It is interesting at this point to note two entries in Clemens's notebooks for 1897 and 1899. In the latter he writes: 'Civilisation is the root of all evil'[23] while in the former he includes this meditation: 'What is civilisation? Clothes. . . . Strip the human race absolutely naked, & it would be a real democracy. But the introduction of even a rag of tiger skin or a cowtail would make a badge of distinction & be the beginning of a monarchy.'[24] This is worth mentioning because on the river Jim and Huck always go naked, and practise a perfect democracy devoid of all style. Tyranny and a minor hierarchy enter with the burlesque royalty of the Duke and King, and Huck's wistful lament—'Sometimes I wish we could hear of a country that's out of kings'[25]—indicates his, and Clemens's, longing for some extra-civilized territory in which there would be no clothes, no degree, no gaudy concealments of evil—no style. For just as Clemens was after a written manner which eschewed romantic adjectival adornment and broke down Ciceronian hypotactic syntax into nude paratactic simple statements—so he yearned for a society rid of style and hierarchy. The two things are of course related. An excess of conventional epithets conceals and colours the empirical facts just as paint hides false fruit and such romantic conventions as feuding give a false dignity and colour to meaningless murder. Similarly a complex syntax which could subsume and organize the variety of the world according to a mental system of references and priorities reflected a society which kept everyone in place by imposing a hierarchy which found a proper station for all and true equality for none. Complex syntax could be autocratic. So Clemens broke it down. Romantic epithets tended to favour the mendacities of social 'style', so Clemens tried to strip his writing bare. All of which, in turn, explain why Huck prefers to go naked, is happiest on the river, and talks in a manner which shows no evidence of having been taught the graces and complexities of 'style'. As he himself says, he was not 'brung up to it'.[26] In a very profound sense he does not belong on the society of the shore. Whenever he ventures into it he always invents a false history for himself, he sometimes dresses up, he adopts any name he can think of and—and this really is significant—he usually forgets what identity he has adopted. Early on having prepared his act as a girl and going into town as Sarah Williams he soon forgets his name, but quite readily slides into the part of a George Peters, 'runaway prentice'. When he arrives at the Grangerfords after the raft crashes with a riverboat he becomes George Jackson and settles in very well as the orphan from an Arkansas farm: but 'when I waked up in the morning, drat it all, I had forgot what my name was'.[27] As Adolphus, the English valet, he is less successful since it is a part imposed on him by the

Duke, but it adds to our feeling that Huck cannot adopt and maintain a consistent authentic role in society. In the marvellous 'Raft Passage' which Clemens foolishly tore out of *Huckleberry Finn* to animate a chapter of *Life on the Mississippi*, Huck hides on a raft to try and discover from the raftsmen's talk where they are. He hears instead a long dismal story about an abandoned child who is thrown into a barrel on the river and then pursues his murdering father on every trip he takes: the child's name is Charles William Albright. When one of the men finds Huck and drags him forward and asks him who he is, Huck, with true inspiration and suggestive identification with the outcast child, says 'Charles William Albright'.[28] And at the end of the book when he arrives at the Phelps's and finds himself welcomed as an expected visitor he tells us: 'I had my mind on the children all the time; I wanted to get them out to one side and pump them a little, and find out who I was.'[29] Huck really has no authentic identity in society: the final irony of his being taken for Tom Sawyer underlines the fact that Tom is distinctly the kind of boy who does have a name, place and identity in society. As long as Huck forces himself to be like Tom he too can stay—as at the end of *Tom Sawyer*—but when his real nature asserts itself he seems to move centrifugally away from society quite automatically. Ideally he sheds his clothes and moves on. By instinct he is a loner. When he plans to escape from both Pap and the widow his programme comes to him quite naturally. 'I guessed I wouldn't stay in one place, but just tramp right across the country, mostly night times, and hunt and fish to keep alive. . . .'[30] It is because he is really in continual instinctive flight—from all societies—that he finds his only true companion in the runaway slave. Both belong on the raft, because 'it doan' *make* no track'.[31] After any involvement with the shore they are both 'mighty glad to get aboard'[32] the raft. 'We said there warn't no home like a raft, after all. Other places do seem so cramped up and smothery, but a raft don't. You feel mighty free and easy and comfortable on a raft.'[33] Whenever Huck is involved in shore life of one kind or another his inevitable comment is 'I wished I was out of there!'[34] He

is always 'sorry I come':[35] when the feud is on 'then I clumb up
into the forks of a cotton-wood that was out of reach, and
watched'.[36] When he smells trouble, and he has an experienced
nose for it, he tries to slide out. Involved in the King's plot to
rob the girls he finds sleep impossible because 'I was in such a
sweat to get through with the business';[37] and more than once
he wishes he had just left things alone, though his instincts, as
we shall see, always drive him to brave attempts to right human
wrongs. When he thinks he has given the Duke and the King the
slip—'the way I lit out and shinned for the road in the dark, there
ain't nobody can tell'.[38] And this brings him back to the raft.
'So, in two seconds, away he went, a-sliding down the river, and
it *did* seem so good to be free again and all by ourselves on the
big river and nobody to bother us.'[39] Unlike Tom neither he nor
Jim have any taste for 'adventures' but much prefer to 'lazy
around'. 'We laid off and lazied'[40] he says in one languorous
reminiscence: or again:

And afterwards we could watch the lonesomeness of the river, and kind
of lazy along, and by and by lazy off to sleep ... we let her alone, and
let her float wherever the current wanted her to ... we was always
naked, day and night, whenever the mosquitoes would let us, the new
clothes Buck's folks made for me was too good to be comfortable, and
besides I didn't go much on clothes, nohow.[41]

The fact that Huck, in his ignorance, can take a word describing
a passive state of mind—'lazy'—and make it into a verb, a
complete activity, is very important to our understanding of him
(just as loafing and sauntering shed central light on Whitman and
Thoreau). The preference for nakedness and the raft is related
to this, and before attempting to explain this syndrome of predilections I want to quote some passages from *A Tramp Abroad*
—written in the same years that Clemens was working on
Huckleberry Finn. Clemens took a raft trip in Germany and
reported it in a curiously lyrical vein, forgetting, absolutely, to
be funny.

The motion of a raft is the needful motion ... it is gentle, and gliding,

and smooth and noiseless; it calms down all feverish activities, it
soothes to sleep all nervous hurry and impatience; under its restful influence all the troubles and vexations and sorrows that harass the
mind vanish away, and existence becomes a dream, a charm, a deep
and tranquil ecstasy. How it contrasts with hot and perspiring
pedestrianism, and dusty and deafening railroad rush, and tedious
jolting behind tired horses over blinding white roads.[42]

Comparable idyllic yearnings are generated by the Alps:

all frets and worries and chafings sank to sleep in the presence of the
benignant serenity of the Alps; the Great Spirit of the Mountains
breathed his own peace upon their hurt minds and sore hearts, and
healed them; they could not think base thoughts or do mean and
sordid things there, before the visible throne of God.[43]

Even the Kandersteg Valley stimulates this sort of desire for
peaceful self-obliteration. 'The spirit of the place was a sense of
deep pervading peace; one might dream his life tranquilly away
there, and not miss it or mind it when it was gone.'[44] Huck too
has an almost pagan sense of the benign moral potency of nature—
though, unlike Emerson, he had an acute sense of its concealed
threats and unpredictable hostilities.

To get at the root significance of this feeling for the raft, for
lazying, for nakedness and relaxation it is worth recalling the
import of the symbolism of the Sabbath Ritual. The ban on all
forms of work not only celebrates God's day of rest after the
labour of creation, it symbolizes a state of harmony between
man and nature, that paradisaical state which existed before
Adam brought sin and work into the world. Work disturbs the
man-nature equilibrium and reveals the extent of our immersion
and imprisonment; the almost immobile 'rest' of the Sabbath is
a temporary escape from time and process, an anticipation of the
Messianic time (which is called the time of 'continuous Sabbath')
of true freedom, peace and harmony. Huck hates to interfere
with the world (he lets the raft go with the current) and all his
instincts are towards the establishing of a precarious pre-
individualistic harmony. He likes to 'smooth people's roads'

and he is endlessly patient of the Duke and King though he can see through their posturing—'it would 'a' been a miserable business to have any unfriendliness on the raft; for what you want, above all things, on a raft, is for everybody to be satisfied, and feel right and kind towards the others. It didn't take me long to make up my mind that these liars warn't no kings nor dukes, at all, but just low-down humbugs and frauds. But I never said nothing, never let on; kept it to myself; it's the best way; then you don't have no quarrels, and don't get into no trouble.'⁴⁵

'Peace in the family'⁴⁶ is what he is after, and this no mere timidity: rather it is the result of an instinctive hunger for the conditions of 'the continuous Sabbath'. (Interestingly enough in one of his Sandwich Islands lectures Clemens had described the place in this way: 'It is Sunday land. The land of indolence and dreams, where the air is drowsy and things tend to repose and peace, and to emancipation from the labor, and turmoil, and weariness, and anxiety of life.'⁴⁷ Late in his life Clemens was to write a story of a nightmare experience of being lost and becalmed—and he called it 'The Everlasting Sunday'. The 'continuous Sabbath' became an ambivalent image for him.) When he and Jim are alone he indeed has intimations of such a state of continuous peace with nature, of a radical unconscious harmony with its pace. 'We had mighty good weather, as a general thing, and nothing ever happened to us at all that night, nor the next, nor the next.'⁴⁸ Such is the even uninterrupted peace which Huck's inner being craves for. He prefers to shed the insignia of 'sivilisation' (clothes) and immerse himself in nature's rhythms by 'lazying' on the raft. But—and this is why *Huckleberry Finn* is in many ways a more probing work than any of the exercises in nostalgia for a lost rapport with nature indulged by Emerson and Thoreau and even Whitman—Huck is forcibly involved with society, thrust into its mire and friction. He seeks to extricate himself from the social mess, but not before he has unwittingly delivered himself of some profound criticisms of it. For as Jim correctly predicts (and Jim and Huck's superstition

163

and belief in signs and portents indicates a reverence and respect for nature) when he interprets the tow-heads:

The lot of tow-heads was troubles we was going to get into with quarrelsome people and all kinds of mean folks, but if we minded our business and didn't talk back and aggravate them, we would pull through and get out of the fog and into the big clear river, which was the free states, and wouldn't have no more trouble.[49]

The second half of the prophecy is wishful thinking. For 'the big clear river, which was the free states' is another way of describing that mythical paradise of freedom, peace and human harmony which Jim and Huck never find: which Clemens (and it broke his heart to discover this) came to see could never be found. It is this basic yearning for a lost paradise which is responsible for various related themes which recur in Clemens's work: the idealization of far away and savage places of youth and the past, the endless moving on, and the recurring sense of exile. Thus in an early manuscript about the Sandwich Islands he starts to transfigure reality into myth by hypnotic superlatives—'the peacefulest, restfulest, sunniest, balmiest, dreamiest haven of refuge for a worn and weary spirit the surface of the earth can offer'.[50] Hence his deliquescent recollection of Jackass Gulch as 'that serene and reposeful and dreamy and delicious sylvan paradise'.[51] He even brought his longing for paradise to Europe with him and thought he caught occasional glimpses of it, in Switzerland for example. Inevitable disillusion leads to endless movement and the continual question 'what to do next?'[52] —with which he significantly starts part two of *Roughing It* after the paradisaical moment of the West had turned sour. After returning from the Sandwich Islands he wrote in his *Notebook* (1866): 'Home again. No—not home again—in prison again, and all the wild sense of freedom gone. City seems so cramped and so dreary with toil and care and business anxieties. God help me, I wish I were at sea again.'[53] Water—the element which moves, which is not built on, which cannot lastingly be interfered with by men; the *uncivilizable* element. It is interesting to note that Clemens's friend Twichell wrote in a letter to a friend: 'Mark is a queer fellow. There is nothing he so delights in as a swift strong stream.'[54] These aspects of Clemens require full-length studies of their own but I wish to point out their relevance to the figure of Huck Finn. For Huck, water—the raft and the river—means more than just an escape from momentary threats. We have said that Huck is forcibly involved with society from time to time, but his most dangerous involvement is an internal affair. Certain social mores have invaded, pervaded his mind; have corrupted his conscience to use Clemens's own formulation. Whenever he stops to think rationally, *socially*, he feels the only goodness lies in betraying Jim. This is a most dramatic metaphor which highlights Huck's midway position between two worlds: the world of men (the shore) and the world of nature (the river —and Jim), and his dilemma of being torn between inculcated morality and instinctive humanity. Clemens himself was obsessed by the curses of conscience and revealingly he writes in one letter of the peace to be found on a raft: 'a conscience in a state of coma, and lazy comfort, solid happiness. In fact there's *nothing* that's so lovely.'[55] The movement of the water could put the conscience in a coma: that was a virtue indeed. And how fruitfully this idea works itself out in *Huckleberry Finn*. It is well known that Huck risks social and religious damnation to save his friend, but it is less often noticed how he arrives at this heroic decision. Listen to him after he has written the betraying letter to Miss Watson and is deliberating whether to send it off:

But I didn't do it straight off, but laid the paper down and set there thinking—thinking how good it was all this happened so and how near I come to being lost and going to hell. And went on thinking. And got to thinking over our trip down the river; and I see Jim before me all the time; in the day and in the night time, sometimes moonlight, sometimes storms, and we a-floating along, talking, and singing and laughing. But somehow I couldn't seem to strike no places to harden me against him, but only the other kind. I'd see him standing my watch on top of his'n, stead of calling me, so I could go on sleeping; and see him how glad he was when I come back out of the fog; and when I come to him again in the swamp, up there where the feud was; and such-like times; and would always call me honey, and pet me, and do everything he could think of for me, and how good he always was; and at last I struck the time I saved him by telling the men we had small-pox abroad, and he was so grateful, and said I was the best friend old Jim ever had in the world, and the *only* one he's got now; and then I happened to look around, and see that paper.[56]

Of course he tears it up; because his whole being has been flooded with a logic superior to that of his social conscience. The flowing mellifluous reminiscence, the abdication of syntax so that he only pauses to let one feelingful memory glide into another, the almost hypnotic harmony which the rhythm and tone of the reminiscences recreate—these are all the result, not of hierarchical, social, rational thought which consults rules and precedents, but of the wayward unhindered currents of 'the sound heart'. Huck's heart has picked up the rhythm of the river, he is attuned to the pulses of nature which he so intimately understands. That is to say that a presocial order of being is feeling through him which melts and dissolves all rational obstructions, asserting instead echoes of a harmonious ideal world which is not based on degree (white man superior to negro) and property (man owning negro, *selling* negro), but on pre-individualistic harmony in which people and days flow into each other in peace and concord. Tom—stuffed with style—thinks Huck has nothing to reflect with. But Huck reflects with something bigger than Tom or his society could understand: he reflects with the river, with nature. It is because of this basic allegiance—which society tries to break but cannot—that Huck seems to have a distant origin, a remote destination, and to move inside a halo of isolation and lonesomeness. (He fits almost perfectly Thoreau's description of the Indian, that figure he spent so many years trying to trace, recapture, and turn into fruitful history and image: 'By the wary independence and aloofness of his dim forest life he preserves his intercourse with his native gods, and is admitted from time to time to a rare and peculiar society with nature.')[57] His basic wildness makes his assimilation by society impossible and any interruption of the balance between himself and nature makes him appear to us with some of the pathetic, though resilient and resourceful reactions, of a trapped animal. His melancholy sensitivity to the moods of nature seems to preclude for ever his adoption by society. For instance when the widow has locked him in his bedroom, nature starts to exert its weird potency over him:

I felt so lonesome I most wished I was dead. The stars were shining, and the leaves rustled in the woods ever so mournful; and I heard an owl, away off, who-whooing about somebody that was dead, and a whippowill and a dog crying about somebody that was going to die; and the wind was trying to whisper something to me, and I couldn't make out what it was, and so it made the cold shivers run over me.[58]

Huck's response has nothing in common with Tom's itch to play hookey on a sunny afternoon; it reveals a profoundly felt emotional contagion between himself and nature. His sympathetic reactions to the suggestivity of nature are of a piece with his tender melancholy in the world of men (lights at night, as Lionel Trilling noted, immediately suggest sick rooms to Huck). He seems, in some uncanny way, to tap the sadness of a race and continent. His reaction after he has lost Jim is little short of cosmic:

When I got there it was still and Sunday-like, and hot and sunshiny; the hands was gone to the fields; and there was them kind of faint dronings of bugs and flies in the air that makes it seem so lonesome and like everybody's dead and gone, and if a breeze fans along and quivers the leaves it makes you feel mournful, because you feel like its spirits whispering—spirits that's been dead ever so many years—and you always think they're talking about *you*. As a general thing it makes a body wish *he* was dead, too, and done with it all.[59]

Such passages, where the naivety becomes the means of transmitting an authentic awe complete the diapason of Huck's total sensitivity to nature, since elsewhere he exhibits a rich, wild, almost voluptuous joy in communing with the more benign moods of nature. His constant attitude towards nature is one of sensitive sustained reverence (a reverence heightened by the colloquial ease with which he talks about it—it makes him seem such a familiar, an intimate). This is what I mean by saying that he reflects with nature. His speech with its wistful or joyful cadences, its haunting evocative rhythms, cannot owe anything to the syntax and categories of society—indeed owes everything to its apparent ability to recall a more primitive manner of speech when man's capacity for wonder was more marked. It is the naive vision which enables Clemens to achieve this. A response not founded on reflection but nourished by natural impulse, a naivety which testifies to an unimpaired heart. As we have seen (as any reading of Clemens's letters, notebooks and works will readily reveal) the notion of the good heart was fundamental to Clemens's thought, at least until the black despair of age overtook him. Rousseauistic though it sounds it was his firm belief in this which enabled him to challenge the corrupt social mentality of his time. It is important to recall that Huck never arrives at a rational repudiation of the idea of slavery: when he tries to think logically society's moral imperatives invade his mind, so much so that he can say of Jim: 'I do believe he cared just as much for his people as White folks does for their'n. It don't seem natural, but I reckon it's so.'[60] The *false* concept of the 'natural' that society has constructed to hide its evil abuse of a minority is stuck in Huck's head; and of course it is just because society's 'nature' is in his head, and real nature is in his heart that his naive bewilderment at his own inner contradictions is so telling. When he grudgingly concedes his heart the victory he immediately relegates himself to a status inferior to society: and for us his humble apologetic self-damnation turns into an excoriating indictment of whatever it was that so corrupted his head. A rational well argued confrontation of social evil can be argued against: but when Huck damns himself for having the virtue of compassion society just seems to cave in like a card-house. Because the whole point about compassion—as opposed to organized charity—is that it is not legalized or ratiocinative: by definition it is impulsive, antinomian, a spontaneous moment of empathy with and sympathy for any suffering thing. And it is because Clemens has made Huck's instinctive compassion such a convincing affair that in his presence we are prepared to believe in the potential natural goodness of man. Huck's authentic, apologetic, unself-conscious habit of compassion vanishes incredulity. He is that rare thing in fiction: the convincing embodiment of an ideal. His compassion strays out over the world: it takes in not only Jim, but a drunk at a circus (while others laugh), murderers, animals, the misguided victims of the feud, the victims of the Duke and King's swindle, and then—marvellously—the swindlers themselves when they get their deserts. His instinct is to help anybody in trouble, no matter how they have mistreated him, and any display of human cruelty sickens him, no matter what the putative rights and wrongs of the matter. As he says when he sees the Duke and King being run out of town. 'Well, it made me sick to see it; and I was sorry for them poor pitiful rascals, it seemed like I couldn't feel any hardness against them any more in the world. It was a dreadful thing to see. Human beings *can* be so awful cruel to one another.'[61] Just as he couldn't find anything hard in his heart against Jim, so he cannot find anything hard in his heart for the whole world. Indeed, and this is a daring stroke which is completely convincing, Clemens makes him feel vaguely to blame for a cruelty which in fact he had only sought to prevent. 'Se we poked along back home, and I warn't feeling so brash as I was before, but kind of ornery, and humble, and to blame, somehow—though *I* hadn't done nothing.'[62] That is not quite sentimental, as it would have been if any vague allusions to a Christ-like taking-the-sins-of-the-world-on-his-own-head had been allowed to intrude: it is simply the unbearable ache which a sensitive heart feels for the unnecessary pain of the world. Huck continually feels ashamed of the human race because to the uncorrupted eye it appears all too often as a shameful thing. If Huck reflected, moralized, and sermonized we would weary of him very soon: but this of course, as Tom Sawyer points out, is the one thing Huck cannot do. But he is almost the only person who cannot. For there is another kind of 'style' ubiquitous on the shore, a style of pulpit oratory which seems to be available as a strategy of verbal deceit to every kind of rogue in the book. Henry Nash Smith has pointed out that 'any character can resort to this pompous language on occasion, even Huck's pap'.[63] Like the stereotyped aesthetic rhetoric we saw Clemens 'reducing', this was a spurious mode of talk, impregnated with religiose clichés, which was used for morally imposing on people: and Huck reduces it in his story, not by any sophisticated arguments or by invoking critical standards of taste, but by an instinctive disaffiliation from it whenever he hears it which is as convincing (and damaging to society) as his compassion. In the last analysis it is Huck's linguistic sincerity which convinces the reader of his complete truth. He can lie and steal—in the world in which he finds himself these are necessary strategies of survival—but he seems quite without the inner equipment which can construct emotional untruths. And this very incapacity makes him an unusually sensitive register of any falseness in the words of the people he is surrounded by. He cannot help it—he winces at the spurious: it is a natural not a conditioned reflex. This instinct ranges from a refusal to accept Tom's 'enchantment' of the facts, to a disgust at the King's grotesque pious fabrications. The naive empiric eye will not see the Emperor's clothes. Huck says 'I couldn't see no profit in it'[64] when Tom suggests his romantic make-believe, and with a simple gesture of repudiating the fictitious he goes on to tell that 'there warn't no Spaniards and A-rabs, and there warn't no camels nor no elephants'.[65] And a more significant rejection of Tom's 'stylizing' of life really marks Huck's crucial separation from Tom's mental habitation. 'So then I judged that all that stuff was only just one of Tom Sawyer's lies. I reckoned he believed in the A-rabs and the elephants, but as for me I think different. It had all the marks of a Sunday school.'[66]

That the Sunday-school type of upbringing was quite inadequate for confronting the realities of the lived-in world is one of Huck's earliest instinctive realizations. Lies. A strong word. Tom's lies are perhaps harmless and trivial (there will always be disagreement about the end of the novel) but Huck is constantly coming up against the adult results of the 'Sunday-school' culture. His Pap's repentance, for instance—tears, confession and new resolutions—takes in the judge: 'the judge said it was the holiest time on record, or something like that.'[67] But that kind of empty, attitudinizing holiness cuts no ice with Huck: his offhand dismissal is marvellously summary. Similarly the sermon he hears with the Grangerfords leaves him unmoved— 'It was pretty ornery preaching—all about brotherly love, and such-like tiresomeness'[68]—yet he himself has more genuine love for his fellow men than any one else in the book, Jim excepted. His cool, contemptuous account of the fanatical prayer-meeting where the King makes his killing reveals how utterly unmoved he was by all the plangent rhetoric. When the King and the Duke set to work to deceive the Wilks girls and their friends they soon have the whole population weeping empty tears ('the place was that damp I never see anything like it'):[69] but for Huck it appears as 'all that kind of rot and slush'[70] and, in a memorable phrase, 'soul-butter and hogwash'.[71] Even the excessive politeness in the house tires him—'all that kind of humbug talky-talk'[72] just as he gets impatient with Tom's final fictional exploitation of Jim's real predicament—'Confound it, it's foolish, Tom'.[73] Huck is the focal point of genuine feelings and words in the book: his disavowal of the false is immediate and subjective, never rationalized. An extension of this which is worth remarking is Huck's suspicion of what Miss Watson calls 'spiritual gifts'[74] and his lack of interest in the biblical stories of Moses and such like because 'I don't take no stock in dead people'.[75] Only the concrete here and now, only what Emerson called 'the nearest and next', the palpable immediacy of the living engaging moment involves his attention and feelings. But for that he is supremely alert, his senses and heart unsullied by Sunday-school rhetoric and holy abstractions, unwarped by considerations of 'style'. Certainly he 'knows' nothing in Tom's terms; his is another form of cognition; and just as certainly he wants 'to be starting something fresh', though in a more profound way than Tom could guess or Huck himself realizes. He wants a society scoured of deceit and hypocrisy, of inequality and cruelty, a land where the sound heart dominates the perversities of the mind, a language unclouded by misleading accretions of rhetoric and romance and capable of an honest unpretentious to-the-pointness which his own way of speaking—such is Clemens's skill—comes close to exemplifying to perfection. We have seen this in his descriptions of nature: one might also with profit compare the operatic burlesque of 'grief' which the King and Duke stage over their dead 'brother' in front of the Wilks's (which works so quickly on the people receptive to rhetorical clichés) and Huck's own elegy over Buck as he performs the touchingly simple last rites on the dead Grangerfords:

When I got down out of the tree I crept along down the river bank a piece, and found the two bodies laying in the edge of the water, and tugged at them till I got them ashore; then I covered up their faces, and got away as quick as I could. I cried a little when I was covering up Buck's face, for he was mighty good to me.[76]

The mass expenditure of aroused sentiment at the Wilks's is merely crass: Huck's quiet understating withholding of grief has the ring of true deep feeling. Clemens as Twain had made the discovery—better few words and clean than many and false: and Huck himself seems to bring back a lost form of honesty into language. The naive narrator is unquestionably veridical: that the forms of truth to which he might have access are definitely limited was only to appear in subsequent adoptions of the strategy, for Huck's kind of insight and response are exactly adequate to his particular environment and moral predicament. In this case the naive eye saw precisely what needed to be seen. And having seen it, and having found a way of saying what he has seen, what else could he do but abandon literature, abandon society, and light out for the unattainable paradise whose non-existence is the ultimate horror for the naive hero: '. . . so there ain't nothing more to write about, and I am rotten glad of it, because if I'd 'a' knowed what a trouble it was to make a book I wouldn't a tackled it and ain't agoing to no more.'[77]

That deserves to be ranked as one of the worst kept promises in literature. Huck made several more attempts to articulate under his own name: and subsequent incarnations have been numerous. What it is necessary to stress is that having perfected the strategy and the language Clemens was never again able to use them to discover new subjects, to produce important art. Since my book so far has concentrated on trying to reveal the gradual emergence of the naive vernacular narrator, the strange fact that this figure produced only one great book—for Huck has relations and descendants but no peers—deserves some careful consideration.

As we have seen, Clemens himself was very much an opportunist when it came to forms and themes. His early important works rely almost entirely on the shape and sequence of a journey (though Europe, out West, down the Mississippi) for such organization and consistency as they reveal. That the journeys all had a latent mythic power, a sort of deep archetypal suggestiveness (an encounter with the old world, an initiation into the new, an exploration of his own and America's past) is one of the facts which raises Clemens's early work above the merely interesting and informative. *Huckleberry Finn* is all but perfectly bound together, structurally by the river, thematically by the important problems (heart and conscience, society and nature, freedom and bondage) which set up an increasingly powerful moral gravitational field, drawing together nearly all the separate incidents and episodes. Clemens really relied for his form on his theme and, in this one case, his theme was so powerfully felt that nearly all the details he selected are relevant and illuminating, pressing contributions to deeper understanding. Even so the book was extremely difficult to write. When his theme landed him in difficulties he had no ideas to help him with suggestions as to various possible arrangements of his material. He chanced his arm—brilliantly—waiting for his imagination to blurt out the next movement of the plot. But his imagination was never so helpful again.

We noticed that Emerson, Thoreau and Whitman all had trouble in finding a form. Emerson's essays are like lay sermons with varying texts which permit a varied speculative meandering;

Thoreau's work usually takes the unpremeditated shape of his 'excursions' or the somewhat more disciplined direction of nature's seasons; Whitman uses a day and an open road, and later the year's calendar, to contain his multitudes. None of these formal principles could be said to be radical, few of them are deeply felt and often the work is not deeply gripped and arranged by them. But then, what formal principles will be suggested by an angle of vision which with open wonder and deliberate simplicity passively absorbs the world? The generosity of its inclusion seems almost necessarily to entail a difficulty in allocating significances, in discovering or imputing significant relationships. Clemens's experiments with naivety were immensely rewarding in terms of language and strategy but they provided him with few formal hints. The problem recurs (and recurs right on up to the present): what form does wonder produce?

Clemens's later work is almost a heap of fragments. Some deeply felt old horror, some unresting problem in the depths of the psyche gave a sort of ferocious concentration to *Pudd'nhead Wilson*, and a genuine anger and bitterness served to shape and tighten a few mordant stories like 'The Man That Corrupted Hadleyburg'; but his newly perfected strategy and language seem not to have helped him at all. To see how inadequate they were when it came to finding fruitful themes and significant forms, we have only to watch Clemens trying, and lamentably failing, to use Huck again to good effect. He tried at least four times—two stories were published, *Tom Sawyer Abroad* (1894) and *Tom Sawyer, Detective* (1896), while two remain as unpublished fragments, 'Huck Finn and Tom Sawyer among the Indians' (c. 1889) and 'Tom Sawyer's Conspiracy' (c. 1897). Henry Nash Smith says of all these pieces that they all 'make the same demonstration. The Lost World was really lost. Adam could not re-enter Paradise, and America in the Gilded Age could not bring back its agrarian past.'[78] What in fact we find is the curious situation of an artist, always uncertain of his real aims, having perfected a new style and strategy and not knowing how to use it. One notes immediately that the name Tom Sawyer appears in every title and the initial fault of all these attempts is that Huck has to tell Tom's stories and not his own. Clemens never let Huck off the leash again and as long as Tom sets the pace and tone Clemens always tends towards superficiality. 'It warn't no use to argue with Tom Sawyer—a body never stood a chance'[79] complains Huck: and Clemens could have said the same about his strange relationship with his boy creation. This whole problem requires separate study, as does Clemens's work written after *Huckleberry Finn*: but one can immediately say that Clemens never again stumbled on that fortunate confrontation of problem and point-of-view which resulted in the simple profundity of *Huckleberry Finn*. He never again discovered a theme which could stimulate the naive vision to demonstrate its peculiar virtues of fruitful clarification: he never again found anything so worth being simple *about* as the problems of the shore and the river, freedom and bondage, sincerity and 'style' which coalesce in *Huckleberry Finn*. 'Huck Finn and Tom Sawyer among the Indians', for instance, toys tentatively with the potentially interesting contrast between Tom's book-learned knowledge of the world and Huck's instinctive pragmatic grasp of it. Tom insists that life among the Indians is a life-long 'circus', a veritable paradise of indolence and nobility: Huck is dubious and after a particularly bloody massacre of some whites by Indians Huck permits himself a quiet irony. 'Tom, where did you learn about Injuns—how noble they was and all that?'[80] The question hits Tom very hard but at last he answers 'Cooper's novels',[81] which really only illustrates an age-old grievance and adds little to Clemens's life-long preoccupation with discrepancies between the idealities of the literature of the official culture and the empirical facts. Perhaps the most remarkable thing that lingers on is Huck's wonderful reaction to nature: not only his almost voluptuous passivity and ability to extract maximum pagan joy from 'lazying' around, but also his feeling for the undercurrents of alien remoteness and hostility in nature. Thus on the desert: 'It was the biggest, wildest, levelest world—

and all dead; dead and still, not a sound. The lonesomest place that ever was; enough to break a body's heart just to listen to the awful stillness of it':[82] and later, after waking up feeling cheerful: 'But I just looked around once over that million miles of gray dead level, and my soul sucked back that brashness and gayness again with just one suck, like a sponge and then all the miserable-ness came back and was worse than yesterday.'[83] Huck's naive senses are indeed like a sponge which can absorb all the confused suggestive radiations which emanate from nature. Here once again the naive vernacular has caught that strange impalpable lyrical sincerity which so distinguishes *Huckleberry Finn*: note how the syntax of the first sentence catches exactly the movements and pauses of the alert involved senses. This clearly is a prose and point of view which can catch the sense at no remove whatever. Such moments constitute an apostasy from the Tom-Sawyer-tone of the story but orthodoxy is quickly restored and Huck shrinks back into his secondary place.

Similarly in 'Tom Sawyer Abroad' Clemens is unable to find a theme to engage Huck's naivety for any but comic results. Once again the opposition between Tom's romantic bookish excesses and the simple candour of Jim and Huck is set up. Tom wants to organize a crusade, Jim and Huck demur. Tom despises their ignorance:

If either of you'd read anything about history you'd know that Richard Cur de Loon, and the Pope, and Godfrey de Bulleyn, and lots more of the most noble hearted and pious people in the world, hacked and hammered at the paynims for more than two hundred years trying to take their land away from them, and swum neck-deep in blood the whole time—and yet here's a couple of sap headed yahoos out of the backwoods of Missourri setting themselves up to know more about the rights and wrongs of it than they did. Talk about cheek.[84]

There are echoes of a serious theme here: the need to abandon traditional attitudes of predatory superiority: but in the story the moral is all too obvious and in no way seriously embodied. Of course the 'country yahoos', the naive vernacular figures, are right, and the learned man is wrong: a moral-pastoral inversion again. Time and again Tom's knowledge, opinions and attitudes, which are the result of standard education, are questioned and challenged by Huck and Jim's naivety. One can see Clemens trying to exploit this strategy of literal-minded innocence and utter simplicity but time and again he only comes up with funny effects: almost like posthumous refinements of the tradition of burlesque. Almost Clemens is back being a stage humorist. But Huck's response to environment is still superbly handled— 'Away in the night, when all the sounds was late sounds, and the air had a late feel, and a late smell, too . . .'[85]—and one realizes anew how much is to be gained by the naive improvising, approximating approach to the task of description. We see through the words to the experiencing narrator: the traditionally hidden process of arriving at a verbal description is now dragged out for the reader to see so that he doesn't receive a finished arrested piece of art but is rather invited to participate in the honest immediacy of the moment of formulation. But if this remains a virtue there are signs of two weaknesses of the naive point of view: one is moral simplesse, the other is sentimentality. The first is best exemplified by a speech from Jim objecting to the necessity to kill while on a Crusade:

De hard part gwine to be to kill folks dat a body hain't been 'quainted wid and dat hain't done him no harm. Dat's it, you see. Ef we wuz to go 'mongst 'em, jist we three, en say we's hungry, en ast 'em for a bite to eat, why maybe dey's jist like yuther people. Don't you reckon dey is? Why *dey'd* give it, I know dey would. . . .[86]

These sentiments of the simple sound heart are of course unimpeachable but they do not occur in a context which would give them that sort of telling, irresistible pungency which such simple goodness must have if it is to have a cutting edge Sentimentality I think can be seen leaking into the naive vernacular style in a long passage in which Huck reveals his feelings about ornithologers. It starts off with that sort of unconscious irony for which Huck is such a good medium:

That's the way people does that writes books about birds, and loves them so that they'll go hungry and tired and take any amount of trouble to find a new bird and kill it. Their name is ornithologers, and I could have been an ornithologer myself, because I always loved birds and creatures; and I started out how to learn to be one, and I see a bird setting on a limb of a high tree, singing with its head tilted back and its mouth open, and before I thought I fired, and his song stopped and he fell straight down from the limb, all limp like a rag, and I run and picked him up and he was dead, and his body was warm in my hand, and his head rolled about this way and that, like his neck was broke, and there was a little white skin over his eyes, and one little drop of blood on the side of his head; and, laws! I couldn't see nothing more for the tears; and I hain't never murdered no creature since that warn't doing me no harm, and I ain't going to.[87]

The passage reveals Huck's true and matchless tenderness and his ethic of non-violence; but somehow there is a disproportionate squeezing out of the last drops of feeling, a perverse lingering over emotionally-loaded details which does not go with Huck's habitual understatement. (In *Huckleberry Finn* he complains that it makes him sick to recall morbid particulars of the feud: there his emotions are tightly controlled and yet much more proportionate to the dreadful human facts.) There is in fact an excessive bid for blurred feeling here. And this is a fault detectable in many writers who have adopted the naive vision as a strategy: the short cut to arousing feelings by an over-insistence on details, an uncalled-for elevation of particulars. After all, Huck did not stop to tell us how his friend Buck looked when he was shot.

Tom Sawyer, Detective suffers like the other stories from a basic uncertainty as to its level of seriousness. It is a detective story, but so is *Pudd'nhead Wilson* and the level of seriousness there is profound. Here once again Huck is involved in a world full of the threat of unmeaning and implacable violence, and the portrait of old Uncle Silas is disturbing and sinister for here one of the most venerable members of the community is threatened with madness. Yet it remains merely a detective story—due to Tom. For Clemens is almost wholly absorbed in giving his protégé clues and thickening the plot merely so that he can have Tom dramatically enlighten everyone at the end. Huck is not really important for wherever he goes he takes with him a sense of the solemn, a heart apt for pity and melancholy, and senses quiveringly open to nature's moods. Tom on the other hand seems only to have a sense of the 'bully'; the two do not go well together and there is an annoying feeling of waste that a narrator of such sensitivity should be employed to transmit the adventures and exploits of Tom. We really draw breath when Clemens makes Huck say to Tom 'I ain't fitten to black your boots'.[88] For the two boys still exemplify completely antipathetic attitudes to life. (One might call them matriarchal and patriarchal respectively: the first indicating a range of attitudes based on acceptance of natural phenomena and issuing in love, passivity, a sense of equality, a habit of mercy, a taste for peace; the second indicating attitudes based on a respect for law and rational thought, productive of active intrusions on nature, development of conscience, and the erection of hierarchies.) Even in this story the difference is clear—for instance when Uncle Silas is arrested for murder Huck gives us the following account. 'It was awful. Aunt Sally and Benny flung themselves at Uncle Silas and hugged him and hung to him, and Aunt Sally said go away, she wouldn't ever give him up, they shouldn't have him, and the niggers they came crowding and crying to the door, and—well, I couldn't stand it.'[89] This is pure Huck, instinctively and readily sympathetic with all suffering wherever he sees at, a true egalitarian of the heart. But Tom?

They took him [i.e. Uncle Silas] up to the little one-horse jail in the village, and we all went along to tell him goodby; and Tom was feeling elegant, and says to me, 'We'll have a most noble good time and heaps of danger some dark night getting him out of here, Huck, and it'll be talked about everywhere and we will be celebrated.'[90]

Tom is the active, responsible, planning one, and his sense of the need for action, for 'interference', tends towards insensitivity in other directions. One indeed wonders what sort of fulfilment Tom was for Clemens. He is the successful one, the hero, the saviour, the bringer of justice, a sort of culture hero: he has the initiative and shrewdness of a capitalist pioneer with none of the sense of guilt. He is the Protestant boy par excellence with the active gifts and contracted feelings characteristic of the type. Huck's area of response is different and somehow prior to Tom's. Huck for instance distrusts and dislikes money, whereas Tom is very aware of the significance of 'fortunes'. In this story they get involved with an outlaw and he shows them some diamonds which his pursuers are after. Huck's response is noteworthy: 'and when the light struck into them they *was* beautiful, sure; why, they seemed to kind of bust, and snap fire all around. But all the same I judged he was a fool. If I had been him I would 'a' handed the di'monds to them pals and got them to go ashore and leave me alone. But he was made different. He said it was a whole fortune and he couldn't bear the idea.'[91] Huck's response is primarily aesthetic: he has no sense of purchasing power. Similarly, he again shows his preference for static somnolent harmonious content over active complex involvements when he states the difference between himself and Tom. 'If you'd lay out a mystery and a pie before me and him, you wouldn't have to say take your choice; it was a thing that would regulate itself. Because in my nature I have always run to pie, whilest in his nature he has always run to mystery.'[92] Childish perhaps: but indicative of a real difference. For Tom, always with a plan afoot or some intent to twist life into melodrama (think of the pointless discord and upset he brings to the Phelps's farm) is too preoccupied with his mental calculations and romantic fantastications to experience real sympathy and to respond to suffering to the full: while Huck, seeking only to achieve a true peace with the world, is rawly exposed to all those things which render such a peace both more desirable and less easy of attainment. Huck, we may say, is *the* passive reflector. Even in this story Huck's darting impulsive sympathy is occasionally visible. When they meet a man on the run for instance and he appeals to them:

'Oh, boys, be good to a poor devil that's being hunted day and night, and dasn't show his face! I've never done you any harm; I'll never do you any, as God is in the heavens; swear you'll be good to me and help me save my life.'

We'd 'a' swore it if he'd been a dog.[93]

Tom because of the opportunities for adventure; Huck because of the sheer irrepressible pity within him. The offhand nature of his phrasing, the absence of all self-congratulatory airs of 'charity'—these are the important qualities. This is how the 'sound heart' responds, or not at all.

Yet all that these stories reveal are glimpses of the possibilities of the style that Clemens had perfected through Huck Finn, the naive vision. Huck remains a voice: a voice of yearning for a lost and unidentified freedom, a voice bemoaning some lost harmony between man and man and man and nature, a voice of sad protest against the deadening encroachments of civilization, a young voice which cannot identify its own emotions and cannot formulate criticisms but which is yet exquisitely sensitive, a perennial voice reminding us for ever of the losses involved in the twin processes of growing up and civilization. Huck seems to voice something of a lost way of life, a simpler if more anarchistic way. (Of course this view of life can easily lead to evasions and escape into deliberate immaturity. One could cite the hero of John Updike's novel, *Rabbit, Run*, Harry Angstrom, who says to a clergyman: 'If you're telling me I'm not mature, that's one thing I don't cry over since as far as I can make out it's the same thing as being dead.'[94] Like Huck he ends by running—just running—away from all the wearying complexities of life in adult society, voicing a nostalgia for some lost vitality, bite and freedom in life. Yet his sense of dissatisfaction is highly equivocal and has none of the lyric yearning, the resonant authenticity of Huck's.) Huck's lament is visionary: the lament of the very principle of youngness, of the state of being not yet committed to a corrupt and complex immobilizing adult world, of nature herself. As here, for example, in a passage which starts in a vein of fidgety childishness and gradually acquires an unsuspected depth:

The frost was working out of the ground, and out of the air, too, and it was getting closer and closer onto barefoot time every day; and next it would be marble time, and next mumblety-peg, and next tops and hoops, and next kites, and then right away it would be summer and going in a-swimming. It just makes a boy homesick to look ahead like that and see how far off summer is. Yes, and it sets him to sighing and saddening around, and there's something the matter with him, he don't know what. But, anyway, he gets out by himself and mopes and thinks; and mostly he hunts for a lonesome place high up on the hill in the edge of the wood, and sets there and looks away off on the big Mississippi down there a-reaching miles and miles around the points where the timber looks smoky and dim, it's so far off and still, and everything's so solemn it seems like everybody you've loved is dead and gone, and you 'most wish you was dead and gone too, and done with it all.

Don' you know what that is? It's spring fever. That is what the name of it is. And when you've got it, you want—oh, you don't quite know what it is you *do* want, but it just fairly makes your heart ache, you want it so! It seems to you that mainly what you want is to get away; get away from the same old tedious things you're used to seeing and so tired of, and see something new. That is the idea; you want to go and be a wanderer; you want to go wandering far away to strange countries where everything is mysterious and wonderful and romantic. And if you can't do that, you'll put up with considerable less; you'll go anywhere you *can* go, just so as to get away, and be thankful of the chance, too![95]

This is the naive voice and in its power to convey a mood, as opposed to initiate an action, it is far superior to anything that Tom stands for. But the naive vision had never again been used to such profound effect as it was in *Huckleberry Finn*: even in these few trivial tales Clemens reveals its limitations. And his note-books are scattered with hints for other stories for Huck. All of them innutrient though revealing. He has the idea to bring Huck back after sixty years from some unknown part of the world and show him to be crazy, thinking he is still a boy again and looking around for old friends: finally to be joined by Tom who looks after him before they both die together in misery because everything fine in life has vanished. Then again, still revealing his hunger for a true democracy like 'the community of saints'[96] on the raft, he has an idea to let Jim tell Huck about Canada, the genuine home of freedom. Then there is later a scribbled suggestion to make Tom sell Huck as a slave: a plot to have them both save an innocent negress just as she is about to be lynched. There is an odd note suggesting the arrival of some hicks whom Huck is either to doubt or believe in, while Tom is to show up the facts of the imposture. And the last mention of Huck in the notebooks returns again to the never-explored idea of having Tom sell Huck as a nigger: left so tantalizingly un-explained one does not know whether Clemens intended it as a sport, a plot to have some of Tom's special brand of 'fun', or whether it might have turned out to be the ultimate betrayal of the outcast by the conformist. What is clear is that he can think of nowhere to take Huck, nothing to involve him fruitfully amongst. He once had something called 'Innocents Adrift'[97] planned and this not only points back to the picaresque figures of innocence, Mark Twain and Huck Finn, but also forward to the series of pointless, fruitless, directionless and ultimately disastrous voyages which fill Clemens's late work. Huck's escape at the end of *Huckleberry Finn* is actually into myth, like Daniel Boone. Perhaps the myth faded with the closing of the frontier, or perhaps unrelenting pessimism finally drove it out of Clemens's heart. He never thought of having Huck 'grow up' in any positive sense, but he couldn't think of anywhere—real or mythic—where he could let Huck indulge his instincts of harmony and equality, and inactive communing with nature, and keep him eternally young.

Huck's curious aloneness, his almost impersonal melancholy (never self-pity), his desire to wander, to leave no tracks, his premature nostalgia as though he had intimations of a paradise of which the very existence is now dubious and the location for-gotten beyond recall, these are recurring characteristics of the naive hero. Perhaps the dilemma is due to the fact—or simply the feeling—that Clemens fixed on in a note when he wrote 'there are no remotenesses, anymore'.[98]

PART III
THE TWENTIETH CENTURY

'Was it grown up to come to the realization that oneself did not matter, that nothing mattered but a kind of consciousness of the wonder of life outside oneself?'

SHERWOOD ANDERSON, *A Storyteller's Story*

CHAPTER 11

GERTRUDE STEIN AND THE COMPLETE ACTUAL PRESENT

The business of art . . . is to live in the actual present, that is the complete actual present, and to completely express that complete actual present.[1]

GERTRUDE STEIN, *Lectures in America*

AFTER Mark Twain, the naive vernacular narrator reappears constantly in American fiction, from the crude and derivative efforts of Don Marquis (*Danny's Own Story*) and Edgar Lee Masters (*Mitch Miller*), up to the sophisticated successes of J. D. Salinger (*Catcher in the Rye*) and Saul Bellow (*Adventures of Augie March*). But a more interesting line of development leads from Twain to Hemingway and it is a development which depends for its success on the separation of the vernacular from the young narrator. The naive vernacular ceases to be an adopted voice and develops into a achieved style; instead of appearing to be spontaneous unarranged talk it is subjected to a rigorous and careful stylization. In this line of development Gertrude Stein played the part of the indispensable provoking theorist. Sherwood Anderson is an early disciple who could not properly absorb her lessons nor resolve his own stylistic problems—thus many of his best stories depend on the retained presence of the naive narrator. Ernest Hemingway learnt what he needed from Stein but pushed beyond her too theoretic experiments and finally turned into a continuously available style what for Mark Twain had been a brilliantly successful strategy which he did not afterwards know how to use or repeat. The aim of this section is to examine some of Stein's more important ideas, Anderson's attempts and difficulties, and Hemingway's success.

Some careful and interesting work has been done on the development of the colloquial style from Twain to Hemingway by

187

Richard Bridgman. He shows that what was necessary for the development of the vernacular into a style was the discovery of its underlying structure: otherwise writers would continue to imitate only its surface mannerisms and perpetuate a sort of pseudo style which was eccentric and formless and unable to address itself to genuine human problems. He stresses the importance of Stein's work and her endless apparently perverse experiments with the whole hidden architecture of colloquial prose—with repetitions, paragraph shapes, unpunctuated movement, sheer sound, etc. He comments:

This 'discontextuated activity' focussed the reader's attention on the surface of the prose by emphasising the appearance of the word, syntactical relationships, prose rhythms, and harmony of sound. Although she did not intend her work for this purpose, Gertrude Stein did colloquial prose a very considerable service by emphasising its submerged patterns. Without her experiments it appears likely that writers working the colloquial vein might soon have had to abandon their work, for men like Damon Runyan were already marketing fool's gold.[2]

Few people these days are greatly moved by much of Stein's work, and yet in her time she attracted a reverence and respect which at least attest to an unusually original and stimulating mind. Picasso liked and looked up to her and indeed she was one of the first to understand what modern painting was trying to accomplish. Sherwood Anderson was always effusive in his praise and insistent on the debt he owed her; and Hemingway, who broke away from her and perhaps attracted her jealousy by an actual achievement she could not emulate, nevertheless confessed that he was very grateful to Stein 'for everything I learned from her about the abstract relationship of words'. I shall try to suggest why I think the reputation of the person is not reflected in the current reputation of the work: here it should be pointed out that she had an unusually penetrating insight into the intellectual climate of her time and a gift for the clarification of ideas and novel experiment. Her ideas ventured beyond what she took from William James, just as her prose changes considerably between the felicitous Henry James imitation of her first novel (which she called *Q.E.D.* and which was recently published as *Things As They Are*) and the post-experimental clarity of *The Autobiography of Alice B. Toklas*. She is more an innovator than an imitator. One forgets, perhaps, how early she was with her ideas and experiments. Her first important experimental work, *Three Lives*, was published in 1905. *The Making of Americans* followed between 1906 and 1908: her important and understanding book on *Picasso* appeared in 1909 while her own work had achieved almost a maximum of experimentation in *Tender Buttons* in 1910–12. For good or bad she was truly original.

What I want to do here is to attempt to draw from her very varied work those of her ideas which might have been seminal and which certainly show that she was well aware of a deep-rooted tendency in American writing. Curiously enough her little book on Picasso contains an unusually lucid statement of certain notions which, no matter how relevant they are to Picasso, are certainly very relevant to American literature. The book is based on the premise that 'nothing changes in people from one generation to another except the way of seeing and being seen'[3] and that 'another vision than that of all the world is very rare. That is why geniuses are rare, to complicate things in a new way that is easy, but to see the things in a new way that is really difficult, everything prevents one, habits, schools, daily life, reason, necessities of daily life, indolence, everything prevents one, in fact there are very few geniuses in the world'.[4] That the artist awakes us out of dulled preceptual habits and offers and enforces new ways of looking at the world, new visual attitudes towards reality, seems to me an insight of perennial relevance: but in this case it is peculiarly relevant in that it leads Stein to take up a question we have seen raised by earlier American writers: namely, what is the most rewarding way to look at the world, the best mode of vision. And in describing Picasso's vision Stein offers us terms relevant to our whole study.

She first compares his way of regarding reality with the way of the child who sees only vivid fragments (one side of its mother's face) and has not learnt to infer the whole. Picasso's struggle was difficult because 'no one had ever tried to express things seen not as one knows them but as they are when one sees them without remembering having looked at them'.[5] But 'he was right, one sees what one sees, the rest is a reconstruction from memory and painters have nothing to do with reconstruction, nothing to do with memory, they concern themselves only with visible things'.[6] The difference between what one can see and what one knows is there, is crucial for Stein and she sees the aim of art as an effort to capture the former: an effort continually interrupted and foiled by reminiscences of the latter. She maintains that, like Picasso, she is trying to look at things as though for the first time and for this reason she works to exclude memory and knowledge from her work.

In the beginning when Picasso wished to express heads and bodies not like every one could see them, which was the problem of other painters, but as he saw them, *as one can see when one had not the habit of knowing what one is looking at,* inevitably when he commenced he had the tendency to paint them as a mass as sculptors do or in profile as children do.[7] [my italics]

The ideas here relate to Thoreau's notion of 'seeing without looking', Whitman's 'first step', and the general American interest in a recovered naivety of vision. All these ideas are the result of the inquiry: how can man establish an authentic first hand relationship with existing reality? Stein too is addressing herself to the problem of how we can establish contact with the 'reality of things that exist'.[8] She thought that the greatest hindrances to this contact were memories of other comparable impressions which blur the uniqueness of the present perceptual instant, and all the associations and thoughts which our minds discharge as soon as we are confronted with an object which we want to recognize and classify. What she wanted, and found in Picasso, were 'things seen without association but simply as things seen'[9] and she comments approvingly that 'only the things seen are knowledge for Picasso'.[10] She wants no interpretation, no reference to other previous 'things seen' no contributions from the storehouse of the mind. For Picasso, she asserts, and we feel her agreement, 'remembered things are not things seen, therefore they are not things known'.[11]

More extreme than Thoreau, Stein has an ideal of what we may call seeing without remembering, without associating, without thinking. She wants the eye to open to the reality of the material world as though it had never opened before: for then we catch reality at its 'realest', unfiltered through the schemata of the sophisticated eye which is dimmed from too long domestication in the world. And even though she does not develop or push the comparison she clearly cites the child's way of looking as exemplary: naivety must be cultivated in order that we may see reality as it is and not as we remember it to be. This takes us back to the problem of how a child does in fact perceive reality. More basically, whether one can in fact see anything clearly at all without the aid of memory, the subtle reawakening of innumerable past visual experiences, is open to doubt. Certainly, words are full of memories—are perhaps pure memory—and the impressions gained by the unremembering eye could never be transmitted by the unremembering voice. For without memory there is no metaphor; and without metaphor we would never have had language. Stein avoids live metaphors but to communicate at all she has to use those dead ones we all use continually in our daily speech. Her ideal properly carried out, if it did not lead to a visual confusion akin to blindness, would certainly lead to silence.

To draw these inferences is perhaps unfair. In fact what Stein wants is to purify the eye, to break old visual habits, to initiate a more vivid commerce between the senses and the real world. That Picasso himself managed to do this is indisputable: that Stein's interest in this relates her to a number of American writers from Emerson onwards is my contention. Perhaps all art ultimately contributes to an endless rediscovery of the world around us and within us. American writing in particular has shown a consistent interest in scraping the grime of old emotions from reality, in shedding complex habits of vision, in cleansing words of those clusters of associations which may produce dullness as often as they contribute richness. To equate seeing things as though for the first time with knowledge as Stein does, is a peculiarly American idea. And having described Picasso in these terms, having dismissed memory as an aid to vision, she adds a further idea which makes us think more of Anderson and Hemingway than Picasso. 'And so then always and always Picasso commenced his attempt to express not things felt, not things remembered, not established in relations but things which are there, really everything a human being can know *at each moment of his existence and not an assembling of all his experiences*'[12] (my italics). A preference for a moment-by-moment notation of impressions is clearly discernible in Anderson and Hemingway: the 'assembling' of experience reveals itself in generalizations and abstractions, just as an interest in the 'relations' between things tends to produce a complex syntax: and it is precisely these two things which their prose attempts to avoid. And of course the naive eye which refuses to remember anything can ill afford to pass by anything: hence the detailed inclusiveness of this way of writing, its moment-by-moment quality. Needless to say a more or less subtle sense of selection must be at work, but the close itemizing contact with the concrete world and the predominantly paratactic syntax which we have remarked in much American writing must be related to this preferred mode of seeing, a mode which separates sensations out rather than assembling them together.

Stein's attack on memory and her related preference for a moment-by-moment notation of experience is also in evidence in her *Lectures in America*, particularly in the one entitled 'Portraits and Repetition'. She discusses what she had attempted in some of her prose portraits and revealingly she turns to the cinema to explain how she managed to make portraits of people 'as they are existing' without having recourse to 'remembering':

Funnily enough the cinema has offered a solution of this thing. By a continuously moving picture of any one there is no memory of any other thing and there is that thing existing. . . . I was doing what the cinema was doing, I was making a continuous succession of the statement of what that person was until I had not many things but one thing.[13]

Just as life never repeats itself, and the cinema doesn't quite repeat itself, so her prose, she claims, does not really repeat itself: rather there is a series of small additions and modifications in her prose, just as there are minute differences in each successive picture flashed on a cinema screen. 'As I told you in comparing it to a cinema picture one second was never the same as the second before or after.'[14] She maintains that 'existing as a human being . . . is never repetition' and goes on to say that 'remembering is the only repetition' just as 'remembering is the only confusion'.[15] The confusion comes from allowing the past to get mixed up with the present, presumably a sullying intrusion which mars the accuracy of our perception of what is actually there in the present. Her ideal is a continuously developing present—complete and actual at any given moment—which is yet a whole, just as an existing thing is a whole or even as a single frame of a film is a whole, although both are made up of many minute parts. What she is against is 'letting remembering mix itself with looking':[16] what she is in favour of is 'moment to moment emphasizing'.[17] As before, the two go together. In a later lecture she makes a simple remark which succinctly hints at her whole theory of prose. 'After all the natural way to count is not that one and one make two but to go on counting by one and one. . . . One and one and one and one and one. That is the natural way to go on counting.'[18] Applied to prose this would mean no 'assembling', no complex 'relating', no accumulation, no interpretation, no comparison, no increasing density of significance. It would mean a prose that, literally, was not additive. Rather language would have to adapt itself to registering the 'complete and actual present' again and again and again: now and now and now—one and one and one. If we hold on to the cinema for an analogy we can see that this will mean a series of still pictures: reading her prose is at times like holding a strip of movie film and looking at each frame separately. Understandably Stein sometimes uses the idea of the still life to explain her intentions and this whole relation between movement and stillness, and their relation in turn to the twin ideas of rejection of memory and the refusal of assembling, must now be looked at rather carefully.

In her lectures on narration Stein took up a very clear hostile attitude towards traditional narrative habits.

When one used to think of narrative one meant a telling of what is happening in successive moments of its happening. . . . But now we have changed all that we really have. We really now do not really know that anything is progressively happening. . . . It is a much more impressive thing to any one to see any one standing, that is not in action than acting or doing anything being a successive thing, standing not being a successive thing but being something existing. That is then the difference between narrative as it has been and narrative as it is now.[19]

She develops this by taking issue with the Aristotelian and time-honoured formulae of a story having a beginning, middle and end:

if you are an American gradually you find that really it is not necessary not really necessary that anything that everything has a beginning and a middle and an ending and so you struggling with anything as anything has begun and begun and began does not really mean that thing does not really mean beginning or begun. I found myself at this time quite naturally using the present participle . . . finally then English writing was entirely that thing, in its poetry as well as in its narrative writing that one thing came after another thing and that not anything existing aroused anyone to feeling but that a thing having beginning and middle and ending made every one have the emotion that they had about everything. . . . The fact that anything was existing was moving around by itself in any way it wanted to move did not arouse any emotion it was only anything succeeding any other thing anything having and beginning middle and ending could and did and would arouse emotion. . . . American writing has been an escaping not an escaping but an existing without the necessary feeling of one thing succeeding another thing of anything having a beginning and a middle and an ending . . . if there is a beginning and ending to anything then it destroys the simplicity of something always happening . . . always beginning and ending is as destructive to existing as never beginning and ending. . . .[20]

To simplify this we may say that Stein is taking issue with narrative which concerns itself with giving an account of purposive action, narrative like a chain of causes and effects leading to a final crisis, narrative which deals with successive things and not existing things. It seems to me that she fails to demonstrate that the existence of a thing cannot be revealed by showing it in action but her intention in making these into mutually exclusive alternatives is fairly clear. It is part of the modern rebellion against conventional plot—it is in Anderson as well—which, it was felt, slighted reality by its habit of erecting a spurious superstructure of eventfulness. Old narrative, so the argument would run, forces the attention to inquire, what has happened, what will happen next, to what resolution does all this tend: it never concentrates on the more basic miracle of what *is*. It ignores the man standing still. Stein's dislike of 'successive' action is not a distrust of all movement: 'it is something strictly American to conceive a space that is filled with moving, a space of time that is filled always filled with moving'[21] she asserts. Movement is inherent in the existing thing, even in its stillness: but in successive narrative, reality is wrenched, suppressed and ignored to fit the traditional arc of beginning, middle and end. Stein is against narrative which fosters a causal time sense, which forces us to ask of the material in front of us—what is happening and why? Better, she would maintain, to develop an art which makes us ponder what is existing, now and for itself. The present participle—the standing man. Memory deflects our attention into the past and thence to the future. Better to seize the moment—in its fullness and in its stillness, a stillness throbbing with latent movement. Her fondness for art is relevant here and it is worth noting that *Lucy Church Amiably* is subtitled 'A Novel of Romantic beauty and nature and which Looks Like an Engraving'. More to the point we should recall that she wrote *Three Lives*, so she tells us, 'looking and looking' at a Cézanne portrait of a woman. Cézanne would indeed seem to exemplify the attitude to reality which Stein spent so much time and care trying to define.

In turning away from academic and classical subjects and

preferring the challenge of still-life painting he spoke revealingly of 'the heroism of the real' and went on to formulate his magnificent phrase about 'the immensity, the torrent of the world in a little bit of matter'. This perfectly explains why his still lives are not still. He needs no reference to heroic actions to convey a dynamic sense of movement and charged reality. Presumably Stein had something like this in mind when she wrote in favour of a style of writing which could catch and hold the existing thing and exclude the successive thing. She wanted a writing that would give, not the thing in history, but the thing-in-itself. It is perhaps illustrative of this strain in her thinking that she could write in one of her lectures: 'I wonder now if it is necessary to stand still to live if it is not necessary to stand still to live, and if it is if that is not perhaps to be a new way to write a novel.'[22]

It is when we come to Stein's specific ideas about writing that we see not only what she was really getting at, but also perhaps why it was that she never really managed to write a work that came up to her ideals. She once wrote 'description is explanation'[23]—a phrase very relevant to Hemingway—but in her later lectures, particularly 'Poetry and Grammar', she redefines description in a way which separates it from the activity as we might understand it. In 'Portraits and Repetition' she tells of looking at something and then trying to find words that looked like the thing under observation:

I became more and more excited about how words which were the words that made whatever I looked at look like itself were not the words that had in them any quality of description. . . . And the thing that excited me so very much at that time and still does is that the words or words that make what I looked at be itself were always words that to me very exactly related themselves to that thing the thing at which I was looking, but as often as not had as I say nothing whatever to do with what any words would do that described that thing.[24]

The idea here—if I understand it correctly—is that if you want to convey a sense of reality, catch the very quality of the thing seen, it is not sufficient to name the object and list its properties. Recreation is not description. Her portraits seem to me for the most part idiosyncratic and unintelligible—too arcane, too sub-jective, or merely too full of private jokes to communicate any recognizable reality. Similarly the prose studies of 'Objects: food: rooms' which make up *Tender Buttons* resist most attempts to find any conventional meaning in them. What is clear is that Stein is not interested in conventional ways of transmitting sense and impressions: rather she seems to want to try and find out how she can manipulate the patterning of the sounds of words to create a verbal still-life so that we may receive the proferred thing itself and not the thing summed up. This example has some novel quality:

A table means does it not my dear it means a whole steadiness. Is it likely that a change.
A table means more than a glass even a looking glass is tall. A table means necessary places and a revision a revision of a little thing it means it does mean that there has been a stand, a stand where it did shake.[25]

However, some recognizable statements are discernible there. In the following example we have mere word play (though it may be fair to say that by playing, literally, with words, writers often discover forgotten properties in them which are later available for more serious employment).

Go red go red laugh white.
Suppose a collapse in rubbed purr, in rubbed purr get.
Little sales ladies little sales ladies little saddles of mutton.
Little sales of leather and such beautiful, beautiful, beauti-ful.[26]

These attempts are obviously too private in their associations and too arbitrary in their procedure: but it seems that a new and careful look is being taken at words themselves, even at the cost of all communicated meaning. And had Gertrude Stein's work matured into real significance she would not have been the first modern artist who had to descend into apparent meaninglessness to emerge with new meanings. Certainly it is worth considering the motivating ideas behind these attempts.

These emerge more clearly in 'Poetry and Grammar'. Her first, and most significant, attack, is on the use of nouns. And here she both makes a valid point and overstates it :

A noun is a name of anything, why after a thing is named write about it. . . . Nouns are the names of anything and just naming names is alright when you want to call a roll but is it any good for anything else. . . . As I say a noun is the name of a thing, and therefore slowly if you feel what is inside that thing you do not call it by the name by which it is known. Everybody knows that by the way they do when they are in love and a writer should always have that intensity of emotion about whatever is the object about which he writes. And therefore and I say it again more and more one does not use nouns.[27]

Adjectives, since their job is to affect nouns, are also 'not really and truly interesting'.[28] From this extreme point of view nouns, with all their qualifying adjuncts, appear as barriers which interpose themselves between the passionate perceiver and the thing perceived. This is valid only if you are considering that crude use of nouns which makes them opaque; mere utilitarian gestures uninhabited by reality. As in a roll call or inventory. There are indeed ways of naming and describing which inhibit, even prohibit, awareness and discourage all sensitivity of response. But to hypothesize an ideal of prose unfurnished with any nouns and adjectives is to recommend a banishment of reality from language which language could not survive. Stein's aim is, however, not so fantastic as that. This is how she phrases her problem : 'Was there not a way of naming things that would not invent names, but mean names without naming them.'[29] She is here lamenting a common phenomenon whereby once we have named a thing (and as always in Stein's use of the word 'thing' she means emotions as well as objects), we tend to forget the reality which lurks or dances beyond the name. Of course there is a way of naming things which embraces and discloses and celebrates that reality—poetry, says Stein. 'So I say poetry is essentially the discovery, the love, the passion for the name of anything.'[30] But—so her argument trends—as the names become dull, common, and opaque, new ways of access to the reality of things must be sought. 'After all one had known its name anything's name for so long, and so the name was not new but the thing being alive was always new.'[31] In face of a continually self-renewing reality we must retain an ever renewed sense of wonder. Look at things as for the first time. Here nouns impede us, they have been around too long. So Stein tries 'looking at anything until something that was not the name of that thing but was in a way that actual thing would come to be written'.[32] Her point is that the name of a thing (the conventional, accredited name) and the actual thing are inevitably separate and different; the former an impoverished substitute for the latter. After looking at something she tries 'creating it without naming it' and so she 'struggled desperately with the recreation and the avoidance of nouns as nouns'.[33] Walt Whitman is singled out for praise—'He wanted really wanted to express the thing and not call it by its name'[34] —and Stein finishes her lecture with her clear conviction that 'the noun must be replaced by the thing in itself'.[35] To answer that words never are nor ever can be things is of course too crude and unsympathetic to Stein's point. We could recall Emerson's distinction between language which is heavy with the bullion of nature and language which has become a false paper currency. Stein's ambition is a manifestation of that compelling reality-hunger which we have seen to be a motivating power in many American writers. Stein wants to create verbal models or constructs which do not point to reality but somehow simulate it and evoke the sheer quality of existing things. It is her method, her idea of banishing the noun, which is open to question. Consider language as a reticulated transparent screen through which we look at the world: the reticulations provide relatively stable shapes—names, notions, species, etc.—which help us to bring into focus and thereby recognize a relatively unstable reality continually in flux. The screen is not reality, but without it reality remains undifferentiated and, to that extent, unseen. Without language we would suffer reality: it would beset us. To perceive the thing we need the word. The word is not the thing, but the word lasts longer than the thing. Stein's idea would seem to be to remove much of this reticulated screen, this patchwork of old names, and to substitute an improvised vocabulary which communicates the present feel of reality without identifying it by recourse to accepted nomenclature. Because names, by virtue of their very acceptance, refer back to the past: and Stein would like to get the past out of language, cleanse words of their dark history, cut them off from those roots which anchor and nourish. Ideally she wants the impossible. Here let me quote Jacques Rivière for his eloquence in making a basic point:

A word can always express more than it means; it has a history. I do not mean simply an etymology: it has a past; it has lived in different works and undergone the influence of its environment; it has had adventures; it has had encounters; it has been helped, supported by other words, or else it has come to their aid, has sustained them; and it retains hazy recollections of all its former companions, like a halo around itself. A thousand phantoms, which we cannot quite recognise, surround it and form its vague, mysterious escort.[36]

It is because so much of the past lies dormant but available in words that we can orient ourselves in current reality. Language is occasionally added to and subtracted from: for the most part it is simply endlessly reshuffled. The great writer manages this reshuffling in such a way as to recall us vividly to reality. He might seek to give us a complete actual present, but he will do it with materials which are saturated with past identifications and insights. The writer brings the past to bear on the present in a new way: indeed it is only by using the old that we can ascertain what is new. It seems to me that Stein confused two separate issues: she wanted to look at reality *as if* for the first time—she then thought it necessary to write about the reality thus perceived without using words which contained dense evidence of previous realities witnessed and wondered at, suffered and seen. Nouns are obviously the main bearers of these past realities—for the word table always refers to yesterday's table—so she struggled to avoid them. Yet we may borrow a Falstaffian reproach for the vast assembly of exiled nouns and imagine them saying to Stein— banish us and you banish the whole world.

Her error was to relegate nouns, theoretically, to poetry. For here she has a point. Concerning her famous phrase she wrote in her lecture:

When I said.
A rose is a rose is a rose is a rose.
And then later made that into a ring I made poetry and what did I do I caressed completely caressed and addressed a noun.[37]

The function of the repetition, I would say, is to take us away from the common word towards the rare reality. It is a way of reasserting what is miraculous in the commonplace. It represents Emerson's wisdom of wondering at the usual. Each time the word is repeated a bit of inertia and impercipience is shaken loose off the noun until the blooming petalled perfumed reality is brought into our minds. This would be a way of ridding language of the dulling encrustations of custom and second-hand reference: being made to hear the word as for the first time we will come to see the rose as for the first time. This sort of repetition aims at replacing habit with wonder. Just so we shall find in some of Hemingway that very simple assertions of the existence of reality—'The river was there.'—can have a tremendously forceful impact. We rediscover the world.

Of course although Stein's theories moved towards a renunciation of nouns and not a forceful re-use of them, in practice she uses them frequently: in a fairly orthodox way in the clear style of *The Autobiography of Alice B. Toklas,* and both in the more conventional statements and the more patterned and stylized parts of *Lucy Church Amiably.* No written style could endure the impoverishment consequent upon a total exclusion of nouns. However it is true that her interest in sheer word-patterning tends to make of her prose a perverse and personal unballasted flow which gives us very little reality. It is as though she experiments nearly all her life and never really puts the results of those experiments to any very fruitful use. Her most famous work is the early story 'Melanctha' which appeared in *Three Lives.*

Here there is a true originality and the words, though patterned and arranged in the interests of calculated repetitions, etc., address themselves directly to palpable realities. It is perhaps one way of commenting on her life's work to say that though she went on to make many more daring experiments she never created a better work of art. Looking back at 'Melanctha' in *Composition as Explanation* Stein wrote this:

In the beginning writing I wrote a book called *Three Lives* this was written in 1905, I wrote a negro story called *Melanctha*. In that there was a constant recurring and beginning there was a marked direction in the direction of being in the present although naturally I had been accustomed to past present and future, and why, because the composition forming around me was a prolonged present. A composition of a prolonged present is a natural composition in the world as it has been these thirty years it was more and more a prolonged present. I created then a prolonged present naturally I knew nothing of a continuous present but it came naturally to me to make one, it was simple it was clear to me and nobody knew why it was done like that, I did not myself although naturally to me it was natural.[38]

In fact the story has a fairly simple narrative line and covers the life of a passionate, confused and suffering negro woman. But it is not presented 'successively' but rather as a series of 'stills'— as Anderson was to address himself to arrested moments. Great use is made of slightly modified repetitions, echoing phrases, and refrains which both serve to organize the prose, and have an incremental effect as more and more of Melanctha's sad experience attaches itself to them (e.g. 'Always Melanctha Herbert wanted peace and quiet, and always she could only find new ways to get excited.')[39] The material of the story happened in time— it deals mainly with painful love affairs—but the story itself does not give the effect of being a trajectory through time. It deposits instants, complete moments, relevant fractions of experience: it describes the past as a series of separate presents so that the feeling is more of 'now and now and now' (the word is used at the start of ten consecutive sentences at one stage) rather than 'then and then and then'. The naive narrating eye is full of wonder (and compassion), not much given to comment and interpretation but more intent on focusing on emotional moments and separating their complexity out into their simple component parts. One and one and one and one.

Jeff Campbell then began again on the old papers. He sat there on the steps just above where Melanctha was sitting, and he went on with his reading, and his head went moving up and down, and sometimes he was reading, and sometimes he was thinking about all the things he wanted to be doing, and then he would rub the back of his dark hand over his mouth, and in between he would be frowning over his thinking, and sometimes he would be rubbing his head hard to help his thinking. And Melanctha just sat still and watched the lamp burning, and sometimes she turned it down a little, when the wind caught it and it would begin to get to smoking.[40]

Jefferson sighed, and then he smiled, and then they were quiet a long time together, and then after some more kindness, it was late, and then Jeff left her.[41]

And they loved it always, more and more, together, with this new feeling they had now, in these long summer days so warm; they, always together now, just these two so dear, more and more to each other always, and the summer evenings when they wandered, and the noises in the full streets, and the music of the organs, and the dancing, and the warm smell of the people, and of dogs and of the horses, and all the joy of the strong, sweet, pungent, dirty, moist, warm negro southern summer.[42]

Syntax and punctuation here are not used for relating and 'assembling' but rather for separating out each moment of existence. The words work outwards to touch and disentangle reality. Here we have a maintained simplicity, a deliberate naivety with no simple first-person narrator present to persuade us to accept the words and point of view as plausible. There is no attempt to catch the audible accents of a personal address: care instead is paid to the subtle control of pace, phrase length, and paragraph organization. The sustained evenness of the narrating tone clearly conceals an intense sympathy, but its main task is to secure and maintain a simple clarity of vision and notation.

Sometimes, indeed, it becomes a pure naivety, an almost excessive spelling out of details which nevertheless plays its part in bringing home the reality of the situation to us. 'Sometimes Jem Richards would be betting and would be good and lucky, and be getting lots of money. Sometimes Jem would be betting badly, and then he would not be having any money.'[43]

The story is genuinely moving and reveals Stein's considerable psychological insight; a talent we must regard as sadly neglected in her subsequent work. For all her theorizing about the need to establish relationships with existent reality, her own prose, mainly because of her distrust of nouns, etc., lost its ability to grope carefully out into the stuff of the world. In one of her lectures she asserts that the American language exhibits a 'lack of connection'[44] with material daily living, and in another lecture she insists that in American writing words 'began to detach themselves from the solidity of anything';[45] to my mind these estimates are only applicable to Stein's own later writing (and possibly to James's later work as she suggests). Her case as a writer and theorizer then presents a contradiction. Obsessed by the need to find a language that would convey directly the existing real thing in itself, she developed a highly mannered style, complicatedly simple yet curiously weightless, full of subtle movement yet fatally uninhabited. Her new way of writing was not a successful communication of her new way of seeing and, as I have tried to suggest, there are certain aspects of her theories which can go some way to explain this failure. Yet many of her ideas were influential, some of her discoveries were put to good effect by later writers, and her intentions place her in a major American tradition of writing and aspiration. She was genuinely aware of the 'seduction (and) ecstasy of things seen'[46] and worked hard to write a prose which could convey 'the rhythm of the visible world':[47] in one of her own good phrases we can say that she herself was moved by 'the emotion of reality'.[48] Anderson made many attempts to catch that emotion, but to feel it genuinely transmitted we shall have to turn to Hemingway.

CHAPTER 12

SHERWOOD ANDERSON'S LITTLE THINGS

In an article for *Dial* written in 1917 significantly entitled 'Apology for Crudity' Anderson tried to clarify his ideas on American writing:

For a long time I have believed that crudity is an inevitable quality in the production of a really significant present-day literature. How indeed is one to escape the fact that there is as yet no native subtlety of thought or living among us? And if we are a crude and childlike people how can our literature hope to escape the influence to that fact? Why indeed should we want it to escape?

We are not subtle enough to conceal ourselves and he who runs with open eyes through the Mississippi valley may read the story of the Mississippi valley.

That is more revealing than it sounds. It places key stress on the vagrant eye and the surface aspects of things, it endorses a predominantly visual response to the world, it requires a child-like response to the American scene.

It is a marvellous story and we have not yet begun to tell the half of it. A little, I think I know why. It is because we who write have drawn ourselves away. We have not had faith in our people and in the story of our people. If we are crude and childlike, that is our story, and our writing men must learn to dare to come among us until they know the story.

Once again the phrase 'crude and childlike'—and if those are the qualities of the subject matter, those must also be the qualities of the prose. For Anderson is after a prose which succumbs to the facts (whatever they are), not a prose which takes issue with them or disdains them.

To be sure the doing of the thing I am talking about will not be easy. America is a land of objective writing and thinking. New paths will have to be made. The subjective impulse is almost unknown to us. Because it is close to life, it works out into crude, broken forms. It leads along a road that such American masters of prose as James and Howells did not want to take, but if we are to get anywhere we shall have to travel that road.

That is a surprising paragraph. At first glance Anderson's prose seems to be aiming at an ideal objectivity, yet he claims that he is working from the subjective impulse and that it is people like James and Howells who were objective. It is hard to say exactly what he means by that: my guess is that he is talking about relative distance from subject matter. James and Howells stand back (or aloof); they reserve the right to evaluate, interpret, offer comment and in general keep their material at a long ironic distance. Anderson wants a new unironic mode of sympathetic involvement with the world, a sort of compassionate merging with the material environment, a new generous proximity of vision. This attitude implies an almost uncritical empathy, as he realizes. 'I do not know how far a man may go on the road of subjective writing. The matter, I admit, puzzles me. There is something approaching insanity in the very idea of sinking yourself too deeply into modern American industrial life. . . . But it is my contention that there is no other road.'[1] It would seem that the writer must sink into his surroundings and then write from inside them as it were: by his intense subjective feeling he somehow empowers the environment to speak for itself. And note that he says that this mode of writing works out into 'crude, broken forms': as crude and broken as experience itself. And indeed how should it be otherwise if the author refuses the privileges of perspective since it is only the withdrawn eye which will perceive patterns: the immersed senses are limited to random sensations, intense but seldom significantly related or additive. Anderson's theory of empathy is clearly related to the qualities of his prose. Consider his description (in *A Story Teller's Story*) of the joy he feels when he is about to start writing:

One has been walking in a street and has been much alive. What stories the faces in the streets tell! How significant the faces of the houses! The walls of the houses are brushed away by the force of the imagination and one sees and feels all of the life within. What a universal giving away of secrets! Everything is felt, everything known. Physical life within one's own body comes to an end of consciousness. *The Life outside oneself is all, everything*[2] [my italics]

Here is not the autocratic artist, battling with his environment, desperately trying to bring it under control and give it some coherence and shape: there is none of the feeling of disputation between man and nature. Here, rather, is a man with an indefinite capacity for sensory response, willingly capitulating to the environment to let it feel through him. This type of artist will become a sponge for single, discrete sensations, absorbing all, rejecting and rearranging as little as possible. Huck Finn has a little of this about him and the child's response has often been used subsequently for its uncritical alertness. It is the naive response which discovers a new world, or rediscovers an old or ignored one; which of course was exactly what Anderson was trying to do. But if his prose strategy sometimes calls to mind Huck Finn it should also remind us of Emerson whose conception of himself as a 'transparent eyeball' is more closely connected to Anderson's deliberately 'naive' empathy than a first glance might reveal. They merge with different material: Emerson abandons himself to a Divine nature, Anderson opens himself to the crudities of small-town life in America. But the receptive stance is similar.

Winesburg, Ohio, published in 1919, is undoubtedly Anderson's most important work and deserves special attention as it was also his most influential work. I want now to try and indicate the particular qualities in Anderson's writing. Perhaps the first thing that strikes one about Anderson's prose is the constant inclusion of seemingly gratuitous details. For instance in the story about Doctor Parcival we are told that he dines at Biff Carter's lunch room. The next sentence reads: 'In the summer the lunch room was filled with flies and Biff Carter's white apron was more dirty than his floor.'[3] And then Biff Carter and his lunch room disappear out of the story for ever. Again, when George Willard takes out Louise Trunnion for a walk the account of his fumbling efforts with her is interrupted by this description of a brick sidewalk: 'Some of the bricks were missing and the sidewalk was rough and irregular.'[4] Why tell us? They don't trip on the sidewalk or make love on its rough surface: it is just that as the author's eye goes over the scene it includes many of the surrounding facts. There is no apparent principle of selection and omission at work. Minor characters suddenly receive a moment of unrelated scrutiny. 'When he laughed he scratched his left elbow with his right hand. The sleeve of his coat was almost worn through from the habit.'[5] That is Edward King who plays no part in the story at all. Such details would be capricious interruption if Anderson was working on a specific theme or up to a discernible dramatic crisis. But he is not. For him there aren't any. No one detail is more or less important than another: all merit attention. The eye is deliberately *not* informed by any selective modes of thinking. It sees without thinking, or perhaps we could fairly say, 'it sees without looking'.

The manner in which Anderson starts and ends a story is also significant:

There were always three or four old people sitting on the front porch of the house or puttering about the garden of the Bentley farm. Three of the old people were women and sisters to Jesse. They were a colorless, soft-voiced lot. Then there was a silent old man with thin white hair who was Jesse's uncle.

The farmhouse was built of wood, a board outer-covering over a framework of logs.[6]

Facts are suddenly thrust before us with no prior introduction. They present themselves to us insisting on their individual importance, an importance always left unexplained, or rather an importance which they are left to explain for themselves. They are never differentiated or appraised. Each fact—about the uncle, about the farmhouse—is separate and of equal importance: there are no connectives but rather a series of isolated impressions. We have the illusion not of Anderson bringing us the world, but of the world appearing to us in its own unpremeditated manner.

Or put it this way: we are given the world seen in the simplest way and not filtered through any exegetical intelligence. The stories take us suddenly into an endless continuum. 'Until she was seven years old she lived in an old unpainted house on an unused road that led off Trunnion Pike.'[7] That is how one story starts. Who is 'she'? asks the reader who is used to the usual elaborate scene setting of the conventional novel. It doesn't matter, says Anderson. Wherever you turn your eye there are things going on: to try and make more out of the chaos of experience than that is to falsify it. Anderson does not bring us a life; he brings us a moment. It is a fragmentary view of life, and it is clear that Anderson's approach can only lead to fragmentation. His vision permits of no plot developments or notable dramatic crises: there are no gestures of summarizing significance, nor do the individual details accumulate to the point of revealing larger meanings. In 'The Philosopher' we read, 'the tales that Doctor Parcival told George Willard began nowhere and ended nowhere',[8] and the same thing could be said of Anderson's tales. Things end, when they do, with a sort of dry abruptness: there is never a feeling of something consummated. 'In the end she married a man who bought and sold real estate and was contented enough.'[9] There is almost a hard dead-pan irony of understatement in this manner of writing. Life tapers off as meaninglessly as this sentence: there are no true endings, only pointless cessations.

Often a paragraph containing or referring to a disaster will end with some comparatively minor and seemingly arbitrary detail of physical description. Unwilling to distribute emphases, intent on confronting only the facts, Anderson's prose has the effect of neutralizing experience: life's intensities come to us muted, potentially dramatic factors appear benumbed. Anderson's refusal to push big emotions and grand climaxes was a real achievement and his almost positivistic attempt to give us only perceived facts or verifiable factors reveals a commendable effort of honesty. At his best he does sometimes achieve that which Joyce said short stories should aim at—an epiphany. Sometimes his 'day of facts' is a 'day of diamonds', though where Emerson's diamonds sparkled of divinity, Anderson's are content to radiate some human significance. But all too often his material is rendered inert and inactive by the way it is assembled, the order in which it appears. Once again we see the problem of form confronting a writer who adopts the naive wondering vision in an effort to rediscover reality. As Anderson said, his form will be 'broken', because life comes to the naive eye unarranged. His difficulty is to find some organizing principle of selection. The book has no insistent time sequence, no dramatic development, no increasing complexity, no knotting and unravelling. Things and people do not develop because they do not inter-mix. (The vague theme of George Willard growing up scarcely binds the book together.) What Anderson aims at is the moment, the mood; something glimpsed rather than something pursued; a fragment arrested rather than life's exfoliating growth. Hence the endlessly localized assembling of facts around separate and barely related nuclei, which produces that curiously stylized and stilted panorama which is the world of this book. It is indeed the world of all his books since his full length novels attempt but fail to transcend his short story method of sudden concentration on an all but static instant.

Consider for a moment the tone of these three passages:

On Saturday afternoons they hitched a team of horses to a three-seated wagon and went off to town. In town they stood about the stoves in the stores talking to other farmers or to the store keepers. They were dressed in overalls and in the winter wore heavy coats that were flecked with mud. Their hands as they stretched them out to the heat of the stove were cracked and red. It was difficult for them to talk and so they for the most part kept silent. When they had bought meat, flour, sugar, and salt, they went into one of the Winesburg saloons and drank beer.[10]

Once he killed a dog with a stick. The dog belonged to Win Pawsey, the shoe merchant, and stood on the sidewalk wagging its tail. Tom King killed it with one blow. He was arrested and paid a fine of ten dollars.[11]

Then he slept and in all Winesburg he was the last soul on that winter night to go to sleep.[12]

Noticeable in all is a reluctance to depart from the simplest basic sentence structure—the minimal (and efficient) means of transmitting information about material scenes and events. But the tone is stranger than that basic schema can account for. In the first passage we get a series of simple physical details, but although they are details of action and movement they come to us curiously stilled, as though seen by a non-participating and almost non-comprehending spectator. Here certainly is a man very close to 'wondering at the usual'. In the second passage the prose has a neutralizing effect: it records a violent incident and drains from it all the violence, all the emotional content, all the fury, and leaves us with a picture stark, sharp, and motionless—as though in crystal. Then in the third passage we are in the presence of an author who can see into every home and who knows every detail of life in the village. (It is amusing to recall that Hemingway's friend Lionel Moise, a journalist, once advised him to be careful over his narrative strategy in the following words: 'no playing dumb observer one paragraph and God Almighty the next'. This is exactly what Anderson often does, though the 'dumb observer' is certainly predominant.) But consider the tone of all those pieces. The minute detail and the summary biography, the whole village and the cracks in a farmer's hand, violent incidents and dull routine—all come to us in the same even tone, arrested and naked of comment. This is not to say that Anderson is writing from a multiple perspective, but rather that there simply is no perspective at all. Or rather it is what I could call the perspective of deliberate naivety: the unprejudiced, awed and undiscriminating eye recording and transmitting all details and information with equal wonder and equal lack of apparent reaction. Of course what may seem like emotionlessness in Anderson's prose might be emotion stunned into silence. The silences between the clean staccato sentences seem at times to be as full of feeling as the silences in a Chehov play. And yet no matter how welcome is the absence of an intrusive bullying authorial rhetoric, it must be said that it is dangerous for any writer to rely on the unsaid as much as Anderson seems to do in this book. Sometimes indeed, like Hemingway at his best, he avoids comment where comment would be superfluous: but at other times he avoids implying any sort of evaluation or reaction at all. If it is a prose which is very humane in its interest in ordinary human doings, it is also a prose which seems helpless to bring any significant light to bear on them. One sometimes has the feeling that Anderson never got over the staggering fact that there was a material visible world at all, and that he never took more than 'the first step'. And if that is true we should not forget that such an attitude and response would have earned Emerson's theoretic approval.

It is perhaps this refusal to comment on, to take any command of, his material that gives Anderson's prose its oddly stylized effect.

Snow lay deep in the streets of Winesburg. It had begun to snow about ten o'clock in the morning and a wind sprang up and blew the snow in clouds along Main Street. The frozen mud roads that led into the town were fairly smooth and in places ice covered the mud. 'There will be good sleighing,' said Will Henderson, standing by the bar in Ed Griffith's saloon. Out of the saloon he went and met Sylvester West the druggist stumbling along in the kind of heavy over-shoes called arctics. 'Snow will bring the people into town on Saturday,' said the druggist. The two men stopped and discussed their affairs. Will Henderson, who had on a light overcoat and no overshoes, kicked the heel of his left foot with the toe of the right. 'Snow will be good for the wheat,' observed the druggist sagely.[13]

The unbroken monotone of the paragraph is perhaps also the unbroken monotony of the village life: the ponderous, yet unimpassioned, almost disinterested tone of the speech echoes perhaps that very tone in village conversation. If it does that then according to Anderson's aesthetic it does enough; yet it is interesting to note how little bulk and momentum is carried by this prose which seems to devote itself to sheer factual clarity.

And indeed we must remind ourselves that objectivity is not what Anderson claims to be after: 'haven't we given ourselves to surface facts long enough?' and 'It is my aim to be true to the essence of things'. In fact Anderson has not so much disappeared *from* his scene as *into* it. His simplicity is not the result of a detached objectivity but stems from a profound subjective identification with the world he writes of. All those random gratuitous details should be faintly luminous with the light of his sympathy—or empathy. This mysticism of detail has a resemblance to the intentions of the Imagists. 'Emotions gather about common things' said William Carlos Williams, and it is a comparable conviction that motivates Anderson's manner of writing. Imagism, in presenting isolated things in such an intensely simple way as to penetrate to their very essence, seems to have been doing what Anderson was also attempting. And just as you could not make an epic out of Imagist poetry so Anderson could never make a novel out of his Imagist prose. Anderson's indiscriminate wonder, his mysticism of detail finally acted as a bar to any developing complexity of insight and judgement. His mysticism itself remained disablingly crude. In the introductory fragment to *Winesburg, Ohio* when he is discussing the 'Book of the Grotesque' by the bed-ridden writer, he writes about the thought that he took away from the book:

All about in the world were the truths and they were all beautiful. The old man had listed hundreds of the truths in his book. I will not try to tell you all of them. There was the truth of virginity and the truth of passion, the truth of wealth and of poverty, of thrift and of profligacy, of carelessness and abandon. Hundreds and hundreds were the truths and they were all beautiful.[14]

This sort of cosmic generalization precludes thought, discrimination, and comparative analysis: on the other hand it allows every aspect of life to be treated as unique, separate and veridical. *Winesburg, Ohio* is intended as a series of truths rather than a series of stories: there is no dramatic interweaving properly speaking, merely the careful annotation of incidents which reveals their 'truth' without reference to any larger scheme of things and detached from any significant causal temporal sequence. From the clearly delineated and minutely observed detail Anderson will suddenly leap to the most vaporous mystical generalization about life, all life everywhere. And in between these two extremes there is nothing: no complex moral attitude towards life, no adjudicating subtleties, no finely drawn discriminations, no nuanced assessment of conduct, no embodied values. There are the cracks in the farmer's hand—and a vague compassion for all men and an even vaguer feeling that all things are beautiful. One is reminded of Emerson's leap from the firkin to the Over-Soul, and in Emerson too we noted a failure to say anything about the complexities of human conduct. (It is true that Anderson does make us aware of such problems as frustration, loneliness, adolescent sex-confusion, failures of communication, but note that these are all individual moods which are almost like secondary qualities of the various characters—a part of their special colour or odour. Anderson's characters are part of his landscape, not dynamic human agents initiating or responding to important actions.) Often Anderson adopts the response of a quivering adolescent sensibility to convey his emotions. Thus when George Willard is out walking one night:

He felt unutterably big and remade by the experience through which he had been passing and in a kind of fervor of emotion put up his hands, thrusting them into the darkness above his head and muttering words. The desire to say words overcome him and he said words without meaning, rolling them over on his tongue and saying them because they were brave words, full of meaning. 'Death', he muttered, 'night, the sea, fear, loveliness.'[15]

This may be an accurate description of an adolescent's mood, moving suddenly from a response to surrounding details to 'a kind of fervor of emotion' which he can only express by murmuring large words. The point is that Anderson himself does no more than this. This is perhaps all a sensitive adolescent can do with his fragmentary sensations and inchoate emotions. He cannot assemble them into anything larger: rather he collapses into an anguished, lyrical, yet essentially inarticulate outpouring of excited approximations. (See for example the story of Tom Foster where he explains why he got drunk: 'It was like making love, that's what I mean. . . . Don't you see how it is? It hurt me to do what I did and made everything strange. That's why I did it. I'm glad, too. It taught me something, that's it, that's what I wanted. Don't you understand?'[16] and so on.) This indeed is the adolescent's dilemma: but it has also become the writer's dilemma because the writer himself has adopted the adolescent's habit of agonizing, fragmentary response. Sharp factual accuracy and blurred emotional fervour: it is a not uncommon combination in the work of writers who have found it desirable to adopt the adolescent response to experience. Some of Anderson's most successful stories indeed preserve the presence of the naive vernacular narrator: such stories as 'I'm a Fool' and 'I Want to Know Why'. Despite what he learned from Stein about the careful choosing and placing of words, the organizing of paragraphs, he never really managed to develop the naive vernacular approach into a style capable of transmitting subtleties of response and awareness which are beyond the blinding momentary sincerities of the adolescent. And indeed Anderson was really most interested in such sincere moments. Perhaps there is one passage more than any other which best points to Anderson's particular area of interest. It occurs when the book climaxes, or refuses to climax, with George Willard's departure:

The young man, going out of town to meet the adventure of life, began to think but he did not think of anything very big or dramatic. Things like his mother's death, his departure from Winesburg, the uncertainty of his future life in the city, the serious and larger aspects of his life did not come into his mind.

He thought of little things—Turk Smallett wheeling boards through the main street of his town in the morning, a tall woman, beautifully gowned, who had once stayed over night at his father's hotel, Butch Wheeler the lamp lighter of Winesburg hurrying through the streets on a summer evening and holding a torch in his hand, Helen White standing by a window in the Winesburg post office and putting a stamp on an envelope.[17]

'He thought of little things'—it is almost a definition of Anderson's style. The passage itself is sensitive and has a welcome air of authenticity in its avoidance of stock emotional attitudinizing. It reminds one of Huck telling about the sound of the man chopping wood coming from the other side of the river: the difference between Anderson and Clemens is that Anderson limits himself to this sort of response. Instead of a sentimentality of large things we approach a sentimentality of little things; instead of a sentimentality of overstatement we find a new and paradoxical sentimentality of insufficient statement (as opposed to controlled understatement). There are hints of all this in *Huckleberry Finn* but the vigorous confrontation of moral problems and the greater dramatic complexity keep them in check, or rather they serve unsentimental ends. It may seem perverse to suggest that there is a sentimentality of detail and insufficient statement, but if we define sentimentality as the assertion of a greater emotion than the presentation of the material warrants then we have some warrant for applying the term to Anderson. Because behind the offered 'little things' there loom large but unarticulated feelings, and this disproportion can be felt throughout the book. Anderson's writing seldom progresses beyond a deliberately naive reduction of experience to its simplest particulars, yet the stoical clippedness of utterance often conceals a vast amount of barely controlled emotionalism. It should not be necessary to add that this is not to say that these feelings are insincere. Anderson's compassion is a real and moving thing: the point is that he develops no satisfactory method of injecting it into his style, of letting it tactfully inform and direct his prose. Anderson's compassion remains vague because it is divorced from perceptive judgement: as the great writers reveal, it is possible, indeed preferable, to keep the assessing faculties operative even when the sympathetic faculties are most engaged. Otherwise compassion precludes understanding, and we need to achieve understanding if our compassion is to develop into a valuable and enduring emotion. Anderson's compassion hovers over his material like a cloud, always threatening to burst and drench it in a lachrymose downpour. His failures are never failures of sympathy, but rather failures of insight and utterance. Certainly we should bear in mind the problem he set himself and which we noted at the start of the chapter: how to write about a certain sort of people in a certain sort of locale without having recourse to artistic schemata which will distort or devalue them. Yet is Anderson's the only way in which an artist can do justice to crude, unsophisticated, inarticulate sections of the community? Think what Tolstoy could make of a farmer or peasant, to say nothing of what Cézanne could make of their faces. The shortcomings of Anderson's writing are a function of his chosen strategy: he sees some things freshly, clearly honestly. But he sees only 'little things', fragments of experience which catch the naive and wondering eye. Ironically enough it is finally his writing which undervalues the people and places he writes about, even though he addresses himself to them with such sympathy, because it is a kind of writing which, though it can make a new and welcome effort of attention, cannot make the necessary effort of penetration.

Anderson's subsequent work is usually more flawed, sentimental and pretentious than *Winesburg, Ohio* but it is worth examining certain passages in some of his more interesting work, such as *Poor White, A Story Teller's Story, Tar: A Midwest Childhood,* and some of the short stories, in order to define more exactly what sort of visual and verbal relationship between himself and the world Anderson attempted to establish.

We have already noted the effect whereby Anderson's descriptions of process and action are curiously devoid of any conveyed sense of movement: similarly when he repeats speech he communicates none of the uneven pressures and quickly changing tempo of ordinary talk. Instead he so stylizes the syntax as to make it seem sedate to the point of silence (e.g. ' "I'm a man. I tell you what I'm a man. Whatever anyone says, I tell you what, I'm a man," he shouted into the void').[18] The arresting effect of his meticulous annotation can be related to a curious preoccupation of Anderson's, a sort of aesthetic dream which is best described in *A Story Teller's Story*. It is worth quoting at length: Anderson is describing his feelings as he sat outside Chartres Cathedral and watched what seemed to be some incipient conflict developing between three people.

The three of them just suddenly came out of the church together and walked away together in silence. That was all. All tales presented themselves to the fancy in just that way. There was a suggestion, a hint given. In a crowd of faces in a crowded street one face suddenly jumped out. It has a tale to tell, was crying its tale to the streets but *at the best one got only a fragment of it.* Once, long after the time of which I am now writing, I tried to paint in an American desert. There was something about the light. My eyes were not accustomed to it. . . . What appeared on the canvas was dull and meaningless. . . . I kept blaming the light. 'Nothing stands still in this light,' I said to myself.

As though anything ever stood still anywhere. It was the artist's business to make it stand still—well, just to *fix the moment*, in a painting, in a tale, in a poem.

Sitting there with my friend, facing the cathedral, I remembered something. On my desk, somewhere back in America, was a book in which I had once written certain lines. Well, I had made a poem and had called it, 'One who would not grow old.' Now it came sharply back: 'I have wished that the wind would stop blowing, that birds would stop dead still in their flight, without falling into the sea, that waves would stand ready to break upon shores without breaking, that all time, all impulse, all movement, mood, hungers, *everything would stop and stand hushed and still for a moment.* It would be wonderful to be sitting on a log in a forest when it happened. When all was still and hushed, just as I have described, we would get off the log and walk a little way.

The insects would all lie still in the ground or float, fixed and silent in the air. An old frog, that lived under a stone and that had opened his mouth to snap at a fly, would sit gaping. *There would be no movement*, in New York, in Detroit, in Chicago down by the stock exchange, in towns, in factories, on farms.

Out in Colorado, where a man was riding a horse furiously, striving to catch a steer to be sent to Chicago and butchered—

He would stop, too, and the steer would stop.

You and I would walk a little way, in the forest, or on a prairie, or on the streets of a town, and then we would stop. We would be the only moving things in the world and then one of us would start a thought rolling and rolling, down time, down space, down mind, down life too. I am sure I would let you do it if later you would keep all of the voices of your mind hushed while I did it in my turn. I would wait ten lives while others did it for my turn.' [19] [my italics]

The suggestive glimpse, the complaint that nothing ever stands still, the dream in which all movement is suspended—this sequence tells us something basic about Anderson's intentions. Look, for instance, at the poem itself and note that he selects unrelated, distinct details and frozen situations. The poem describes the very effect that Anderson's prose has on the world: it stops it. People make gestures and open their mouths but oddly enough there is no movement and no noise. In a letter to James Boyd written in 1939 he said:

From time to time an impulse comes to me. I would like to write the story of a man during an hour of his life, *without physical action*, the man sitting, or standing, or just walking about. All that he is that made him what he is. I have this temptation and at the same time realize that man is best understood by his actions. [20] [my italics]

In a subtler way than he outlines in the letter Anderson gives in to this 'temptation' in his general prose style. For the main thing missing from Anderson's stories is 'action' in the dramatic sense of the word: his fictional world is composed of glimpses rather than events. He himself was aware of his gift and predilection for the trapped and arrested fragment, as he reveals when he describes how his mind is 'filled with fragmentary glimpses of life caught and held. . . . The little fragments caught in the field of my fancy are like flies caught in molasses—they cannot escape.' [21] His interest in glimpses is also indicated by his habit of frequently omitting the verb from his sentences.

In the tenement districts of American cities among the poor in small towns, strange things to be seen by a boy. [22]

Horses trotting around a race track in an Ohio town on a Sunday morning in the summer, squirrels running along the top of a worn fence, apples getting ripe in orchards. [23]

Anderson's wondering eye is capable of registering states but not of pursuing situations, and an arrested world would give his wonder more scope: he could itemize the myriad miracles of the world at his leisure with no concern for their order of inclusion. A world brought to a standstill, all significant action eliminated (or ignored), and its totality reduced to intensely seen fragments: this is not all of Anderson's work but it is a large part of it.

The paratactic shortness of Anderson's sentences has often been noted and their very shortness and avoidance of complex subordinate clauses demonstrates the fragmentary nature of his vision. As an extreme example of how his particular attention works, note how, in the following simple piece of description, Anderson makes three sentences out of information which most writers would easily have handled in one: 'The bars were in place and window shades were drawn over the windows. Above the door that faced the road there was a large sign. "Keep out. This Means You," the sign said.'[24]

With scrupulous care the multiple sensation is separated into its contributing parts; we follow the movements of an eye which refuses to take in more than one aspect of reality at a time. We are pushed out among things and denied all the shorthand summaries and appraising compressions which words make possible. This can produce an effect of looking at the world anew, it can force us to re-evaluate our simplest sensations and perceptions (as Hemingway at his best does): however the strategy requires great tact in the selection of the aspects of the world to be so carefully re-examined and the sensations of the man to be so deliberately retarded. Anderson seldom has this tact and then we see the dangers and drawbacks of the naive wondering vision when it is not under the strictest control of the author who must so carefully direct and curtail it. It produces no form because it gets lost among equally interesting particulars: it is also almost fatal to plot progression which relies on a certain kind of mobility and skirting of inessentials—and indeed in his long novel Anderson all too often gives the impression of a sort of bemused listlessness in the recounting tone. (Jonson, advocate of brevity and compression, noted, quoting Quintilian, that 'there is a briefness of the parts sometimes that makes the whole long'. And when he says long he means tediously and unnecessarily drawn out.) But Anderson had a special feeling for the potentialities of the sentence. He once wrote:

There are sentences written by all writers of note in all countries that have their roots deep down in the life about them. The sentences are like windows looking into houses. Something is suddenly torn aside, all lies, all trickery about life gone for the moment. It is what one wants, what one seeks constantly in one's own craftsmanship, and how seldom it comes.[25]

Sentences like windows: again the insistence on the snatched glimpse, the sudden stare which somehow fastens on to a deeply truthful particular. One could see Anderson's short unrelated sentences as part of prolonged quest for the significant detail, the wondering eye testing everything that it alights on.

As well as seeing the sentence as an agent of isolation, a tool for separating the significant glimpse off from its blurring context, Anderson had a particular attitude towards words themselves which requires some attention. He is most revealing in a passage about Gertrude Stein:

How significant words had become to me! At about this time an American woman living in Paris, Miss Gertrude Stein, had published a book called 'Tender Buttons' and it had come into my hands. How it had excited me! Here was something purely experimental and dealing in words separated from sense—in the ordinary meaning of the word sense—an approach I was sure the poets must often be compelled to make.

He then describes how he played with a painter's colours one day:

I shifted the little pans of color about, laid one color against another. I walked away and came near. Suddenly there had flashed into my consciousness, for perhaps the first time in my life, the secret inner world of the painters. . . . Very well then, the words used by the tale-teller were as the colors used by the painter. Form was another matter. It grew out of the materials of the tale and the teller's reaction to them.

... And words were something else. Words were the surfaces, the clothes of the tale.... Would the common words of our daily speech in shops and offices do the trick?

Stein's book was, for Anderson, a literary experience equivalent to seeing the painter juxtapose his colours. 'Here were words laid before me as the painter had laid the color pans on the table in my presence.... Perhaps it was then I really fell in love with words, wanted to give each word I used every chance to show itself at its best.'[26]

This points to some interesting conclusions. First of all he is trying to escape from the conventions dominating his chosen genre: he despises the artificial language and plots of contemporary stories ('those bastard children of De Maupassant, Poe and O'Henry') and wants to take plots whose shape is determined by his actual environment and words spoken in that environment. But notice the divorce between words and form. Form emerges from the fragments of experience which compose his material: words are surfaces of things. And when he talks of words separated from sense he does not mean, as some symbolist poets have meant, words emptied of all denotative function, but rather words used more like pointillist spots of paint than agents in ratiocinative discourse. Words depict the scattered glimpses that the eye registers. They do not impose form on formless material. It is this attitude to words which gives his prose that curious clean aseptic quality, as though each one was surrounded by a margin of space. It is this desire to give each word equal prominence that accounts for the almost total suppression of syntax in Anderson's prose, for syntax relates and subordinates. Anderson's ideal unit is not even the sentence: it is the single word representing the surface of a single seen thing. Emerson found 'bare lists of words' suggestive, and just as Anderson's attitude towards reality is latent in some of Emerson's ideas, so too does Anderson's prose have a distant relationship to Emerson's way of writing: both give equal prominence to a series of juxtaposed but not inter-acting particulars.

Anderson's ability to be hypnotized almost into a trance by the isolated glimpse is well exemplified in the following passage from *A Story Tellers' Story* in which he describes how he watched the beginnings of a domestic quarrel through his window (significantly enough):

They were in the garden unconscious of me and I was unconscious of a dinner being put on a table downstairs in my house, unconscious of any need of food I would ever feel again, unconscious of the regime of my own household, of the affairs of my factory. A man and a woman in a garden had become the centre of a universe about which it seemed I might think and feel in joy and wonder forever.[27]

One random scene, one 'little thing' can soak up all his attention: this, if you like, is both the gift and danger of the habit of wonder. For Emerson a 'little thing' could lead him through to the Over-Soul. Anderson has the same sort of quality of response without the assured philosophic penetration. His little things never quite turn into revelations or coherent symbols. The wondering eye finds these things infinitely precious without being able to relate them to any larger scheme of values. The response is truly child-like, as Anderson reveals when he adopts the narrative mask of a youth as he often does with real success. Here, for instance, in 'Man Who Became a Woman':

Perhaps you know how a person feels at such a moment. There are things you think of, *odd little things* you had thought you had forgotten. Once, when you were a kid, you were with your father, and he was all dressed up, as for a funeral or Fourth of July, and was walking along a street holding your hand. And you were going past a railroad station, and there was a man standing. . . . Or maybe, when you get jammed up as I was that night, and can't get things clear about yourself or other people and why you are alive, or for that matter why anyone you can think of is alive, you think, not of people at all but of other *things you have seen and felt*—like walking along a road in the snow in winter, perhaps out in Iowa, and hearing soft warm sounds in a barn close to the road, or of another time when you were on a hill and the sun was going down and the sky suddenly became a great soft-coloured bowl. . . . As I say, there I was anyway, up there alone with that horse in that warm stall in the dark lonesome fair ground and I had that feeling about being sick at the thought of human beings and what they could be like.[28] [my italics]

We can catch the accents of Huck Finn there, but the interesting thing to note is that it is in the adolescent's manner of noting or recalling 'odd little things' that Anderson has found his most comfortable mode of writing. To say that Anderson is childish is to say nothing to the point: but to say that he seemed most at ease with what he considered to be the child's manner of assimilating the world—wondering at its endless stream of 'little things', hoarding cherished sensations—is to say something with relevance for a great deal of modern American literature.

Anderson's interest in the child's mode of responding to the world is most obviously revealed in his autobiography *Tar* which is concerned with his own childhood. One passage must be quoted in full. 'He' refers to young Tar, Anderson himself, left alone as a small child.

He sat on the box near the door of the barn. Was he glad to be alone? One of those odd things happened that were always happening later when he was grown. A particular scene, a country road climbing over a hill, the yard of a railroad seen from a bridge in a city at night, a grass-grown road leading into a wood, the garden of a deserted tumble-down house—*some scene that, outwardly at least, had no more meaning than a thousand other scenes* swept by his eye, perhaps on the same day, *printed itself with the most minutely worked out details on the walls of his mind.* The house of his mind had many rooms and each room was a mood. On the walls pictures were hung. He had hung them there. Why? *Some inner sense of selection had perhaps been at work.*[29] [my italics]

What is interesting is the relationship he suggests that exists between the seemingly random, minutely registered detail and a total emotional mood; a relationship which seems vague and perhaps unconscious. This feeling that one minutely detailed scene can stand for and reprovoke a whole mood bears some relation to Eliot's concept of the 'objective correlative' and it partially explains Anderson's reason for caring so reverently about seemingly gratuitous details. Of course there is a risk that what the detail does for him it does not do for the reader: the failure then would be in the art of depiction, its inability to transcend the purely personal, the subjectively mnemonic. It could be a failure to move beyond a perfected and cultivated 'child's' manner of reaction. The whole of *Tar* reveals a happy reimmersion in childhood experience, experience recalled from a child's point of view. And a most interesting example of the way Anderson's mind worked is provided by his description of the child's reaction to the concept of God:

People talked about God. There wasn't anything very definite in Tar's mind. Lots of times you do something—like carrying that straw from the threshing inside your shirt all afternoon (it tickling you) and you don't know why you do it.
There is a lot to think about you never can really think about.[30]

Can only think about, we might suggest, if it is translated down into simple sensory particulars and vivid instances. Still turning over the word 'God' Anderson continues:

If you sit at the edge of a cornfield and an orchard and you have a little fire and it is almost night and there is a cornfield and the smoke goes up lazy and slow toward the sky and you look up . . .[31]

Those dots at the end of the passage are Anderson's and they are significant. In effect they imply that there is an endless continuum of vivid perceptual and sensory experiences and singular moods; but there is nothing more to be said about them, nothing to be inferred from them—nothing, perhaps, to be learned from them, except a manner of awed meditation. Let us move from Tar on to the grown artist, talking about himself in his preface to *Horses and Men*. Anderson is looking at an apple.

Did you ever have a notion of this kind—there is an orange, or say an apple, lying on the table before you. . . . What subtle flavours are concealed in it—how does it taste, smell, feel? Heavens, man, the way the apple feels in the hand is something—isn't it? . . . The point is that after the form of the apple began to take my eye I often found myself unable to touch it at all. . . . There I sat, in the room with the apple before me, and hours passed. I had pushed myself off into a world where nothing has any existence. Had I done that, or had I merely stepped, for a moment, out of the world of darkness into the light.[32]

'The wise man wonders at the usual'—Anderson's 'naive' mysticism follows Emerson's prescription to the letter and it seems closely related to his adolescent reverence for the single vivid item. An incident at the end of *Poor White* really offers us a most suggestive image for Anderson's art. Hugh McVey, the childish inventor, has gradually come to the realization that in submitting to the methods of industrialization and mass production he would seriously compromise himself, and the purity and perfection of his creative ideas would be irreparably soiled. He is told to check up on the models of a rival firm and incorporate any new ideas they may have into his own plans. He refuses to do this, though he does visit other machines from reasons of pure interest. On one such visit to Sandusky he takes a walk by the bay shore after his business is completed.

Some brightly colored stones attracted his attention and he picked several of them up and put them in his pockets. In the station at Pittsburgh he took them out and held them in his hand. A light came in at a window, a long slanting light that played over the stones. His roving, disturbed mind was caught and held. He rolled the stones back and forth. The colors blended and then separated again.[33]

Later in his journey he takes the stones out.

In the smoker Hugh sat, again playing with the colored stones held in his hand. There was relief for his mind in the stones. The light played continually about them, and their color shifted and changed. One could look at the stones and get relief from thought. Raising his eyes he looked out of the car window. The train was passing through Youngstown. His eyes looked along grimy streets of workers' houses clustered closely about huge mills. The same light that had played over the stones in his hand began to play over his mind, and for a moment he became not an inventor but a poet. The revolution within had really begun. A new declaration of independence wrote itself within him. 'The Gods have thrown the towns like stones over the flat country, but the stones have no color. They do not burn and change in the light,' he thought.[34]

This offers us a simple but revealing parable for Anderson's picture of the dilemma, need, and strategy of the contemporary artist. Surrounded by a reality which man has dulled and sullied the writer will seek out and cherish a few little things which for him still have a sort of luminous beauty. These things will be part of reality (as opposed to a deliberately unreal artifact) but they will be only those things which stimulate this child-like capacity for wonder. These he will gather together and, as he later wrote in *A Story Teller's Story*, they will 'glisten and shine outside the muddle of life'.[35] In that latter book he discussed the incident in these terms: 'To the child man, the American who was the hero of my book and, I thought, to myself and to many other American men I had seen, they were something a little permanent.'[36] The arrested thing, impulsively and subjectively selected by the wondering 'child man' (sic) and retained for secret comfort: perhaps what Anderson's prose was always seeking was the solace of the brilliant detail, the consolation of the loved particular. Perhaps he would have been willing to borrow a line from T. S. Eliot and say with reference to the reassurance afforded him by his pebbles, his particulars—'These fragments I have shored against my ruins.'

CHAPTER 13

ERNEST HEMINGWAY'S UNHURRIED
SENSATIONS

ONE of the richest chapters in *Death in the Afternoon* is the last, in which Hemingway describes all those things he has not managed to get into the book but which he thinks deserve a place: and of course in the very enumeration of the missing material he is in fact inserting it. This whole chapter seems to me to provide a most interesting point of departure for a discussion of Hemingway's whole attitude towards experience, but before pursuing that discussion I must quote at some length from the chapter itself. This will give us a preliminary clue to the structure of reality as perceived by the Hemingway eye.

If I could have made this enough of a book it would have had everything in it. The Prado, looking like some big American college building with sprinklers watering the grass early in the bright Madrid summer morning; the bare white mud hills looking across toward Carabanchel; days on the train in August with the blinds pulled down on the side against the sun and the wind blowing them; chaff blown against the car in the wind from the hard earthen threshing floors; the odour of grain and the stone windmills. . . .

It should have the smell of burnt powder and the smoke and the flash and the noise of the traca going off through the green leaves of the trees, and it should have the taste of horchata, ice-cold horchata, and the new-washed streets in the sun, and the melons and beads of cool on the outside of the pitchers of beer; the storks on the houses in Barco de Avila and wheeling in the sky, and the red-mud colour of the ring; and at night dancing to the pipes, and the drum with lights through the green leaves and the portrait of Garibaldi framed in leaves. . . .

There ought to be Astorga, Lugo, Orense, Soria, Tarragona, and Catalayud, the chestnut woods on the high hills, the green country and the rivers, the red dust, the small shade beside the dry rivers and the white, baked clay hills; cool walking under palms in the old city

228

on the cliff above the sea, cool in the evening with the breeze; mosquitoes at night, but in the morning the water clear and the sand white; then sitting in the heavy twilight at Miro's; vines as far as you can see, cut by the hedges and the road; the railroad and the sea with pebbly beach and tall papyrus grass. . . .

Let those who want to save the world *if you can get to see it clear and as a whole. Then any part you make will represent the whole* if it's made truly. The thing to do is work and learn to make it. No. It is not enough of a book, but still there were a few things to be said. There were a few practical things to be said.[1] [my italics]

The reality of the world can best be attested to by certain experienced sensations—smells, feels, above all sights—not classified or related or theorized about, but simply put one alongside the other; separate yet cohabitating, their original sharp clarity undiminished and unblurred. The syntax is essentially paratactic because that is how the vision operates. And Hemingway has got all those impressions into his book, got them in in a manner which looks rather like Whitman's loose lines contracted into imagist incisiveness, and yet got them in in a manner which seems to him not to be the proper mode of inclusion. It is as though he feels he has not had any warrant for giving us those sensory particulars although they mean so much to him. They represent a veritable treasure-trove of unused particulars, an unspendable horde which he yet feels moved to display. There is a similar moment in 'The Snows of Kilimanjaro' where the dying writer thinks over those things which he had not written about and which somehow could not be committed to paper. I give only a very short sample: 'you could not dictate the Place Contrescarpe where the flower sellers dyed their flowers in the street and the dye ran over the paving where the autobus started and the old men and the women, always drunk on wine and bad marc; and the children with their noses running in the cold; the smell of dirty sweat and poverty and drunkenness at the Café des Amateurs and the whores at the Bal Musette they lived above.'[2] There is a great deal more, all of it taken up with set scenes, perceived fragments, place names, and occasionally very abrupt incidents. This is Hemingway's wealth: meticulously retained sensations of the scattered munificence of the world. Hemingway has Clemens's gift of vivid recollection: he too can 'call it all back and make it as real as it ever was, and as blessed'; and, in these passages at least, he, like Clemens, can do little more with it than 'call it all back'. Once again the problem of form arises. How is the writer to organize, distribute and employ the harvest of valued particulars which the wondering eye has garnered for him? The two pieces quoted manage, by skilful and quite legitimate legerdemain, to bring the details before us with no form but the flow of rapt reminiscence. This interesting phenomenon permits us to speculate on Hemingway's criteria for inclusion: which details did get properly into his work, and why? Or put in another way: what is the function of the registered particular in Hemingway's fiction? Is it just one of a random inventory—as the publishers who rejected the short prose pieces which composed the first *in our time* doubtless thought—or does it have real artistic work to do? To what end does the Hemingway eye work? It will be worth bearing in mind those italicized words: see things clearly and the part, the particular, will represent the whole. Remember Emerson's words: 'the truth-speaker may dismiss all solicitude as to the proportion and congruency of the aggregate of his thoughts, so long as he is a faithful reporter of particular impressions.' Hemingway is repeating, as an artistic principle, what Emerson prescribed as a philosophic strategy: be faithful to the particular and the over-all pattern and meaning will emerge of their own accord. What we must examine is the use Hemingway made of the clear particulars which his naive wondering eye afforded him. Let us take two examples from his short stories, examples of the scrupulous itemization of sensory details, and try to suggest why they are where they are, just those details in just that order:

They were seated in the boat, Nick in the stern, his father rowing. The sun was coming up over the hills. A bass jumped, making a circle in the water. Nick trailed his hand in the water. It felt warm in the sharp chill of the morning.[3]   ('Indian Camp')

There was no breeze came through the open window. The American lady pulled the window-blind down and there was no more sea, even occasionally. On the other side there was glass, then the corridor, then an open window, and outside the window were dusty trees and an oiled road and flat fields of grapes, with grey-stone hills behind them.[4]   ('A Canary for One')

The first passage occurs just after the child has been brought into contact with death for the first time: thus the delight in physical movement, the rising sun, the leaping fish, the touch of water and the feel of morning air are absolutely relevant to the boy's state of mind at that particular moment. It is a moment of intense awareness of the livingness of live things and the delights of the senses. The second passage describes the railway carriage which contains a couple on the point of break-up and an insensitive hard talkative American woman who makes the journey peculiarly agonizing. We learn the facts only at the end; but such passages as this bring home to us the claustrophobic, oppressive feeling in the compartment. The elimination of sea and breeze, the eye listlessly, desperately seeking some outlet through two windows and noting, with that curious lucidity which can come at moments of stifling tension, the details of the outer landscape: being given so much we are given as it were the environmental truth of the situation, as opposed to the psychological truth of it. Not the inward facts, but how the inward facts determine the registering of the outward scene.

One could easily list the particular moments that Hemingway chooses to focus on in his short stories and nearly always they will be found to be moments of crisis, tension and passion. This is not to say that they are epiphanies in Joyce's sense, but rather that they deal with moments of pain, shock, strain, test, moments of emotional heightening of some kind. It may be an ageing courageous bull fighter facing and succumbing to his last bull, it may be a man listening to his wife say that she is leaving him to go off with a woman: the subject matter varies widely, the emotional pitch of the characters is almost uniformly high. And it is at such moments that the details of the encompassing world seem saturated with relevance in an unusually intense way. They do not become symbolic, it is a weakness in the later Hemingway that he pushes them too far in that direction: they can be full of mute menace (as rain, for instance, always is in his stories): but usually they function as the recipients of the characters' intense attention. The character's emotion and the surrounding concrete details inter-permeate. In *A Farewell to Arms* there are at least three detailed accounts of meals, detailed to an extent which would be boring if they were simply meals taken by habit for sustenance. But they occur—immediately before the hero is bombed; while he and Catherine are enjoying a snatched few moments of ecstasy away from the war; and while he is waiting to hear the result of her fatal delivery. In the first case the vividness is retrospective: the moment frozen and etched in the memory before the shattering upheaval. In the other two cases the mundane minutiae are included because the intensity of the hero's emotions has so sharpened his sensory faculties that details are elevated from the mundane to the significant. It is as though anything he touches or smells or sees becomes a temporary reflector, even container, of his emotion. The scrupulous registration of details will give the most accurate morphology of the feeling. Only sensory evidence is veridical, and then only when the accounting senses have been pressured into a state of raw hyper-lucidity. Think of Hemingway's major characters: an emasculated man in love with a near nymphomaniac, a man torn between a ruinous war and a doomed though ecstatic love, a man on a particularly dangerous guerilla mission, a dying soldier terribly in love with life, an old fisherman in pursuit of the biggest fish he has ever seen: all but the last living in countries far from home. What the hero of *For Whom the Bell Tolls* ponders to himself is in some way relevant to them all: 'I know a few things now. I wonder if you only learn them now because you are oversensitized because of the shortness of the time?'[5] Most of Hemingway's characters (and a very large number of major characters in American fiction) exhibit this 'over-sensitization' in the face of the world. In Robert Jordan's own case it is the danger of his mission and the love of Maria that sensitize him, prompting his senses to an almost awed alertness and efficient clarity. For instance, when he is waiting to dynamite the bridge he not only scrutinizes his tactical objective with a crisp military objectivity, his eyes receive whatever nature offers to etch on them. A squirrel for instance:

A squirrel chittered from a pine tree below him and Robert Jordan watched the squirrel come down the tree trunk, stopping on his way down to turn his head and look toward where the man was watching. He saw the squirrel's eyes, small and bright and watched his tail jerk in excitement. Then the squirrel crossed to another tree, moving on the ground in long, small-pawed, tail-exaggerated bounds.[6]

The book abounds in such brilliantly perceived particulars: it is because the sights, smells, sounds and tastes are recorded with such resonant accuracy that the book has such a rich surface texture. It is because it contains little more than that that it lacks any overarching structure. It is interesting to see how Hemingway tries to give his material an externally derived historical significance which the book in fact belies: 'that bridge can be the point on which the future of the human race can turn'[7] argues Jordan to himself to invest his task with a sense of purpose. But Hemingway's and Hemingway's heroes' interest lies elsewhere. They are not interested in the capillary movements of history, in progress, in the slow erosions and rehabilitions of time, in the fall and survival of societies. They are committed to their own moment-by-moment experience and what Jordan says of his relationship with Maria could be said by all of them of their relationship with the world: he intends to 'make up in intensity what the relation will lack in duration and continuity'.[8] And they would agree that if your senses are properly attuned and at work 'it is possible to live as full a life in seventy hours as in seventy years'.[9] And because of this belief in the great truth and value of the intense momentary sensory experience the Hemingway hero is committed to 'the now'. 'You have it *now* and that is all your whole life is; now. There is nothing else than now. There is neither yesterday, certainly, nor is there any tomorrow.'[10] Such

233

an attitude is at bottom indifferent (though not hostile) to the large palpable social historical stirrings around it. Jordan, admittedly, thinks these thoughts within the shadow of a possible death: but in fact the words serve to define an attitude towards experience which is not only shared by all other Hemingway heroes but has also a number of precedents in American literature (as we noted in the introduction and the chapter on Gertrude Stein). And of course it is this elevation of intensity over continuity, the 'now' over history, and the evidence of the senses over the constructs of the mind that determines the whole point of view and strategy of Hemingway's prose and explains his essential preoccupation with what we might call the 'oversensitized hero'.

Having glanced at some of the reasons for Hemingway's concentration on concrete sensory particulars we should now examine in more detail the whole anti-abstract, anti-metaphysical, indeed anti-intellectual tendency of his writing. The famous passage in *A Farewell to Arms* does not need to be requoted in full but let us remind ourselves of the last sentence. 'Abstract words such as glory, honor, courage or hallow were obscene beside the concrete names of villages, the numbers of roads, the names of rivers, the numbers of regiments and the dates.'[11] The interesting thing to note about this is that for Hemingway 'courage' was a quality of major importance. It is the word not the thing that he is objecting to. As we can see for instance, if we take this passage from *Death in the Afternoon*. 'If qualities have odours, the odour of courage to me is the smell of smoked leather or the smell of a frozen road or the smell of the sea when the wind rips the top from a wave. . . .'[12] Abstract concepts only have any meaning for Hemingway if they are translated into sensory particulars. Hemingway's prose is based, among other things, on a 'nausea of untruth' and for him the only verifiable truth is the evidence of the senses. Hence his prose is calculated to resist any tendency towards abstract words which somehow suggest that qualities and meanings have a super-personal life of their own, irrespective of individual incarnation and sensory recognition.

Hemingway denies the Platonic idea of 'Courage'—but there is a certain smell to a brave man, an unmistakable odour to his actions which he will testify to and describe by comparing it to other natural sensations. This, of course, avoids any theoretic analysis of the quality, and it is this avoidance of analytic explanation which is one of the striking aspects of Hemingway's style. Meticulous description takes its place. As Gertrude Stein once affirmed: 'description is explanation'. For Hemingway it might be better to say: description is definition. Let us here examine two more passages on subjects which are most apt for metaphysical speculation, life and death:

Dying was nothing and he had no picture of it nor fear of it in his mind. But living was a field of grain blowing in the wind on the side of a hill. Living was a hawk in the sky. Living was an earthen jar of water in the dust of the threshing with the grain flailed out and the chaff blowing. Living was a horse between your legs and a carbine under one leg and a hill and a valley and a stream with trees along it and the far side of the valley and the hills beyond.[13]

(For Whom the Bell Tolls)

Death is a lot of shit, he thought. It comes to you in small fragments that hardly show where it has entered. It comes, sometimes, atrociously. It can come from unboiled water; an un-pulled-up mosquito boot, or it can come with the great, white-hot, clanging roar we have lived with. It comes in small cracking whispers that precede the noise of the automatic weapon. It can come with the smoke-emitting arc of the grenade, or the sharp, cracking drop of the mortar.[14]

(Across the River and Into the Trees)

In the first piece, to define 'Life' Sordo lists for himself certain life-full moments: no speculations about origins, purposes, values, but cherished memories of the senses, concrete fragments of the seen and relished world which are all he has to put up against the vasts nothingness of non-existence. In the second piece the ageing colonel can only get at 'Death' by recalling the numerous specific instances and occasions of its coming. Sordo, asking himself about Life, thinks of a hawk in the sky: the colonel, asking himself about Death, thinks of shrapnel in the air. This is how the Hemingway hero prefers to think, for this much at least is true.

We said, of the Transcendentalists, that they scrutinized the minute particulars of the world because they believed that any such particular could act as a sort of avenue through which the eye could pass, penetrating to the vast hinterland of coherent cosmic benevolence. Hemingway's characters scrutinize particulars for rather different reasons. To try and pin these reasons down it will help us to recall one of Hemingway's best short stories, 'A Clean, Well-Lighted Place'. This story concerns itself simply with two waiters discussing an old man who likes to sit late at night drinking in their clean, well-lit cafe. The young waiter finds him a mere nuisance, but the old waiter understands him and his desire to stay at the cafe late. Because he too is at one 'with all those who do not want to go to bed. With all those who need a light for the night'.[15] He respects the old man because of his clean and decorous behaviour: 'This old man is clean. He drinks without spilling. Even now, drunk.'[16]—and he starts to meditate on the nature of his own dislike of the darkness. 'What did he fear? It was not fear or dread. It was a nothing that he knew too well. It was all a nothing and a man was nothing too. It was only that and light was all it needed and a certain cleanness and order.'[17]

This is as near to a metaphysic as Hemingway ever presents to us satisfactorily, and if we had only this hint it should illumine for us a great deal that is important in his work. For the old waiter, for Hemingway, Existence is an incomprehensible void inhabited by concrete particulars perceptible to the senses. In place of vague consoling speculations about the meaning of the infinite nothingness which surrounds human life, the Hemingway hero prefers to overcome his horror of vacancy by a ritual of orderliness and cleanliness in small things. In the living, in the writing. Only this will give him any meaning. When Jordan discovers in himself a yearning for 'small and regular things'[18] he has moved a long way towards this crucial discovery. And we can see the old waiter's philosophy in action at the death of the colonel in *Across the River and into the Trees*. Knowing his death is imminent he decides to get into the back seat of the car, with all the animal instinct for the dignity of privacy at moments of physical crisis. His last act—his last comment to the world, in effect—is extremely eloquent. More eloquent than his words of instruction to the driver. 'That was the last thing the Colonel ever said. But he made the back seat all right and he shut the door. He shut it carefully and well.'[19] (Cf. also the suicide of Loyola in *Death in the Afternoon*: 'he dived well and cleanly with his hands tied while they walked with him praying.')[20] No spillage, no sloppiness, no outcry or mess: rather, a continuing attachment to that essential ritual of meticulousness in practical details which compose the only aspect of life on which the Hemingway hero can pin his faith. You don't know where you're going, but you shut the door cleanly behind you. Under the circumstances —the circumstances of vanished belief—it is all you can do.

Death is the dissolution into nothingness. As the dying writer in 'Snows of Kilimanjaro' discovers: 'And just then it occurred to him that he was going to die. It came with a rush; not as a rush of water nor of wind; but of a sudden evil-smelling emptiness. . . .'[21] The moment of death, for the Hemingway hero, is the testing moment when he is agonizingly poised between the wondrous plenitude of the world and the oncoming smell of black emptiness. The only way he can maintain himself is by orienting himself in the world just as he had done during his life. Thus in 'A Way You'll Never Be' Nick Adams, thinking he is dying, fights to get the facts of his past straight and in order. 'If it didn't get so damned mixed up he could follow it all right. That was why he noticed everything in such detail to keep it all straight so he would know just where he was. . . .'[22] More remarkable is Jordan's death as he waits for the opposing soldiers to appear. He knows death is a matter of moments—and his task is to keep a proper inner control.

Think about Montana. *I can't.* Think about Madrid. *I can't.* Think about a cool drink of water. *All right.* That's what it will be like.

Like a cool drink of water. *You're a liar.* It will just be nothing. That's all it will be. Just nothing. Then do it. *Do it.* Do it now. It's all right to do it now.[23]

But no matter how justified suicide might appear to the sceptical mind it betokens a terrible collapse of achieved stance for the Hemingway hero: earth-bound, earth-committed, he must await earth's recall and not anticipate it. As Jordan thinks to himself, recalling his father who committed suicide: 'Anyone has a right to do it. . . . But it isn't a good thing to do. I understand it, but I do not approve of it. *Lache* was the word.'[24] (A passage which makes Hemingway's own suicide unusually terrible, even though he did do it to avoid the mess and indignity of failing senses and senile weakness.) So Jordan settles himself down for one more soldierly act of defiance and usefulness. Having set himself a proper task he regains control of himself. 'He was completely integrated now and he took a good long look at everything. Then he looked up at the sky. There were big white clouds in it. He touched the palm of his hand against the pine needles where he lay and he touched the bark of the pine trunk that he lay behind.'[25]

That last act of communion is one of the most moving things in Hemingway: the senses taking their farewell from all the truth they have ever known; the wounded individual, his dignity unimpaired, preparing himself for the slide into nothingness with a final feel of the earth. Jordan takes death 'straight',[26] without religion, his attitude to life summed up with poignant simplicity as he says to himself: 'It is only missing it that's bad.'[27] This is all far more eloquent than the slangy metaphysics of the justifiably outraged hero of *A Farewell to Arms*: 'They threw you in and told you the rules and the first time they caught you off base they killed you.'[28] In thinking like this the hero has detached himself from the only certainties, the certainties of the senses. He speaks more profoundly than he realizes when, earlier in the book, he decides: 'I was not made to think.'[29] Thought has a way of spiralling up and away from our concrete surroundings. That is why at various key points in *The Old Man and the*

Sea the fisherman fights against the onset of thought. The following three quotations come from various parts of the book but they add up to an important tenet in Hemingway's creed. 'He rested sitting on the unstepped mast and sail and tried not to think but only to endure. . . . There is no sense in being anything but practical though, he thought.'[30] . . .'Think of what you can do with what there is.'[31] A basic distinction must be made between the ordinary intelligence which interprets difficulties, formulates intentions, and modifies actions, etc.; and the sort of vague speculation, metaphysical or theological, etc., which the fisherman is countering. It is, of course, only this latter form of thought which the Hemingway hero tries to avoid. The significant similarity of that last intention with the pragmatist line of thought need only be noted here. The point is that for the Hemingway hero only concrete things are 'true' and only practical tasks efficiently undertaken and rigorously seen through offer any meaning and salvation: salvation from the crippling and undermining sense of nothingness which is his perpetual nightmare. This notion of what we might call the pragmatic redemption of life is nicely illustrated in *The Sun Also Rises* when Jake goes out of his way to explain all the technicalities of bullfighting to Brett 'so that it became more something that was going on with a definite end, and less of a spectacle with unexplained horrors'.[32] One could use that as a summary of the intention of Hemingway's prose and the behaviour of his heroes. Life, for Hemingway, is all too often a 'spectacle with unexplained horrors': think of the amount of sheer physical suffering and human damage and cruelly capricious disaster there is in his work. The ambition, the necessary thing, is to try and make it, momentarily at least, 'something that was going on with a definite end'. Getting a gun into position, handling a fishing boat properly, even closing a car door—such things offer a temporary defence against the darkness: every functional grip on the concrete world creates an area of light, a small and saving illusion of meaningfulness. (A comparison with Conrad could be advanced here.)

An interesting and key passage occurs in *The Sun Also Rises*.

Jake is meditating to himself on the meaning of the world. 'Perhaps as you went along you did learn something. I did not care what it was all about. All I wanted to know was how to live in it. Maybe if you found out how to live in it you learned from that what it was all about.'³³ That last sentence reveals more of a philosophy than is at first apparent. It points not only to the particular Hemingway ethic—'grace under pressure'—but also suggests that the only meaning to be found lies in the relationship of man to the environment he is immersed in. And to learn how to *live in it* it is essential first of all to learn how to *look at it*. The proper sort of visual relationship with the world is neatly brought out in the same book by a comparison between Jake and Cohn's response to a Spanish cathedral. Cohn is the Hemingway anti-hero: he breaks every rule in the book and it is surely intentional that even his way of looking at the world is shown to be very different from Jake's, particularly as Hemingway has gone to some pains to tell us that Cohn educated his responses according to the most debased romantic pretentious literature. 'We went out into the street again and took a look at the cathedral. Cohn made some remark about it being a very good example of something or other, I forget what. It seemed like a nice cathedral, nice and dim, like Spanish churches.'³⁴ Cohn sees the cathedral through the orthodox learned concepts: Jake limits himself to his own sensory responses. Later his response to the interior of the cathedral is reminiscent of Huck Finn's tone of voice. 'It was dim and dark and the pillars went high up, and there were people praying, and it smelt of incense, and there were some wonderful big windows.'³⁵ Here again is the wandering, wondering eye; the intensely personal vibration in face of concrete phenomena; the priority given to the itemizing senses over the classifying mind. Another, not so different, example of this preferred mode of vision can be taken from *Across the River and Into the Trees*. The colonel reminisces about past battles. 'All that winter, with a bad sore throat, he had killed men who came, wearing the stick bombs hooked up on a harness under their shoulders with the heavy, calf-hide packs and the bucket helmets.

They were the enemy.'[36] The 'enemy' is a concept which slips through our minds too easily, leaving no definite marks. The colonel breaks the generalizing word down into its concrete manifestations. 'Baroque' (if that was Cohn's word) and 'enemy' are, alike, words which carry within them very little of the bullion of sensory evidence. Jake and the Colonel avoid them, preferring to deal with the multiple component details with which the senses have to work.

Having noted this exclusive trust in the single perceptual event we can move on to consider two important aspects of Hemingway's work: the related problems of how to see and how to experience. The bull-fighter provided Hemingway with a metaphor of life-long validity. The isolated individual confronting the challenge of a powerful and hostile nature, pitting his craft and character against it to the point of death: such is the Hemingway hero as well as the toreador. And the way the toreador uses his eyes at the moment of crisis will have relevance for all other Hemingway characters. Thus in 'The Undefeated' we read: 'Walking forward, watching the bull's feet, *he saw successively* his eyes, his wet muzzle, and the wide, forward-pointing spread of his horns'[37] [my italics]. 'He saw successively ...'—not a writer's mannerism but a fighter's strategy, an essential means of orientation at the crucial and demanding moment. Sensations should not be collapsed together and pressed into generalizations: rather they are to be delicately and carefully separated out and each given their individual contours. (Stein's theories, of course, corroborate and clarify this intention.) Experience should be as little pre-judged as possible. Jordan is connected with the Communist party, but this allegiance is not allowed to prejudice his senses: 'nobody owned his mind, nor his faculties for seeing and hearing, and if he were going to form judgments he would form them afterwards'.[38] It is as though the intimacy between the world and the eye was something holy and not to be disturbed by any nagging interruptions from the prescribing mind. Once again, judgement is postponed in the interests of wonder. In this connection the Colonel's game in

Venice is relevant. He likes to try and get from one part of the city to another without having recourse to any mathematical calculations in the way of counting streets, etc. 'It is a sort of *solitaire ambulante* and what you win is the happiness of your eye and heart.'[39] It is a way of not taking reality for granted, of not substituting habit and number for the ever-renewed activity of the eye. It is a way of forcing your senses to travel *through* the dense and dazzling medium of the world instead of merely sliding over it, blind, in a hurry to be at the next rendezvous. Significantly Hemingway says, of the Colonel's way of looking at the market, that it was 'as though he were enjoying the Dutch painters, whose names no one remembers, who painted, in perfection of detail, all things you shot, or that were eatable'.[40] What the bull-fighter does for strategic reasons, the retired colonel now does for aesthetic ones: but either way the senses are at full stretch, with a maximum of attention, and a minimum of interfering pre-conceptions. It is a visual stance related to Thoreau's ideal of 'seeing without looking'. It was because Hemingway thought that this was the only way to get at 'the truth'—such truth as he would give any credence to—that he made use of the young Nick Adams in many of his early stories, though not, we should note, as a naive narrator. Having perfected a vernacular style he can dispense with a vernacular 'voice'. What Hemingway makes use of is Nick's 'first chastity of mind'[41] which wonderingly notes the details without being tempted away into the blurring habits of theorizing. If there is a symbolic 'first man in the world' hidden inside the name 'Adams' it is only because Nick retains that essential integrity of the senses even when confronted with the most brutal disillusioning scenes. He is the ideal Hemingway 'eye' and if, for example, you look at the first few paragraphs of 'A Way You'll Never Be', which offer a scrupu-lously and horrifyingly detailed picture of a battlefield, you will notice that they are prefaced by the phrase 'Nicholas Adams saw'.[42] The essential virtue of this sort of eye is best expressed in Jordan's admonition to himself while he awaits his death. 'Keep it accurate, he said. Quite accurate.'[43] Accurate in the parts, we might add, accurate as far as the senses can honestly testify. No further. The rest is nada.

This explains, from another angle, why so much of Hemingway's prose is restricted to scenery and environment, for this is the one known and knowable quantity in any situation: this the unprejudiced eye can quite properly assimilate, whereas there are no senses which can so surely annotate the dubious internality of the people involved in the scene. Hemingway wrote in *The Green Hills of Africa*: 'But if I ever write anything about this it will just be landscape painting until I know something about it. Your first seeing of a country is a very valuable one.'[44] The scenery—the first seeing: a lot of what is really good in Hemingway is based on these two factors. It is interesting to recall that both of Hemingway's last ageing heroes indulge in reveries connected with a feeling for 'place'. The Colonel's dreams, for instance, are usually about places. 'We live by accidents or terrain, you know. And terrain is what remains in the dreaming part of your mind.'[45] And the old fisherman's dreams: 'He no longer dreamed of storms, nor of women, nor of great occurrences nor of great fish, nor fights, nor contests of strength, nor of his wife. He only dreamed of places now and of the lions on the beach.'[46] The lions are an important part of his personal mythology—nature, beautiful, strong, and at play—but for the rest: places. Because, we might infer, what the senses remember and retain of the external world forms a firm residue of truth in the heart and mind of man. Given Hemingway's philosophy it follows that for him only concrete things, perceptible manifestations of nature, have certain value: 'the earth abideth forever'[47] is the important phrase from Ecclesiastes which prefaces *The Sun Also Rises*. Thus when any Hemingway hero starts to indulge his memory it instinctively seeks back, not for episodic continuity or vague congenial atmospherics, but simply for things the senses had registered and then stored away, for 'little things' in Anderson's phrase. Thus, for example, Robert Jordan finds consolation in calling back to mind 'something concrete and practical';[48] it may be his Grandfather's well-oiled sabre, or the arrows his father kept in his office 'and

243

how the bundle of shafts felt when you closed your hand around them'.[49] And this is not useless day-dreaming. Jordan elsewhere thinks of 'the confidence that had come from thinking back to concrete things'.[50] A clearly recalled concrete impression was an aid to self-possession. When Nick Adams thinks he might be dying ('Now I Lay Me') his mind will only dwell on accurate retained impressions; whatever blurs is abandoned. 'I would think of a trout stream I had fished along when I was a boy and fish its whole length very carefully in my mind; fishing very carefully under all the logs, all the turns of the bank, the deep holes and the clear shallow stretches, sometimes catching trout and sometimes losing them.'[51] He thinks about other things occasionally: 'Finally, though, I went back to trout-fishing, because I found that I could remember all the streams and there was always something new about them, while the girls, after I had thought about them a few times, blurred and I could not call them into my mind and finally they all blurred and all became rather the same and I gave up thinking about them almost altogether.'[52] When memories start to run into each other they lose that sharp distinctness which serves to guarantee the authenticity of the unique and valued instant. As Hemingway himself states it in *Green Hills of Africa* it is imperative 'that one memory does not destroy another'.[53] Rather they should be kept separate and thus preserved with a sort of cordon sanitaire round them guarding against contamination and confusion. In the African book itself the narrator, between hunts, starts to recall his Paris life, and does so in a manner analogous to all the other Hemingway heroes we have mentioned:

and I remember the look of that apartment, how it was arranged, and the wall paper, and instead we had taken the upstairs of the pavilion in Notre Dame des Champs in the courtyard with the sawmill (*and the sudden whine of the saw, the smell of sawdust and the chestnut tree over the roof with a mad woman downstairs*)[54]

and so on—just like the last chapter of *Death in the Afternoon*. This is how the Hemingway hero remembers, or not at all.

We have considered how the Hemingway hero sees and recalls those sights; we should now add something about his manner of experiencing the world. And the first essential condition of true experience is that he should be alone. Let us look again at Robert Jordan, the Hemingway hero who comes nearest to involving himself significantly with history, via the communist party. And to see his attitudes in their most revealing context let us consider this quotation from the communist critic George Lukacs. He wrote: 'the developmental tendencies of history partake of a higher reality than the "facts" of mere experience'.[55] This is the orthodox Marxist belief: that there is a higher, objective 'truth' contained in the movements of history which surpasses the 'mere' truth accessible to the senses, the empiric facts of our day-to-day surroundings. Yet it is precisely this kind of 'truth' that Jordan embraces and the higher 'historical' truth which he renounces, or least invests little faith in: 'all people should be left alone and you should interfere with no one. So he believed that, did he? Yes, he believed that. And what about a planned society and the rest of it? That was for the others to do'.[56] Jordan never tries to 'think' the future; instead he intensely 'feels' the present. One example must suffice though every page abounds with them:

They were walking through the heather of the mountain meadow and Robert Jordan *felt* the brushing of the heather against his legs, *felt* the weight of his pistol in its holster against his thigh, *felt* the sun on his head, *felt* the breeze from the snow of the mountain peaks cool on his back, and, in his hand he *felt* the girl's hand firm and strong, the fingers locked in his.[57] [my italics]

Against the assurance of the felt thing, the consoling artifacts of the intellect fade into irrelevance.

To find any truth a man must be alone, alone with his senses and the seen world. Hence the specific renunciation of social engagement in *Green Hills of Africa*. 'If you serve time for society, democracy, and the other things quite young, and declining any further enlistment make yourself responsible only to yourself, you exchange the pleasant, comforting stench of comrades for *something you can never feel in any other way than by yourself'*[58] [my italics]. This, among other reasons, is why the old fisherman has to be utterly alone when he takes on the big fish.

> My choice was to go there to find him beyond all people. Beyond all people in the world. . . . Aloud he said, 'I wish I had the boy.'
> But you haven't the boy, he thought. You have only yourself.
> . . .[59]

Only what the isolated self can do on its own is valuable, only what the isolated ego can perceive for itself is true. To have any significant experience the Hemingway hero must, in one sense or another, for one reason or another (a wound for instance), be 'beyond all people'. Any peace he makes with the world will be personal rather than social, not communal but 'separate'.[60] Having discussed the relationship between the hero and the world in Hemingway's work I want now to suggest how this had a direct shaping influence on the prose style of his work. For since syntax is simply vision in action, the preferred manner of arranging perceptions, we can expect to find the ethics of the eye reflected in the order of the words. And one of the most notable aspects of Hemingway's prose is the way it avoids summary and insists on recording sequences in detail. A good example is this passage from *The Sun Also Rises*:

> After a while we came out of the mountains, and there were trees along both sides of the road, and a stream and ripe fields of grain, and the road went on, very white and straight ahead, and then lifted to a little rise, and off on the left was a hill with an old castle, with buildings close around it and a field of grain going right up to the walls and shifting in the wind. I was up in front with the driver and I turned around. Robert Cohn was asleep, but Bill looked and nodded his head.[61]

Jake notes everything carefully, reverently, meticulously as the bus travels through the beautiful countryside: each glimpse is caught in its transient perfection. Cohn, typically, lacks the Hemingway eye and reveals his insensitivity by sleeping. But Bill understands; no words need to be exchanged between people who know how to look at the natural world. And the prose makes permanent the attentive wonder of the senses: it mimes out the whole process, impression by impression. How far Hemingway will take this can be demonstrated by such examples as the following: 'The red door of the ring went shut, the crowd on the outside balconies of the bull-ring were pressing through to the inside, there was a shout, then another shout.'[62] Not 'there were some shouts': that would be summary, a collapsing together of separate moments. The pause in reality must reappear in the prose. It was part of the truth of things. This pursuit of the exact progress of the senses is everywhere in evidence in Hemingway, even in his earliest work, as for example in the story 'The Three-Day Blow'. 'They stood together, looking out across the country, down over the orchard, beyond the road, across the lower fields and the woods of the point to the lake.'[63] Out, down, beyond, across—as the eye shifts its direction and focus, the prose follows it. As a result the prose very often has recourse to the words 'then' and 'and', and participles: these become important structural factors. They serve to thrust the reader much closer to the actual moment.

Here we should quote again from Robert Jordan: 'but if there is only now, why then now is the thing to praise and I am very happy with it.'[64] Hemingway's practice of unravelling the instant, of hugging the details of a sequence with his whole attention, is not merely the developed habit of a graphic news reporter, no matter how much Hemingway owes to his early journalism. It is a reflection of his faith in the ultimate veracity of the attuned and operating senses and the unsurpassable value of the registered 'now'. As Jordan realizes: '*Now*, it has a funny sound to be a whole world and your life.'[65] A moment is 'a whole world': this is why Hemingway explores its geography with such delicate care. Perhaps we can understand why Hemingway's prose always works to extract and arrest the significant fragments from the endless continuum of sense impressions which constitutes experience. His unflagging efforts to discover and hold 'the real thing, the sequence of motion and fact which made the emotion'[66] constitute a creed and not a gimmick. Hemingway's style has been called 'matter-of-fact' as though its laconic understatement was its main achievement: but we could more accurately rephrase that and say his style was after the facts of matter, those items of the material world which prompted and provoked the attention of his characters. In this he could be compared with Thoreau who, we recall, also made it his aim to 'front only the essential facts', to ascertain 'the case that is'. And it is surely significant that in Hemingway's later work the facts tended to become fabulous, to expand into myth—just as Thoreau asserted they would do if seen properly.

Hemingway wanted to 'isolate and state' the facts not out of mere documentary interest, but because of his conviction that only thus could you preserve and bestow permanence upon those important moments when a man's senses confronted the world and responded to it with maximum emotion and honesty. To try and state the emotion as opposed to that which provoked it seemed to Hemingway a misconceived undertaking. His ironic comments on 'erectile' writing were aimed at that sort of subjective romantic-mysticism which distorts a man's vision of reality. For when a man is in this febrile state 'all objects look different. They look slightly larger, more mysterious, and vaguely blurred.'[67] Blurred writing is the ultimate aesthetic sin for it constitutes an irreverence towards the external world and probably indicates an internal mendacity and self-deception. This is what is implied in his cryptic phrase: 'Prose is architecture, not interior decoration, and the Baroque is over.'[68] 'Baroque' here is used to cover that sort of writing where the author has behaved 'egotistically', either by inserting his ideas in the form of prolonged intellectual discussions, or by a display of metaphorical pyrotechnics which is not purely functional to the work in hand. It is perhaps an ill-chosen word and certainly it indicates a rather narrow approach to literature. But at least Hemingway was sincere and consistent: prose should aim at depicting the external world (architecture) and not be abused in the interests of self-display (interior decoration). Hemingway valued perception more than inflated self-generated excitement in writing: his interest was not in the subjective self which makes a world of its own, but in the objective world which makes and moves the outward-looking self. This is not to say that he was a mere positivist with no values or illusions to mobilize his attention: the aim is rather to continually check what we believe in against what we can see. Hemingway would agree with the ageing colonel : 'you can cut out everything phony about the illusion as though you would cut it with a straight-edge razor.'[69] One is reminded of Blake's advice to 'circumcise away the indefinite'.

His concern, then, with edge, clarity, distinct contours, and accuracy is profoundly connected with his whole attitude towards life. It is no mere coincidence that we can find the best clues to Hemingway's ideal of 'style' in his descriptions of the bull-fighter and the fisherman. Consider the praise for Romero's manner of fighting in *The Sun Also Rises*:

Romero never made any contortions, always it was straight and pure and natural in line. . . . Romero's bull-fighting gave real emotion, because he kept the absolute purity of line in his movements and always quietly and calmly let the horns pass him close each time. He did not have to emphasise their closeness. . . . Romero had the old thing, the holding of his purity of line through the maximum of exposure. . . . It was all so slow and so controlled.[70]

Add to that these comments from *Death in the Afternoon*. Bravery, asserts Hemingway, 'should be a quality whose presence permits the fighter to perform all acts he chooses to attempt, unhampered by apprehension. It is not something to club the public with'.[71] And later: 'Killing cleanly and in a way which gives you aesthetic pleasure and pride has always been one of the greatest enjoyments of a part of the human race.'[72] If we also bear in mind the old fisherman who does everything 'as cleanly as possible',[73] who elevates 'precision'[74] into an ethic and who asserts 'It is better to be lucky. But I would rather be exact'[75]—then we have a sufficient vocabulary to discuss Hemingway's prose. Without any strain the bull and the fish can be seen as representative of the experience of the world which the artist has to confront and master—beautiful, powerful, and dangerous; sometimes fatal to the challenger, the man seeking to dominate through his 'craft'. Those who do manage to kill the bull, land the fish, must employ cleanliness and precision (we should here remember the old man in the café for whom these virtues were the sole source of consolation in life): there must be no false histrionics, no mere flourishes, no eye-catching exhibitionism. Every gesture must be absolutely focused on the job in hand: every move must be unhurried, unhampered, and controlled. The beauty and vitality of a work of art will depend on the maximum exposure of the artist to experience, the linear clarity and purity with which he gradually asserts his control over the experience, and the exhilarating cleanliness and exactitude with which he finally demonstrates his mastery over his material in 'the kill'. The idea of maintaining a 'purity of line through the maximum exposure' applies equally to Hemingway's prose and Romero's bull-fighting.

With all this in mind we can reconsider those prose sketches which originally formed the book *in our time* and subsequently served as contrasting prefaces to the short stories which made up the revised *In Our Time*. They do not represent Hemingway's most important work but in some ways they were his most original creations. They all deal with scenes of violence, usually either connected with war or with bull-fighting. From one point of view they are early studies of how, by selection, repetition, spacing and patterning, the vernacular could be turned into an impersonal objective style as opposed to a confessional subjective voice. Also they are exercises in the unhysterical treatment of horror, attempts to achieve maximum factual clarity when confronted by scenes which are most calculated to stimulate a writer to emotional rhetoric. They are not cold or indifferent; rather they attempt to find just those facts which first made the writer's emotion and which will recreate that emotion in the reader. They try to make us 'see' it, because if we see it in the proper way we will feel about it in the proper manner. To this end they employ two of Hemingway's most important stylistic strategies. What he calls 'the profundity of unseen detail' and described with the famous metaphor of the iceberg,[76] and what he referred to when he said to the old lady (in *Death in the After-noon*) 'It is years since I added the wow to the end of a story'.[77] We might rephrase this latter as the avoidance of contrived climax. If the writer selects the right details he will activate the power of a large number of other details without having to enumerate them: the economy of the art will increase the impact of the material. And the material is in itself so significant that it needs no literary devices to re-shape it to secure a stock response. That is the burden of these two tenets of Hemingway's faith. Here is one of those prose sketches:

They shot the six cabinet ministers at half-past six in the morning against the wall of a hospital. There were pools of water in the court-yard. There were wet dead leaves on the paving of the courtyard. It rained hard. All the shutters of the hospital were nailed shut. One of the ministers was sick with typhoid. Two soldiers carried him down-stairs and out into the rain. They tried to hold him up against the wall but he sat down in a puddle of water. The other five stood very quietly against the wall. Finally the officer told the soldiers it was no good trying to make him stand up. When they fired the first volley he was sitting down in the water with his head on his knees.[78]

The rigour of selection is extreme: the messy business of a squalid execution is reduced to a few arrested particulars, denuded down to its environmental essentials, those which somehow are responsible for the quality of the incident. We are not told of a man's misery and fear: we do see him sitting in a puddle with dead leaves and blind windows around him. What is interesting to note is that the purity of the line somehow both emphasizes and compensates for the impurity of the material. To have it stilled, focused and mastered like that testifies to some radical honesty of the eye. The strategy is that of the naive eye which records without comment, seemingly without full comprehension, and which therefore catches the living details in the quick, before any rhetoric of shame or disgust has intervened. Art can never miti-gate real horrors, but there is a way of looking at them which consoles us by its unblinking integrity and which at the same time shows us the horror in full without 'clubbing' us with it. Hemingway at his best can do that. On the other hand it must be pointed out that a complete reliance on a selection of details to stimulate a major emotion—such as pity, terror—can come dangerously close to sentimentality, that sentimentality of 'little things' we noted in Anderson. For instance one of the sketches which deals with a chaotic retreat ends like this: 'Women and kids were in the carts couched with mattresses, mirrors, sewing machines, bundles. There was a woman having a kid with a young girl holding a blanket over her and crying. Scared sick looking at it. It rained all through the evacuation.'[79] This comes close to that sort of journalism which when, for instance, writing up a train crash, selects one or two 'moving' details to achieve a quick front-page pathos. No one questions the truth of it, but somehow we feel our emotions are being too crudely roused, we resent the facility with which we are shocked, we feel that the very material which makes us feel sick is being cheapened by such improper synecdoche. For there is certainly a way of making the part stand for the whole which is debasing. Hemingway is not guilty of this, but there is that in his style which occasionally moves in that direction. It is a risk any writer must run if he refuses to avail himself of complex conceptual thought and the whole range of analysing, comparing, and placing powers which the fine intellect has at its disposal. It is an honourable risk, but the hazards are very real; not only for the artist trying to write, but also for the man trying to live. This is not the place to discuss Hemingway's code, his scale of values, his ethics: but if there is a simplifying tendency to them, if we feel human conduct cannot be so easily assessed and reduced as Hemingway's categories will allow, part of the reason must be that he tried to attend only to his senses. The disregard of mind not only sharpened those senses until they were a miraculously sensitive instrument, it also imposed a great strain on them, with the result that the range of his emotional response stayed small—either sensuous contentment (fun, ecstasy) or a sort of stunned shock and disillusioned horror which just manages to conceal itself behind the compacted concrete details of the prose. This combination of wonder and horror is very common in American literature.

Most of what we have said about Hemingway can be seen exemplified in one of his finest short stories—'Big Two-Hearted River'. Nick Adams returns to the fishing grounds of his youth after some hurtful and shocking experience, presumably war. Both parts of the story annotate this return; the re-establishment of an harmonious and therapeutic intimacy with nature; the flight from bad memories and unpleasant thoughts; the re-immersion of the senses into the miraculous plentitude of an unspoiled world. He arrives to find a burnt-out territory where there was once a town: but where man's objects are transient, nature is permanent.

The river was there. It swirled against the log piles of the bridge. Nick looked down into the clear, brown water, colored from the pebbly bottom, and watched the trout keeping themselves steady in the current with wavering fins. As he watched them they changed their positions by quick angles, only to hold steady in the fast water again. Nick watched them a long time. . . . It was a long time since Nick had looked into a stream and seen trout.[80]

The first part of the story covers his slow eager progress towards the river; the river which it is wonderful to find existing, 'permanent and of value'[81] as Hemingway said of another stretch of water in another book. And it is Nick's quiet reverent wonder in face of the seen world that gives this story the air of a sort of improvised and private ritual. 'Nick was glad to get to the river.'[82] Making the camp is done with equal care. The smoothing of the earth, the folding of the blankets, the pegging of the canvas, each act is kept separate, crystallized in a short sentence, religiously attended to—by Nick, by the words. Because a good camp is a 'home',[83] that ever-desired thing which is so basic in Hemingway ('where a man feels at home, outside of where he's born, is where he's meant to go').[84] Nick is back where he should be. 'Already there was something mysterious and home-like. Nick was happy as he crawled inside the tent. . . . It was a good place to camp. He was there, in the good place. He was in his home where

253

he had made it.'[85] The getting of water and the cooking of food are all reproduced with a loving handling of details which recalls Huck Finn's delight in the minutiae of life. Over coffee his mind starts to get active: 'His mind was starting to work. He knew he could choke it because he was tired enough.'[86] After that, like a banished uninvited guest the mind never troubles him again. His senses are in sole command. The second part recreates his first day's fishing, a wonderful gradual merging of man and nature: man on his own—for 'Nick did not like to fish with other men on the river'.[87]

He sat on the logs, smoking, drying in the sun, the sun warm on his back, the river shallow ahead entering the woods, curving into the woods, shallows, light glittering, big water-smooth rocks, cedars along the bank and white birches, the logs warm in the sun, smooth to sit on, without bark, grey to the touch; slowly the feeling of disappointment left him.[88]

The specific disappointment of losing a fish: the larger disappointment, we feel, with all that is bad, cruel and ugly in the world. As his senses and the scene intermingle—the syntax serving to bring them into harmonious proximity—Nick Adams recovers a content, a feeling of at-one-ness with the earth, of which his recent life in the world of men has robbed him. However the menace of deep shadows and infected darkness is still there in the world:

Beyond that the river went into the swamp. . . . In the swamp the banks were bare, the big cedars came together overhead, the sun did not come through, except in patches; in the fast deep water, in the half light, the fishing would be tragic. In the swamp fishing was a tragic adventure. Nick did not want it.[89]

That is the dark barren place, the earthly terrain of nada, the opposite of the clean well-lighted place which, in this case, is not a café but simply the sun-drenched world offering its sharp and well-lit particulars to the disciple's reverent eye. It is this patch of dismal foreboding shadow in the story which gives a sort of retroactive enhancement to the concrete details of the world which Nick has been so lovingly appropriating with his sensitized attention. Seen against the dark depths of the swamp the well-lit facts become vivid values. For the swamp is a warning hint of many things: of growing up, of disillusion, of that territory 'across the river and into the trees', death and nada itself. Because of this ineradicable surrounding threat, Nick seeks to establish contact with the concrete world, by careful touch and by careful sight. In this way he manages to 'give concrete filling to the empty "mine"' in Hegel's terminology, i.e. he fills the mine of consciousness with the positive stuff of existence. By limiting himself to a sort of scrupulous sense-certainty Nick revitalizes his senses, he refurnishes his mind, he replenishes his consciousness with a rich concrete content which will keep the void at bay. And this is why he so carefully relishes and even prolongs, every sensation that nature offers him. 'Nick climbed out onto the meadow and stood, water running down his trousers and out of his shoes, his shoes squelchy. He went over and sat on the logs. *He did not want to rush his sensations any.*'[90] [my italics] That last sentence is one of the most important in the whole of Hemingway. It explains the conduct of his main characters, it explains the structure of his prose, it even hints at his total philosophy. Our sensations of the phenomenological world are the most precious, the most truthful, the most necessary things we have. We must not rush them. That is why, to stress it again, Hemingway's prose is essentially outward-looking, close to the ground, acutely alert in the face of the texture and contours of the objective world, reverently sensitive in its notation of the perceptions of the senses. And Nick's careful re-immersion into the natural real world, as well as recalling Thoreau and Huck Finn, evokes some comparison with D. H. Lawrence's feeling for nature, evidenced in such statements as this from his letters. 'It is a great thing to realize that the original world is still there— perfectly clean and pure.'[91] And Hemingway would probably have agreed with Lawrence when he went on to lament: 'It is this mass of unclean world that we have superimposed on the clean world that we cannot bear.'[92] Hemingway's syntax works to disentangle each precious single sense impression: it is if you like the syntax of sensation. His prose attempts to establish and preserve 'everything a human being can know at each moment of his existence and not an assembling of all his experiences' as Stein put it. By deliberately not hurrying his sensations Hemingway wonderfully attests reality and finds a way of orienting and stabilizing man in a world which is, after all, only a teeming flux surrounded by a gaping nothingness.

In the work of the Transcendentalists two of their major beliefs were that a true reverence for the world would not attempt to tamper with 'the arrangement in the cabinet of creation' and that 'sinners must needs reason; saints behold'. Hemingway covers experiences that the Transcendentalists scarcely conceded the existence of: but basically his attitude is similar to theirs. 'A country was made to be as we found it',[93] he asserted after his African trip. And the old colonel, looking again at Venice, finds it as wonderful as when he 'had seen it first, understanding nothing of it and only knowing that it was beautiful'.[94] A proper reverence for the world precedes intellectual understanding; indeed, attempts to understand it, to reduce it to reason, may lead to a loss of that reverence, a dulling of the sense of beauty. Similarly the concrete natural world is best seen and arranged according to its original topography: man's reworking interference, literally with machines and metaphorically with certain kinds of art, is ultimately a desecration. Ultimately man, civilized man, is the fallen part of a beautiful world. The old fisherman respects the great fish as 'more noble and more able',[95] if less intelligent, than himself: he feels that 'Man is not much beside the great birds and beasts'.[96] Similarly, Hemingway in Africa wrote an indictment of man and his spoliation and ruination of the paradisaical world:

A continent ages quickly once we come. The natives live in harmony with it. But the foreigner destroys. . . . Our people went to America because that was the place to go then. It had been a good country and we had made a bloody mess of it and I would go, now, somewhere else as we had always had the right to go somewhere else and as we

ERNEST HEMINGWAY

had always done. . . . We always went in the old days and there were still good places to go.[97]

Except that there are not any more: apart from odd precarious refuges. Hemingway wanted to follow Huck into unspoiled mythical territories, but for the race as a whole that is no longer possible: as Clemens had felt before him. But Nick Adams, like Huck, has moments when he reachieves that fading rapport with nature, and then the prose of their creators sheds all complexity of thought and follows the naive, wondering eye as it enters into a reverent communion with the earth that abideth forever.

PART IV
HENRY JAMES

'*The active, contributive close-circling wonder, as I have called it, in which the child's identity is guarded and preserved, and which makes her case remarkable exactly by the weight of the tax on it, provides distinction for her, provides vitality and variety, through the operation of the tax—which would have done comparatively little for us hadn't it been monstrous.*'

HENRY JAMES, Preface to *What Maisie Knew*

CHAPTER 14

THE CANDID OUTSIDER

He noted that the water-colours on the walls of the room she sat in had mainly the quality of being naives, and reflected that naïveté in art is like a zero in a number: its importance depends on the figure it is united with.[1]

HENRY JAMES, *The Lesson of the Master*

HENRY JAMES was the first, and still by far the greatest, writer to inquire into the fate of wonder when it is introduced into the clotted complexities of society and the turbulence of time. For James is quite as interested in the naive wondering vision as any American writer. But rather than allow it the passive meditation prescribed by Emerson, James forced it—condemned it, even— to work on exclusively human, social material. None of his characters can withdraw to Walden Pond; none of them can flee 'down river'; none of them are even allowed that saving reimmersion into nature which Nick Adams enjoys by his 'river'. In James's work the naive eye cannot afford to be passive: more than that, he seldom reveals it as being completely authoritative or reliable. It is a point of view with its own special value, pathos and vulnerability: but it is one point of view among others. It is never the only, or even the prevailing perspective. Thus it is worth noting from the outset that although James created many literary children, he rarely let one of them speak for him- or herself: he never ceded his narrative prerogative to a naive character. The tactical and technical reasons for this we can examine later: here I just want to stress that in his work the naive point of view is never the only, or even the prevailing perspective. For whereas Emerson believed in a *uni*verse, the profound unity of which could be discerned by an innocent humility of vision; James, if we may borrow a term from his brother, believed in a *multi*verse,

261

the multiplicity of which is testified to by the variety of interpretations one phenomenon can provoke. Proust's felicitous
sentence—'The universe is true for us all and dissimilar to each
of us'—would have been perfectly understood by James, for,
like Proust, he too believed that there is 'not one universe, there
are millions, almost as many as the number of human eyes and
brains in existence, that awake every morning'. (One can see
James exploiting this notion very simply in the story called
'The Point of View'.) James made use of 'naïveté' from first to
last, from Daisy Miller to Maggie Verver, but the fruitful zero is
always surrounded by a cluster of 'numbers'—characters more
weighty with experience, more identifiable by appetite, more
fixed in prejudice than the buoyant, valuable yet vulnerable zero.
Number and zero constantly serve to place each other, to form a
complex number, finally coming to rest in a configuration which
gives a relative contextual significance to each, which each in his
separateness could not have discerned.

To see how James departed from the Emersonian view of the
world it is revealing to turn to a review he wrote of Cabot's
Memoir of Emerson in 1887. Claiming that 'we know a man
imperfectly until we know his society'[2] James points to the
'singular impression of paleness', the want of colour, which the
book reveals. And the pallor of the book represents precisely
the shortcoming of the society of which Emerson was a member.
In Emerson's own life there were no 'passions, alternations,
affairs, adventures':[3] in his society 'the bribes and lures, the
beguilements and prizes, were few.'[4]

We seem to see the circumstances of our author's origin, immediate
and remote, in a kind of high, vertical moral light, the brightness of a
society at once very simple and very responsible. The rare singleness
that was in his nature (so that he was *all* the warning moral voice,
without distraction or counter-solicitation), was also in the stock he
sprang from. . . .[5]

Although 'he was introduced to a more complicated world'—
on three visits to Europe—'his spirit, his moral taste, as it were,
abode always within the undecorated walls of his youth'.[6]

James's point in all this is that 'the will, in the old New England society, was a clue without a labyrinth'.[7] He elaborates this most significantly, going on to emphasize the curious fate of 'the primitive New England character' and 'its queer search for something to expend itself upon'. Thinking of that character and that society we get, writes James, 'the impression of a conscience gasping in the void, panting for sensations, with something of the movement of a landed fish'.[8] In such a barren, colourless society a man like Emerson dwelt 'with a ripe unconsciousness of evil'[9] and thus could develop 'a special capacity for moral experience—always that and only that'.[10] (James, by the way, was still complaining of the colourlessness of American life when he revisited it in later years—see *The American Scene*.) A moral sense with no vision of evil; a conscience with no confronting sensations to work on; a fish without an element; a clue without a labyrinth—such was the Emersonian, the New England mind. And one can see at once that James decided to take that conscience and push it into a labyrinth, dazzle it with impressions, engulf it with sensations, bewilder it with alternatives, distract it with counter-solicitations. The Emersonian vision was removed from the thin vertical simple light in which it could thrive without challenge, and introduced into a complex society. The gasping fish was made to swim—even to drowning—and in this context it is notable how very often James has recourse to images of water, swimming, and floating, to describe the difficulties of living and self-orientation in a complex society. More than one Jamesian protagonist is 'swamped' by waves of novel sensations. It is thus that the unexpended conscience is stimulated to maximum activity. In place of the sort of untroubled self-reliance in a vacuum which Emerson represented, James shows us characters desperately trying to orient themselves in novel and richly bewildering circumstances. We watch them trying to make correct inferences, trying to read the signs aright, quickly weighing alternatives, assessing other people's knowledge, sifting various and perhaps contradictory impressions; and finally making decisions which are momentous perhaps only because of

263

the amount of deliberation that preceded them. There is a very good case, for instance, for seeing Isabel Archer as a true Emersonian whose self-reliant mind is dislodged from a static timeless isolation and forced to move into time and society, perhaps to her ultimate destruction. Where Emerson advocated and practised a passive serenity, James developed a strategy of bewilderment. This is a key word in his critical writing and he imagines the ideal reader demanding the following: 'Give us in the persons represented, the subjects of bewilderment (that bewilderment without which there would be no question of an issue or of the fact of suspense) as much experience as possible'.[11] James alludes confidently to something Emerson would not have understood, namely 'our own precious liability to fall into traps and be bewildered'.[12]

He found precedent for his preoccupation with the labyrinth in Hawthorne, and, in writing his critical biography of him, James fastens on his concentration on 'the moral and spiritual maze'. Revealingly he applauds Hawthorne's imagination which is 'always engaged in a game of hide and seek in the region in which it seemed to him that the game could best be played—among the shadows and substructions, the dark-based pillars and supports of our moral nature'.[13] And in a memorable sentence he wrote: 'Emerson, as a sort of spiritual sun-worshipper, could have attached but a moderate value to Hawthorne's cat-like faculty of seeing in the dark.'[14] Images of dark corridors, mazes, labyrinths, mines, wells, etc., proliferate throughout James's work and clearly he himself developed the cat-like faculty he ascribed to Hawthorne. Yet despite his admiration for Hawthorne's work, it was too stark, too remote, too insistently allegorical, too suprasocial to satisfy James's mind which focused best on the minute complexities of social living. America lacked the 'complex social machinery' which he, as a writer, needed to provide him with his themes, so he turned to 'the denser, richer, warmer European spectacle'.[15] If only to provide a deep element for those naive 'landed fish' who were, after all, his fellow-countrymen.

From a distance the theme of the blank, quivering American

sensibility immersed and involved in the European order seems indeed to be basic to James's fiction. From the wide-eyed, socially non-comprehending candour of Daisy Miller to the perpetually open eyes of Adam Verver; from Daisy Miller's death in the miasmic atmosphere of Rome to Milly Theale's turning to the wall in Venice; from the succumbing of Roderick Hudson to the suicide of Grace Mavis on board the 'Patagonia'; from the undamaged return of Christopher Newman to the perverse yet enlightened renunciation of Lambert Strether; from the confident dismissal of Europeans by Bessy Alden and Pandora, through the precarious victory of Francie Dosson, on to the new kind of mastery of a shattered European society as managed by Mrs Gracedew and Maggie Verver: in all these repeated and developed themes the dramatic interlocking of a new sensibility with an old civilization is the fulcrum. In his introduction to *The Reverberator* James was very explicit about the discerned possibilities of this theme, the 'lurid contrast' of the two types, the unpreparedness of the American and the amount of necessary response called forth by a masterful and possibly threatening European society. More interestingly he singles out 'the younger, the youngest' of his American types and suggests how 'their share of the characteristic blankness underwent what one might call a sea-change'. 'Conscious of so few things in the world, these unprecedented creatures—since that is what it comes to for them—were least of all conscious of deficiences and dangers; so that, the grace of youth and innocence and freshness aiding, their negatives were converted and became in certain relations lively positives and values.'[16] That the very blankness of the naive point of view might, in certain circumstances, reveal itself as a source of 'positives and values' is a part of James's insight that the value of the zero depends upon its status and function in a specific locale. What these positives and values might be we shall have occasion to discuss later, but here I want to suggest that we consider the international theme not as basic, but as a dramatization of James's root interest. It provided him with metaphors more than it provoked him to history. To see this more clearly we can turn to his introduction to the volume of the collected works which contained *A London Life*, for here he specifically discounts the primary value of the international opposition.

Looking back, James now questions the very premisses on which some of his work has been based, calling attention to 'the international fallacy' and lamenting 'the scant results . . . promised by confronting the fruits of a constituted order with the fruits of no order at all'. It is as though he was having doubts about his own recurring theme.

We may strike lights by opposing order to order, one sort to another sort; for in that case we get the correspondences and equivalents that make differences mean something; we get the interest and the tension of disparity where a certain parity may have been in question. Where it may *not* have been in question, where the dramatic encounter is but the poor concussion of positives on one side with negatives on the other, we get little beyond a consideration of the differences between fishes and fowls.[17]

Yet this constitutes no indictment of his own work since, as he pointed out, there are situations in which apparent negatives are activated into strident or bewildered positives. If James really had shown us a series of innocent Americans blankly succumbing to their European doom he would merely have been a melodramatist. But he was always more than that, just as his theme was always more than merely America and Europe. He gives us the clue in this same introduction, maintaining that

it wasn't after all of the prime, the very most prime, intention of the tale in question that the persons concerned in them should have had this, that or the other land of birth; but that the central situation should really be rendered—that of a charming and decent young thing, *from wheresoever· proceeding*, who has her decision and her action to take, horribly and unexpectedly, in the face of a squalid 'scandal'. . . .[18]

James goes on to say that he was always interested in the effect of London on people and that it seemed easy to evoke an American in order to measure the registered impression it might make. But London was simply a metaphor for a dense conglomeration of sensations and values, a massive aggregate of experiential possibilities, the most bewildering territory for the human sensibility to traverse: and the American visitor also has a more than geographic significance: 'the impression was always there that no one so much as the candid outsider, caught up and involved in the sweep of the machine, could measure the values revealed. Laura Wing must have figured for me thus as the necessary candid outsider. . . .'[19] Candid outsiders are not, of course, new in literature. Since Goldsmith's Chinese Citizen of the World and Voltaire's Ingenu the strategy of naive external comment has been part of the standard repertoire of satire. Huck Finn is a type of candid outsider though his range of response transcends the satiric mode. But James's interest is far away from satire, though it can include ironic mutual illumination. His interest (or perhaps one should always say with James, one of his main interests) is epistemological. How—when confronted with the task to any degree—do people assimilate, construe and interpret experience: in what way do they absorb and assemble the endless flow of sensations which swarm to them from the world? How do we—and perhaps this involves the quiet after-question, how *should* we—look at the world? The enforced response, the 'process of vision' of the candid outsider, attracted him as a theme not because it was American, nor even because it was moral and innocent, but because it allowed him to study what he elsewhere calls 'the strain of observation and the assault of experience'. It permitted him to scrutinize unanticipated collisions of sensibility and data when those collisions were at their freshest, their most revealing, their most meaningful. Much of James's most important drama goes on just behind the eye.

This is why—to return to *A London Life*—James took himself to task for a lapse which would not have bothered another novelist. The lapse consisted of the direct account of an interview between Lady Davenant and Wendover, the only item in the book not refracted through the consciousness of Laura Wing. This interview, and it is clearly on James's conscience, 'breaks the chain of the girl's own consciousness'. Why is this so drastic an error? Because James does not want to 'make my attack on the spectator's consciousness a call as immediate as a postman's knock. This attack, at every other point, reaches that objective only through the medium of the interesting girl's own vision, own experience, with which all the facts are richly charged and coloured. That saturates our sense of them with the savour of Laura's sense—thanks to which enhancement we get intensity.'[20] This seemingly slight point has many far-reaching implications. James is not interested in communicating directly to the reader what actually happened in the way of material incident. Nor is he interested in showing us the possible discrepancies between what actually happened and the sensitive girl's impression of what happened. Rather, he wants to involve us in the moment-by-moment efforts on the part of the candid outsider to discern and decide, to infer and interpret. Not the facts, but the facts saturated with the deciphering efforts and emotional predispositions of a proximate, involved naivety. James never celebrates the inactive naive vision: he shows that vision bewildered and at work. And just as the syntactical nudity of Emerson's style reflects his theories of passivity and non-interference and the absence in his work of any sense of the complexities of human community; just so the increasing syntactical complexity in James's work testifies to his interest in eyes and minds continually active, alert, condemned to the effort of endless response in a multi-faceted world of beguiling and deceiving brilliance. In this world the naive eye can no longer afford merely to saunter. Daisy Miller's eyes receive a significant amount of emphasis. They are 'singularly honest and fresh'; her glance is 'perfectly direct and unshrinking': they are devoid of mockery and irony; they 'wander' continually, are 'constantly moving'.[21] In the revised version of the story for the collected works James added touches to emphasize those eyes. They 'gleamed in the darkness'[22] as she asks Winterbourne to take her out in a boat: more significantly when Winterbourne finally reveals he has lost faith in her purity when he finds her with Giovanelli in the Colosseum one evening 'he felt her lighted eyes fairly penetrate the thick gloom of the vaulted passage—as if to seek some access to him she hadn't yet compassed'.[23] These are the touching, inquiring eyes of a wild spontaneous creature who desperately peers through the social gloom to try and find out why she is so condemned, so judged and banished. By the time he wrote *A London Life* (1889) James's interest in those naive eyes had increased. He makes them yield a richer parable. Let us now turn to an examination of Laura Wing in that novel. Her story, briefly, is this. She has come over to England to stay with her sister and brother-in-law. At first impressed by the amenities of an old civilization she is horrified to discover that her sister is involved in a probably adulterous relationship, that her husband does not seem to care greatly, and that society connives at these dark goings-on with a circumspection and tact which forever borders on moral indifference. Counselled in the ways of social stoicism by Lady Davenant and tentatively proposed to by a young American, Wendover, she finally runs away from the whole pack of them when her sister finally does elope with another man. A good enough story, and one which many writers would have used to show the outrage of innocence at a corrupt society. But for James it is not so simple. His focus—apart from the lapse mentioned above—is on Laura's assessing and uncertain eye, her dubiety of vision rather than society's explicit dubiousness of conduct. The novel opens with her considering the internal changes one year in London has wrought. 'A year ago she knew nothing, and now she knew pretty well everything. . . . The place was the same but her eyes were other: they had seen such sad bad things in so short a time. Yes, the time was short and everything was strange.'[24] But does she 'know everything'—are such eyes reliable? Laura's shifts of appraisal are exemplified in the difference between her preconceived judgements and her actual impressions. For instance there is a friend of her sister's called Lady Ringrose whom she is sure is part of a corrupt circle around her sister. 'She knew who Lady Ringrose was; she knew so many things to-day that when she was younger—and only a little—she had not expected ever to know. Her eyes had been opened very wide in England and certainly they had been opened to Lady Ring-rose.'[25] But what is her reaction when she finally meets Lady Ringrose? 'Laura found her with surprise no such Jezebel but a clever little woman with a single eye-glass and short hair who had read Lecky and could give useful hints about water-colours.'[26]

If her eyes are opened too wide in some directions, in others she seems not to have peered closely enough. Her sister, Selina, answering Laura's accusations, asks her whether she has realized how far short of pure her husband is. Laura says she knows nothing about that.

'So I perceive—as I also perceive that you must have shut your eyes very tight.'[27]

She turns her lamp too strongly in some directions, leaving related areas in comparative twilight; the result of this is a warped vision, an uneven distribution of visual emphasis. Her eye glares or misses, a disabling tool in the penumbras of society. 'It was new work for our young woman to estimate these shades—the gradations, the probabilities of horridness. . . .'[28] At one stage her desperation leads her to an attempted refusal to 'see' at all: 'She drifted on, shutting her eyes, averting her head and, as it seemed to herself, hardening her heart.'[29] At another stage she feels she knows nothing, as opposed to the 'everything' of her earlier confidence.

'Oh, Lady Davenant, I don't know and I don't understand!' Laura broke out. 'I don't understand anything any more—I have given up trying.'[30]

At other times she feels afraid of what knowledge might be unerringly approaching her way. Nevertheless the instinct to pursue her sister with the claims and reproaches of an uncompromising conscience remains uppermost. For Laura has the eye of conscience which is what, precisely, she feels her depraved sister to lack. 'The organs of vision Selina was prepared to take oath she had not misapplied were, as her sister looked into them, an abyss of indefinite prettiness. The girl had sounded them before without discovering a conscience at the bottom of them. ....'[31] Yet Laura's conscience, it is suggested, might be too rigid (and Laura, like Emerson, is 'all the warning moral voice', though unlike Emerson she is faced with 'distraction and counter-solicitation'). While she is waiting one night to pounce on Selina with high-minded reproaches, Laura has a moment of doubt:

Was she wrong after all—was she cruel by being too rigid? Was Mrs Collingwood's attitude the right one and ought she only to propose to herself to 'allow' more and more, and to allow ever, and to smooth things down by gentleness, by sympathy, by not looking at them too hard? It was not the first time that the just measure of things seemed to slip from her hands as she became conscious of possible, or rather of very actual, differences of standard and usage.[32]

Rigidity, inflexibility, intransigence—these are bad characteristics in the Jamesian world. The rigorous imposition of moral preconceptions and social prejudices on the organic stuff of life is usually shown to be either ill-advised or cruel, and always impoverishing. It is Winterbourne's social stiffness and acquired rigidity of prejudice that prevents him from fully appreciating the real spontaneous quality of Daisy Miller. (He cannot dance— Daisy loves to.) It is the father's cruel rigidity which crushes Catherine Sloper's chances for a fuller life in Washington Square, it is the desire to manage and manipulate which makes Mr Flack such an obnoxious and dangerous presence in *The Reverberator*. It is Gilbert Osmond's cold, calculated abuse of Isabel Archer's natural vitality which means a possible death for her; it is the dogmatic stiffness of Waymarsh's moral judgements which Strether disaffiliates himself from in the interest of a fuller vision of life; it is the icy possessive dominating rigour of Olive Chancellor which threatens to divert Verena Tarrant into a sterile death-in-life. The examples of the variety of more or less damnable rigidities in James's work could be extended. The point to catch is that there is also a rigidity of conscience which James came increasingly to feel might be bruisingly misapplied. The world of social appearances has a claim to make against those who insist on extracting the concealed fault and damning it in isolation.

Laura Wing drives Selina to distraction with her moral 'harrying' and James drops the hint that her probity might be 'barbarous'. The balanced, perhaps rather cynical, Lady Davenant calls her 'high strung' and certainly there is something neurotic and hysterical in her over-reaction to things and her general sense of omen and disaster. Her drop into total indictment—'it's all black darkness'[33]—is clearly meant to be excessive, and we may recall what we said, à propos of Whitman among others, that when the naive innocent eye *is* disabused it is liable to collapse into extremes of paralysed despair. Her eye has no flexible apparatus for sorting out the subtle varieties of nuance: if things are not all good, then they are all bad.

This is what I meant by suggesting that the final number which *contains* the 'zero' of naive judgement is a subtler affair than the zero on its own. The verdict of the whole book is not coterminous with Laura's own condemnation. It is not that Laura Wing is wrong as to her facts—Selina *is* having an affair with Captain Crispin, the established norms and decencies of English life do contain hidden principles of corruption—but rather that she is excessive as to her response to the facts, misguided as to the light she sees them in. Bemused fish that she is, she does not learn to swim in society. The point is amusingly made near the end when, at the height of her moral indignation and despair, one of the children suggests that Lionel (Selina's husband) should 'take her by the waistband and teach her to "strike out"'.[34] Lionel himself, creature of his element that he is, recommends a glass of port. Laura however talks of killing herself. In the context—and the context is all—this is clearly disproportionate; just as her final flight to the banks of the Rappahanock (with its flavour of some distant wild unspoilt paradise) from the squalid world which centres on 'the Court of Probate and Divorce' is not only a gesture of repudiation on Laura's part, but also a revelation of her own undigestibility as far as society is concerned.

We must return to Laura's eyes and her general groping apprehension of the dark areas of society. One passage in the book is almost a microcosmic reduction of the whole affair. She

is having a day out with Mr Wendover and is so enjoying herself
that she is inclined to a more benevolent view of society and a
more tolerant assessment of her sister. A rain shower drives them
into a museum where they stroll around in amiable patience.

One of the keepers told them of other rooms to see, of objects of high
interest in the basement. They made their way down—it grew much
darker and they heard a great deal of thunder—and entered a part of
the house which presented itself to Laura as a series of dim, irregular
vaults, passages, and little narrow avenues, encumbered with strange
vague things, obscured for the time but some of which had an
ambiguous sinister look, so that she wondered the keepers could quite
bear it. 'It's very fearful—it looks like a cave of idols!' she said to her
companion; and then she added, 'Just look there—is that a person
or a thing?'[35]

The descent, the darkness, the general atmosphere of an under-
ground maze (concealing, perhaps unconsciously, a hint of
forbidden and frightening sexual orifices), the general unnerving
dubiety of things in this subterannean haze, the 'otherness' of
the things and people yet to be seen, the unrecognizability of
close relations (for that sinister 'thing' is her own sister engaged
in an illicit rendezvous)—all these comprise the theme of the
whole book as well as of the specific scene. And so great is
Laura's shock that her incipient tolerant good humour vanishes
and she makes an awkward neurotic flight. Her shock is only
increased by her next view of Selina—sitting in a carriage waiting
to go out to dinner 'in pure white splendour'.[36] So white to
society—so black at heart. This is what Laura quite literally
cannot assimilate, cannot 'stomach' we might say.

The situation is repeated in the key scene of the book—at the
Opera. Laura, Selina, Wendover and another man, Booker, are
sitting in a box, when Selina suddenly excuses herself and asks
Booker to take her to visit another friend on the other side of the
House. After some hushed manoeuvring and some conspiratorial
to-and-froing Laura suddenly realizes that Selina is in a box with
Lady Ringrose, without Booker but with a mysterious third
person. Her interest in the Opera vanishes and those morbid,

HENRY JAMES

anxious eyes start straining once more. 'She watched them earnestly, tried to sound with her glass the curtained dimness behind them.'³⁷ Having decided that Selina is with the wicked Crispin, Laura surrenders to her bottomless repugnance and excessive nervousness. She feels all the eyes of the theatre staring at her, mocking her ('She had recognised many faces already and her imagination quickly multiplied them'),³⁸ she is distracted with the calm and gallant Wendover: in the interval 'Laura tried more than ever to see with her glass'.³⁹ Her morbidness, her multiplying imagination so jostles and disturbs her apprehension of things that the whole place becomes 'a blur and a swim'.⁴⁰ Quite unbalanced by her realization that Selina has deceived her again and is in fact planning something with Crispin, Laura makes a half-crazed proposal to the baffled Wendover, and then collapses into the depths of world- and self-loathing. James has managed to invest the whole scene with an atmosphere of rich ambiguity so that everything appears at once normal and yet full of omen. Ominous, that is, to Laura's feverish imagination which cannot hold the world around her in any perspective. Moralities seem to shade off into immoralities all round her so that her feeling of failure ('She scarce knew what she feared, scarce knew what she supposed')⁴¹ is, in one important sense, simply the failure of the candid outside eye to acquire any sustained clarity, any contoured accuracy in its visual handling of the world. Her stance—straining her eyes into the circumambient and peopled dimness—is classically suggestive, and her reaction to the events, her terror, her shame, her flight, should not be taken as a sound moral comment so much as external evidence of an intense inward disorder. A disorder resulting from moral eye strain. (As Proust noted: 'moral uncertainty is a greater obstacle to an exact visual perception than any defect of vision would be.') The plight—and this is one of James's finer insights —of the innocent eye is not so much its horror at what it sees, as its bewilderment at what it only half sees. That bewilderment leads to unease, and that an excess of conscience and immature imagination can magnify unease into horror is of course an important part of the story. But we must realize that the resultant horror is by no means proportionate to the initially half-seen data: it is the result of some mental addition, some imaginative multiplication. After all there are enough hints in the opera scene to allow us to feel that what Laura sees as a miasma of evil could also, very easily, be seen as a comedy of errors.

Some critics take the revulsion of the innocent as the reliable, the James-endorsed response. And indeed, as we have said, Laura is right about the central fact: Selina does run off with Crispin. But I think we can challenge the notion that Laura's reaction is the necessarily sound, the necessarily right one. In his preface to the short story 'The Marriages' (written two years after *A London Life*) James describes how easily he got his subject. The story is about a daughter who is so attached to the memory of her dead mother that she fears any idea of a second marriage on the part of her father. Granted the intensity of this apprehension, writes James, 'granted that, the drama is all there—all in the consciousness, the fond imagination, *the possibly poisoned and inflamed judgment*, of the suffering subject'[42] [my italics]. Adela Chart, the daughter, not only suspects her father of wishing to marry Mrs Churchley, she takes the step of poisoning Mrs Churchley's mind against her own father when the engagement is announced. She conceives of this act in an heroic light, a gesture of devotion to the dead mother (and how many characters in James do worship at 'The Altar of the Dead') though it causes only trouble in her family and the premature decline of her father. At the end she is so distressed by the results of her courageous mendacity that she visits Mrs Churchley to try and make amends. She then discovers that her lies were not the cause of the broken engagement, though she herself as a person probably was. Thus the story: but, as James said, the drama is in the consciousness of Adela. From the start she is peering, interpreting, exaggerating, misconstruing. Often the 'horrible clearness in her mind'[43] is the result of a most perverse distortion. Her observation suffers from an excess of misplaced ardour, ardour for the dead mother instead of concern for the happiness of the living father. When she hears of the engagement and the light way her worldly brother has taken it, she goes through inner paroxysms rather like Laura Wing's:

When he had gone Adela locked herself in as with the fear that she should be overtaken or invaded, and during a sleepless feverish memorable night she took counsel of her uncompromising spirit. She saw things as they were, in all the indignity of life. The levity, the mockery, the infidelity, the ugliness, lay as plain as a map before her; it was a world of gross practical jokes, a world *pour rire*; but she cried about it all the same.[44]

A comparable excess is to be found in her loathing of other people: the not ungenerous Mrs Churchley becomes 'that queen of beasts'[45] to the 'inflamed judgement' of Adela. Yet her inner sense of heroism and high morality do not go uncontested. When her brother hears what she has done to avert what seemed like a happy marriage all round, he stands 'incredulous and appalled'.

'You invented such a tissue of falsities and calumnies, and you talk about your conscience?'

More outspokenly he leaves her with what is, for James, some fairly strong language: 'You raving maniac!'[46] The cry is worth remembering for the idea that the diseased, hypertrophied imagination might have something maniacal about it was a theme James was to probe in *The Sacred Fount*.

Is there any attitude open to shocked naivety which does not involve the extremes of timid flight or disastrous interference? At the start of *A London Life* Laura Wing looks to Lady Davenant to teach her to be a stoic: 'she wanted rather to be taught a certain fortitude—how to live and hold up one's head even while knowing what things horribly meant. A cynical indifference—it wasn't exactly this she wished to acquire; but weren't there some sorts of indifference that might be philosophic and noble?'[47] This stoicism she signally fails to learn, but at least she realizes that it is one attitude left open to the innocent eye which can never properly absorb society, can never really come to terms with the welter of nuances which the world imposes on them. It is perhaps this sort of stoicism that Hemingway's hurt laconic toughs are trying to practise.

In concentrating on *A London Life* I have wanted to suggest that although James continually uses the innocent, the candid outside eye as a strategy he is not necessarily using it to enforce a facile condemnation of society. He took the untutored eye— so revered by the Transcendentalists—and subjected it to a dynamic, unprogrammed education. And watching the naive person assimilating, misconstruing, digesting, regurgitating, concentrating, omitting, as he or she was faced with the task of visually appropriating the world, James learnt something profound about the whole question of veridical knowledge, about the whole problem of verifying impressions. His study took him towards epistemological scepticism and towards a new morality of vision which I wish to explore in the next section.

CHAPTER 15

THE RANGE OF WONDERMENT

The case being with Maisie to the end that she treats her friends to the rich little spectacle of objects embalmed in her wonder. She wonders, in other words, to the death—the death of her childhood; after which (with the inevitable shift, sooner or later, of her point of view) her situation will change and become another affair, subject to other measurements and with a new centre altogether.

HENRY JAMES, Preface to *What Maisie Knew*[1]

Her vocation was to see the world and to thrill with enjoyment of the picture.

What Maisie Knew[2]

Life claimed her and used her and beset her—made her range in her groping, her naturally immature and unlighted way from end to end of the scale. . . . She was absolutely afraid of nothing she might come to by living with enough sincerity and enough wonder.

James on his cousin Minny Temple[3]

THE concept of 'wonder' was as important for James as it was for Emerson, though its uses, its difficulties, its destiny are very differently estimated by each writer. James submitted the naive vision, the unimpaired habit of wonder, to the sort of social tests which Emerson's metaphysical preoccupations took little account of. That the wondering eye was bound to give way to some more sophisticated manner of observation is a fact that James, unlike Clemens, took as axiomatic and not necessarily wholly a bad thing. He knew that there were some things which the naive wondering eye could not see or could only misinterpret, that it might glare too strongly for charity, too wrongly for justice; yet that, withal, there might be a definite loss involved in its capitulation to a more settled savoir-faire, a duller worldliness. His analysis of the naive eye was never simple and to appreciate its full subtlety and richness, and the lessons he made it yield, I intend to attempt a careful examination of *What Maisie Knew*. It is interesting to note that Maisie has certain characteristics in common with Huck Finn. She is unwanted, 'orphaned' and abused: yet she is 'the gentlest spirit on earth'.[4] Unlike Laura Wing she is gifted with a quality of bravery which is distinctly Huck-like. She is 'thoroughly game' and is notable for her 'small stoicism', even an 'unformulated fatalism'[5] which endures without complaining. She is both excluded and exploited by more powerful agents than herself and is as thoroughly 'mixed' with the more selfish, violent elements of humanity as Huck was with the King and Duke. And just as Huck was heroic for Jim, so, in a different but not less notable way, Maisie is 'heroic' for the kind but spineless Sir Claude. More closely analogous, she has an 'instinct for keeping the peace' and to this end often practises 'the pacific art of stupidity',[6] cultivating a tactful 'blankness' in the interests of general harmony and self-preservation. More, there is a definite pathos in her innocence which, because of her situation, is 'an innocence so saturated with knowledge and so directed to diplomacy'.[7] Yet she is unspoiled by knowledge, and none of the surrounding badness rubs off onto her. Like Huck she is a sort of permanent 'castaway' but unlike Huck she cannot escape her doom. For her there is no reprieve by myth. In as much as she is a child 'she could surrender herself to the day'[8] and she neither plans for the future nor regrets the past. But her sensitivity to the present empirical world is at least as remarkable as Huck's ('the actual was the absolute, the present alone was vivid'),[9] and she too would probably prefer pie to mystery. This is not to say that either writer was attempting to celebrate 'the saintly child' notion, though it is to point out that both were very interested in the positive virtues of childhood. If Maisie and Huck do not represent 'the only decency' in their respective worlds, they both deserve the praise that James lavishes on Maisie in his preface when he writes of her

flourishing, to a degree, at the cost of many conventions and proprieties, even decencies, really keeping the torch of virtue alive in an

279

HENRY JAMES

air tending infinitely to smother it; really in short making confusion
worse confounded by drawing some stray fragrance of an ideal
across the scent of selfishness, by sowing on barren strands, through the
mere fact of presence, the seed of the moral life.[10]

Yet clearly the books are very different, and James's interest
significantly diverges from Clemens's. One way to realize this
is to examine James's reason for *not* allowing Maisie to tell her
own story, for not adopting that first-person child's persona
which was Clemens's artistic salvation. In the preface he recalls
his intention. 'The one presented register of the whole complexity would be the play of the child's confused and obscure notation
of it, and yet the whole, as I say, should be unmistakably, should
be honourably there, seen through the faint intelligence.' Yet he
decides not to allow Maisie to tell the story herself for the following reasons: 'The infant mind would at best leave great gaps and
voids'; and 'small children have many more perceptions than they
have terms to translate them'[11] (remember how often Huck
apologizes for not having the words to transcribe his impressions).
James therefore addressed himself to the question of giving 'the
whole situation surrounding her, but of giving it only through
the occasions of her proximity and attention; only as it might
pass before her and appeal to her, as it might touch and affect her,
for better or worse, for perceptive gain or perceptive loss'[12]
(not moral gain, note). The focus is indeed on Maisie: 'it is her
relation, her activity of spirit, that determines all our own concern
—we simply take advantage of these things better than she herself'[13] (spirit, not conscience: James chooses his words carefully).
To the end of securing ampler comprehension of Maisie's
'activity of spirit' James reserves the right to describe things
beyond her comprehension: 'our own commentary constantly
attends and amplifies'[14] (without, be it here noted, inserting
final moral judgements: James intends to fill out the picture, not
to introduce judicial pronouncements and verdicts).

This is central to an understanding of James's interest in, and
use of, the wondering naive eye. One should notice that what
facilitated Clemens's satisfactory articulateness is seen here as a

280

limiting, strangling hindrance by James. Unlike Clemens he chose not to abandon 'the heights of analytic omniscience'[15] for the first person child-like stance. He wants to make the naive zero central, but he wants the adult reader to see the neighbouring numbers; numbers which Maisie cannot make out, but which show up in a fierce clarity by reason of their proximity to the luminous zero. James intends, for instance, that we shall understand the French conversation which reveals that Sir Claude has spent the night with Mrs Beale, at the same time as we realize that to Maisie it is merely a buzz of impressive exotic European sound. 'The child's confused and obscure notation' of its environing complexities was used by Clemens as well to obtain important effects: for example, Huck's mistaken reaction to the circus clown, and to the Grangerford household. But Clemens did not share James's interest in cognitive difficulties, in the subtle relationship between epistemology and judgement. Huck's confused notation, like his confused ratiocination, always makes an unmistakable moral point about the society around him, its cruelty, its deceptions. Maisie's 'small expanding consciousness' gives us satiric and moral insights as well, but it also takes us deep into the central problem of vision; and the way she registers a varied range of impressions allows James to consider questions of aesthetic apprehension and attitude which did not interest Clemens. To be sure, one of the glories of *Huckleberry Finn* is its luminous moral authority; firm but never forced, supple yet ultimately uncompromising; humane, undogmatic, unforgettable. James simply has a different kind of book in mind which nevertheless does pursue a complex moral problem—the problem of the ethics governing vision.

The lesson of *What Maisie Knew* is richer than that of *A London Life* because James has separated the naive eye and the voice of 'conscious conscience' so that candour and condemnation are not combined in one sensibility. Maisie offers us incomparably more positives than Laura Wing. Maisie, the child abandoned by her real parents and exploited by adulterous step-parents, has more incentive and more need to use her eyes than any other Jamesian character. They are, as it were, all she has got. 'It was to be the fate of this patient little girl to see much more than she at first understood.'[16] Hence those ever open, inquiring eyes. James calls her 'gravely-gazing soul' a 'boundless receptacle'[17] into which the impressions of the world are poured, and as she grows older she enjoys her pathetic privilege of being the unwanted witness. 'She saw more and more; she saw too much.'[18] In a curious way she is both dangerously *in* and helplessly *out* of the 'wild game of "going round"'[19] which society seems to be. Her 'sharpened sense of spectatorship' acts as 'a sort of compensation for the doom of a peculiar passivity. It gave her often an odd air of being present at her history in as separate a manner as if she could only get at experience by flattening her nose against a pane of glass.'[20] This image is picked up later: 'She was to feel henceforth as if she were flattening her nose upon the hard window-pane of the sweet-shop of knowledge.'[21] She has to content herself with 'delightful little glimpses'.[22] She *sees*—but always more than she can understand or formulate. The question we must ask is how much of what she sees can she transform into knowledge—in fact what does she know? To get at this we must consider rather carefully the nature of the world she lives in.

It is a world saturated with tortuous ambiguities. Nothing remains separate, distinct or clear. 'To be "involved" was of the essence of everybody's affairs.'[23] This web of involvement acts as a continual obstacle to clarity: social relations become a 'system of dodges',[24] a confusing muddled game which Maisie has to attempt to understand in much the same way that she has to puzzle over 'the cards and counters and bewildering pamphlets' that Sir Claude gives her. Certain key words help to emphasize the uncertainty of events about her. People are always 'squaring' other people, and the ideal state of affairs would seem to consist of a world where everyone was 'squared' to everyone else's satisfaction. Maisie picks on the word as describing the sought-for Utopia. After Sir Claude and Mrs Beale have discussed certain problems and possibilities she chimes in with an engaging naivety. 'Maisie, giving a sigh of relief, looked round

THE RANGE OF WONDERMENT

at what seemed to her the dawn of a higher order. "Then
everyone will be squared!" she peacefully said.'[25] Shortly after
that the precarious structure of social squarings collapses:
'Hadn't they at last to look the fact in the face?—it was too
disgustingly evident that no one after all had been squared.
Well, if no one had been squared it was because everyone had
been vile.'[26] Similarly the idea of freedom recoils with malicious
irony. Towards the end of the book a provident release seems
imminent for all parties: but Maisie discovers that the more 'free'
they claim to be, the less safe everything seems. 'The strangest
thing of all was what had happened to the old safety. What had
really happened was that Sir Claude was "free" and that Mrs
Beale was "free", and yet that the new medium was somehow
still more oppressive than the old.'[27] In this world of dodges,
squarings, illusory freedom, and unexpected unease, Maisie has
to make her way. Her world is consequently well described as
'phantasmagoric'. 'She was taken into the confidence of passions
on which she fixed just the stare she might have had for images
bounding across the wall in the slide of a magic-lantern. Her
little world was phantasmagoric—strange shadows dancing on
a sheet. It was as if the whole performance had been given for
her—a mite of a half-scared infant in a dim theatre.'[28] James
maintains this 'phantasmagoric' texture of Maisie's world by
continually likening it to the theatre, pantomime, the Arabian
nights, etc. He goes to a great deal of trouble to recreate the child's
angle of vision at important moments in the book, and he continually strives to make us realize how Maisie must see the
world from her diminished and limited vantage point; usually
not taking in the whole scene or person but only certain isolated
features. Embraced by her mother she is only conscious of being
lost 'amid a wilderness of trinkets':[29] asked by her father whether
she wishes to accompany him to America her first reaction is to
notice his shoes. Maisie 'for a minute looked at his shoes, though
they were not the pair she most admired, the laced yellow
"uppers" and patent-leather complement'.[30] Visual objects often
bulk larger than abstract issues. The child's eye has a minimum

of perspective. 'His presence was like an object brought so close to her face that she couldn't see round its edges.'[31] So many presences have 'vague edges': and at the important dinner attended by Mrs Beale and Mrs Wix, James is careful to remind us that Maisie was most aware of Mrs Beale's shoulder and elbow. This relative absence of perspective, this foreshortened upward view of the world is worth emphasizing; because, although Maisie would 'know' a very great deal if she were an adult, if we remember her limited outlook, her stature, her vague indiscriminating attention, then we realize how hard it would be for her to read the signs correctly—if at all. And just as people are seen in distortion, so their actions seem utterly inconsequential. People visit regularly for some reason—and then inexplicably stay away. They change their relationship with her most capriciously (a governess becomes a mother) and show her annoyance and affection, attention and indifference in an arbitrary manner which Maisie is at a loss to comprehend. They approach and fade like fish in a murky aquarium: she is suddenly face to face with new figures, suddenly aware of the absence of old ones. People, in general, are never where you might expect them to be. In such a world even personal pronouns become a source of ambiguity. '"She" of course at Beale Farange's had never meant any one but Ida, and there was the difference in this case that it now meant Ida with renewed intensity.'[32] Maisie has to read the emotional temperature by assessing the emphasis given to pronouns, a difficult task. As with what she sees, so with what she hears. Out of the confused social murmur sudden phrases detach themselves and come to her ears with a clarity which is as baffling as the previous inaudibility for want of a context: 'she found in her mind a collection of images and echoes to which meanings were attachable—images and echoes kept for her in the childish dusk, the dim closet, the high drawers, like games she wasn't big enough to play'.[33] Precisely: she lacks the terms, the concepts, the rules of the game, a knowledge of the stakes. She is the recipient of innumerable impressions: but she lacks any coordinating key.

Hence her occasional feelings of 'terrifying strangeness',[34] and hence too, the comic-grotesque nature of the world she lives in. Take for instance the brief appearance of Mr Perriam, one of Ida's friends. We register him as a bloated banker: to Maisie he is as exotic as 'a heathen turk' because of certain strange characteristics such as his eyes like 'billiard-balls',[35] and the diamond-studded hand which pulls at the strange moustache. The nature of the world Maisie lives in is best brought out by the scene at the Exhibition which acts as a lurid metaphor for the mundane life which precedes and succeeds it. For Maisie the Exhibition means 'a collection of extraordinary foreign things in tremendous gardens, with illuminations, bands, elephants, switchbacks and side-shows, as well as crowds of people among whom they might possibly see some one they knew'.[36] And at the Exhibition, with its tantalizing colourful side-shows from which, as from society, Maisie is debarred, there occurs that weird pantomimic moment when Mrs Beale encounters, not Sir Claude whom she seeks, but her husband:

The companions paused . . . before the Flowers of the Forest, a large presentment of bright brown ladies—they were brown all over—in a medium suggestive of tropical luxuriance, and there Maisie dolourously expressed her belief that he would never come at all. Mrs Beale thereupon, though she was discernibly disappointed, reminded her that he had not been promised as a certainty—a remark which caused the girl to gaze at the Flowers through a blur in which they became more magnificent, yet oddly more confused, and by which, moreover, confusion was imparted to the aspect of a gentlemen who at that moment, in the company of a lady, came out of the brilliant booth. The lady was so brown that Maisie at first took her for one of the Flowers; but during the few seconds that this required . . . she heard Mrs Beale's voice, behind her, gather both wonder and pain into a single cry.

'Of all the wickedness—*Beale*!'

He had already, without distinguishing them in the mass of strollers, turned another way—it seemed at the brown lady's suggestion. Her course was marked over head and shoulders, by an upright scarlet plume, as to the ownership of which Maisie was instantly eager. 'Who is she?—Who is she?'[37]

Out of the colourful welter of confusion emerge unexpected figures, with unexpected companions, eliciting unexpected reactions (just like everyday society for Maisie); and what impresses Maisie most is—that scarlet feather; she certainly wants to find out who owns that. The fact that a strange brown lady should be with her father is less arresting. The different comments made about this woman by the adult and the child are revealing.

Maisie took it in. 'She's almost black,' she then reported.
'They're always hideous,' said Mrs Beale.[38]

The adult speaks with personal bitterness and implied moral astringency: Maisie is no more, and no less, confused by it all than by her usual life. Her response is to the surface: the secondary qualities rather than the substance—colour rather than weight. The whole evening has a curious dream-like flow and unpredictability for Maisie and her final reaction—'It was still at any rate the Arabian Nights'[39]—indicates that it is not the moral depravity of the participants that has struck her but the exotic confusion of the scene. James's point, it seems to me, is to emphasize the unreal, fluid, luridly-lit, oddly-angled quality of Maisie's perceptual world; to make us share its sudden close-ups and strange disappearances, its shufflings and shocks, its inexplicables and imponderables. What Maisie most wants to do is to make some sense of this world, to read the clues correctly, to make the fragments cohere in meaningful and consistent configurations: not to submit it to moral evaluation. This book is about the difficulty of knowing, not the difficulty of judging; about the reversals of expectation, the difficulties of prognostication, the disappointment of illusions and hopes which are the lot of the naive mind. As in Laura Wing's world there are unexpected dark places: 'Everything had something behind it: life was like a long, long corridor with rows of closed doors.'[40] When Maisie expects friendship from her mother, she suddenly receives a wholly unexpected hostile stare. 'It reminded her of the way that once, at one of the lectures in Gower Street, something in a big jar that, amid an array of strange glasses and bad smells, had been promised as a beautiful yellow and was produced as a beautiful black.'[41] In a world where what should be most reliable is inexplicably reversed, what can Maisie, 'a mite of a half-scared infant in a great dim theatre', possibly 'know'?

Yet James clearly infers that her mental grasp of the world is constantly growing stronger. At one point in her youth she has had 'a small smug conviction that in the domestic labyrinth she always kept the clue',[42] though as it turns out each addition of light seems only to widen the horizons of encompassing darkness. However her acuteness certainly grows. 'The little girl's interpretations thickened':[43] she is, at times, 'receptive and profound'.[44] At the start of Chapter Twelve we read: 'It may indeed be said that these days brought on a high quickening of Maisie's direct perceptions, of her sense of freedom to make out things for herself.'[45] Yet too often enlightenment leads to more enigma. If at one stage she is claiming, insouciantly, bravely— 'Oh yes, I know everything!'[46]—one of her last pathetic cries is— 'I don't know—I don't know.'[47] She thinks she is approaching knowledge: actually she is increasing in her ability to 'read' possible interpretations into events, to 'attach meanings' to things, to 'read the unspoken into the spoken',[48] to 'make out things'. She develops a 'sense' rather than a sureness 'of the relations of things',[49] and it is her 'reflexions' which 'thicken'[50] rather than her knowledge of verifiable facts. She is acquiring a map, a picture, building a mental construct; she is coming to terms with 'the strain'[51] of observation. Yet the strain is everywhere apparent, as the very shape of this quotation reveals:

It had become now, for that matter, a question of sides, there was at least a certain amount of evidence as to where they all were. Maisie of course, in such a delicate position, was on nobody's; but Sir Claude had all the air of being on her's. If, therefore, Mrs Wix was on Sir Claude's, her ladyship on Mr Perriam's and Mr Perriam presumably on her ladyship's, this left only Mrs Beale and Mr Farange to account for. Mrs Beale clearly was, like Sir Claude, on Maisie's, and papa, it was to be supposed, on Mrs Beale's. Here indeed was a slight ambiguity, as papa being on Mrs Beale's didn't somehow seem to place him quite on his daughter's. It sounded, as this young lady thought, very much like puss-in-the-corner, and she could only wonder if the distribution of parties would lead to a rushing to and fro and a changing of places. She was in the presence, she felt, of restless change. . . .[52]

This is hardly clear knowledge, and it is a long way round to that last rather helpless conclusion. Small wonder that she often experiences what we can call a vertigo of uncertainty, the feeling being likened variously to being on 'a prancing horse'[53] and on a swing. Maisie is astray in a world of perpetually disintegrating and reforming relationships, a world open to a theoretically infinite number of interpretations. There is of course one thing which determines Maisie's groping ignorance, one missing clue without which the whole tangled web of adult involvements will remain forever incomprehensible—sex. She has picked up all the terms, but she does not understand the matching substance. There is 'impropriety'; people can be 'compromised'; some people are called 'bad': these things she knows, but it is a purely verbal knowledge. For Maisie such words remain almost non-referential. And as long as the ramifications of sexual appetite are still a mystery her world will remain phantasmagoric, full of sudden events and activities and precipitating motives and mixed consequences which she will never fathom. In a sense the book hinges on what Maisie does *not* know. And in Maisie's difficult life James, it seems to me, has demonstrated the impossibility of any clear, confident appraisal of the world—an impossibility inherent in the fluid mutational character of the world and the necessary limits of vision. In one passage James describes Maisie teasing her doll for her innocence: as the doll is to Maisie, so is Maisie to the adult world. It is an image which suggests the relativity of all knowledge. This is what I mean by his epistemological scepticism. Yet, it might be objected, some information is clear to us and surely intended as absolute. Beale and Ida are selfish heartless brutes, Mrs Beale is a plausible bitch, and Sir Claude is a weak-minded, if pleasant man, who can be distracted from Maisie's plight by the well-turned leg of a fisherwoman. This much, surely, is clear. Maisie is an affectionate child who yearns for a world of matching love, who retains a sort of Platonic ideal of the good mother and the good father and is willing to pretend (in two moving interviews) that they are good and lovable if only to satisfy her intuition of a possible better state of affairs. She is an innocent whose ideals finally have to succumb to the grubby sordid facts of a far from ideal social actuality, who is immersed in a world not good enough for her, whose wonder must give way to harsher modes of judgement. So much is certainly in the book, yet this book is about more than disillusioned innocence. For, as stated, this is Mrs Wix's version of Maisie and her world and all that happens. Mrs Wix 'knows' all this, and yet it is very open to question whether Mrs Wix is the most reliable moral and veridical centre of the book. But before turning to that crucial figure we must stress the vulnerable state of the ignorant, innocent Maisie.

This vulnerability—which makes the drawing room a place of inquisition to her uncomprehending smallness—is well brought out by recurrent references to hands and teeth. A few examples will suffice to show how this works. Here for instance we gather her vivid awareness of Sir Claude's hand. 'She clung to his hand, which was encased in a pearl grey glove ornamented with the thick black lines that, at her mother's, always used to strike her as connected with the way the bestitched fists of the long ladies carried, with the elbows well out, their umbrellas upside down.'[54] The whole point of this rather minute description is to remind us of Maisie's eye-level: to recall to us what a big part hands play in her life, how large they must bulk to her vision. Quite simply she is always being taken by the hand. The strange Captain she meets in the park with her mother puts out 'a big military hand which she immediately took':[55] when her father snatches her away from the Exhibition she is most conscious of 'his arm about her':[56] when her mother appears in Folkestone on that extraordinary journey of self justification we read: 'They sat together while the parent's gloved hand sometimes rested sociably on the child's and sometimes gave a corrective pull to a ribbon too meagre or a tress too thick.'[57] There are some solacing hands, even if the solace contains the hint of a future betrayal; as on her last walk with Sir Claude when they nearly, but not quite, make their escape to Paris. 'The only touch was that of Sir Claude's hand, and to feel her own in it was her mute resistance to time. She went about as sightlessly as if he had been leading her blindfold.'[58] Then there is that hand which will finally retain possession of Maisie, the hand of Mrs Wix. 'That hand had shown altogether, these twenty-four hours, a new capacity for closing.'[59] The description is not without its chilling, ominous intent. This 'hands' theme reminds us that she is an orphan, an abandoned child (left by her mother alone in 'the empty garden and the deeper dusk'[60] in one of James's more pregnant phrases) who shows an infinite readiness of allegiance, an innocent who offers trust and affection to a scheming, selfish, manipulating world: it serves to emphasize how passive she is.

The 'teeth' theme reminds us of the sense of threat which exists for Maisie in the world around her. The most prominent are her father's. When he first calls to take Maisie away from her mother, he shouts at Ida, picking up his daughter and 'showing his teeth more than ever at Maisie as he hugged her'.[61] Behind the ostensible affection there lurk the fangs of selfish hunger. James elsewhere calls them 'shining fangs' and if the word is half-jocular to us it must be taken as referring to something which is half-sinister to Maisie. When he finally abandons Maisie his teeth are prominent. 'Her father's teeth, at this, were such a picture of appetite without action as to be a match for any plea of poverty.'[62]

Teeth and hands: appetite and appropriation we might say. Maisie in her vulnerable ignorance is the focus of many base adult emotions, but in particular she attracts two which James deprecated above all others. The sort of social selfishness which wishes to possess and use, and a type of self-righteous moralism which hungers to subdue and thwart. The last scene in the book clarifies her unfortunate position between these two forces.

Mrs Beale is hysterically clutching at Maisie, trying to detain her, presumably because of some money which has now been settled on her; and Mrs Wix is beckoning sternly from the door. Maisie, still the victim of an intermittent bewildered terror, is threatened by selfish appetite and spiritual appropriation. Sir Claude's genial tolerance is self-confessedly no force at all, too weak to help the child in her hour of need. Mrs Beale we can recognize for what she is: her affection is more plausible than real, a scheming implement rather than a generosity. But should the trust that she forfeits necessarily attach itself to the ugly, gauche, worthy yet ludicrous Mrs Wix? She voices the uncompromising claims of the 'moral sense' and Dr Leavis is at least half won over by her rhetoric when he offers the opinion that 'perhaps it is as well that Maisie . . . should enter adolescence under that kind of responsible tutelage'.[63] But for James morality is not such an easy business as the edict-mongering Mrs Wix makes out. In his *Autobiographies* James, recalling his father's distaste for 'prigs', describes a parental bias which he himself shared:

Thus we had ever the amusement, since I can really call it nothing less, of hearing morality, or moralism, as it was more invidiously worded, made hay of in the very interest of character and conduct; these things suffering much, it seemed, by their association with the conscience— the *conscious* conscience—the very home of the literal, the haunt of so many pedantries.[64]

Mrs Wix is the embodiment par excellence of 'the conscious conscience' and I think we are to infer that Maisie's character will 'suffer much' by close association with it, by enforced subjugation *to* it. But to justify this point of view some detailed attention must be paid to Mrs Wix from the time of her first appearance. Maisie is first frightened of her but feels that at least she has been a proper mother, which is more than can be said of Ida. But the dominant impression she gives is one of 'greasy greyness', she looks 'cross and cruel' and in dress reminds Maisie of 'a horrid beetle'.[65] She is addicted to cheap fiction and, more significantly, she wears thick glasses through which she squints myopically at the world and which testify to a permanent obliquity of vision. That she calls them 'her straighteners'[66] seems to indicate that she is given to imposing a rigid rigorous pattern on a world less clearly marked and plotted than she thinks. Throughout the book Mrs Wix 'intensely waited' for Maisie, as though waiting to make an ultimate claim of possession. She is against Maisie knowing, seeing, or hearing anything from the surrounding world, and is hysterical in her apprehensions of contamination. She is always excessive in her condemnations and interpretations (perhaps because of a neurotic love for Sir Claude) and it is that gentle man who gives us a clue to her habits of mind when he says of her moralizing: 'the situation isn't after all quite so desperate or quite so simple.'[67] Her tastes are drab and severe and testify to a permanent suspicion of the joys of the senses. In the church of her choosing there are 'no haloes on heads, but only, during long sermons, beguiling blacks of bonnets'.[68] She has no capacity for wonder and ideally would like to close Maisie's eyes for good. Yet Maisie's supreme virtue is her very unprejudiced inquiringness. James describes Maisie as 'only, more than anything else, curious'[69] and so it is not surprising that the presence of Mrs Wix sometimes depresses her. 'Was the sum of all knowledge only to know how little in this presence one could ever reach it?'[70] Maisie wants to 'see' the world: Mrs Wix wants to prevent her seeing and make her 'judge' it. Mrs Wix's desire to protect is also a desire to possess; and that possessiveness includes an instinct to arrest, to impose a state of sensory imprisonment. Maisie has no 'moral sense' at least as those words operate in Mrs Wix's vocabulary. Her qualities belong to a pre-moral or trans-moral realm. In her ignorance she is all potential, all readiness, all humanity. What is innate is her spontaneous affection, her appetite for the new, her aptitude for life, her unprejudiced uncondemning eye which is hospitable to the whole spectrum of sense impressions. Shortly after being abandoned by her mother she can take solace from the 'intoxicating poetry' of society. 'Everything about her, however—the crowded room, the bedizened banquet, the savour of dishes, the drama of figures—ministered to the joy of life.'[71] Maisie can see haloes, whereas Mrs Wix simply cannot see all there is to be seen (she is expert at extracting certain traits for acerb condemnation) and refuses to try. Maisie on the other hand wants nothing better than a chance to see—and accept—everything. This is brought out on her first visit to Europe, always a significant confrontation in James's work. Maisie's first emotion when she reaches Boulogne is 'the great ecstasy of a larger impression of life'. There is no timidity or fearful holding back: this is her world. 'She recognised, she understood, she adored and took possession; feeling herself attuned to everything and laying her hand, right and left, on what had simply been waiting for her.'[72] The descriptions of the scenes as they appear to Maisie's rapt eye evoke the sensuous delight of the work of the French Impressionists. 'The place and the people were all a picture together, a picture that when they went down to the wide sands, shimmered, in a thousand tints, with the pretty organisation of the *plage*, with the gaiety of spectators and bathers, with that of the language and the weather, and above all with that of our young lady's unprecedented situation.'[73] The atmosphere is analogous to a Monet canvas with its diffuse, almost deliquescent delight in magical effects of light. It is a world which, to Maisie's eye, 'prances' with sheer joy of being. It is this feeling which allows us to call Maisie's response to the world instinctively 'aesthetic' as opposed to the ethical rigidifying vision of Mrs Wix. 'Her vocation was to see the world and to thrill with enjoyment of the picture': the terminology gently insists that Maisie's response to the world with all its impartial eagerness and expanding openness to new sensations is more akin to that of the artist than that of the moralist. What then of Mrs Wix who works to narrow the girl's mind, to make it contract, to teach it disgust, jealousy, and rejection? As the rich foreign vistas open up to Maisie, Mrs Wix returns to the attack again and again. 'Haven't you really and truly *any* moral sense?' Mrs Wix puts this question twice as they are sitting by the sea one late afternoon and they agree that this is a thing 'Maisie absolutely and appallingly had so little of'. The setting is important: the seascape and the indolent beauty of the shore seem to make of Mrs Wix's moral ranting a discordant note. Maisie here feels that she is approaching 'knowledge', but it is not the kind Mrs Wix has in mind.

It came to her in fact as they sat there on the sands that she was distinctly on the road to know Everything. . . . She looked at the pink sky with a placid foreboding that she soon should have learnt All. They lingered in the flushed air till at last it turned to grey and she seemed fairly to receive new information from every brush of the breeze.[74]

The capitalized 'Everything' and 'All' describe the confidence of the young exfoliating senses in their first excited exposure to a wider world. This kind of knowledge is inclusive, it is a knowledge which will 'overflow' with the sheer brim-fullness of gratefully received impressions. This is knowledge learnt from the texture of things, the sensuous surface of the world: Mrs Wix's is a knowledge which works towards exclusion, refusal, and condemnation. There is one masterly scene in which James demonstrates the implications and rights of the two views, the two sets of values. Mrs Wix, after an ecstatic outpouring of her devotion for Maisie and a reminder of all the horrors she has undergone for her, finishes by apologizing a little for the quarrel they had over Mrs Beale (whom Maisie refused to hate to order).

'What I did lose patience at this morning was at how it was that without your seeming to condemn—for you didn't, you remember!—you yet did seem to *know*. Thank God, in his mercy, at last, *if* you do!'
    The night, this time, was warm and one of the windows stood open to the small balcony over the rail of which, on coming up for dinner, Maisie had hung for a long time in the enjoyment of the chatter, the lights, the life of the quay made brilliant by the season and the hour . . . the casement was still wide, the spectacle, the pleasure were still there and from her place in the room . . . the child could still take account of them. She appeared to watch and listen; after which she answered Mrs Wix with a question. 'If I do know—?' 'If you do condemn.' The correction was made with some austerity. It had the effect of causing Maisie to heave a vague sigh of oppression and then after an instant and as if under cover of this ambiguity pass out again upon the

balcony. She hung over the rail; she felt the summer night; she dropped down into the manners of France. There was a cafe below the hotel, before which, with little chairs and tables, people sat on a space enclosed by plants in tubs; and the impression was enriched by the flash of the white aprons of waiters and the music of a man and a woman who, from beyond the precinct, send up the strum of a guitar and the drawl of a song about 'amour'. Maisie knew what 'amour' meant too, and wondered if Mrs Wix did: Mrs Wix remained within, as still as a mouse and perhaps not reached by the performance. After a while, but not till the musicians had ceased and begun to circulate with a little plate, her pupil came back to her.

'Is it a crime?' Maisie then asked.

Mrs Wix was as prompt as if she had been crouching in a lair. 'Branded by the Bible.'[75]

The passage is incomparably subtle. There is the rich gay life outside full of movement, music, chatter, and lights, and there is the silent Mrs Wix withdrawn out of hearing (truly she is never 'reached by the performance'—she is temperamentally out of earshot); and the child wandering between the two. She looks longingly at the outside scene, but then has to return to Mrs Wix although she feels an oppression to reside with her in contrast to the promise of brilliant release down among the life of the quay. She simply wants to acquaint herself with the phenomenological world ('she was mainly curious', 'her vocation was to see the world'), not to 'condemn' it: in this she and the Bible are at odds. The low-church Old Testament cast of mind of Mrs Wix is significant: at one point she regrets she is not a Catholic. If we borrow the wider secular application of that title we realize that she lacks a breadth, a wide embrace, and is bitterly narrow and excluding in her response to life. Her eyes can see no haloes, none of the blessedness of life: only the vileness and the threats. Is this figure really the desirable mentor and cicerone for Maisie? For all the emotions which she seeks to introduce into Maisie's generous mind are essentially antipathetic to life. In particular she teaches her a jealousy which is quite foreign to her nature. In the last scene of the book Mrs Wix, in appealing to Maisie's 'moral sense', is in effect appealing to the projection of herself which she has attempted to fasten on to Maisie's plastic sensibility. She has attempted to remake and fix the child in her own image—a cardinal Jamesian sin: she works to bracket and edit her spontaneity. It is utterly right that in her final crisis of choice Maisie should lose the newly inculcated 'moral sense'. It is simply not her manner of appraising life, she is not given to such simplifying reductions of experience. For a moment, indeed, she thinks she can catch the odour of the moral sense emanating from Mrs Wix.

Then it left her, and, as if she were sinking with a slip from a foothold, her arms made a short jerk. What this jerk represented was the spasm within her of something still deeper than a moral sense. She looked at her examiner; she looked at the visitors; she felt the rising of tears she had kept down at the station. They had nothing—no, distinctly nothing—to do with her moral sense. The only thing was the old flat shameful schoolroom plea. 'I don't know—I don't know.'[76]

Her plight is not one which is solved by recourse to ethical terms; nor, indeed, could it be solved by capitulating to the selfish Mrs Beale. Mrs Wix, seeing Maisie's confusion, accuses Sir Claude of killing her moral sense, but Sir Claude is a man who knows the good when he sees it even if he cannot follow it, and he is more confident in word than deed.

'I've not killed anything . . . on the contrary I think I've produced life. I don't know what to call it—I haven't even known how decently to deal with it, to approach it; but, whatever it is, it's the most beautiful thing I've ever met—it's exquisite, it's sacred.'[77]

We can name it: it is an eagerness of acceptance, a generosity of assimilation, an incorruptible unselfish curiosity, a desire to celebrate rather than categorize life, a preference for seeing it 'prancing' rather than having it submitted to rigorous moral judgement. It is in fact that 'spontaneity of life' which, as Quentin Anderson has shown in his book *The American Henry James*, James valued above all other things and set up as the supreme virtue against the vice of various modes of appropriation by which spontaneity is always threatened. It is Mrs Wix's hand which finally leads Maisie away: yet it is not really her choice, and she has to be led to her side, thus maintaining the theme of external compulsion and direction right to the end. The adult world has provided her with no adequate guardians or companions. Sir Claude alone appreciates her and realizes that 'some lovely work of art or nature had suddenly been set down among them'[78] but he is a man weakened by his state of sexual thralldom and he cannot turn his appreciation into constructive help. It can be conceded that perhaps Mrs Wix is a better guardian than Mrs Beale but this is not James's point. As we watch Maisie returning to 'The grey horizon that was England'[79] in a state of subservience to the no less grey Mrs Wix we must feel that what is in store for her is a progressive diminution, a devivification, a contraction of her sacred range of wonderment. No adult in the book is to be wholly endorsed, though doubtless some are meant to be wholly deplored: but the threatened end of Maisie's 'wonder' is to be lamented.

James, rather schematically, has shown us a world dominated by sexual appetite in which the alternative responses seem to range from a disdaining renouncing, desperate and myopic moralism, to an extreme of selfish, unscrupulous, hypocritical pursuit of personal satisfaction. Not that Mrs Wix is completely immune to the blandishments of the social-sensual world: not that Mrs Beale is completely without feeling for Maisie. But neither properly appreciate Maisie's real virtues. One wants to snatch her, the other to blind her: neither allow for her true 'vocation'. Maisie's response is, for James, preferable to either. The very incompleteness of her knowledge makes her gentle and open where others are peremptory and shut, and it seems to me that in celebrating Maisie, James was doing more than eulogizing the child. He was saying something very important about what he considered to be the most fruitful attitude to experience:

Experience is never limited and it is never complete; it is an immense sensibility, a kind of huge spider-web of the finest silken threads suspended in the chamber of consciousness, and catching every airborne particle; it is the very atmosphere of the mind . . . it takes to itself the faintest hints of life, it converts the very pulses of the air into revelations.[80]

A famous passage but worth juxtaposing with Maisie. For given that belief certain preferences follow. Life will not be assessed according to *a priori* edicts, but rather by *a posteriori* inferences, and it will be loved rather than exploited. In James one is made to feel that to approach experience with a set of ethical imperatives is to mutilate life in advance. True virtue lies in opening oneself to as many as possible of the swarm of impressions which life offers, and then behaving in a manner dictated more by aesthetic unselfish considerations than by prescribed rules of conduct or perverse self-seeking. In a word, virtue is to celebrate life and to love its endless flow, not to appropriate it or attempt to arrest it—with a hand, with a code. Quentin Anderson formulates one of the basic questions of James's fiction in the following way: 'Is life to be loved for the wondrous appearances which love can create, or is it to be loved as a snatching game, an awful cannibalistic, gothic, nursery tale?'[81] Maisie is a victim of the 'snatching game' yet given the dubiety, the necessary incompleteness of knowledge, her spontaneous aesthetic appreciation of all that lies in her path is the one response in the novel which James would completely endorse. Her 'wonder' is an important mode of cognition.

At this point we might examine more generally James's vision of the fate of the naive eye, the doom of the unprejudiced habit of wonder. Most interesting in this respect is the curious ending to the next major novel he wrote after *What Maisie Knew*, that is *The Awkward Age*. Although to sum up the book is to violate its incomparable subtlety we may say that it hinges on an examination of two different sorts of innocence. Nanda is a sort of grown-up Maisie, though the 'oppressive' social fogs, the adult 'malaria' in which she lives and through which she moves is a more suffocating and sordid medium than Maisie's world. She is the girl who has been too carelessly 'initiated', who 'knows everything' (that ironic recurring phrase in James), and yet whose 'precious freshness of feeling'[82] seems uncorrupted by the squalid ethos to which her eyes are so candidly, so clearly open.

298

Yet she is rejected as soiled by the fashionable world in the character of Vanderbank. He feels that she has been too long steeped in a poisonous atmosphere to which, it must be pointed out, he has himself largely contributed. The other girl, Aggie, is brought up in a way of which Mrs Wix would surely approve. She 'isn't exposed to anything', she has been kept from coming 'downstairs' by her socially scrupulous mother, the Duchess. Her eyes are blinkered and averted from any tell-tale evidence of the adult world. She reads history 'that leaves the horrors out': she has been deliberately tooled and shaped and finished 'like some wonderful piece of stitching'[83] (rather as Osmond turns Pansy into a doll): she is sedulously preserved from all pollution. Unlike Nanda who is plain (and whose photograph is framed in white wood) Aggie is pretty (her photograph is framed in fur) and she seems, in all external appearances, to be the ideal sweet and simpering innocent, while Nanda appears to be all too horribly *au fait* with the dark concealed undergrowths of motive and behaviour of the adult world. On Nanda's own evidence 'the beauty of Aggie is that she knows nothing—but absolutely, utterly: not the least little tittle of anything.'[84] Nanda on the other hand is not so young as she looks, according to the Duchess who says of her: 'Of course she's supposedly young, but she's really any age you like: your London world so fearfully batters and bruises them.'[85] Aggie is brought up in a garden of innocence, apart from the contaminated society in which she is subsequently to live; whereas from the first Nanda recognizes that 'we're in society, aren't we, and that's our horizon'[86] and faces the fact by not feigning a sly ignorance but accepting things as they are for what they are. Hence her 'crude young clearness',[87] a clearness, we might add, which is not 'muddied' by what it sees and learns.

Two innocents: the real and the apparent, the plainly honest and the prettily plausible, the seemingly ignorant and the seemingly knowledgeable; what happens to them? At this point we must mention the strange Mr Longdon. He is a Jamesian spectator, 'a fresh eye, an outside mind',[88] in this case not from

America but from an ideal past of taste, kindliness, and decorum. He once loved Nanda's grandmother and he recognizes in Nanda the possibilities for perfection that he had loved in that woman: but although Nanda is for him like a Gainsborough portrait the age is no longer the age of Gainsborough and Nanda has to grow up in a London that 'has neither time, nor taste, nor sense for anything less discernible than the red flag in front of the steam-roller'.[89] Longdon spends much of his time trying to appraise the respective innocences of Nanda and Aggie through the murk of a society with which he no longer feels in sympathy. (Significantly he often takes his glasses off—as though apprehensive of too much involvement.) There is one key moment when his eye compares the two girls. He is approaching Aggie:

Since to create a particular little rounded and tinted innocence had been aimed at, the fruit had been grown to the perfection of a peach on a sheltered wall, and this quality of the object resulting from a process might well make him feel himself in contact with something wholly new. Little Aggie differed from any young person he had ever met in that she had been deliberately prepared for consumption and in that, furthermore, the gentleness of her spirit had immensely helped the preparation. Nanda, beside her, was a northern savage, and the reason was partly that the elements of that young lady's nature were already, were publicly, were almost indecorously active. They were practically there, for good or for ill; experience was still to come and what they might work out to still a mystery; but the sum would get itself done with the figures now on the slate. On little Aggie's slate the figures were yet to be written; which sufficiently accounted for the difference of the two surfaces. Both the girls struck him as lambs with the great shambles of life in their future; but while one, with its neck in a pink ribbon, had no consciousness but of being fed from the hand with the small sweet biscuit of unobjectionable knowledge, the other struggled with instincts and forebodings, with the suspicion of its doom and the far-borne accent, in the flowery fields, of blood.[90]

What becomes of Aggie can best be described by reference to a certain tropical fish which when seen below the water is a most rare and exquisite colour, but which once brought to the surface and exposed to the air loses its colours very rapidly in exchange for a sort of filthy drabness. When Aggie does finally come down stairs and out into society, it is 'with a bound—into the arena'.[91] Even before her honeymoon is over she is engaging in adulterous sexual games of tooth and claw with a predatory vigour and immorality which justifies James's strong animal imagery. So much for the traditional 'innocent'. Nanda moves in the opposite direction: the more she sees and knows, the more society conspires to exclude and abandon her. There is real pathos in the manner in which her fate starts to take on a definite shape towards the end of the book until she finally returns 'upstairs': her 'punishment', as it were, for having had an open eye and habitual candid lucidity about the world, her punishment for having 'unlearned surprise'[92] and for not practising a false ingenuousness. Of the two girls there can be no question which one attracted James, as there is finally no question which one receives Mr Longdon's approval. It is only at that point where naivety has to struggle with the onset and onslaught of knowledge and experience that life, for James, becomes truly interesting since it offers a challenge which, if met honestly and not dodged hypocritically, can result in the dignity of accurate insight, the morality of considered choice. Innocence, in this world, is something far other than the surface blush of a fruit which, tendered never so carefully, often proves to be rotten before half ripe. It is a quality of response to inevitable experience: it can be exposed and submerged in a corrupt and complex medium but it need not be contaminated or undermined if it retains a generous unselfish attitude of wonder.

But Nanda is not finally left to suffocate upstairs. Mr Longdon, who can see the fineness in her, offers a different, and to us, very interesting avenue of escape. He finally rejects London Society as being too vulgar, too merely clever and facetious, too threatening, and he holds up a surviving alternative. Objectively this alternative is represented by his house in Suffolk. He invites Nanda down there saying:

'I want to show you . . . what life *can* give. Not, of course . . . of this sort of thing.'

'No—you've told me. Of peace.'

'Of peace,' said Mr Longdon. 'Oh, you don't know—you haven't the least idea. That's just why I want to show you.'[93]

The atmosphere in his rural retreat is one of singular purity. Everything in the house seems somehow transcended simply by being the appurtenances of Mr Longdon's pure life. 'Everything, on every side, had dropped straight from heaven, with nowhere a bargaining thumb mark, a single sign of the shop.'[94] Mr Longdon has remained untainted by the age of commerce, trade, and urban expansion and its concomitant deleterious effects on the simplicity of man. He is, and the phrase is immensely suggestive, 'a great gardener—I mean really one of the greatest'.[95] It is as though he preserves and tends a lost corner of paradise. The weeks that Nanda spends in this blissful retreat she speaks of as being the happiest she had spent anywhere. When Vanderbank finally abandons her Mr Longdon comes to her rescue and invites her to come away with him, presumably to his rural paradise, though he also imposes one rather stern condition. 'You understand clearly, I take it, that this time it's never again to leave me—or to *be* left.'[96] He is indeed offering a retreat: a total retreat from social life, from its battles and nightmares, but also from its richness and fulfilments. Nanda however is well schooled in renunciation. Early on in the book she seems lucidly aware of her doom and she says of marriage: 'I shall be one of the people who don't. I shall be at the end . . . one of those who haven't.'[97] She has had her 'one crowded hour of glorious life'[98] but—and here we approach a basic Jamesian theme—just because she opened her eyes to all of it, just because of her honest wonder and interest, just because of her unprejudiced lucidity of vision, she seems to forfeit all rights of participation, all the privileges of consummation. The end of her days of wondering involvement is even more certainly decreed than Maisie's. James wrote this novel shortly after moving into Lamb House at Rye, a wonderful old house with a magnificent walled garden to which he loved to flee from London society. James in the form of Mr Longdon has entered this novel to rescue Nanda; as though,

THE RANGE OF WONDERMENT

recognizing the value of her attitude toward life and the pathos of her predicament, he could not bear to see her so foolishly undervalued and so callously marooned.

A third girl who is doomed to suffer because of what a corrupt society seems to have made of her is Julia Bride in the late (1909) strange astringent story of that name. Here James does not equivocate at all about the nature of the society that has served her so ill. Julia has met a fine sensitive man worthy of her but seems likely to lose him because of her mother's scandalous past and her own six broken engagements which were more thrust upon her than solicited. The story is simply her efforts to find someone to tell a 'lie' for her to her young man, an outward lie which would be the essential truth, namely that she is basically a decent and fine girl. In the process she realizes how ruinous society has been for her.

Something in the girl's vision . . . worked, even at the moment, to quicken once more the clearness and harshness of judgment, the retrospective disgust, as she might have called it, that had of late grown up in her, the sense of all the folly and vanity and vulgarity, the lies, the perversities, the falsification of all life in the interest of who could say what wretched frivolity, what preposterous policy, amid which she had been condemned so ignorantly, so pitifully to sit, to walk, to grope, to flounder, from the very dawn of her consciousness.[99]

In desperation she seeks help from one of her old boy-friends, but even as she listens to him assenting to help her she realizes that his profound vulgarity will alienate her young man from her for once and for all. She knows she is slipping to 'some doom as yet incalculable', she feels 'the fascination of the abyss'[100] as she drops away from all hope, and she sees the ruins of her future with 'grim lucidity'.[101] She is a minor Jamesian 'seer' of sensibility and openness who moves towards a banishment as sure, if not a death so swift, as Daisy Miller's. She has had to grope like Maisie, she has been forced to early awareness like Nanda, she has been more squalidly involved and used than any of them, and the clearness with which she sees all this seems to grow precisely as her exclusion from the 'good' life becomes more sure.

303

Most of the true 'wonderers' seemed doomed to a fate of exclusion in James, and if exclusion is not enforced a gesture of renunciation often takes its place. Maisie is taken by the hand back to England: Strether returns of his own volition to America. It might seem absurd to suggest that Maisie and Strether are both examples of the naive eye: yet both do learn to view the world with true inclusive wonder, both show themselves worthy spectators of at least 'one crowded hour of glorious life' and both leave the scene, like Nanda, though neither is so fortunate as to be rescued by the author. James's account of his interest in Strether could be made to cover many Jamesian characters with only slight qualifications. Thus in the preface to *The Ambassadors* he writes:

Would there yet perhaps be time for reparation?—reparation, that is, for the injury done his character; for the affront, he is quite ready to say, so stupidly put upon it and in which he has even himself had so clumsy a hand? The answer to which is that he now at all events *sees*; so that the business of my tale and the march of my action, not to say the precious moral of everything, is just my demonstration of this process of vision.[102]

I suggest that this description relates Strether to Maisie and several other characters addicted to seeing and wondering. Writing about the girl 'in the cage' James makes an interesting grouping:

The range of wonderment attributed in our tale to the young woman employed at Cocker's differs little in essence from the speculative thread on which the pearls of Maisie's experience, in this same volume— pearls of so strange an iridescence—are mostly strung. She wonders, putting it simply, very much as Morgan Moreen wonders; and they all wonder, for that matter, very much after the fashion of our portentous little Hyacinth of 'The Princess Casamassima,' tainted to the core, as we have seen him, with the trick of mental reaction on the things about him and fairly staggering under appropriations as I have called them, that he owes to the critical spirit. He collapses, poor Hyacinth, like a thief at night, overcharged with treasures of reflexion and spoils of passion of which he can give, in his poverty and obscurity, no honest account.[103]

THE RANGE OF WONDERMENT

Hyacinth is an interesting case. His descent is a mixed one: the justly vengeful yet destructive energies of his mother mingling with the aristocratic fineness and culpable decadence of his father. He is gifted with an aesthetic sensitivity which no one appreciates and forced into alignment with a socialist anarchy with which he cannot sympathize. A snatched visit to Europe offers him a positive transcending vision of the sheer plenitude, the endless possibilities of life: 'a sudden sense overtook him, making his heart sink with a fund of desolation—a sense of everything that might hold one to the world, of the sweetness of not dying, the fascination of great cities, the charm of travel and discovery, the generosity of admiration.'[104] Yet his social situation works against this generous exfoliation of the senses and forces him to be destructively partisan. Committed to murdering a man in the interests of the party cause he instead commits suicide, making thereby the supreme 'effort of renunciation'. As Frederick Crews has commented: 'he must die because with his new vision there is no place left for him to live.'[105] Not dissimilarly, Morgan Moreen in 'The Pupil' dies in the 'morning twilight of his childhood', his morality and vision at once too fine and too frail to survive in the fifth-rate social world to which he is condemned. His embattled and foredoomed integrity has much in common with the artist and his death betokens more than the premature expiration of innocence. Strether also attains a vision which society cannot contain and his somewhat perverse return to America is perhaps a symbolic suicide, analogous to Hyacinth's more final act. Those who live on in the Jamesian world are usually those who have more appetite than imagination; whose 'seeing' is calculating and perhaps cruel; who wonder, if at all, suspiciously and not generously; who are too energetically end-seeking to appreciate the delights of passive appreciation. For the truly naive eye, the habit of wonder, there is no place in the social centre of the world: it must either give way to some more worldly perspective on the world, or flee, or die. And yet—and this links James with Emerson and Thoreau—it is the naive wondering eye which most

20   305   TRW

generously celebrates and responds to the full range of experience. It omits nothing: even if admission costs no less than everything.

The intimate connection between comprehensiveness of vision and renunciation of participation is discernible in James's work almost from the first. There is in fact a most instructive shift visible in the attitudes of Roderick Hudson and Isabel Archer towards life, a shift worth examining here as it throws light on James's later work. When Rowland Mallett first visits Hudson in America he admires one of his statues which shows much promise: it is a young Water-drinker.

'Tell me this,' said Rowland. 'Did you mean anything very particular by your young Water-drinker? Does he represent an idea? Is he a pointed symbol?'

Hudson raised his eyebrows and gently stroked his hair. 'Why, he's youth, you know; he's innocence, he's health, he's strength, he's curiosity. Yes, he's a lot of grand things.'

'And the cup is also a symbol?'

'The cup is knowledge, pleasure, experience. Anything of that kind.'

'Then he's drinking very deep,' said Rowland.

Hudson gave an approving nod. 'Well, poor wretch, you wouldn't have him die of thirst, would you?'[106]

The novel is all here in little. Rowland becomes Hudson's patron and helps him to go to Europe where Hudson duly drinks very deep of the cup of life and dies as a result of the corrupting liquor. Isabel Archer has an almost artistic hunger to become acquainted with the full range of life, but there is a significant difference in her attitude as is brought out in this conversation with Ralph. He speaks first.

'You want to drain the cup of experience.'

'No, I don't want to touch the cup of experience. It's a poisoned drink. I want only to see for myself.'

'You want to see, but not to feel.'[107]

This not only throws significant light on Isabel's character, showing why she makes the fatal mistake of marrying Osmond: it also reveals something of that growing suspicion of the dangers of passion and participation which James exhibits in his later work. The artist type in particular cannot maintain his comprehensive vision *and* drink the cup of experience. Thus Strether refuses the offered draught. And if we turn briefly to James's very late work, *The Ivory Tower*, we can see this idea fully developed.

The story concentrates on a young man called Gray who returns to America after being brought up in Europe: he is an artist figure (James was toying with the idea of making him a writer) but in returning to America he inherits vast sums of money. The point of the novel was to be the way he lets his friend carefully rob him of all his money so that he can in fact hold back from all involvements in society. As is consistent with late James, society here has become an abysmal thing (and this is not to be taken as mere anti-Americanism). It is a jungle of 'greedy wants, timid ideas and fishy passions'[108] as one character lightly proclaims; it is all 'senseless sound and expensive futility'.[109] It is full of poison, and this is why Mr Betterman leaves his money to Gray. Because Gray has always loathed money and the greedy bustle of the market. Betterman hopes Gray will come and redeem society. But Gray has all the instincts of withdrawal. In the scene in which he picks up the too-obvious symbol of the Ivory Tower he says: '*Isn't* it an ivory tower, and doesn't living in an ivory tower just mean the most distinguished retirement?'[110] And much later in the book Gray makes a remark which has widespread implications for James's work: 'for the situation to have a sense, I take it, one must sit in one's tower alone.'[111] What James calls 'the eccentricity of Gray's holdings-off'[112]— from money, from marriage—indicate his wish to create a character who lacks all worldly appetites and aspirations and who is, as it were, all consciousness, all detached appreciation: an intelligence without a proper world to inhabit. James has a rather striking image in his notes for the continuation of the novel. He is discussing Gray:

His 'culture', his initiations of intelligence and experience, his possibilities of imagination, if one will, to say nothing of other things, make for me a sort of figure of a floating island on which he drifts and bumps and coasts about, wanting to get alongside as much as possible, yet always with the gap of water, the little island *fact*, to be somehow bridged over. All of which makes him, I of course desperately recognise, another of the 'intelligent', another exposed and assaulted, active and passive 'mind' engaged in an adventure and interesting in *itself* by so being.[113]

The island which cannot attach itself to the continent, the mind which lacks a suitable world: these images give us some telling hints as to James's vision of the artists' relation with society. More clearly we can see that for James, the artist figure *had* to remove himself from the world in order to attain to a true vision of the Whole. By 'holding-off' Gray can appreciate even his betrayal—'the beautiful way in which it falls into the general ironic apprehension, imagination, appropriation, of the Whole, becomes for him *the* fact about it'[114]—and James continues his notes to give us a really vital insight, not only about Gray, but about all those other renouncing, non-participating protagonists we have noted. 'He really enjoys getting so detached from it as to be able to have it before him for observation and wonder as he does. . . .'[115]

The connection between detachment, wonder, and art is clearly revealed, and it is this connection which I wish to examine in the next chapter.

CHAPTER 16

THE SUBJECTIVE ADVENTURE

Her consciousness, if they let it alone—as they of course after this
mercifully must—was, in the last analysis, a kind of shy romance.
Not a romance like their own, a thing to make the fortune of any
author up to the mark—one who should have the invention or who
could *have the courage; but a small scared starved subjective satis-*
faction that would do her no harm and nobody else any good.

HENRY JAMES, *The Story in it*[1]

But if nothing was more impossible than the fact, nothing was more
intense than the vision. What may not, we can only moralise, take
place in the quickened muffled perception of a young person with an
ardent soul?

HENRY JAMES, *In the Cage*[2]

'WONDER' has another meaning which we have not yet mentioned but which for James was closely related to the meaning
of it we have discussed so far. You can 'wonder *at*'—and you
can also 'wonder *about*'. As well as the attitude of awed and
reverent openness, there is the habit of speculation: the word
connotes both, and clearly one activity can easily give way to the
other. There is a small but significant shift from a passive to an
active mood, the idea of uninterrupted sensory reception giving
way to the energized imagination which adds and provides out
of its own stirring abundance. That James was interested in this
sort of imaginative activity can be demonstrated at once by
turning to his preface to *The Aspern Papers*. Discussing the way
he developed the hint which resulted in 'The Turn of the Screw'
he writes:

The thing had for me the immense merit of allowing the imagination
absolute freedom of hand, of inviting it to act on a perfectly clear field,

309

with no 'outside' control involved, no pattern of the usual or the true
or the terrible 'pleasant' . . . to consort with. . . . I find here a perfect
example of an exercise of the imagination unassisted, unassociated—
playing the game, making the score, in the phrase of our sporting day,
off its own bat.

He goes on to talk suggestively of that 'annexed but independent
world in which nothing is right save as we rightly imagine it'.[3]
Clearly, as an artist, he felt that imaginative speculation could
create 'truths' not verifiable in the empirically received world.
Speculation can mean anything from mere factual conjecture—the
whereabouts of X and Y at a compromising moment, say—to
imaginative construction or rather, if I may coin a word for
James's benefit, imaginative superstruction. 'Speculation' was
a key word for James and it is perhaps fitting that the etymology
of the word gives us *specula*—a watch tower, and *speculari*—to
watch. More than that, of course, the word means to reflect,
conjecture, theorize: it also means, to borrow the OED phrasing,
'to undertake a business enterprise or transaction of a risky
nature in the expectation of considerable gain'. And a speculum
is a reflector for seeing inside people, a surgical aid. Perhaps it is
perverse to push so many varieties of connotation, but I think
we can profitably bear in mind the idea of the isolated spectator
in his tower; a hint of that tool which reveals the concealed
inwardness of people; and the notion of risk and gain—though
in James the dangers and profits are imaginative rather than
pecuniary.

To illustrate the connection between wonder and speculation
in James, and the close relationship between the naive eye and the
artist which I have alluded to before, I want to examine two short
novels which seem to me central to his work and hitherto unjustly
neglected and ignored.

The first of these is *In the Cage*, completed the year after *What
Maisie Knew* (i.e. in 1898) and three years before the second novel
I wish to study, *The Sacred Fount*. *In The Cage* concerns a young
girl who works as a telegraphist in one of the busiest parts of
London; and before entering the book there are two aspects of

the heroine's situation which we should note. First, the heroine by virtue of her situation is physically almost completely immobilized. She moves around and sees far less than Maisie and any trip to France is virtually out of the question. All of her significant activity—except (perhaps) for one notable walk—takes place in her imagination, and here she is far more active than Maisie. Secondly, this is the only book where James gives us a heroine completely excluded from any participation in that area of society which habitually interested him. As he wrote in his introduction to this story, he had become interested in 'the question of what it might "mean" . . . for confined and cramped and yet considerably tutored young officials of either sex to be made so free, intellectually, of a range of experience otherwise quite closed to them'.[4] There is no question of the immersion of the 'candid outsider', nor even of the physical involvement of the much-handled Maisie. Nor is there any question of her suffering the sort of fatality which overtakes Hyacinth Robinson or Morgan Moreen who, among other reasons, seem to die for want of a proper world to move in. Her actual physical world is real and solid, but elsewhere and irrelevant by virtue of its impoverished low position in the social scale. It consists of Mr Mudge and Chalk Farm: that is where, physically, she is condemned to 'live'. But her imagination lives in Mayfair and it is that which interests James. Finally it might be added that, like the narrator of *The Sacred Fount*, and unlike most other major Jamesian characters, the heroine of *In the Cage* remains unnamed from start to finish. She is more of a presence, a principle, an activity, than a personality and identity. These considerations alone, plus the story's important chronological place in James's work, allow us to see more in its material than the rather sentimental interest of a sensitive girl condemned to a lower-class life, indulging in upper-class day-dreams. James has isolated something in this story for special scrutiny. He has devised a situation and manipulated the mechanics of the plot in a way that will exclude all movements and gestures, all situational complexities which might distract from a single focusing: a focusing this time not, as with

Maisie, on the wondering eye, but on the wondering imagination. If it was Maisie's vocation to 'see', then it is the vocation of this heroine to have visions. Put it another way. Maisie was, to a certain extent, on the outside looking in, through a pane of glass. The telegraphist is on the inside looking out: she is 'in the cage', the cage of her isolated imagination. Maisie was to some extent debarred from entering the sweet-shop of society: this girl is trapped inside her own head. This is what I mean by the narrowing of focus evident in this story.

Right from the start the heroine's situation, predicament and stance are so suggestive as to be symbolic. 'It had occurred to her early that in her position—that of a young person spending, in framed and wire confinement, the life of a guinea-pig or a magpie—she should know a great many persons without their recognizing the acquaintance.'[5] That 'framed and wired confinement' suggests a more than local separation and aloneness of the experiencing ego, but if we are alert enough to pick up the hint of the 'magpie' (and James never wastes his similes) we should be prepared for someone who has a predilection for the snatching up and hoarding of precious brilliant things, things which might adorn the lonely nest and console the outcast. There is another important hint in the first paragraph. Her function, we learn, was mainly to 'count words as numberless as the sands of the sea, the words of the telegrams thrust, from morning to night, through the gap left in the high lattice, across the encumbered shelf that her forearm ached with rubbing'.[6]

Telegrams: cryptic hints from the outside world, highly charged fragments from the bustle of society, random dislocated shreds of significance saturated with limitless possible meanings: the heroine's vocation is to *receive*, and in her imagination to *decipher*, telegrams. Her task is that of a Jamesian protagonist reproduced in an extreme physical form. The clues which she receives are more enigmatic and elliptical than the clues which, say, Strether has to work on. But in essence the predicament and aspiration are the same. Given this young, naive yet sensitive telegraphist, what does James make of her? In a word—the

Jamesian artist, though seen in comic and pathetic perspective. It is really interesting to see just how much of the artist James makes her:

she had a whimsical mind and wonderful nerves; she was subject, in short, to sudden flickers of antipathy and sympathy, red gleams in the grey, fitful needs to notice and to 'care', old caprices of curiosity. . . . She was perfectly aware that her imaginative life was the life in which she spent most of her time. . . . What *she* could handle freely, she said to herself, was combinations of men and women . . . there were long stretches in which inspiration, divination and interest quite dropped. The great thing was the flashes, the quick revivals, absolute accidents all, and neither to be counted on nor to be resisted.[7]

Her dominant feeling is that there are innumerable 'impressions to be gathered' and more important to her, even than marriage, is 'her actual chance for a play of mind'. She has an 'instinct of observation' and she postpones the marriage that would take her out of the shop on the grounds that 'where I am I still see things'.[8] In her job as a telegraphist 'she had seen all sorts of things and pieced together all sorts of mysteries': she has 'an extraordinary way of keeping clues',[9] a curiosity that goes out 'with a rush':[10] she also has a tendency which James was accused of himself. 'Sometimes she put in too much—too much of her own sense.'[11] Thus on the basis of a few telegrams between some ladies and gentlemen 'she read into the immensity of their intercourse stories and meanings without end'.[12] One message will prompt a dozen conflicting theories. One good-looking Captain Everard with his multiplicity of signatures seems to be a universe in himself. On the basis of a few telegrams from this man and the woman who accompanies him, the heroine provides romantic crises, climaxes, ecstasies, disasters and destinies for an ever-expanding social world. Truly she justifies Yvor Winters's comment on *The American*: 'There is a marked tendency in this book on the part of James and his characters alike to read into situations more than can be justified by the facts as given, to build up intense states of feeling, on the basis of such a reading, and to judge or act as a result of that feeling.'[13] Certainly when

HENRY JAMES

we see what the heroine does with the Captain's mundane civility
—'Oh yes, hasn't it been awfully wet?'—we may wonder whether
James wants us to regard his heroine as pathetically absurd, or
even neurotic. 'That was a specimen of their give and take; it fed
her fancy that no form of intercourse so transcendent and distilled
had even been established on earth. Everything, so far as they
chose to consider it, might mean almost anything.'¹⁴ And of
course we are reminded that she feeds herself on cheap novels 'all
about fine folks'. With her compulsive appetite for 'framing
pictures' of an absent glamorous world, is she simply a comic
parody of the Jamesian artist? Certainly she is at least that; yet
James has subjected the habits of her imagination to a scrutiny
which lifts the book above mere parody. The book is a genuine
exploration into the activities of the speculative imagination,
not a joke.

If James heard the start of an anecdote that stimulated his
imagination he would ask his raconteur to discontinue, in case
more facts inhibited his growing vision. (The pinch of snuff, the
germ—these are typical metaphors.) Again we find his heroine
emulating her master in an extreme manner. Upon the first
appearance of Captain Everard she is so distracted by the glory
of the apparition that she cannot even read his telegrams while
she is counting the words. 'His words were mere numbers, they
told her nothing whatever; and after he had gone she was in
possession of no name, of no address, of no meaning, of nothing
but a vague sweet sound and an immense impression. . . . Yet
she had taken him in; she knew everything; she had made up
her mind.'¹⁵

Her sense of knowing everything—a sense which relates her to
so many of James's heroes and heroines—is sometimes so intense
as to give her a kind of vertigo. Sometimes she sees the world
'as through rippled shallow sunshot water';¹⁶ the mundane and
the banal take on a fluid brilliance for her. Yet this sense of knowledge is based on a minimum of acquaintance with any physical
facts. When the captain does come into the shop it torments her
that she cannot 'touch with him on some individual fact'.¹⁷ She

314

does not even know the correct state of the weather outside, and James's phrasing of this ignorance perhaps encourages us to discern in it a larger unawareness. She has to guess at the climate, 'betraying how little she knew, in her cage, of whether it was foul or fair'.[18] Of course this lack of actual experience, of empirical evidence, serves to emphasize her exclusion—virtually from 'life'. Two of James's images for this state again seem to reflect back to his conception of the artist. 'The nose of this observer was brushed by the bouquet, yet she could never really pluck even a daisy.'[19] And later we read that she could be 'stupified' by 'the revelation of the golden shower flying about without a gleam of gold for herself'.[20] The important connection to note is that it is precisely because she has to feed herself on 'whiffs and glimpses' that the girl finds 'her divinations work faster and stretch further'.[21] Imaginative activity seems to take place in inverse proportion to experience. And imaginative activity can reach a state where it no longer seeks corroboration from life, indeed may find any more evidence an unwelcome distraction. Thus at the climax of the book when the Captain enters in obvious distress, the telegraphist first of all realizes 'how much she had missed in the gaps and blanks and absent answers': but just the sight of the Captain is enough for her imagination. 'This was vivid enough, and after an instant she knew it was all she wanted. She wanted no detail, no fact. . . .'[22] Facts may be disputed, but you cannot argue with the intensity of a vision. As the tow-line is to the glider so is the world of history to that of the imagination: the former drops away once the latter is in flight.

But there is still one more aspect of the relation between the imagination and the physical world which James hints at in this book and which gives us an important clue in approaching *The Sacred Fount*. First of all, because of her 'knowledge' (i.e. the world's telegrams and what her imagination adds by way of creative interpretation) she enjoys a 'triumphant vicious feeling of mastery'.[23] It is like a comic echo of the Faustian 'knowledge enormous makes a God of me'. Secondly this feeling of mastery

HENRY JAMES

gives way to a vague feeling that her dreams are so intense as to have a creative power, as though her visions got back in amongst the facts and influenced them for its own ends. At one moment at least her imagination seems to have a vaguely Prospero-ish ability to conjure up décor and players and direct the scene. This occurs when she takes an evening walk with the intense yet half unacknowledged hope that she might meet the Captain. She has dreamed and dreamed, and suddenly the dream is upon her. There he is: and he is as nice to her and appreciative of her help as she could have ever wished. He even manages to hint that there are stronger feelings there. If this was one of James's ghost stories he might have made this sudden apparition of the Captain more hallucinatory, like the various spectral appearances in *The Turn of the Screw* which may also be ascribed to an intense disordered imagination. As it is he amiably equivocates by saying that 'it was almost rich enough to be but the positive creation of a dream'.[24] But the hint is there. And after the meeting her fancy works even harder so we read of 'the frenzy of her imagination',[25] a frenzy in which she can turn all factual scraps into evidence of their intimate relationship. Pathetically, when the Captain does not even bother to look at her when he comes into the shop she imagines his eyes have answered her own advice to keep quiet by implying to her: 'I'll do whatever you say; I won't even look at you—see, see!'[26] The imaginative super-structure has supplanted the real world altogether.

Yet at one crucial moment she is able to give the Captain a piece of actual information which he needs desperately, something he had written on an old telegram, and the dénouement of the story reveals that the heroine's surmises had not all been wildly wrong. Exactly what nexus between the real and the imagined James intended to establish is not clear. Clearly he does not want the imagination to be regarded as a mere instrument of day-dreaming. It has its truths. More importantly, the heroine, the person who exercises her imagination to the full, feels 'like the very fountain of fate'.[27] Does life in fact spring out of the sacred fount of the imagination? The idea is certainly not absent

316

from James's later work. Of course the heroine is seen in a comic perspective. An ironic light is thrown on her by her friend Mrs Jordan who has a menial job arranging flowers for aristocrat's tables and yet—'She spoke as if, for that matter, she invited the company. "They simply *give* me the table—all the rest, all the other effects, come afterwards."'[28] Of course James intends us to smile at the idea of a telegraphist who feels imaginatively responsible for Mayfair society. In conversation with Mrs Jordan the telegraphist makes the following claim: 'I doubt if you "do" them as much as I! Their affairs, their appointments and arrangements, their little games and secrets and vices—those things all pass before me.'[29]

This claim to a thoroughness in the 'doing' of society is an amusing echo of the sort of thing James discusses in his prefaces. But there are other aspects to the telegraphist which are more serious. For one thing, the heroine has a very ambivalent attitude towards high society. Sometimes she regards it as 'the high reality', a sort of poetic perfection of humanity: yet in her 'talk' with the captain she firmly condemns that society's shortcomings: 'Your extravagances, your selfishness, your immorality, your crimes.' And in a relaxed moment with Mrs Jordan she dismisses them all. 'They're *too* real! They're selfish brutes.'[30] This dual attitude towards the summit of society—a spur to the imagination, an outrage to the moral sense—reflects a dualism in James's own work. And finally it is not the opposition between low and high society that we are left with so much as a qualified praise of the imagination itself. It is precisely because the heroine is so irremediably excluded that her imagination can be examined in such isolation: it is all she has got. For her 'reality . . . could only be ugliness and obscurity, could never be the escape, the rise'.[31] She is a captive, and 'the amusements of captives are full of a desperate contrivance'.[32] Are her desperate contrivances mere imagined wish-fulfilments, a compensation for the dullness of Mr Mudge and Chalk Farm? Or is, perhaps, her predicament only that of any sensitive person projected in an extreme form? After all she has what mere day-dreamers are not noted for: the 'heroism of sympathy',[33] a sort of generous, feeling, empathy which James greatly admired.

We may speak, then, with some certainty of the consolations and the risks of the imagination, and note the fact that it is intimately related to that important virtue, sympathy. But what are the positive gains? Where is the profit of the speculation? In this connection there is an apt passage concerning the heroine's visit to Bournemouth with Mr Mudge and their visits to the band-stand, the noisy centre of the town life. 'She preferred to sit at the far end, away from the band and the crowd; as to which she had frequent differences with her friend, who reminded her often that they could have only in the thick of it the sense of the money they were getting back. That had little effect on her, for she got back her money by seeing many things, the things of the past year, fall together and connect themselves, undergo the happy relegation that transforms melancholy and misery, passion and effort, into experience and knowledge.'[34]

Mr Mudge leads a purely physical existence: he voices the claims of the creature who wishes to join the herd. The heroine prefers to remain away from it all; considering her money well spent if she can be left to her work of imaginative reconstruction, allowing the mind to find order and connection where it will, endowing the arbitrary with a sense of sequence, redeeming life from chaos, transforming suffering into wisdom, making facts serve the need of vision. This book is certainly minor, but it is important. For here in miniature James has submitted the habit of speculation to a comic examination and at the same time asserted its virtues and purpose. As a person the telegraphist must go away with Mr Mudge to Chalk Farm: but as a principle she represents for James the predicament and function of the artist. The price she has to pay is exclusion from participation—indeed it is the very condition of her work: the profit is however large— the imaginative transformation of the world. The action of the story is, wrote James, 'simply the girl's "subjective" adventure':[35] she is one of those few people for whom consciousness in itself is 'a romance', one of those rare and privileged people who are gifted with 'the critical impulse and the acuter vision'.[36] But this book by no means exhausted James's analysis of speculative wonder. It was more of an ironic sounding of the theme. And some of his remarks in the preface to this work point the way his inquiry was to take him. Discussing his interest in 'wonderment' —wonderment which has been sparked into activity—he affords himself some general considerations. 'To criticise is to appreciate, to appropriate, to take intellectual possession, to establish in fine a relation with the criticised thing and make it one's own. The large intellectual appetite projects itself thus on many things, while the small—not better advised, but unconscious of need for advice—projects itself on few.'

James goes on to damn with faint praise all the 'non-speculative' people in the world:

Their example is much to the point, in the light of all the barren trouble they are saved; but somehow, after all, it gives no pause to the 'artist', to the morbid imagination. That rash, that idle faculty continues to abound in questions, and to supply answers to as many of them as possible; all of which makes a great occupation for idleness. To the fantastic scale on which this last-named state may, in favouring conditions, organise itself, to the activities it may practise when the favouring conditions happen to crop up in Mayfair or in Kensington, our portrayal of the caged telegraphist may well appear a proper little monument.[37]

A larger monument appeared in 1901: *The Sacred Fount*, which is James's most sustained and penetrating exploration of the habit of wonder or, as he more significantly and equivocally calls it, 'the morbid imagination'.

The theme of the book is not so esoteric as some critics have made out: it fits in with one of James's recurring preoccupations. Briefly: the narrator tells of a weekend visit to a country house called Newmarch. On the train going down he notes that a man, Gilbert Long, whom he once considered dull and stupid, now seems bright and intelligent. He also notes that a lady, Grace Brissenden, whom he knows to be old, seems in fact to be growing younger and more vivacious with her years. On later meeting her husband, Briss, he fancies him to be old and exhausted. ('It was he who was old—it was he who was older—it was he who was oldest.')³⁸ On the strength of these impressions the narrator starts to construct a theory, a theory which at first is helped by equivocal hints from other people. The theory is based on the idea of the depletion and appropriation of human energy, particularly between the sexes. The 'sacred fount' of the life force is 'like the greedy man's description of the turkey as an "awkward" dinner dish. It may be sometimes too much for a single share, but it's not enough to go round.'³⁹ Thus in any marriage one person will be a taker, the other a giver.

'One of the pair,' I said, 'has to pay for the other.'

A conversation with Mrs Brissenden draws out the point more clearly. She speaks first:

'One of them always gets more out of it than the other. One of them—you know the saying—gives the lips, the other gives the cheek.'
'It's the deepest of all truths. Yet the cheek profits too,' I more prudently argued.
'It profits most. It takes and keeps and uses all the lips give.'⁴⁰

It is those characters in James who 'take and keep and use' the sacred life energy of another person who are the real villains. Whether one cares to think of Olive Chancellor trying to draw Verena Tarrant into her freezing orbit, or Gilbert Osmond exploiting Isabel Archer for his sterile ends, or the more minor cruelty exercised by Lady Beldonald in 'The Beldonald Holbein' or the 'atrocity of art' with which Mrs Grantham takes her revenge on the innocent Lady Gwyther (in 'The Two Faces'), the general fault common to all is that they batten on other people, use them, exploit them, make them over for their own ends, instead of reverencing their unique and independent jet of life. They turn life into an 'awful game of grab'. The narrator's theory, then, is related to a central Jamesian concern, and in the light of his theory he is sure that just as Briss is 'paying' for his wife, so some lady must be paying for the unbelievably enhanced and energized Gilbert Long. His improvement is such that she must be paying a great deal: she must be almost drained of her own spirit and wit. So he sets about looking for 'the right idiot'[41] —right, that is, for his theory. One could almost put it this way: he is trying to find warrant for writing a James novel.

Newmarch is no ordinary country house. It is 'a place of charm so special as to create rather a bond among its guests'.[42] It is sometimes discussed in theatrical terms ('an ample stage') and it is clearly more emblematic than real: 'life became a mere arrested ramble or stimulated lounge, and we profited to the full by the noble freedom of Newmarch, that overarching ease which in nothing was so marked as in the tolerance of talk. The air of the place itself, in such conditions, left one's powers with a sense of play; if one wanted something to play at one simply played at being there.'[43] It is a sort of ideal world in which people are released from all material contingencies and provided with a setting which most encourages and allows them to indulge their talent for forming relationships. 'Was *any* temporary colloca-tion, in a house so encouraging to sociability, out of the range of nature?'[44] It has all the appearance of being James's version of the Platonic idea of 'society'. Certainly all the challenges which James found in society are here in an extreme form. The atmo-sphere of the house is one of 'clear dimness and rich gleams'[45] and in this ambiguous brilliant dusk the relationship between appearances and reality is almost preternaturally difficult to infer and establish. Every room leads to another room—there are 'great chains' of rooms—and everybody seems a possible screen for somebody else until the whole place seems to be composed of nothing but screens, and every spoken thing seems a mask for an unspoken gesture of sinister portent. The consensus of gracious forms at some times seems to be an expression of mankind's finest social instincts; and at other times it seems a prolonged massive charade of non-expressive and concealing postures. At times the atmosphere of the house is distinctly oppressive, as when the narrator walks out into the garden and finds the air 'a sudden corrective to the grossness of our lustre and the thickness of our medium, our general heavy humanity'.[46] More remarkable is the narrator's meditation in the garden:

We were all so fine and formal, and the ladies in particular at once so little and so much clothed, so beflounced yet so denuded, that the summer stars called to us in vain. We had ignored them in our crystal cage, among our tinkling lamps; no more free really to alight than if we had been dashing in a locked railway-train across a lovely land.[47]

That society might be abysmal, that it might be a condemnation and a sentence, a suffocating and wearying imprisonment—these pessimistic feelings are part of the late James's ambivalent attitude towards society. Newmarch is the social world, and the narrator goes back into it to continue his quest: but while, as a house, it is not so horrifying as Atreus' palace in *Agamemnon* or the guilt-saturated mansion of *Rosmersholm*, it is a place more of darkness than light and there is the hint of something mephitic in the thick social air.

In its populated gloom the one thing necessary is some guiding light, and since society has come to ignore the stars and prefer the inadequate substitute of its 'tinkling lamps' the narrator's quest is really for some sort of better illumination—in every sense of that word. When he speaks of 'raking the gloom for lights'[48] he reveals himself in his most suggestive stance. All his ideas and fancies are spoken of in terms of light: 'a blaze of suggestion', 'the flame of the fancy', 'sparks were what we wanted'[49] and so on. His theory acts as 'a torch in the darkness': as he says 'I start, for my part, at any rate, quite in the dark—or in a darkness lighted, at best, by what you have called the torch of my analogy'.[50]

We have noted other Jamesian characters who had to try and orient themselves in the gloom, as an example we may recall Laura Wing peering through the half-lights of the Opera House. In this work, too, the importance of eyesight is stressed continually. From the start he 'watches with curiosity', he is always attracted by the prospect of there being 'something for me to see'.[51] He always wants 'a glimpse', a word to which he recurs and which, as with the girl in the cage, seems to indicate a preferred mode of seeing. For glimpses stimulate the imagination as a revealed panorama seen in absolute clarity would not. He talks of 'seeing depths' in things, and he talks of a 'general, amiable consensus of blindness' around him in such a way as to dignify and sanctify his dedication to the holy task of 'the very act of seeing'.[52] He likes to 'watch and watch' and lives in a separate 'world of observation' to such an extent that he attracts the accusation 'You see too much',[53] a possibility to which we will return. His point is 'that one couldn't know anything without seeing all':[54] but in this case 'seeing', unlike the faculty exercised by early Jamesian protagonists, but like that of the girl in the cage, is a source of visions. 'Observation breeds ideas' as he succinctly puts it, and he elsewhere talks of 'the momentum already acquired by the act of observation'.[55] His 'extraordinary interest in my fellow-creatures'[56] stimulates his eye, and seen glimpses promote imagined speculations. And speculation—this is the main point—is a source of illumination.

It is important to note that, as with the girl in the cage, seeing, speculating, creating are related activities. 'To see all this was at the time, I remember, to be inhumanly amused as if one had found one could create something. I had created nothing but a clue or two to the larger comprehension I still needed, yet I positively found myself overtaken by a mild artistic glow.'[57] More, at one crucial point, the lady Mrs Server, whom he suspects to be the missing character in his scheme and with whom he is possibly infatuated, seems to appear at the dictates of his imagination. 'It was exactly as if she had been there by the operation of my intelligence. . . .'[58] At the time of this meeting Newmarch has become like some 'castle of enchantment' and he is reminded of the 'days of fairy-tales and of the childish imagination of the impossible'. In those days, he goes on, 'I moved in a world in which the strange "came true"'.[59] By extension he feels there is now a touch of 'wizardry' in his own imaginative version of the world. 'I had thought it all out, and to have thought it was, wonderfully, to have brought it.'[60] With such a build-up when Mrs Server finally appears in 'the thin suffusion of twilight' there is something vaguely hallucinatory about her presence. Even more than the Captain's appearance to the telegraphist do we feel that this encounter might be an overspill from the 'wealth' of his imagination into the world of fact. At this point we should more clearly establish what is the motivating force behind the narrator's strenuous activity, what drives him to his compulsive watching, his endless envisioning? What does he mean when he speaks of being 'on the scent of something ultimate'?[61] A key statement occurs early in the book:

I was just conscious, vaguely, of being on the track of the law, a law that would fit, that would strike me as governing the delicate phenomena—delicate though so marked—that my imagination found itself playing with. A part of the amusement they yielded came, I daresay, from my exaggerating them—grouping them into a larger mystery (and thereby a larger 'law') than the facts, as observed, yet warranted; but that is the common fault of minds for which the vision of life is an obsession.[62]

He talks about wanting 'absolute certainty' and claims the right 'to judge of what other people did'. He also refers to 'the sense of a discovery to be made' and his 'sense of reality':[63] and we may be sure that he means the reality that lies muffled and obliterated under the thick pile of appearances. He wants to get at the underlying pattern, to tease out the deeper meaning. He claims that 'the more things I fitted together the larger sense, every way, they made'.[64] For him, only those things which cohere can signify; the random, the contingent, the unrelated cannot yield up a meaning. It is in making things 'hook up', in finding a theory which will embrace the facts, that he finds 'the joy of the intellectual mastery of things unamenable, that joy of determining, almost of creating results'.[65] Like the girl in the cage he represents an activity rather than an involved character. 'I alone was magnificently and absurdly aware— everyone else was benightedly out of it.'[66] He is one of the privileged and perhaps cursed few who care to be conscious, who seek for the higher awareness, who catechize and interrogate the surfaces of the world in an effort to perceive the core of meaning. Yet though he is after an explaining law, he is also desirous of constructing a picture. That is to say he also wants to add something to the world, in particular those symmetries and harmonies which are alien to its gratuitous configurations. 'Things in the real had a way of not balancing; it was all an affair, this fine symmetry, of artificial proportion.'[67] The desire to account for things leads on to the instinct to alter them or add to them in the interests of an ideal of 'composition'. The narrator continually discusses his ambition in the terms of painting and he explicitly compares his chosen task to that of the painter Obert. 'I only talk as you paint.'[68] He talks of 'fresh accessions' enriching 'the picture' and often alludes to 'my gallery'. He views chance collocations with a painter's eye and at moments his desire for composition supersedes his need for elucidation. So, referring back to his avowed search for a law, we see that he wants to establish both the laws which explain actual human events, and also the laws which govern the act of artistic creation. The idea which relates these two aspirations is that of 'analogy': the ideally composed artistic world can shed illuminating light on the fractured imperfect physical world. 'Our world is brazen: the poet only delivers a golden.' Thus Sir Philip Sidney, and without exploring the neo-platonic implications we can see that James is continuing a long aesthetic debate: the question of the relationship between the brazen and golden worlds, between fact and vision.

There is little doubt that the narrator epitomizes the artistic instinct. The comparative triviality of his initial line of inquiry—is Gilbert Long having an affair which is in some way nourishing him with unexpected energy?—extends to the whole question of discerning or imposing a principle of order in or on the world. He talks about his theory very much as many great critics have talked about a work of art: 'that special beauty of my scheme through which the whole depended so on each part and each part guaranteed the whole.'[69] He wants and works to elicit a golden world from the brazen one. And as he talks about his golden world he continually implies that it is fragile, insubstantial, but precious. He refers to his constructed theory, his composed picture, as 'a great glittering crystal palace', 'a palace of thought', 'the kingdom of thought I had won';[70] though Mrs Brissenden who most nearly understands him and most grievously threatens him refers to his speculations as 'houses of cards'.[71] He makes his 'flight into luminous ether'[72] and in those rarified territories of the imagination he constructs a delicate artifact which orders and ordains the lower world. But the risk is great. Having made his brilliant construction he concedes: 'but there was no objective test to which I have yet exposed my theory.'[73] Random scraps of information and alternative points of view continually threaten his 'whole airy structure'.[74] He is often made to 'tremble for the impunity of my creation',[75] and he comes to object to the possibility of verifying his vision. He does not wish 'to expose to the world, to defend against the world, to share with the world, that now so complex tangle of hypotheses that I have had for convenience to speak of as my theory'.[76] He is in the position of the alienated artist, cherishing his product, and nervously guarding it against what Yeats called 'the brutality, the ill-breeding, the barbarism of truth'. (And Yeats too constructed 'A vision' as 'a last act of defense against the chaos of the world'.) His highly-organized vision becomes self-sealing and so far from explaining the life around him it becomes a consolation to set over against that life, a preferable extension of creation. If the facts do not fit the theory, why so much the worse for the facts. That is the feeling.

The relation of the narrator's art to reality is, then, a curious one. He starts his theory from a 'recognized fact'—the change in Gilbert Long—but from then on facts seem to become more of a menace and less to be desired. He says quite early to Ford Obert: 'If I had a material clue I should feel ashamed: the fact would be a deterrent.'[77] The 'affluence' of his vision is based on 'amazingly little evidence'.[78] In fact the less of one seems to mean more of the other. 'It would have been almost as embarrassing to have to tell them how little experience I had had in fact as to have had to tell them how much I had had in fancy.'[79] This clearly relates him to the girl in the cage. One 'straw' picked up from the world of fact yields him a rich harvest of imagined 'possibilities'. And in the interests of his theory he sometimes misses things which actually happen, and sometimes reads what does not happen into the actual. When a recalcitrant indigestible fact seems imminent it induces intense nervousness in the narrator. 'Things *had*, from step to step, to hang together',[80] that is the ambition, the need: but at crucial moments they seem, worryingly enough, 'to hang a little apart'.[81] The slightest hint can set his fantastic imagination to work—the swish of a skirt, the stoop of a back—for to him the world is seething with suggestiveness. He is perhaps a fanatic (Santayana defined fanaticism by saying it was when you redoubled your effort having forgotten your aim), but the crisis comes when he is confronted with a fact which not only can not be assimilated, dissolved in the 'solution' of his theory, but which also threatens to demolish his imaginative superstructure. This is what happens at the end. His whole theory has come to be based on the fact that Mrs Server must be the poor woman who is 'paying' for Long. But Mrs Brissenden comes to assure him that Long is in fact having an affair with Lady John, a talkative, self-possessed woman who will not fit the requirements of his theory at all. There is in fact something hard, ruthless, and dominating about Mrs Brissenden and she is referred to in terms of brass as opposed to the gentler more fragile Mrs Server who by contrast seems porcelain. And it is her brass— a base compound—which shatters the pure crystal of his theory. Her harsh assurance as to the *facts* leaves his vision completely dismantled—'a pile of ruins'.[82] It is possible that she is lying, or working for her own ends, but her very presence, and what she comes to stand for, are inimical to his careful 'embroidery' work, his artistic instincts, his search for a hidden logic. For she embraces a random, unpredictable world: she disdains his imaginative efforts to describe and prescribe for the real world. 'Things are not . . . gouged out to *your* tune.'[83] If his theory fails, his vision vanishes, and art, as it were, loses out to life.

In this book James has subjected the activities of the 'morbid imagination' to their most damaging criticisms. James allows certain key questions to be raised concerning the narrator's habit of speculation. Is this activity necessary, is it pernicious? Should he stop? Can he stop? Is he neurotic or even mad? Is he so obsessed with Mrs Server as to see the world in a distorted manner? These are the sort of questions which James allows to be raised around the narrator. He himself sometimes feels that his curiosity is 'wanting in taste'. When Mrs Brissenden in the early part of the story takes up his theory, but with some added malice, and says 'we want a fool', he suddenly feels gloomy and says 'Do we really want anyone at all?'[84] At certain contented moments at Newmarch he feels that there is no 'application' for 'a transcendent intelligence' and that 'we existed . . . to be really what we looked'.[85] At other moments his 'estimate of the value of perception'[86] undergoes a sudden reversal. He suddenly 'wished to unthink every thought with which I have been occupied for twenty-four hours'.[87] Certainly he thinks it a bad thing to communicate his visions to other people, which would only make them 'begin to vibrate, to crack and split, from within'.[88] If imagination and speculation are a curse then it is one the narrator feels he must bear alone. More than once he proclaims his readiness to 'give up everything'. At times he envies 'the state of exemption from intense obsessions',[89] and desires to 'break off sharp' from his own. But he cannot remain detached, he cannot make himself impervious to suggestion. His imaginative speculation seems to work autonomously, independent of his social-physical presence. The fact that it might be an obsessional activity is supported by his moments of intense excitement and anxiety, the sudden absurd agitation of the nerves to which he is liable. And at one moment it is hinted that there is something predatory in the way his imagination follows and rides other people. Then there are the various comments of the other characters on the narrator.

Gilbert Long says he has got Briss 'on the brain' and will not join in his speculations. The artist Obert after following him for a while drops out. 'It isn't any of one's business, is it?'[90]—a sentiment the author himself seconds. Lady John accuses him of having 'the imagination of atrocity', of trying to be a providence. 'You can't be a providence and not be a bore.'[91] Many complain of his constant questioning and his habit of trying to involve them in his meditative speculations. But it is Mrs Briss who voices the most damning sequence of charges. 'You see too much'—'You talk too much!'—'you're abused by a fine fancy' —'I think you're crazy'.[92] Since the narrator himself refers to his 'private madness' James clearly intends to allow the idea of the abnormality if not the insanity of art to lie like a vein through the novel. It is, we might say, the verdict of the practical world, the people who make themselves at home amongst the surface facts. 'Crazy' is Mrs Briss's last word for the narrator and if that seems like a comic exaggeration we can be sure that she intends the less extreme charge that he is 'an intelligent man gone wrong'.[93] Does he inquire too curiously? 'The state of my conscience was that I knew too much—that no one had really any business to know what I knew.'[94] But what kind of knowledge is it that disdains facts and winces at proffered information? It is imaginative penetration, the attempt to ensnare the essence by speculation, the registering of nuances and possibilities and suggestions which afford faint intimations of a profounder level of reality. But of course all this labour might be misdirected; it might have its origins in some inward disorder, the unhealthy hypertrophy of the speculative faculty; it might spring from unacknowledged passions gone sour; it might interfere with living in the empirical world—'the lap of the actual'. It might be a menace, an intrusion for less 'conscious' people; it might lead to a valuation of art over life or an impotent solipsism; it might take a man out of the world in a number of ways. These are some of the risks for the subjective adventurer. What are the gains? Are we to dismiss the narrator as 'crazy' along with Mrs Briss, or does James make him stand for a set of attitudes and activities that he valued, despite the attendant risks? Valued, perhaps, because those very risks made the activity heroic?

If 'art is our flounderings shown',[95] as Colonel Voyt suggests in 'The Story in it', then the narrator's attempts to chart the tangled relations of the people around him has at least the value of drawing up a tentative map for a troubled sea. Even if the flounderings are due to the ineradicable predatory instincts of men and women, still it is better to have a pattern of pursuit and carnage than no pattern at all. Any light is at least a minor triumph against the darkness. But as the narrator comes to realize 'the condition of light . . . was the sacrifice of feeling'.[96] Exclusion from participation—and this relates him to the other protagonists we have studied— is 'the price of the secret success, the lonely liberty and the intellectual joy'.[97] It is what his 'priceless pearl of an inquiry' costs: to save it he is willing to 'harden my heart'.[98] Pearl and crystal in preference to—a live woman? We are at least allowed the hint and should take away with us some sense of the price the narrator talks about. But if his willingness to pay the price is not simply obsessional, then his sense of exclusion must be due to an awareness of some higher allegiance, some more exacting responsibility. His 'providential supervision'[99] of the social world, even if it only goes on in his head, does have a value, and is a real responsibility. For in some way he is the one who strives to see among the blind, the upholder of consciousness among the unconscious. Excluded from the frame of society he is its artist: out of reach of its physical embraces he is its conscience. He is what Conrad said James himself was: 'the preserver, the keeper, the expounder, of human experience.'[100] That is why his 'curiosity matters'. First of all because it is the only way he can appease his inner drives. 'The satisfaction of my curiosity is the pacification of my mind.'[101] But more than that, even among the wreck of his theory he can salvage his 'understanding'. And this is an important passage: 'I couldn't save Mrs Server, and I couldn't save poor Briss: I *could*, however, guard, to the last grain of gold, my precious sense of their loss, their disintegration and their doom.'[102] Only understanding can develop a sense of values: the narrator is not, after all, a nosey-parker. Rather he is the person whose heightened awareness and delicate sensibility introduce into the callous indifference of unconscious life a sense of good things spoiled and cruelties perpetrated, of fine things destroyed and horrors achieved. He is accused in the book of not only seeing 'horrors' but liking them, and it is possible to see some of his curiosity as illicit, almost prurient: but his own answer is that before condemning them he likes to 'look them first well in the face'.[103] But if 'knowing', whether through inference or in imagination, is his vocation, then a proper distribution of pity is closely involved in it. The speculation might not be *for the sake of* sympathy, but there is sympathy in the speculator and in the very manner of the speculation. And this idea that here might be different kinds of curiosity, different ways of seeing, different modes of speculation, different sorts of 'knowledge', brings us to what I think is one of the most important tenets in James's work.

There is a moment early in the book when the narrator gets Mrs Brissenden to share his theory about the hidden source of Gilbert Long's improvement. But as he listens to her speculating he suddenly has a sense of the cruelty in her being so 'keen' to indict Mrs Server. Perhaps in this he is only seeing his own fault writ large, perhaps he is emotionally involved with Mrs Server: or perhaps he is realizing that there are at least two different kinds of 'attention' that one can pay the world. He defends observation, speculation, reflection—'reflection was the real intensity'[104] —but he is shocked at the gleam of cruelty in Mrs Bissenden's manner of mentally pouncing on victims and fools. She lacks the artistic, the sympathetic motive. To emphasize these two different ways of *looking* at the world I want to turn to the relatively simple story of 'The Patagonia'. There is also a narrator to that story, and he tells of an ocean crossing made in the company of Mrs Nettlepoint, her son Jasper, and a rather lonely girl named Grace Mavis who is crossing with them to finally marry her fiancé in France. He too is an observer, and there is something in his character that 'makes me, in any situation, just inordinately and submissively *see* things'.[105] And in the

HENRY JAMES

curious atmosphere of the boat—detached from land entanglements as Newmarch is detached from the material limitations
and impositions of day-to-day city existence—his speculations
take on an almost creative resonance. If one substitutes the idea
of Newmarch for the boat in the following passage—down to
its being like a stage on which relationships can be developed—
then the relevance of this story should become clear.

One had never thought of the sea as the great place of safety, but now
it came over one that there's no place so safe from the land. When it
doesn't confer trouble it takes trouble away—takes away letters and
telegrams and newspapers and visits and duties and efforts, all the
complications, all the superfluities and superstitions that we have
stuffed into our terrene life. The simple absence of the post, when
the particular conditions enable you to enjoy the great fact by which
it's produced, becomes in itself a positive bliss, and the clean boards
of the deck turn to the stage of a play that amuses, the personal drama
of the voyage, the movement and interaction, in the strong sea-light,
of figures that end by representing something—something moreover
of which the interest is never, even in its keenness, too great to suffer
you to slumber. I at any rate dozed to excess, stretched on my rug with
the French novel, and when I opened my eyes I generally saw Jasper
Nettlepoint pass with the young woman confided to his mother's care
on his arm. Somehow at these moments, between sleeping and waking,
I inconsequently felt that my French novel had set them in motion.[106]

Yet in this dreamy proto-fictional world on which the narrator
finds it so interesting to 'exercise' his mind, a real event of
palpable physical tragedy is germinating. For Grace Mavis is
obviously falling in love with Jasper—a selfish young man who is
sporting with her to pass the time—and as obviously dreads her
impending marriage. The narrator, sympathetic through his
very speculations about her state of mind, takes it upon himself
to issue some advice and reproach to Jasper, who is offended but
who then leaves the girl alone. Very alone. 'There was an odd
pang in seeing her move about alone; I felt somehow responsible for it and asked myself why I couldn't have kept my hands
off.'[107] Is he an interfering busy-body, or does he act from insight
and pity and imagination? I think we are meant to feel more of

332

the latter. Certainly when the dream is over, reality intrudes in the ugliest way. The narrator says to Grace shortly before the ship docks: 'The first sight of land, at sea, changes everything ... it always affects me as waking up from a dream. It's a return to reality.'[108] The dream-like French romance gives way to a tragic suicide: for Grace Mavis jumps from the ship at night. It is such events, such unpleasant cruel twists to existence that James alluded to in his famous phrase—'the Medusa face of life'. These are things which art is helpless to prevent and unable to fully explain: it can only console by recording the loss and lamenting the waste. This is the narrator's function. His type of observation and curiosity in one sense do a great service to life: they provide that sort of sympathetic generosity of appreciation and the 'dignity of judgment' without which life remains an unreclaimed and unrecorded mess, an unmapped jungle of appetites. But there is another kind of observation at work on the boat. The loathsome Mrs Peck who is the busy-body supreme, hungry for derogatory tit-bits, quick to spread damning rumours, always keen to spot out something to castigate in public with malicious glee. She also pays attention, is an observer, perhaps even a 'creator' of sorts, since her vicious gossip may have driven the lonely Grace Mavis to her suicide. The narrator's benevolent meditative speculation bestows a benediction on life: he endows it with significance and invests it with an inner emotional logic where the surface shows only a squandering chaos. He may perhaps be mocked a little because he is 'so full of signification' but at least, as he himself protests, 'I had taken really no such ferocious ... note as Mrs Peck'.[109] In contrast to his artistic speculations there is a ferocity of attention which mars what it touches, which destroys what it regards. This sort of attention has a withering effect: it takes life away.

If I wanted to sum up the virtues which these narrators—and the artist in general—represented for James, I would pick on Natalia Haldin's compliment to the old Western language teacher in *Under Western Eyes*. 'There is a way of looking on which is valuable.' For James, like Conrad, was one of those few

HENRY JAMES

men who, to use Conrad's fine phrase, 'know how to look at their kind'.

This might seem a long way from the Jamesian 'candid outsider' or his employment of characters given to a sort of tolerant, generous wonder in the face of life. Yet it is those very virtues of the 'wondering' hero which James carries over into his portrait of the artist, that other sort of wonderer. He too has that tolerance, that generosity, that sort of compassionate desire to 'know' which stops short of the abuse of others, which celebrates rather than violates the world around him. There is a distinct progression from the figure of Daisy Miller, to Maisie, on to the girl in the cage, and thence to the narrator of *The Sacred Fount*: but the progression does not break the relationship. Some deeply sympathetic attitude to life is common to all of them. From one point of view James is a consummate artist in a European context: but it is also fruitful to see him and his attitude to the world and to art, as one of the finest and subtlest products of a distinctly American tradition.

The 'wonderer' has to see for himself; as Emerson intimated when he asked 'why should not we also enjoy an original relation to the universe?' Emerson's universe, however, neglected society. James forced his 'wonderers' to inhabit the human world where, not content with taking society's current version and evaluation of things, they have to see and assess everything for themselves. And they start from scratch. It is a typical American undertaking as I have tried to show. And if James shows his two great late 'wonderers' as unapt for normal social living (Strether withdrawing into sterile silence to muse over the mixed wealth of his garnered impressions, the narrator of *The Sacred Fount* risking madness in his effort to turn the fruits of his wondering into art), then that is a part of his comment on the fate of wonder in the dangerous social world, as opposed to the safe isolation of, say, Walden Pond.

The Jamesian artist who pays for his privileged vision by renouncing all participation in the physical world, who is forever marooned on his 'floating island' of heightened imaginative

334

consciousness, who is addicted to the 'phantasmagoric' at the expense of the 'evidential' (James's own terms),[110] who in following out his inferences risks losing all normal contact with facts—this figure is bound to attract the accusation of insanity. And our age has come to see that there might indeed be something pathological in the feverish activity of the artist. But if it is madness it is a sacred madness. As James himself realized and expressed in the unforgettable words of the dying artist Dencomb, in 'The Middle Years': 'We work in the dark—we do what we can—we give what we have. Our doubt is our passion and our passion is our task. The rest is the madness of art.'[111]

AFTERWORD: WONDER AND ALIENATION—
THE MYSTIC AND THE MOVIEGOER

As for willing *the world into shape—better chaos a thousand times than any 'perfect' world.* . . . . *To me chaos doesn't matter so much as abstract, which is mechanical, order. To me it is life to feel the white ideas and 'oneness' crumbling into a thousand pieces, and all sorts of wonder coming through.*

D. H. LAWRENCE, *Letters*

MANY times during the course of this book we have had occasion to discuss the varying importance ascribed by different writers to clearly perceived particulars and vague philosophical generalizations. And indeed the relationship between minute details and vast affirmations has worried, haunted even, the American imagination in a particular way. Tocqueville discerned this when he made his shrewd observation that the American mind tends to oscillate between ideas that 'are all either extremely minute and clear or extremely general and vague'. His explanation was that, whereas European society inherited a communally shared group of attitudes, social gestures and institutions, which provided a sort of known scaffolding to mediate between the individual and the state; in America 'each citizen is habitually engaged in the contemplation of a very puny object; namely, himself' and if he looks away from the self he sees only 'the immense form of society at large or the still more imposing aspect of mankind. . . . What lies between is a void'.[1] This is no place to discuss the validity of the offered explanation, but adapted to American literature the insight is very interesting. It points to that very phenomenon we have noted in various writers: namely the shift from the minutely scrutinized particular to the large and often vague affirmative generalization, from the material to the metaphysical, from the concrete to the mystical. Now this is not, of course, necessarily an adverse observation: for it points not only to the worst of Emerson and Anderson, but also to what makes

336

Moby Dick one of the greatest novels ever written. Generalizations about national literatures are naturally suspect and always
dangerous. But if we can say that, in general, the English novel
has preferred to address itself to the observation of social realities
and the formulation of moral comment; and that the French novel
tends to bring experience to the point where it will furnish us
with a valid intelligent generalization about social phenomena and
personal emotions; then we can, tentatively, go on to say that the
American writer tends to start from a closely perceived sub-social
or non-social reality and attempts to move towards some sort of
metaphysical and philosophical generalization. It strains to kick
over the pail and accept the horizon, to move from the vase of
pigment to the vase of ether—to reintroduce two of Emerson's
relevant phrases. Of course qualifications clamour to be made
immediately. From Twain to Hemingway there were writers
who constantly sought to avoid such generalizations. And yet
Twain's own late work is full of brooding metaphysical statements,
Sherwood Anderson often breaks into the accents of a faltering
Transcendentalist, and even Hemingway, whose best work is
strong with the effort of avoiding such generalizations, shows a
tendency in his later work to allow assertion to overtake perception. And the remainder of Tocqueville's point stands up very
well, for between the lone American self and the rest of the world
there is, indeed, very often a void (although Emerson, I
suppose, would have called it an absence of distraction and interference between the self and the Over-Soul). Leave out James
for the moment (though he is not exactly the social novelist many
take him to be) and how many major American writers have in
fact taken their material from society? Of the great formative
works of the American imagination one is set on a river (*Huckleberry Finn*), one on an open road (*Song of Myself*), one on the sea
(*Moby Dick*), and one by a pond (*Walden*). *The Scarlet Letter*,
it is true, confronts some of the complexities engendered by
nature and society, yet even in this book one of the most important
figures is Hester, alienated in the forest.[2] The value of Tocqueville's initial insight is nicely corroborated by a worried entry in

Thoreau's *Journals* in which he reminds himself of the need to correct a dangerous disposition. 'Let me not be in haste to detect the *universal law*; let me see more clearly a particular instance of it.'³ This haste towards generalizations seems to have had a peculiar magnetism for American writers at the same time as they have shown a real genius for the unbiased notation of concrete particulars. These paradoxical pulls, whether seductive or imperious, can of course produce a really valuable binding sort of tension; so that in, say, *Moby Dick*, you have the tremendously exciting feeling of concrete realities constantly pushing and dragging you far down into Truth, and Truth as constantly thrusting you back and abandoning you to reality. And it is part of Melville's genius that he realized so profoundly the limits of metaphysics and the limitlessness of life, so that he can make generalizations about the limitations of generalizations. 'For Faith and philosophy are air, but events are brass. Amidst his gray philosophizings, Life breaks upon a man like the morning.'

But when the tension slackens and one inclination asserts an uncontested dominance over a writer the dangers are clear to see: heaps of particulars, amassed with zeal but unassimilated by the writer's imagination; or facile generalizations, up-lifting or sombre as taste will have it. Particulars are of course the indispensable material of art, but the writer must apprehend them, possess them, saturate them with imagination and insight. Generalizations can constitute the peak of art, its dignity, its morality, its truth, but they must be earned, bled for, perhaps despaired of, and then clutched with true gratitude. They should arrive singed with battle, since only on the very exceptional do they descend like a dove. Now in some ways the tradition which I have attempted to describe in this book shows an increasing suspicion of un-earned generalizations. It started with the fairly uncomplicated optimism of the Transcendentalists who could find God in a stone, and it moved on to the unwilling scepticism of a Sherwood Anderson who found no manifest divinity or Law but only private consolation in the truth and beauty of a few pebbles. Where Emerson saw all fragments of concrete reality as being potentially transparent to some superior Reality, Hemingway saw only detached details of matter, marooned in a meaningless void. Emerson's wondering is a constant act of worship; Hemingway's lucid scrutiny betokens a continuing effort of orientation. Emerson praised God by looking through matter; Hemingway saved himself by holding onto it. Emerson believed what he could infer; Hemingway relied only on what he could see and touch. Instead of the consolations of religion we have the consolations of sensation (and in James, as we have suggested, the consolations of speculation). And yet I have suggested that a certain mode of vision—the habit of wonder, the cultivation of a naive eye—relates the writers I have discussed where questions of faith would separate them. For a particular way of regarding reality may answer different needs and be employed to different ends. Thus, for the Transcendentalists the wondering eye was an instrument of the orthodox; later it became a strategy for the alienated. Huck Finn lights out, Nick Adams makes a separate peace, Sherwood Anderson walks out of his business office and fills his work with an aching sense of lostness, exclusion and banishment—even Henry James is detached from the continent of contemporary reality and exists like a wise castaway on his island of wonder. The list could be extended through many more contemporary writers, but we have said enough to make the shift in pattern clear. But if the pattern has shifted, it has not been totally broken. Underneath all the changing philosophical and religious beliefs there is an abiding manner of visually taking hold of the world which in some ways relates such disparate writers as Emerson and Hemingway, despite their very different convictions and conclusions. This manner, this sensory stance, is indicated as clearly by Emerson's creed—'the wise man wonders at the usual'—as it is by Sherwood Anderson's conclusion that 'nothing mattered but a kind of consciousness of the wonder of life outside oneself'.[4] It is this way of regarding reality which constitutes the tradition I have tried to describe.

Finally I want to make some comments on two contemporary writers to demonstrate how this tradition (and the connection between alienation and wonder) continues to operate in the absence of any major writer to give if fresh impetus or fertile redirection.

The fact that most of J. D. Salinger's heroes—if that is the word—are children, or at least child-like to the extent that they are emotionally not assimilated into the adult world, brings him immediately into line with one of the more obvious aspects of the tradition I have tried to establish. But the fact that nearly all his young protagonists, with the exception of Holden Caulfield, are geniuses, even mystics, is a rarer and more interesting phenomenon. In fact it is their torment and their salvation as we shall see. The scope of Salinger's work was adumbrated in the short story called 'De Daumier-Smith's Blue Period' where the young sensitive 'artistic' narrator has two experiences, or two responses to the same scene. At two different moments in the story he stops in front of a display-window of orthopaedic appliances. His first reaction is 'hideous':

The thought was forced on me that no matter how coolly or sensibly or gracefully I might one day learn to live my life, I would always at best be a visitor in a garden of enamel urinals and bedpans, with a sightless, wooden dummy-deity standing by in a marked-down rupture-truss. The thought, certainly, couldn't have been endurable for more than a few seconds.[5]

His second reaction occurs when he stops to watch a young woman change the truss on the wooden dummy. Embarrassed by his presence she falls down, but recovers herself and continues to lace up the truss:

It was just then that I had my Experience. Suddenly (and I say this, I believe, with all due self-consciousness), the sun came up and sped towards the bridge of my nose at the rate of ninety-three million miles a second. Blinded and very frightened—I had to put my hand on the glass to keep my balance. The thing lasted for no more than a few seconds. When I got my sight back, the girl had gone from the window, leaving behind her a shimmering field of exquisite, twice-blessed, enamel flowers.[6]

Nausea at the stubborn base creatural materiality of the world can only be overcome by a transcendental experience in which the very same dull mess of things is transformed and consecrated—by the eye of the beholder. The world that Salinger sees is so ugly, so devoid of spirit and grace, so befouled by phoney or filthy humanity, so larded with muck, that the only way his sensitive characters can rescue themselves from paralysing despair and return from the far margins of alienation, is to undergo a miraculous transformation (or receive a miraculous vision) which—Salinger would have us believe—enables them to assert that it is all beautiful, all holy, all good. The eye which is offended and sickened to the point at which it would like to exclude everything, is redeemed by the eye which wonderingly beholds an endless flow of beatific visions. Thus in another early short story called 'Teddy' we are introduced to a young sage (who has been through many incarnations—hence his wealth of ancient wisdom) telling his older friend that man should 'vomit up' all 'logic and intellectual stuff' and start to learn 'the real ways of looking at things'.[7] He has this proper knack of vision and he explains how it works:

'I was six when I saw that everything was God, and my hair stood up and all that,' Teddy said. 'It was on a Sunday, I remember. My sister was only a very tiny child then, and she was drinking her milk, and all of a sudden I saw that *she* was God and the *milk* was God. I mean all she was doing was pouring God into God, if you know what I mean.'[8]

This is to take generalizations to the very edge of meaninglessness. And perhaps it is just worth noting that the little scrap of divinity, his sister, kills Teddy by pushing him into an empty swimming pool to break his skull. She is, in fact, the only murderous child to stray into Salinger's fictional world, and she and her type have been subsequently banished so that Salinger can indulge undisturbed his favourite contrast of pure child against 'crumby' adults and talk about them as our 'guests' who 'belong to God'.

Holden Caulfield is the most plausible and human of Salinger's young heroes. His sense of alienation, his disgust at the sordidness and falsity of the adult world, his sudden grasps at tiny moments of precious lyricism are attributes accounted for, and even authenticated by, the awkward adolescent stage he has reached. But for all the surface resemblances he is no Huck Finn, and mainly for the following reason. Huck indeed has a quick intuitive sense of the false and the vile when he brushes up against it, but he also has resilience, energy, and a tough sense of joy. Holden exists in a permanent state of trembling neurotic apprehensiveness at the *potential* 'phoneyness' of everyone and everything. At a theatre, for instance, he cannot enjoy the show because he keeps worrying that the actor is 'going to do something phoney every minute':[9] listening to 'all the phonies' applaud a pseudo French singer in a night club 'you got to hate everybody in the world, I swear you did'.[10] His revulsion is uncontained, uncontainable. His sister Phoebe sums him up when she cried 'You don't like *anything* that's happening'.[11]

But he asserts that he does: odd random 'little things' which he secretes in his memory much as Hugh McVey slipped the pebbles into his pocket; things which 'glisten and shine outside the muddle of life'. They include two nuns he meets, the girl who kept all her kings in the back row, a happy dusk spent throwing a ball around, talking to Phoebe and, of course, watching her riding the carousel. 'I was damn near bawling, I felt so damn happy, if you want to know the truth. I don't know why. It was just that she looked so damn *nice*, the way she kept going round and round in her blue coat and all. God. I wish you could've been there.'[12] This sort of scene comes off, where the blankly asserted beatific visions do not, because the mood, the sudden welling-up of an inexplicable life-joy, lies plausibly within the compass of an adolescent's response. The book as a whole is a success, not only because it is sometimes wonderfully funny and acute in its quick darting attacks on the 'phonies' of the world, not only because it does seem to convey the confused range of inchoate adolescent emotions moving so quickly from revulsion to wonder, but because the vernacular intimacy of the child (or adolescent) narrator sets a limit to what Salinger can assert and

Holden's confessional sincerity is never intruded on. Holden is a true wonderer, not a false mystic. But it should be noted how far alienation has gone even in this book. Holden has nightmare feelings that he will never reach the other sides of streets; worse, that he will disappear. He cannot tie himself into reality satisfactorily at any point. He writes to us from a mental home. So much for the fate of a person acutely aware of the lurking falsity of the modern world and sensitive to its fugitive beauties. So far from lighting out for the territory he must lie down on the analyst's couch. Not only is he trapped but he is, we feel, too sensitive, too sick even, for flight.

In his as yet uncompleted series of stories about the Glass family, Salinger not only reveals to the full the contradictions in his attitude to the world, but he also makes an attempt to pass beyond them. The all too brilliant Glass children are essentially artist types by virtue of the superior insight, their remorseless and penetrating candour, their sense of or quest for some form of spiritual beauty, and, more simply, the uncanny talent imputed to them. Their common problem, almost without exception, is how to stop hating and despising the sloppy, phoney, mediocre world which hems them in and stinks in their nostrils until a total nervous breakdown seems imminent. *Franny and Zooey* shows Franny brought to this point of breakdown, and then reveals how she was retrieved from the edge of the abyss by her brother Zooey: it shows how guilt and nausea give way to the beatific vision.

Her problem is the standard Salinger one. Everything seems so 'tiny and meaningless and—sad-making': she is sick of the feel of 'ego' all round her (and inside her): she is driven desperate by the realization that whatever you do, no matter how apparently individual, it will turn out to be just another type of conformity. Worse than that she hates herself for being so 'cavilling and bitchy': guilt brings on waves of self-loathing. She has only one refuge from this overwhelming sense of disgust: she retires to a lavatory and mumbles her pilgrim's prayer. The aim of this prayer, as she explains to her boorish Ivy League date, is that after sufficient repetition 'you get to see God'.[13] And in a world so utterly crass, selfish and ugly, Franny needs to see God very much. Zooey reveals Him to her.

His therapy includes a long indictment of Franny's attitude to the world. He attacks her 'blanket attack' (admitting however that she is ninety-eight percent correct!), he rebukes her for despising people personally, he accuses her of being greedy for spiritual treasure. He can do all this with a fairly keen tongue because he is very much the same type himself. He too hates himself because 'I sit in judgment on every poor, ulcerous bastard I know':[14] because he picks and rails at people's opinions and values 'and everything'. He is either 'a goddam *seer* or a human hatpin'[15] and, like his author, he is more convincing as the latter than the former. The mysticism is theoretic, the hate is real: the one is a forced gesture of atonement, the other is the forked tongue of true scorn. However, he brings Franny round to his way of thinking. He admits that the pair of them are freaks: 'we're the Tattooed Lady'[16] as he puts it. And, as entertainers, they must reconcile themselves with what they call 'the Fat Lady'[17] who is plain, average, untattoed, ugly, probably cancerous, humanity. They must love what they despise, and emotionally embrace that from which they feel most alienated. Under the hovering influence of the memory of Seymour—their saintly elder brother—Zooey brings Franny to the point where she can see all life as consecrated, and all humanity as Christ. As artists they had both come to hate their audience because of 'the goddam "unskilled laughter" coming from the fifth row'[18] (as Holden found 'People always clap for the wrong thing').[19] The audience is that terrible endless mass of obtuse, insensitive, phoney, complacent, acquisitive, soulless people who compose the shoddy fallen world in which the exquisitely sensitive *Glass* children (fragile, pure, clean, etc.) must warily make their way. Apparently their only method of reconciliation is to leap from loathing to love, to replace the eye of revulsion with the eye of reverent wonder like the boy in front of the orthopaedic display window. Look once and you see the Fat Lady ('very thick legs, very veiny'): look twice—'Ah, buddy, Ah, buddy. It's Christ Himself. Christ Himself, buddy.'[20] The alienated wonderers are saved by the generous scope of their vague generalizations.

Without in any way impugning the sincerity of Salinger's mystical beliefs, I am suggesting that he tries to solve his problems by having recourse to the easy unearned generalization. He condemns 'blanket' attacks on humanity, but blanket acceptance and affirmation are not very much more fruitful as far as art is concerned. I think the point can be made another way by considering the style of the book. Salinger still has, as he always had, a fine eye for the informing detail, the lyrical fragment. Thus Zooey can gaze out of a window and become absorbed in a small uncontrived scene between a child and her dog: his response is a sort of inarticulate delight which, simple as it is, is preferable to his mystical vaporizings. 'God damn it', he said, 'there are nice things in the world—and I mean *nice* things. We're all such morons to get so sidetracked.'[21] This is like one of Holden's 'little things': a rare rescued delightful detail. So throughout the book there are many details, particularly of the home in which the Glass family live. But the mystical generalizations do not arise out of them, are not ignited by them: there is no sense of tussle or interpenetration or interdependency. Rather the details are arbitrarily encamped round the generalizations: they do not generate them, they enclose them in a vain effort to relate them to the ground. A nice symbol for the relationship is provided by Zooey's explanation of the significance of the endless cigars he smokes. 'The cigars are ballast, sweetheart. Sheer ballast. If he didn't have a cigar to hold on to, his feet would leave the ground.'[22] But art does not work that way. It always has a profound gravitational pull earthwards no matter how much upward elevation and aspiration run through it. The particulars of the real world are not mere ballast but the very ground of its being, not something to hold it down but the very stuff without which it would not have arisen in the first place. Philosophy works in its own way and makes its own constructs, but it may be said that in a work of art as direct philosophic assertion increases, reality ebbs and art

345

dwindles. Reality should never be an excuse for offering philosophic generalizations, though it may very well provoke a man into mining for them. As Salinger increasingly uses it as an excuse and not a source, so his work ceases to be art. This is not to say, of course, that his philosophy—offered separately as philosophy—may not be extremely satisfactory to some people. But, if one may offer so extreme a judgement, he is ceasing to be an artist for the same reason that so few of the Transcendentalists ever started to become artists—generalizations satisfied them more than reality challenged them.

Salinger's later stories about Seymour simply confirm this trend. Seymour is the real saint of the family, and the most interesting aspect of the two long stories about him ('Raise High the Roof Beam, Carpenters' and 'Seymour: an Introduction') is the description of his efforts to insert himself into the circumambient reality which deep down he abhors and despises. Here we see the old Salinger guilt working itself out in an extreme form and finally having recourse to the extremest measures, first of reconciliation and then of escape. The introduction to Seymour establishes, between embarrassing outbursts of aggressive apology and truculent defensiveness, the saintliness of the young Seymour. There are many examples of his supreme gift of finding God everywhere: let the following suffice. Buddy, his younger brother is giving the account. 'My brother, for the record, had a distracting habit, most of his adult life, of investigating loaded ashtrays with his index finger, clearing all the cigarette ends to the sides—smiling from ear to ear as he did it—as if he expected to see Christ himself curled up cherubically in the middle, and he never looked disappointed.'[23] Seymour's poems (for he was a great poet we are told) illustrate this gift. Understandably he prefers the eastern haiku genre to anything occidental and analytic. As Buddy explains, 'a Chinese or Japanese poet's real forte is knowing a good persimmon or a good crab or a good mosquito bite on a good arm when he sees one'.[24] That is, he has an eye which is extremely sensitive to the lyrical detail and capable of a mood of sustained, uninterfering, uninquiring wonder. As

Emerson had asserted, the real poet should be passive before his material: Buddy echoes him. 'The true poet has no choice of material. The material plainly chooses him, not he it.'[25] Seymour writes poems which reach out to hold, cherish and wonder at the rare exquisite detail. Or rather, since selection would indicate choice, he is like a sacred sponge which absorbs 'the usual' and finds it wonder-full.

But he is guilty about his poetry. He feels that

the poems read as though they'd been written by an ingrate of sorts, someone who was turning his back—in effect, at least—on his own environment and the people in it who were close to him. He said he ate his food out of our big refrigerators, drove our eight-cylinder American cars, unhesitatingly used our medicines when he was sick, and relied on the U.S. Army to protect his parents and sisters from Hitler's Germany, and nothing, not one single thing in all his poems, reflects these realities. Something was terribly wrong.[26]

This almost reads like Salinger's uneasiness and an attempt to disarm criticism by anticipating it. This is the remorse of the alienated artist—and the evasive mystic. The only compensation he can offer is to bestow a benefaction on all things, indiscriminately, and assert 'that all we do our whole lives is go from one little piece of Holy Ground to the next'.[27] Indiscrimination, indeed, is a key word in Seymour's attempt to reconcile himself to the world. In the earlier story we were told of his marriage and two entries in his conveniently found diary reveal the rationale behind this gesture. He is marrying—and surely has deliberately sought out—the most vapid conventional inane type of bourgeois girl whose motives for marrying are simply the clichés of the modern world. Seymour knows this but argues himself into a gesture of acceptance. The diary comments on his fiancée's motives for marrying:

But are they despicable? In a way they must be, but yet they seem to me so human size and beautiful that I can't think of them even now as I write this without feeling deeply, deeply moved. He [i.e. Buddy] would disapprove of Muriel's mother, too, She's an irritating, opinionated woman, a type Buddy can't stand. I don't think he could see her for what she is. A person deprived, for life, of any understanding or taste for the main current of poetry that flows through things, all things. She might as well be dead, and yet she goes on living, stopping off at delicatessens, seeing her analyst, consuming a novel every night, putting on her girdle, plotting for Muriel's health and prosperity. I love her. I find her unimaginably brave.[28]

The hat pin having done its deflating work, the seer blesses the victim with words like 'beautiful' and 'brave'. (In an even more amusing piece of sophistry in the later story, Seymour, worried by Christ's injunction to call no man fool—for, like his author, he sees the world to be full of them—finds the following solution: 'there are no fools. Dopes, yes—fools, no.')[29] This is how Seymour emancipates himself from what an analyst tells him is his 'perfection complex'. He records in his diary some comments on his conversation with the analyst:

Much talk from him, and quite intelligent, on the virtues of living the imperfect life, of accepting one's own and other's weaknesses. I agree with him, but only in theory. I'll champion indiscrimination till doomsday, on the grounds that it leads to health and a kind of real, enviable happiness. *Followed purely* it's the way of the Tao, and undoubtedly the highest way. But for a discriminating man to achieve this, it would mean that he would have to dispossess himself of poetry, go *beyond* poetry. That is, he couldn't possibly learn or drive himself to *like* bad poetry in the abstract, let alone equate it with good poetry. He would have to drop poetry altogether. I said it would be no easy thing to do![30]

Seymour's marriage is an attempt to abandon poetry, to go beyond poetry, to couple with all that most offends him, to find holy what he knows to be dead. But the attempt failed, for, as we know from the early story 'A Perfect Day for Bananafish', Seymour has recourse to suicide. Having tried to marry the world, Seymour chooses, like many other saints, to die to it. Whether he does this through an excess of sheer wonder (the beautiful innocence of the child on the beach) or from an unbearable loathing of the soulless ugliness of his wife's way of life, or because of the unsustainable contrast between the two, does not really matter. Seymour is the saint, the great poet, the man who suspects people of 'plotting to make me happy',[31] the man most raw to the myriad tiny beauties of life, the man who finds all ground to be holy ground and no man to be a fool. And Seymour puts a bullet through his right temple. Alienation cannot very well go much further. Seymour's mystical generalizations have not finally managed to reconcile him to modern reality.

In mentioning Walker Percy's *The Moviegoer* my aim is not to extol an undiscovered masterpiece but simply to take a recent, talented first novel and show how unmistakably it relates itself to the lines of development we have discussed in this book. Binx Bolling, the narrator, is a sort of American Outsider. But the manner of his rebellion and the form of his alienation differ from those of his French counterpart. His desire is to preserve a sense of wonder: his dread is the feeling of being 'cut loose metaphysically speaking'[32] (very much as Hemingway dreaded *nada* and Sherwood Anderson shivered to feel that all life might simply be 'a vastness and emptiness').[33] He aspires to find some sort of lodgement and anchorage in the world without inwardly capitulating to the false standards and dead values and empty gestures of the world's inhabitants, even though outwardly, as we shall see, he is quite willing to imitate them, to appear as one of the herd. His sense of alienation is often brought out in the manner in which he describes other people, people who are utterly and complacently at home in the world, people who, to use Anderson's phrase, have 'no sense of strangeness, no wonder about life'.[34] For example, the dull efficient business man, Eddie Lovell who looks out on the world and sees no mystery. 'He understands everything out there and everything out there is something to be understood.'[35] The accurate yet utterly detached, cool way in which he describes such people is reminiscent of the strategy employed by Camus in *L'Étranger* of which Sartre very shrewdly said:

M. Camus has a method ready to hand. He is going to insert a glass partition between the reader and his characters. Is there anything

349

sillier than a man behind a glass window? Glass seems to let everything through. It stops only one thing: the meaning of his gestures.
The glass remains to be chosen. It will be the Outsider's mind, which
is really transparent, since we see everything it sees. However, it is so
constructed as to be transparent to things and opaque to meanings.[36]

(One might add that a child's mind is often 'transparent to things
and opaque to meanings' and it is not surprising that the child has
so often been employed in recent fiction as a vehicle for a sense of
alienation.)

Percy's narrator, to all outward appearances utterly normal
and conventional, moves through society feeling like a Jew. 'We
share the same exile. The fact is, however, I am more Jewish
than the Jews I know. They are more at home than I am. I
accept my exile.'[37] (Norman Mailer has given us the white negro,
now we have the gentile Jew.) He laughs and talks with people
as occasion demands, but 'all the friendly and likable people seem
dead to me; only the haters seem alive'.[38] (A conclusion Salinger
shied away from.) Even as he describes, without acrid comment,
the nice people he meets, we see them as corpses through the cold
glass of his mind. Only with his cousin Kate does he feel real
sympathy, and she is in the process of having a nervous breakdown not dissimilar to Franny's since she too feels that everything is 'so—no 'count, somehow'.[38] When, at the end of the
book, Binx's aunt arraigns him in the name of all the traditional
values and virtues of which she herself is a dignified upholder he
can only remain silent. He does not disagree with her bitter indictment of the modern world, he simply cannot think of anything to
say. She attacks him and denounces what she considers his new
solution to life's problems:

Your discovery, as best as I can determine, is that there is an alternative
which no one has hit upon. It is that one finding oneself in one of life's
critical situations need not after all respond in one of the traditional
ways. No. One may simply default. Pass. Do as one pleases, shrug,
turn on one's heel and leave. Exit.[39]

In all this he is a straight outsider, a man alienated from his
neighbours and unable to subscribe to their values, allegiances

and verdicts. His solution however—an extreme one, indeed—
is to try and become as ordinary as possible, to carve a reliable
niche for himself in normality and routine. He has given up
ambition, abandoned the 'old longings', taken a suburban apartment, addicted himself to television and filled his wallet with
'identity cards, library cards, credit cards'. 'It is a pleasure to
carry out the duties of a citizen and to receive in return a receipt
or a neat styrene card with one's name on it certifying, so to
speak, one's right to exist.'[40] He gives himself up wholly to his
business, making money and dating his secretaries. But his
motives have nothing in common with Seymour's desire to bless
and embrace what he secretly despises. Binx Bolling's aim is to
keep the nightmare of metaphysical lostness and unreality at bay.
The worst threat—and travelling from place to place makes the
threat acute—is that one day he may wake up and 'find himself
No one and Nowhere'.[41] This is why, unlike most American
heroes, he hates to travel. A visit to Chicago disturbs him greatly,
leading him to assert:

Every place of arrival should have a booth set up and manned by an
ordinary person whose task it is to greet strangers and give them a
little trophy of local spacetime stuff—tell them of his difficulties in
high school and put a pinch of soil in their pockets—in order to insure
that the stranger shall not become an Anyone.[42]

Like Zooey he needs ballast: but not to prevent his premature
ascension to heaven, only to stave off the complete dissolution of
his identity. It is this need which makes him mark his cinema seat
with his thumbnail. It is a way of reminding himself that he was
Some where at Some time, and not Any where in Any time.
    It is for this reason that he is a moviegoer, that he remembers
incidents from films more vividly than he can recall incidents
from his own life. It is not that films give romance where romance
is lacking, nor that they offer the escape of a dream world.
Rather they render fixed and inevitable what in life seems to him
to be fluid and contingent. He is fascinated by the 'peculiar
reality' of movie stars, and movies themselves bestow images of

351

reality on a world which seems in danger of losing any conviction as to its very existence. In particular if you see your own world in a film, then your world is 'certified'. He explains:

Nowadays when a person lives somewhere, in a neighbourhood, the place is not certified for him. More than likely he will live there sadly and the emptiness which is inside of him will expand until it evacuates the entire neighbourhood. But if he sees a movie which shows his very neighbourhood, it becomes possible for him to live, for a time at least, as a person who is Somewhere and not Anywhere.[43]

That it requires the movies to give man this certification of the reality of his own world merely indicates what deserts of unreality the modern alienated wonderer finds himself stumbling through.

But there is one big difference between the American Movie-goer and the French Outsider. For there recurs to Binx Bolling 'the possibility of a search'.[44] Now, it is hard to think of many major American novels which do not in some way incorporate in them the notion of a search, a quest, a more than physical journey—whether one thinks of Captain Ahab or Augie March, Huck Finn or Albert Strether or Jay Gatsby. For Binx Bolling the search is finally for a true wonder, a maintained curiosity, an inviolable sense of reality. Of course the 'search' has nothing to do with a spell of world-wide sightseeing (he loathes the idea of a *wanderjahr* very much as Zooey detests 'any kind of so-called creative type who gets on any kind of a ship').[45] The search is into the 'here and now', not away from it. He first had the idea of a search when he came to his senses after being wounded in the war. 'Six inches from my nose a dung beetle was scratching around under the leaves. As I watched, there awoke in me an immense curiosity. I was onto something. I vowed that if I ever got out of this fix, I would pursue the search. Naturally, as soon as I recovered and got home, I forgot all about it.'[46] The idea recurs to him one morning when he suddenly sees the odds and ends on his dressing table as though for the first time. He wonders at them, insignificant scraps though they are. 'What was unfamiliar about them was that I could see them. They might have belonged to someone else.'[47] This is to cease to take reality for granted, to be restored to a sense of the miraculousness as well as the gratuitousness of the stuff around us. He then defines the search in the following way:

The search is what anyone would undertake if he were not sunk in the everydayness of his own life. This morning, for example, I felt as if I had come to myself on a strange island. And what does such a castaway do? Why, he pokes around his neighbourhood and he doesn't miss a trick.

To become aware of the possibility of the search is to be onto something. Not to be onto something is to be in despair.[48]

The terms are vague but the main point is clear. To be sunk in everydayness, to be bored, blasé, or complacently unaware of mystery, to have lost the sense of wonder—is to be dead. More interesting for our purpose is the narrator's description of the two different kinds of search he has conducted. There was the vertical search: 'During those years I stood outside the universe and sought to understand it. . . . The only difficulty was that though the universe had been disposed of, I myself was left over.'[49] This search had been concerned with discovering the governing laws of life from books like *The Expanding Universe* and *The Chemistry of Life*. These laws could not, however, explain the mystery of his own presence. So he moved to the horizontal search. 'As a consequence, what takes place in my room is less important. What is important is what I shall find when I leave my room and wander in the neighbourhood. Before, I wandered as a diversion. Now I wander seriously and sit and read as a diversion.'[50] The two terms neatly echo the conflict of inclination we noted in so many American writers, a desire to pierce the sky wrestling with an instinct to align themselves with the ground. Binx Bolling's decision to move to the horizontal search is of a piece with Thoreau's resolution to turn away from the Universal Law and seek for truth in particular instances. With the vertical search you approach that Universal Law: 'you understand more and more specimens by fewer and fewer formulae. . . . Of course you are always after the big one, the new key, the secret leverage point, and that is the best of it.'[51] Except that the perceiving enraptured individual gets left out. Whereas with the horizontal search, as Kate interprets it, 'if you sit back here and take a little carcass out of the garbage can, a specimen which has been used and discarded, there remains something left over, a clue.'[52] The scrap from the garbage can—the pebble by your foot: it is yet another expression of the recurring American resolution to start with the nearest and next, the potluck of the day, the small proximate particular.

The habit of wonder is, for Binx Bolling, superior to all scientific and intellectual modes of inquiry: and here we see a typical American suspicion or prejudice discharging itself. Thus he once tried to do scientific research to please his aunt; but his interest faded and 'I became extraordinarily affected by the summer afternoons in the laboratory'. His co-worker became a dedicated and successful scientist.

Yet I do not envy him. . . . For he is no more aware of the mystery which surrounds him than a fish is aware of the water it swims in. He could do research for a thousand years and never have an inkling of it. By the middle of August I could not see what difference it made whether the pigs got kidney stones or not (they didn't incidentally), compared to the mystery of those summer afternoons.[53]

And later, when his aunt insists on praising his 'analytical mind' he takes pains to inform us that 'I have never analysed anything'.[54] Only wondered at everything. Even an old dilapidated cinema fills him with 'a secret sense of wonder about the enduring, about all the nights, the rainy summer nights at twelve and one and two o'clock when the seats endured alone in the empty theater. The enduring is something which must be accounted for. One cannot simply shrug it off'.[55] This refusal to shrug off the mystery of life and the concomitant suspicion of all inquiry without wonder, is, of course, very sympathetic. It is just worth noting, however, that once the hero (and this applies now to many American books) has opted for this stance of reverent wonder to the exclusion of all other forms of response, there is very little he can do except reiterate his sense of wonder. This can lead to the repetitious and ultimately boring, even unconvincing enthusiasm of a Jack Kerouac. It can lead, as we have seen throughout the book, to endless formal problems—what shall the artist do with what he wonders at apart from list it? To set up 'wonder' as the *only* adequate response to reality is impoverishing, and to assert that it alone can approach the rare mystery of life is untrue. Binx Bolling can no more 'account' for the endurance of an old cinema than a scientist can account for the miraculous fact that the matter he explains exists at all. But there can surely be forms of science not divorced from wonder just as there can be intellectual activity not devoid of reverence: to set up such simplifying antinomies seems to me an unfortunate late-romantic sentimentality. In terms of the book we nevertheless feel the rightness of Binx Bolling's preferences and his sense of wonder is balanced by his intelligence, his irony, and his well-regulated dislike for the moribund niceness of the society which surrounds him.

The novel solution of this alienated wonderer is to hide himself deep inside ordinary society, for there he can wander incognito, secretly raging against 'the great shithouse of scientific humanism',[56] with his 'nose for merde'[57] and his eye for wonder as his two most precious assets. One could say that, in a different way, Salinger also employs those highly developed organs. And so does Huck Finn, and Nick Adams, and the young narrator of Sherwood Anderson's 'I want to know why'—the list extends itself. If we call the two responses wonder and horror we can draw in many of Henry James's protagonists: substitute 'a suspicion of society' for horror, and Emerson, Thoreau and Whitman appear without incongruity. What all these writers stress in their various ways is the radical importance of a true way of seeing; the generous, open, even naive, undulled and reverent eye—as opposed to the self-interested squinting and peering of the greedy utilitarian social eye, and the cold myopia of the scientific, analytic eye. Their ideal is an eye of passive wonder. 'Saints Behold' announced the Transcendentalists: 'perpetual observation, perpetual acquiescence' was Emerson's favourite stance: 'You might say of a philosopher that he was in this world as a spectator'[58] wrote Thoreau: Whitman wanted to be 'in and out of the game, watching and wondering at it': 'observe perpetually' advised James. Sherwood Anderson simply 'wanted to spend my life walking about and looking at things':[59] the Moviegoer likes to 'listen to people, see how they stick themselves into the world':[60] 'Judgment is second to wonder' for Saul Bellow's first narrator:'WATCH' was Seymour's favourite word in the Bible.

Emerson almost wrote a creed for all the writers we have discussed when he stressed the prime importance, for the artist, of 'revelation, always a miracle, which no frequency of occurrence or incessant study can ever familiarize, but which must always leave the inquirer stupid with wonder'.[61] But as the wonderer has become more and more alienated, the things miraculously revealed to him are not always such as will leave him 'stupid with wonder': sometimes he is stupefied with nausea, sometimes paralysed with horror. These reactions may be called 'first step' reactions; and perhaps we may just hazard the generalization that, finding themselves the new inhabitants of a new world (a world which had not been properly looked at before), American writers had first of all to see 'like children' before they could go on to see like men. The strange fact is that very few of them managed to make that development. Scott Fitzgerald's remark that the lives of American writers have no second acts could perhaps be adapted to read—American writers find it extremely difficult to take second steps. From the start European models offered them almost no help with their basic problem—how to absorb and arrange American experience. The 'first step' of somehow assimilating the clamorous undifferentiated stuff around them required tremendous energy and effort and often seems to have exhausted American writers. If there is a sort of habit of itemizing discernible in Whitman and other writers then that is because itemization is at least the beginning of differentiation; and without differentiation art is impossible and man is the mere victim of impressions which yield no meanings, of things which express no values. But this primal act of differentiation and assimilation will not, of itself, produce art. For that there is required some sense of ordered form. And it is noticeable that American writers have found it unusually difficult to discover helpful modes of organization, fruitful forms which will guide without enslaving, encircling devices which will aid in the necessary ordering of intensities.

It may seem rather arid and conservative to insist on the value and necessity of form, almost abstractly considered; but I should stress that I am far from insisting on the superior value of any one particular sort of form. Rather, by 'form' I mean some prior notion of shaping intent, some initial focus which directs vision without determining results. I mean that which produces architecture and not mere aggregates. Since the very protoplasmic stuff of life is not aimless but on the contrary exhibits a formative capacity, a regulatory purposive activity, an indefatigable tendency towards complex but stable organization, it is perhaps inevitable that art must have at least as much organization if it is to live. If we do uphold organic theories of art then it should be to insist that a work of art exhibits, not as much waywardness as nature's processes, but as much self-maintaining and co-ordinated structure as nature's products. But a work of art is more than a work of nature. Nature organizes herself to survive; art is organized to discover and display meanings and values. And without some sense of form that indispensable work of discovery can scarcely begin. The formed work perpetuates values and meanings: the unformed work records sensations and accidents.

Nearly all American writers have found it difficult to move beyond the first step, to find satisfactory forms. This phenomenon poses a problem which is obviously beyond the scope of this book. But we are in a position to offer a few tentative partial explanations. The passive wonder which constitutes the preferred mode of vision of so many of the writers we have discussed is a valid strategy of assimilation, but of itself it can neither generate nor discover form. It can isolate and vivify details and facts; but if, as Emerson advised, you ask the fact for the form, the fact has a habit of not answering. As so much American writing demonstrates. For although passivity may promote a state of rich appreciation, it can never produce the means of embodying and projecting that appreciation: passivity can never effect that necessary transformation of private impressions into communicated values. Art is inherently active: passive creation is a contradiction in terms. Art is indebted to the natural given world for its materials: but it adds to nature new arrangings which reveal significances. It forcefully separates things from chaos and flux and sets them in new contexts, new configurations which radiate and preserve values and insights. And to achieve this a positive act of inquiry and penetration is required. Sheer awareness must give way to something more active if it is to develop a style. This leads us to our second clue.

Many American writers have shown a persistent antipathy to 'analysis'. (Of course from one point of view this can be subsumed under the general romantic nineteenth-century distaste for 'analysis': but there is something specially, and significantly, virulent and programmatic, even fearful, in the American attitude.) In American writing the word is nearly always used pejoratively, and a deep-rooted hostility to the analysing faculties is as obvious in Salinger's and Percy's novels as it is in Emerson and Thoreau. (A typical gesture of repugnance can be found in a letter from Mark Twain to Howells written in 1885 where he complains that George Eliot 'analyzes the guts' out of 'motives and feelings'.) When Baudelaire affirmed that 'genius is nothing more or less than *childhood recovered* at will' he was expressing an appreciation of the rapture of infantile habits of perception and response which many American writers have shared. But Baudelaire went on to add these significant words: 'a childhood now equipped for self-expression with manhood's capacities and *a power of analysis which enables it to order the mass of raw material which it has involuntarily accumulated.*' (My italics—the passage can be found in his essay 'The Painter of Modern Life'.) Here, as I suggested at the outset, is a major difference between European and American literature since the romantic movement. In American writing one hears much about 'recovered childhood' but very little about the ordering 'power of analysis' which Baudelaire deemed indispensable to artistic creation: the result is, I maintain, that we often meet with a great deal of 'involuntary accumulation'. Mind and intellect are too often the villains in American literature. Yet, as Thomas Mann said, 'mind is life's self-criticism': it is also an important agent of life's self-evaluation. It is ultimately perverse and crippling to deny it an important part in the creation of works of art. Without some sort of analysis there can be no second steps, no fully realized form. It is the necessary prelude to a new synthesis. Of course these observations by no means exhaust the problem. Hawthorne and Melville were both active inquirers and courageous analysts, and yet they too had difficulty in finding enabling forms. In Hawthorne's case it would seem that there was so much guilt attached to analysis that his appalled conscience unsettled and unnerved his probing mind until the stable form of *The Scarlet Letter* finally gives way to the unbalanced confusion of *The Marble Faun*. Melville also seems to have experienced some of this guilt. *Moby Dick* does after all explore the fatal blasphemy of a Faustian man—though, of course, it took a Faustian man to write it. This great book indeed does have a profound inner organization which easily contains any surface shifts and inconsistencies: the relentless focus and indelible imprint of a great mind and imagination at full stretch are everywhere in evidence. Yet *Pierre* reveals that same mind perturbed and harassed to a point where it can no longer organize its materials: things get out of proportion, perspective fails, and the form all but tears itself to pieces. *Billy Budd* and a few of the short stories display a compressed unremitting relevance which indicates Melville's intermittent mastery of form: but the long years of silence and the unprofitable experiments with verse lead one to suspect that a prolonged inability to find satisfactory forms had a stifling effect on the greatest of all American imaginations. Henry James could never have written anything as great as *Moby Dick*, but his endless preoccupation with problems of form and his serene employment of the intelligence did enable him to produce consistently and continuously. He took step after step and made discovery after discovery. Scott Fitzgerald was perhaps the only successor to James who did justice to the attitude of wonder and also moved towards an increasingly profound analysis of it—its shortcomings and frailties, its poetry and its fate. He responded to 'the dream', but turned an increasingly acute eye to the 'foul dust' that 'floated in the wake'. Into the figure of Gatsby he put much of what he admired in America: a 'heightened sensitivity to the promise of life . . . an extraordinary gift for hope, a romantic readiness'.[62] There is something in Gatsby's generous, ideal aspirations which transcends their sordid base and survives their squalid destiny. His hopes are visionary, even though his end is coldly actual. ' Out of the corner of his eye Gatsby saw that the blocks of the sidewalk really formed a ladder and mounted to a secret place above the trees—he could climb to it, if he climbed alone, and once there he could suck the pap of life, gulp down the incomparable milk of wonder.'[63] Fitzgerald is remarkable because he never blinks the gaudiness and sentimentality, indeed the almost majestic vulgarity of Gatsby's imagination, yet he can catch what is truly lyrical and valuable and rare in the spirit behind it. He never fell into cynical disillusion even though he went on to show how inwardly fallible and outwardly foredoomed the wondering idealist was. Like those Dutch sailors he thought that America brought man 'face to face for the last time in history with something commensurate to his capacity for wonder'[64] and he celebrated that capacity at the same time as he traced it to its doom. His early work is over-ebullient, too romantic, vulnerable: but his later work shows a sober, compassionate analytic power which points, not to the indignity of the 'crack-up', but to a growing artistic maturity. It does seem as though Fitzgerald's determination to explore the *limits* of wonder, to celebrate the poetry of its willingness *and* draw the perspectives of its fate, helped him towards an increasingly firm formal control of his material.

Of course none of the works we have examined is totally without form and where we think we can detect faltering or failure we may be in the presence of some exciting and enriching experiment, some challengingly new form. But often this form has been one which does not countenance further explorations and facilitate further discoveries. Few of the writers we mentioned found forms which would help to stimulate a deepening complexity of response. How many great American writers have really triumphed only in one book!

Despite the many difficulties American writers have had to face, American literature is already immensely rich and fertile. However, one might fairly make a certain limiting judgement on its very real wealth by suggesting that it has often shown an inability to move beyond one particular syndrome of responses —wonder keeling over into horror, delight switching to disillusion, revulsion locked with awe. It has shown itself, perhaps, too suspicious of the analytical intellect, too disinclined to develop a complex reaction to society, too much given to extreme reactions, too hungry for metaphysics. In style it has, at times, been too sedulous in its indiscriminate attention to details, or too apt to avoid complexity by leaping to the refuge of vague generalizations. And yet all these shortcomings are but the extremes of its virtues: its great personal integrity, its noble refusal of complacency and compromise, its compassion and generosity and humour, its energy, its unremitting craving for reality and its reverent love for the world. It was with no idle phrase that Scott Fitzgerald described America as 'a willingness of the heart'.[65] At their best the writers we have discussed do what all artists should do—replenish and revivify our vision of the world. They approach with awe areas of existence which most men are prepared to exploit or ignore; they give the world back into our reinvigorated keeping, they enhance reality for us. An indispensable wonder comes through.

REFERENCES

INTRODUCTION

1 Rousseau, *Emile* (Everyman's Library, Dent, London, 1961), p. 54.
2 *Ibid.* p. 71.   3 *Ibid.* p. 172.
4 *Ibid.* p. 70.   5 *Ibid.* p. 131.
6 *Ibid.* p. 165.   7 *Ibid.* p. 166.
8 *Ibid.* p. 232.   9 *Ibid.* p. 153.
10 *Ibid.* p. 201.   11 *Ibid.* p. 134.
12 Rousseau, *Confessions* (William Glaisher, London, 1925), p. 524.
13 Rousseau, *Emile*, p. 238.   14 *Ibid.* p. 172.
15 Wordsworth, *Intimations of Immortality*, ll. 110–11.
16 Wordsworth, *The Prelude*, Book XI, l. 126.
17 *Ibid.* Book II, ll. 247–50.   18 *Ibid.* Book I, ll. 589–90.
19 *Ibid.* Book VII, l. 712.   20 *Ibid.* Book XI, ll. 235–40.
21 *Intimations of Immortality*, l. 5.
22 John Stuart Mill, *Autobiography* (World's Classics, Oxford, 1958), p. 116.
23 *Ibid.* pp. 117 and 121.
24 Carlyle, *Sartor Resartus* (Chapman & Hall, London, 1870), p. 40.
25 *Ibid.* p. 41.   26 *Ibid.* p. 41.
27 *Ibid.* p. 41.   28 *Ibid.* p. 135.
29 *Ibid.* p. 42.   30 *Ibid.* pp. 159–60.
31 Ruskin, *Elements of Drawing* (Smith Elder & Co., London, 1857), pp. 6–7.
32 Ruskin, *Modern Painters* (Everyman's Library, Dent, London): Preface to Second Edition, vol. I, p. xi.
33 Baudelaire, *Œuvres Complètes* (Pléiade, Paris, 1951), p. 880.
34 Bliss Perry (ed.), *The Heart of Emerson's Journals* (Dover Publications, New York, 1958), p. 59.
35 *Ibid.* p. 124.   36 *Ibid.* p. 331.
37 *Ibid.* p. 108.
38 Quoted in *Emerson: An Organic Anthology*, ed. Stephen Whicher (Riverside Press, Cambridge, Mass., 1960), p. 492.
39 Perry Miller (ed.), *The Transcendentalists: An Anthology* (Harvard University Press, 1950), p. 304.
40 Walker Percy, *The Moviegoer* (Popular Library Edition, New York, 1962), p. 42.
41 Saul Bellow, *The Dangling Man* (Vanguard Press, New York, 1944), p. 29.
42 Sherwood Anderson, *Tar, A Mid-Western Childhood* (Boni & Liveright, New York, 1926), p. 166.
43 Quoted by Wayne Booth in *The Rhetoric of Fiction* (University of Chicago Press, 1961), p. 338.
44 Emerson, *Complete Works* (Houghton Mifflin, Boston and New York, 1903), Vol. III, p. 274.
45 *Ibid.* vol. II, p. 318.   46 *Ibid.* vol. II, p. 11; vol. III, p. 61.

47 Emerson, *Complete Works*, vol. VII, p. 183.
48 *Ibid.* vol. II, p. 64.   49 *Ibid.* vol. II, pp. 125–6.
50 *Ibid.* vol. III, p. 171.
51 Transcript of a talk given to The Choate School, Wallingford, Conn. In *Oxford Anthology of American Literature* (Oxford), p. 1446.)

CHAPTER I

1 Perry Miller (ed.), *The Transcendentalists: An Anthology*, p. 98.
2 Perry Miller's illuminating inquiries into this subject are too well known to need enumerating here; but see in particular his *Errand Into The Wilderness* (Harvard University Press, 1956), p. 184 *et seq.*
3 Miller (ed.), *Transcendentalists*, pp. 322–3.
4 *Ibid.* p. 165.   5 *Ibid.* p. 165.
6 *Ibid.* p. 46.   7 *Ibid.* pp. 136–7.
8 *Ibid.* p. 309.   9 *Ibid.* p. 306.
10 *Ibid.* p. 312.   11 *Ibid.* p. 330.
12 Quoted by Charles Fiedelson, Jr, in *Symbolism and American Literature* (University of Chicago Press, 1953), p. 128.
13 Miller (ed.), *Transcendentalists*, p. 152.
14 *Ibid.* p. 146.   15 *Ibid.* p. 54.
16 *Ibid.* pp. 189–90.   17 *Ibid.* p. 208.
18 *Ibid.* p. 295.   19 *Ibid.* p. 296.
20 *Ibid.* p. 85.
21 Emerson, *Complete Works*, vol. XI, p. 21.
22 Miller (ed.), *Transcendentalists*, p. 317.
23 *Ibid.* p. 135.   24 *Ibid.* pp. 292–3.
25 *Ibid.* p. 292.

CHAPTER 2

1 Henry Nash Smith, 'Emerson's Problem of Vocation', *New England Quarterly*, vol. XII (March–December 1939).
2 For more sympathetic treatment of Emerson's handling of the problem of pain and evil see 'The House of Pain' by Newton Arvin (*Hudson Review*, vol. XII, No. 1, Spring 1959) and 'Emerson's Tragic Sense' by Stephen Whicher (*American Scholar*, vol. XXII, Summer 1953).
3 *Works*, vol. XII, p. 10.   4 *Journals*, VIII, p. 550.
5 *Works*, vol. I, pp. 73–4.   6 *Ibid.* vol. II, p. 147.
7 *Ibid.* vol. I, p. 3.   8 *Ibid.* vol. I, p. 4.
9 *Ibid.* vol. III, p. 92.   10 *Ibid.* vol. I, pp. 127–8.
11 *Ibid.* vol. I, p. 330.   12 *Ibid.* vol. II, p. 269.
13 *Journals*, X, p. 238.
14 Sherman Paul, *Emerson's Angle of Vision* (Harvard University Press, 1952), p. 73.

15 *Journals*, V, pp. 310–11.
16 Paul, *Emerson's Angle of Vision*, p. 75.
17 A. G. McGiffert (ed.), *Young Emerson Speaks* (Houghton Mifflin, Boston, 1938), p. 48.
18 Quoted by Leo Marx in his edition of Thoreau's *Excursions* (Corinth Books, New York, 1962), p. xiii.
19 *Works*, vol. III, p. 59.   20 *Ibid.* vol. III, p. 236.
21 *Ibid.* vol. I, p. 63.   22 *Ibid.* vol. IX, p. 181.
23 *Ibid.* vol. II, p. 354.   24 *Ibid.* vol. III, p. 285.
25 *Ibid.* vol. I, p. 74.   26 *Ibid.* vol. I, p. 10.
27 Quoted by F. O. Matthiessen, *The American Renaissance* (Oxford, 1941), p. 62.

28 *Works*, vol. I, p. 8.   29 *Ibid.* vol. III, p. 178.
30 *Ibid.* vol. I, p. 40.   31 *Ibid.* vol. III, p. 170.
32 *Ibid.* vol. I, p. 338.   33 *Ibid.* vol. I, p. 339.
34 *Ibid.* vol. IX, p. 166.   35 *Ibid.* vol. I, p. 139.
36 *Ibid.* vol. II, p. 48.   37 *Ibid.* vol. II, p. 49.
38 *Ibid.* vol. II, p. 319.   39 *Ibid.* vol. II, p. 329.
40 *Ibid.* vol. III, pp. 75–6.   41 *Ibid.* vol. III, pp. 185–6.
42 *Ibid.* vol. I, p. 73.   43 *Ibid.* vol. II, p. 325.
44 *Ibid.* vol. III, p. 244.   45 *Ibid.* vol. II, p. 335.
46 *Ibid.* vol. II, p. 171.   47 *Ibid.* vol. II, p. 302.
48 Quoted by F. O. Matthiessen in *The American Renaissance*, p. 58.
49 *Works*, vol. I, p. 43.   50 *Ibid.* vol. III, p. 17.
51 *Ibid.* vol. II, p. 101.   52 *Ibid.* vol. II, p. 101.
53 *Ibid.* vol. X, p. 474.
54 Quoted by Feidelson, Jr, in *Symbolism and American Literature*, p. 150.
55 Quoted by Norman Foerster in 'Emerson on the Organic Principle in Art', *PMLA*, XLI (1926).
56 *Works*, vol. II, p. 334.   57 *Ibid.* vol. I, p. 75.
58 *Ibid.* vol. III, p. 88.   59 *Ibid.* vol. I, p. 82.
60 *Ibid.* vol. I, p. 9.   61 *Ibid.* vol. III, p. 196.
62 *Ibid.* vol. III, p. 92.   63 *Ibid.* vol. III, p. 28.
64 *Ibid.* vol. II, p. 367.   65 *Ibid.* vol. II, p. 369.
66 *Ibid.* vol. I, pp. 111–12.   67 *Ibid.* vol. II, p. 290.
68 *Ibid.* vol. III, p. 183.   69 *Ibid.* vol. I, p. 38.
70 *Ibid.* vol. II, p. 354.   71 *Ibid.* vol. II, p. 355.
72 *Ibid.* vol. I, p. 85.   73 *Ibid.* vol. I, pp. 29–30.
74 *Ibid.* vol. I, p. 26.   75 *Ibid.* vol. I, p. 31.
76 *Ibid.* vol. I, p. 98.   77 *Ibid.* vol. III, p. 17.
78 *Ibid.* vol. III, pp. 17–18.   79 *Ibid.* vol. III, p. 22.
80 *Ibid.* vol. III, p. 237.   81 *Ibid.* vol. III, p. 171.
82 *Ibid.* vol. I, pp. 43–4.   83 *Ibid.* vol. II, p. 17.
84 *Ibid.* vol. I, pp. 111–12.   85 *Ibid.* vol. III, p. 172.
86 *Ibid.* vol. III, p. 229.   87 *Ibid.* vol. IV, p. 55.
88 *Ibid.* vol. IV, p. 56.   89 *Ibid.* vol. II, p. 315.
90 *Ibid.* vol. II, p. 330.   91 *Ibid.* vol. II, p. 330.
92 *Ibid.* vol. III, p. 173.

CHAPTER 3

1 Thoreau, *Complete Works* (Houghton Mifflin, Riverside Press, Boston and New York, 1906), vol. XV, p. 296.
2 *Ibid.* vol. XII, p. 133.   3 *Ibid.* vol. VII. pp. 247–8.
4 *Ibid.* vol. II, p. 123.   5 *Ibid.* vol. VII, p. 150.
6 *Ibid.* vol. VIII, p. 150.   7 *Ibid.* vol. VIII, p. 160.
8 *Ibid.* vol. X, p. 351.   9 *Ibid.* vol. XVIII, p. 371.
10 *Ibid.* vol. VII, p. 28.   11 *Ibid.* vol. VII, p. 35.
12 *Ibid.* vol. IX, p. 231.   13 *Ibid.* vol. VII, p. 253.
14 *Ibid.* vol. VII, p. 391.   15 *Ibid.* vol. I, p. 40.
16 *Ibid.* vol. VIII, p. 203.
17 Walt Whitman, *Leaves of Grass.* First version ed. M. Cowley (Viking Press, New York, 1959), p. 15.
18 Lawrence Durrell (ed.), *The Best of Henry Miller* (Heinemann, London, 1960), p. 363.
19 Wallace Stevens, *Collected Poems* (Knopf, New York, 1954), p. 386.
20 *Works*, vol. VIII, p. 160.   21 *Ibid.* vol. XIII, p. 46.
22 *Ibid.* vol. XIV, pp. 43–4.   23 *Ibid.* vol. XI, p. 45.
24 *Ibid.* vol. IX, p. 107.   25 *Ibid.* vol. XI, p. 293.
26 *Ibid.* vol. II, p. 313.   27 *Ibid.* vol. XVI, p. 125.
28 *Ibid.* vol. XIX, p. 30.   29 *Ibid.* vol. II, p. 109.
30 *Ibid.* vol. VIII, pp. 306–7.   31 *Ibid.* vol. VIII, p. 324.
32 *Ibid.* vol. VIII, pp. 290–1.   33 *Ibid.* vol. II, p. 366.
34 *Ibid.* vol. I, p. 285.   35 *Ibid.* vol. XVII, p. 18.
36 *Ibid.* vol. XVIII, p. 371.   37 *Ibid.* vol. XV, p. 362.
38 *Ibid.* vol. VIII, p. 168.   39 *Ibid.* vol. II, pp. 100–101.
40 *Ibid.* vol. II, pp. 108–9.   41 *Ibid.* vol. II, p. 360.
42 *Ibid.* vol. II, p. 107.   43 *Ibid.* vol. XIX, p. 145.
44 *Ibid.* vol. VIII, p. 43.   45 *Ibid.* vol. XV, p. 205.
46 *Ibid.* vol. I, p. 408.
47 Quoted by Sherman Paul in 'A Fable of the Renewal of Life', Introduction to *Walden* (Houghton Mifflin, Boston, 1957).
48 *Ibid.*   49 *Ibid.*
50 *Works*, vol. IX, p. 99.   51 *Ibid.* vol. IX, p. 311.
52 *Ibid.* vol. I, p. 92.   53 *Ibid.* vol. II, p. 159.
54 *Ibid.* vol. I, p. 6.   55 *Ibid.* vol. II, p. 106.
56 *Ibid.* vol. VIII, p. 419.   57 *Ibid.* vol. VIII, p. 419.
58 *Ibid.* vol. IX, p. 107.   59 *Ibid.* vol. I, p. 107.
60 Emerson, *Journals*, vol. VII, p. 29.
61 Quoted by F. O. Matthiessen in *The American Renaissance*, p. 35.
62 *Works*, vol. VII, p. 312.   63 *Ibid.* vol. XVIII, p. 389.
64 *Ibid.* vol. II, p. 357.   65 *Ibid.* vol. VIII, p. 302.
66 *Ibid.* vol. XIII, p. 73.   67 *Ibid.* vol. VII, pp. 487–8.
68 *Ibid.* vol. II, p. 5.   69 *Ibid.* vol. II, p. 367.
70 *Ibid.* vol. II, p. 127.   71 *Ibid.* vol. II, pp. 3–4.
72 *Ibid.* vol. II, p. 339.   73 *Ibid.* vol. II, p. 153.
74 *Ibid.* vol. II, p. 332.   75 *Ibid.* vol. II, p. 156.

76 *Works*, vol. II, p. 346.   77 *Ibid.* vol. XIX, p. 30.
78 Leo Marx, Introduction to *Excursions* (Corinth Books, New York, 1962),
    p. xiii.
79 *Works*, vol. XV, p. 205.

CHAPTER 4

References are either to *The Complete Writings of Walt Whitman*, ed. R. M.
Bucke, T. B. Harned, & H. L. Traubel (G. P. Putnam's, New York, 1902), to
be referred to as *Works*; or to an edition of the original version of *Leaves of Grass*
by Malcolm Cowley (Viking Press, New York, 1959), to be referred to as *LG*;
a simple line reference refers to *Song of Myself*.

 1 *LG*, ll. 1251–2.   2 *LG*, Introduction, p. viii.
 3 *LG*, l. 499.   4 *LG*, ll. 27–9.
 5 *LG*, ll. 1225–7.   6 *Works*, vol. I, p. 130.
 7 *LG*, Introduction, pp. 9–10.   8 *Works*, vol. I, p. 163.
 9 *LG*, Introduction, p. 8.   10 *LG*, l. 352.
11 *LG*, p. 9.   12 *LG*, p. 5.
13 *LG*, p. 5.   14 *LG*, pp. 6 and 16.
15 *LG*, p. 6.   16 *LG*, p. 11.
17 *LG*, p. 13.   18 *LG*, p. 17.
19 *Works*, vol. IX, pp. 34–5.   20 *Ibid.* vol. IX, p. 35.
21 *Ibid.* vol. IX, p. 35.
22 W. B. Yeats, *Essays and Introductions* (Macmillan, London, 1961), p. 503.
23 D. H. Lawrence, *Selected Literary Criticism* (Heinemann, London, 1955),
    p. 90.
24 *LG*, l. 1308.   25 *LG*, p. 7.
26 *LG*, p. 21.   27 *LG*, p. 138.
28 *loc. cit.*   29 *loc. cit.*
30 *loc. cit.*   31 *loc. cit.*
32 *Works*, vol. I, pp. 9–10.   33 *LG*, l. 1194.
34 *Works*, vol. V, p. 140.   35 *Ibid.* vol. V, p. 137.
36 *Ibid.* vol. V, p. 137.   37 *LG*, p. 17.
38 *LG*, p. 9.   39 *Works*, vol. III, p. 46.
40 *Ibid.* vol. V, p. 136.   41 *Ibid.* vol. I, p. 16.
42 *Ibid.* vol. I, p. 20.   43 *Ibid.* vol. I, pp. 25–6.
44 *Ibid.* vol. II, p. 226.
45 *The Letters of W. B. Yeats* (Rupert Hart-Davis, London, 1954), p. 903.
46 *Works*, vol. II, p. 233.   47 *Ibid.* vol. II, p. 34.
48 *Ibid.* vol. II, p. 34.   49 *LG*, l. 72.
50 *LG*, ll. 140–5.   51 Emerson, *Works*, vol. III, pp. 40–1.
52 *Works*, vol. III, p. 50.   53 *LG*, l. 5.
54 *LG*, l. 51.   55 *LG*, ll. 66–70.
56 *LG*, l. 40.   57 *LG*, l. 1082.
58 *LG*, l. 67.   59 *LG*, l. 1265.
60 *LG*, ll. 801–2.   61 *LG*, l. 840.
62 *LG*, l. 953.   63 *LG*, l. 1179.

64 *LG*, l. 1198.   65 *LG*, l. 1206.
66 *LG*, l. 1336.   67 *LG*, ll. 1327–30.
68 *LG*, l. 75.   69 *LG*, l. 100.
70 *LG*, l. 1326.   71 *LG*, l. 714.
72 *LG*, l. 832.   73 *LG*, l. 841.
74 *LG*, l. 169.   75 *LG*, l. 176.
76 *LG*, ll. 177–82.   77 *LG*, l. 312.
78 *LG*, ll. 305–6.   79 *LG*, ll. 300–1.
80 *LG*, l. 712.   81 *LG*, l. 736.
82 *LG*, ll. 765–6.   83 *LG*, l. 226.
84 *LG*, ll. 877–8.   85 *LG*, ll. 896–7.
86 Emerson, *Works*, vol. III, p. 194.   87 *LG*, l. 236.
88 *LG*, l. 63.   89 *LG*, l. 110.
90 *LG*, l. 125.   91 *LG*, ll. 499–502.
92 *LG*, l. 495.

CHAPTER 5

1   Perry Miller (ed.), *The Transcendentalists: An Anthology*, p. 326.
2   *Ibid.* p. 57.   3   *Ibid.* p. 112.
4   See Glenn Hughes, *Imagism and Imagists* (Stanford University Press, 1931), pp. 56, 61, 45, 68.
5   Miller (ed.), *Transcendentalists*, p. 322.
6   William Carlos Williams, *Collected Earlier Poems* (New Directions, New York, 1951), p. 90.
7   *Ibid.* p. 91.   8   *Ibid.* p. 277.
9   See Hughes, *Imagism and Imagists*, p. 67.
10 Miller (ed.), *Transcendentalists*, p. 372.
11 Sherwood Anderson, *Poor White* (Huebsch, New York, 1920), pp. 365–6.
12 Sherwood Anderson, *A Story Teller's Story* (Grove Press, New York, 1951), p. 270.
13 Ernest Hemingway, *A Farewell to Arms* (Scribner's, New York, 1929), p. 196.
14 William Carlos Williams, *Paterson* (New Directions, New York, 1951), p.11.

CHAPTER 6

1   Emerson, *Works*, vol. IX, p. 185.
2   Johnson J. Hooper, *Simon Suggs' Adventures* (American Book Co., New York, 1928), p. 41.
3   George Washington Harris, *Sut Lovingood* (Dick & Fitzgerald, New York, 1867), pp. 106–7.
4   *Ibid.* p. 174.   5   *Ibid.* pp. 261–2.

CHAPTER 7

1   H. N. Smith & W. G. Gibson (eds.), *Mark Twain–Howells Letters* (Harvard University Press, 1960), vol. II, p. 641.
2   *Ibid.* vol. I, p. 46.

3 Mark Twain, *Complete Works*, ed. A. B. Paine (Gabriel Wells, New York, 1922), vol. II, pp. 282–3.
4 *Ibid.* vol. XIX, p. 107.
5 *Ibid.* vol. XXXIV, p. 113 (quoted by Paine in a footnote).
6 H. N. Smith (ed.), *Mark Twain of the Enterprise* (University of California Press, 1957), p. 35.

7 *Ibid.* p. 94.
8 *Ibid.* p. 94.
9 *Ibid.* p. 9.
10 *Ibid.* p. 105.
11 *Ibid.* p. 105.
12 *Ibid.* p. 113.
13 *Ibid.* p. 132.
14 *Ibid.* p. 134.
15 *Ibid.* p. 139.
16 *Ibid.* p. 182.
17 *Works*, vol. I, p. 27.
18 *Ibid.* vol. I, p. 84.
19 *Ibid.* vol. I, p. 233.
20 *Ibid.* vol. I, p. 1.
21 *Ibid.* vol. I, p. 2.
22 *Ibid.* vol. I, p. 50.
23 *Ibid.* vol. I, p. 80.
24 *Ibid.* vol. I, p. 80.
25 *Ibid.* vol. I, p. 34.
26 *Ibid.* vol. II, p. 45.
27 *Ibid.* vol. II, p. 238.
28 *Ibid.* vol. II, p. 240.
29 *Ibid.* vol. I, p. 204.
30 *Ibid.* vol. II, p. 352.
31 *Ibid.* vol. II, p. 353.
32 *Ibid.* vol. II, p. 352.
33 *Ibid.* vol. I, p. 170.
34 *Ibid.* vol. I, p. 42.
35 *Ibid.* vol. II, p. 323.
36 *Ibid.* vol. II, p. 351.
37 *Ibid.* vol. I, p. 216.
38 *Ibid.* vol. II, p. 277.
39 *Ibid.* vol. II, p. 240.
40 *Ibid.* vol. II, p. 214.
41 *Ibid.* vol. II, p. 243.
42 *Ibid.* vol. II, p. 242.
43 *Ibid.* vol. II, p. 242.
44 *Ibid.* vol. I, p. xxi.
45 *Ibid.* vol. III, p. 73.
46 *Ibid.* vol. III, p. 82.
47 *Ibid.* vol. III, p. 85.
48 *Ibid.* vol. III, p. 86.
49 *Ibid.* vol. III, p. 129.
50 *Ibid.* vol. III, pp. 129–31.
51 *Ibid.* vol. III, p. 130.
52 *Ibid.* vol. III, p. 161.
53 *Ibid.* vol. IV, pp. 14–15.
54 *Ibid.* vol. III, p. 33.
55 *Ibid.* vol. III, p. 127.
56 *Ibid.* vol. III, p. 127.
57 *Ibid.* vol. III, p. 28.
58 *Ibid.* vol. III, p. 139.
59 *Ibid.* vol. III, p. 145.
60 *Ibid.* vol. III, p. 163.
61 *Ibid.* vol. IV, p. 8.
62 *Ibid.* vol. IX, p. 11.
63 *Ibid.* vol. IX, p. 11.
64 *Ibid.* vol. IX, pp. 12–13.
65 *Ibid.* vol. X, p. 88.
66 *Ibid.* vol. X, p. 40.
67 *Ibid.* vol. X, p. 232.
68 *Ibid.* vol. IX, p. 93.
69 *Ibid.* vol. IX, p. 155.
70 *Ibid.* vol. X, p. 170.
71 *Ibid.* vol. XII, pp. 78–80.
72 *Ibid.* vol. XII, p. 479.
73 *Ibid.* vol. XII, p. 111.
74 *Ibid.* vol. XIII, pp. 163–4.
75 *Ibid.* vol. VIII, p. 121.
76 See also Leo Mark, 'The Pilot and the Passenger: Landscape Conventions and the style of Huckleberry Finn', *American Literature*, vol. XXVIII, No. 2 (May, 1956).
77 *Oxford Book of American Verse* (Oxford, 1950), p. 113.
78 *Works*, vol. XIII, p. 48.
79 *Ibid.* vol. XIII, p. 49.
80 *Ibid.* vol. XIII, pp. 67–8.
81 *Ibid.* vol. XIII, p. 166.
82 *Ibid.* vol. XIII, p. 165.

83 T. S. Eliot, 'American Literature and the American Language', *Washington University Studies. New Series, Language and Literature*, No. 23 (St Louis, 1953), pp. 16–17.

CHAPTER 8

MTP: Mark Twain Papers, University of California, Berkeley

1   *Mark Twain–Howells Letters*, vol. I, p. 338.
2   *The Autobiography of Mark Twain*, ed. Charles Neider (Harper, New York, 1959), p. 176.
3   *Mark Twain–Howells Letters*, vol. II, p. 778.
4   *Ibid.* vol. I, p. 231 (quoted in a footnote); also MTP DV 4, pp. 368–72.
5   *Ibid.* vol. II, p. 705.   6   *Autobiography*, p. 176.
7   Smith, *Mark Twain of the Enterprise*, p. 58.
8   *Ibid.* p. 65.   9   *Works*, vol. I, p. 93.
10 G. Santayana, *Winds of Doctrine* (*Studies in Contemporary Opinion*, Dent, London, 1913), p. 201.
11 *Works*, vol. III, p. 9.   12   *Ibid.* vol. III, p. 9.
13 *Ibid.* vol. III, p. 62.   14   *Ibid.* vol. II, p. 65.
15 *Ibid.* vol. III, p. 241.   16   *Ibid.* vol. III, p. 155.
17 *Ibid.* vol. III, p. 169.
18 H. N. Smith, *Mark Twain* (Harvard University Press, 1962), p. 64.
19 *Works*, vol. IV, p. 42.   20   Smith, *Mark Twain*, p. 69.
21 Notebook 28a (I), 15 May 1895–23 Aug. 1895, Typescript 8 MTP. Copyright © 1963 by the Mark Twain Company.
22 *Works*, vol. VII, pp. 242–3.
23 *Mark Twain–Howells Letters*, vol. I, p. 26.
24 *Works*, vol. IX, pp. 16–17.   25   *Ibid.* vol. IX, p. 205.
26 *Ibid.* vol. IX, p. 207.
27 Notebook 28a (I), Typescript 35 (1895), MTP. Copyright © 1963 by the Mark Twain Company.
28 *Works*, vol. IX, p. 206.   29   *Ibid.* vol. VIII, pp. 54–5.
30 *Ibid.* vol. VIII, p. 190.   31   *Ibid.* vol. VIII, pp. 227–8.
32 *Ibid.* vol. VIII, p. 222.   33   *Ibid.* vol. VIII, p. 290.
34 *Ibid.* vol. VIII, p. 289.
35 *Mark Twain–Howells Letters*, vol. I, pp. 91–2.
36 Notebook 15, 26 July 1880–Dec. 1881, MTP TS, p. 2. Copyright © 1963 by the Mark Twain Company.

CHAPTER 9

1   Emerson, *Works*, vol. II, p. 334.
2   *Mark Twain–Howells Letters*, vol. II, p. 665.
3   *The Autobiography of Mark Twain*, ed. Charles Neider, pp. 12–13.
4   *Works*, vol. XXXV, p. 773.   5   *Autobiography*, p. 40.

6 *Mark Twain Notebooks*, ed. A. B. Paine, p. 319; also Notebook 31 (II), 13 Dec. 1896–6 Jan. 1897, MTP TS, p. 50. Copyright © 1963 by the Mark Twain Company.

7 *Mark Twain–Howells Letters*, vol. II, p. 686 (see footnote).

8 *Mark Twain Notebooks*, ed. Paine, p. 319.

9 *Autobiography*, p. 71. 10 *Ibid.* p. 37.

11 *Ibid.* p. 74. 12 *Ibid.* p. 126.

13 *Works*, vol. XXXVII, p. 146.

14 Notebook 31 (II), 13 Dec. 1896–6 Jan. 1897, MTP TS, pp. 41–3. Copyright © 1963 by the Mark Twain Company.

15 William Dean Howells, *Indian Summer* (Ticknor, Boston, 1886), p. 75.

16 *Ibid.* p. 92. 17 *Ibid.* p. 149.

18 *Ibid.* p. 277. 19 *Ibid.* pp. 371–2.

20 *Ibid.* p. 44.

21 Henry James, *The Ambassadors* (Macmillan, London, 1923), vol. I, p. 190.

22 Henry James, *Hawthorne* (Cornell University Press, 1956), p. 114.

23 *Autobiography*, p. 121.

24 *Mark Twain–Howells Letters*, vol. II, pp. 534–5.

25 Smith, *Mark Twain of the Enterprise*, pp. 136–7.

26 Mark Twain, *The Celebrated Jumping Frog of Calaveras County and other sketches* (Webb, New York, 1867), p. 31.

27 *Ibid*, pp. 32–3.

28 Letter to Wattie Bowser, 20 March 1880. First published in *Houston Post*, Sunday, 7 Feb. 1960.

29 *Mark Twain–Howells Letters*, vol. II, p. 369.

30 *Ibid.* vol. I, p. 105. 31 *Works*, vol. XXVI, p. 254.

32 *Ibid.* vol. XXVI, p. 254. 33 *Ibid.* vol. XXVI, p. 254.

34 *Autobiography*, p. 202. 35 *Ibid.* p. 202.

36 *Mark Twain–Howells Letters*, vol. I, p. 138.

37 *Ibid.* vol. II, p. 492 (footnote).

CHAPTER 10

1 *Works*, vol. XIX, p. 49.

2 *Ibid.* vol. XIII, p. 20. (Unless otherwise stated all references to *Works* in this chapter will be to vol. XIII and only the page number will be given.)

3 p. 333. 4 pp. 93, 324, etc.

5 pp. 12, 337, etc. 6 p. 341.

7 p. 18. 8 p. 46.

9 p. 326. 10 pp. 330–1.

11 p. 364. 12 p. 341.

13 p. 345.

14 See Leo Mark, 'Mr Eliot, Mr Trilling and Huckleberry Finn', *American Scholar*, XXII (Autumn 1953).

15 p. 294. 16 p. 332.

17 W. J. Cash, *The Mind of the South* (Vintage Books, New York, 1960), p. 50.

18 p. 138. 19 p. 139.

20 p. 150. 21 p. 148.

22 p. 241.
23 Notebook 32b (II), 24 Sept. 1897–Aug. 1899, MTP TS, p. 63. Copyright © 1963 by the Mark Twain Company.
24 Notebook 32b (I), 22 June 1897–24 Sept. 1897, MTP TS, p. 28. Copyright © 1963 by the Mark Twain Company.
25 p. 215.   26 p. 270.
27 p. 138.   28 *Works*, vol. XII, p. 30.
29 p. 308.   30 p. 36.
31 p. 61.   32 p. 100.
33 p. 162.   34 p. 81.
35 p. 95.   36 p. 158.
37 p. 247.   38 p. 282.
39 p. 283.   40 p. 59.
41 pp. 164–5.   42 *Works*, vol. IX, p. 107.
43 *Ibid.* vol. X, pp. 41–2.   44 *Ibid.* vol. X, p. 48.
45 p. 174.   46 p. 174.
47 Walter Francis Frear, *Mark Twain and Hawaii* (Chicago, 1947), see Appendix D2, Sandwich Islands Lecture, p. 436.
48 p. 90.   49 pp. 118–19.
50 MTP DV 111. Copyright © 1963 by the Mark Twain Company.
51 *The Autobiography of Mark Twain*, ed. Charles Neider, p. 139.
52 *Works*, vol. IV, p. 1.
53 Quoted by Paine in his Biography: *Works*, vol. XXX, p. 289.
54 *Works*, vol. XXXIV, p. 337 (see footnote).
55 *Ibid.* vol. XXXV, p. 558.   56 pp. 296–7.
57 Thoreau, *Works*, vol. I, p. 55.   58 p. 17.
59 p. 303.   60 p. 215.
61 p. 321.   62 p. 322.
63 H. N. Smith, Introduction to *Huckleberry Finn* (Riverside Press, Cambridge, Mass., 1958), p. xxiv.
64 p. 17.   65 p. 18.
66 p. 20.   67 p. 31.
68 p. 152.   69 p. 227.
70 p. 228.   71 p. 228.
72 p. 238.   73 p. 337.
74 p. 15.   75 p. 2.
76 p. 160.   77 p. 80.
78 H. N. Smith, 'Mark Twain's Images of Hannibal', *University of Texas Studies in English*, vol. XXXVII (1958).
79 MTP DV 303. Copyright © 1963 by the Mark Twain Company.
80 *Ibid.*   81 *Ibid.*
82 *Ibid.*   83 *Ibid.*
84 *Works*, vol. XIX, p. 10.   85 *Ibid.* vol. XIX, p. 18.
86 *Ibid.* vol. XIX, pp. 10–11. 87 *Ibid.* vol. XIX, p. 41.
88 *Ibid.* vol. XIX, p. 159.   89 *Ibid.* vol. XIX, p. 189.
90 *Ibid.* vol. XIX, p. 189.   91 *Ibid.* vol. XIX, p. 151.
92 *Ibid.* vol. XIX, p. 134.   93 *Ibid.* vol. XIX, p. 137.
94 John Updike, *Rabbit, Run* (André Deutsch, London, 1961), p. 106.

95 *Works*, vol. XIX, pp. 126–7.
96 Lionel Trilling, *The Liberal Imagination* (Secker & Warburg, London, 1951), p. 110.
97 Notebook 27, 4 March 1893–13 July 1894, MTP TS, p. 23. Copyright © 1963 by the Mark Twain Company.
98 Notebook 29 (II), 8 Apr. 1896–28 Apr. 1896, MTP TS, p. 37. Copyright © 1963 by the Mark Twain Company.

CHAPTER 11

1 *Lectures in America* (Random House, New York, 1935), pp. 140–5.
2 Unpublished Dissertation at the University of California on the development of the colloquial style from Mark Twain to Hemingway.
3 *Picasso* (first published in French by Librarie Floury, Paris, 1938; Beacon Press, Boston, 1959), p. 10.

4 *Ibid.* p. 43.
5 *Ibid.* p. 15.
6 *Ibid.* p. 15.
7 *Ibid.* p. 18.
8 *Ibid.* p. 18.
9 *Ibid.* p. 35.
10 *Ibid.* p. 35.
11 *Ibid.* p. 35.
12 *Ibid.* p. 35.
13 *Lectures in America*, p. 176.
14 *Ibid.* p. 187.
15 *Ibid.* p. 179.
16 *Ibid.* p. 196.
17 *Ibid.* p. 196.
18 *Ibid.* p. 227.
19 *Narration* (University of Chicago Press, 1935), pp. 17, 19–20.
20 *Ibid.* pp. 23–5, 44.
21 *Lectures in America*, p. 161.
22 *Ibid.* p. 172.
23 *Ibid.* p. 142.
24 *Ibid.* pp. 191–2.
25 *Tender Buttons* (Calire Marie, New York, 1914), p. 26.
26 *Ibid.* p. 27.
27 *Lectures in America*, pp. 209–10.
28 *Ibid.* p. 211.
29 *Ibid.* p. 236.
30 *Ibid.* p. 235.
31 *Ibid.* pp. 236–7.
32 *Ibid.* p. 237.
33 *Ibid.* p. 238.
34 *Ibid.* p. 241.
35 *Ibid.* p. 246.
36 Jacques Rivière, *The Ideal Reader* (Horrill, London, 1962), pp. 40–1.
37 *Lectures in America*, p. 231.
38 *Composition as Explanation* (Hogarth Press, London, 1926), p. 16.
39 *Three Lives* (Grafton Press, 1909; Modern Library, New York, 1933), pp. 89, 207.
40 *Ibid.* p. 119.
41 *Ibid.* p. 142.
42 *Ibid.* p. 154.
43 *Ibid.* p. 217.
44 *Lectures in America*, p. 53.
45 *Narration*, p. 10.
46 *Picasso*, p. 13.
47 *The Autobiography of Alice B. Toklas* (Literary Guild, Harcourt Brace, New York, 1933), p. 145.
48 *Narration*, p. 44.

CHAPTER 12

1   *Dial* Magazine, 8 Nov. 1917.
2   *A Story Teller's Story* (first published by Huebsch, New York, 1924; Grove Press, New York, 1951), p. 290.
3   *Winesburg, Ohio* (Heubsch, New York, 1919), p. 41.
4   *Ibid.* p. 53.   5   *Ibid.* p. 117.
6   *Ibid.* p. 55.   7   *Ibid.* p. 166.
8   *Ibid.* p. 41.   9   *Ibid.* p. 205.
10 *Ibid.* p. 57.   11 *Ibid.* p. 117.
12 *Ibid.* p. 196.   13 *Ibid.* p. 184.
14 *Ibid.* p. 4.   15 *Ibid.* pp. 221–2.
16 *Ibid.* p. 267.   17 *Ibid.* p. 303.
18 *Poor White* (Huebsch, New York, 1920), p. 113.
19 *A Story Teller's Story*, pp. 402–4.
20 *Letters of Sherwood Anderson*, ed. and sel. Howard Mumford Jones (Little, Brown, Boston, 1952), p. 441.
21 *A Story Teller's Story*, p. 439.
22 *Tar: A Mid-West Childhood* (Boni & Liveright, New York, 1926), p. 107.
23 *Ibid.* p. 157.   24 *Poor White*, pp. 108–9.
25 *A Story Teller's Story*, p. 328.   26 *Ibid.* pp. 359–62.
27 *Ibid.* p. 317.
28 *Horses and Men* (Huebsch, New York, 1923), pp. 215–17.
29 *Tar*, pp. 54–5.   30 *Ibid.* p. 195.
31 *Ibid.* p. 196.   32 *Horses and Men*, p. ix.
33 *Poor White*, p. 363.   34 *Ibid.* pp. 365–6.
35 *A Story Teller's Story*, p. 408.   36 *Ibid.* p. 408.

CHAPTER 13

1   *Death in the Afternoon* (Cape, London, 1932), pp. 254, 255, 258, 259, 261.
2   *The First Forty-Nine Stories* (Collier, New York, 1938), p. 167.
3   *Ibid.* p. 193.   4   *Ibid.* p. 435.
5   *For Whom the Bell Tolls* (Scribner's, New York, 1940), p. 381.
6   *Ibid.* p. 433.   7   *Ibid.* p. 43.
8   *Ibid.* p. 168.   9   *Ibid.* p. 166.
10 *Ibid.* p. 169.
11 *A Farewell To Arms* (Scribner's, New York, 1929), p. 196.
12 *Death in the Afternoon*, p. 248.
13 *For Whom the Bell Tolls*, pp. 312–13.
14 *Across the River and Into the Trees* (Scribner's, New York, 1950), pp. 219–20.
15 *The First Forty-Nine Stories*, p. 480.
16 *Ibid.* p. 479.   17 *Ibid.* p. 481.
18 *For Whom the Bell Tolls*, p. 367.
19 *Across the River and Into the Trees*, p. 307.

20 *Death in the Afternoon*, p. 258.   21 *First Forty-Nine Stories*, p. 162.

22 *Ibid.* p. 507.   23 *For Whom the Bell Tolls*, p. 470.

24 *Ibid.* p. 338.   25 *Ibid.* p. 471.

26 *Ibid.* p. 468.   27 *Ibid.* p. 468.

28 *A Farewell to Arms*, p. 350.   29 *Ibid.* p. 221.

30 *The Old Man and the Sea* (Scribner's, New York, 1952), pp. 50, 65.

31 *Ibid.* p. 122.

32 *The Sun Also Rises* (Scribner's, New York, 1926), p. 173.

33 *Ibid.* p. 153.   34 *Ibid.* p. 92.

35 *Ibid.* p. 99.

36 *Across the River and Into the Trees*, p. 32.

37 *The First Forty-Nine Stories*, p. 355.

38 *For Whom the Bell Tolls*, pp. 136-7.

39 *Across the River and into the Trees*, p. 185.

40 *Ibid.* pp. 191-2.   41 *For Whom the Bell Tolls*, p. 239.

42 *The First Forty-Nine Stories*, p. 500.

43 *For Whom the Bell Tolls*, p. 466.

44 *The Green Hills of Africa* (Scribner's, New York, 1953), p. 193.

45 *Across the River and into the Trees*, p. 123.

46 *The Old Man and the Sea*, p. 27.

47 *The Sun Also Rises*, facing title page.

48 *For Whom the Bell Tolls*, p. 336.   49 *Ibid.* p. 336.

50 *Ibid.* p. 340.

51 *The First Forty-Nine Stories*, p. 461.

52 *Ibid.* p. 469.

53 *The Green Hills of Africa*, pp. 235-6.

54 *Ibid.* p. 70.

55 Quoted by Morris Watnick in his essay on Lukacs collected in *Revisionism: Essays on the history of Marxist Ideas*, ed. L. Labedz (Allen & Unwin, London, 1962), p. 159.

56 *For Whom the Bell Tolls*, p. 163.   57 *Ibid.* p. 158.

58 *The Green Hills of Africa*, p. 148.

59 *The Old Man and the Sea*, pp. 55-7.

60 *The Sun Also Rises*, p. 204.   61 *Ibid.* p. 204.

62 *Ibid.* p. 204.   63 *The First Forty-Nine Stories*, p. 213.

64 *For Whom the Bell Tolls*, p. 166.   65 *Ibid.* p. 166.

66 *Death in the Afternoon*, p. 10.   67 *Ibid.* p. 56.

68 *Ibid.* p. 182.

69 *Across the River and into the Trees*, p. 232.

70 *The Sun Also Rises*, pp. 174, 226. 71 *Death in the Afternoon*, p. 93.

72 *Ibid.* p. 220.   73 *The Old Man and the Sea*, p. 107.

74 *Ibid.* p. 35.   75 *Ibid.* p. 36.

76 *Death in the Afternoon*, p. 183.   77 *Ibid.* p. 174.

78 *in our time* (Paris, 1924), ch. 6, p. 14.

79 *Ibid.* ch. 3, p. 11.

80 *The First Forty-Nine Stories*, pp. 308-9.

81 *The Green Hills of Africa*, p. 149.

82 *The First Forty-Nine Stories*, p. 311.

83   *The First Forty-Nine Stories*, p. 313.
84   *The Green Hills of Africa*, p. 284.
85   *The First Forty-Nine Stories*, p. 313.
86   *Ibid.* p. 316.   87   *Ibid.* p. 323.
88   *Ibid.* p. 325.   89   *Ibid.* p. 329.
90   *Ibid.* p. 325.
91   D. H. Lawrence, *Collected Letters* (Heinemann, London, 1962), ed. H. T. Moore, vol. I, p. 358.
92   *Ibid.* vol. I, p. 358.
93   *The Green Hills of Africa*, p. 284.
94   *Across the River and into the Trees*, p. 31.
95   *The Old Man and the Sea*, p. 70.
96   *Ibid.* p. 75.
97   *The Green Hills of Africa*, pp. 284–5.

CHAPTER 14

All references are to the edition of Henry James's work published by Macmillan & Co. in London 1920–, unless otherwise stated. These volumes are not numbered, so in each case the title of the volume will be cited.

1   *Lesson of the Master Etc.*, p. 48.
2   Henry James, 'Emerson', reprinted in *The American Essays of Henry James*, ed. Leon Edel (Vintage Books, New York, 1956), p. 53.
3   *Ibid.* p. 52.   4   *Ibid.* p. 57.
5   *Ibid.* p. 54.   6   *Ibid.* p. 56.
7   *Ibid.* p. 61.   8   *Ibid.* p. 62.
9   *Ibid.* p. 56.   10   *Ibid.* p. 57.
11   *Critical Prefaces by Henry James*, ed. R. P. Blackmur (hereafter to be referred to as '*Prefaces*') (Scribner's, New York, 1934), p. 64.
12   *Ibid.* p. 63.
13   Henry James, *Hawthorne* (reprinted by Cornell University Press, 1956), p. 22.
14   *Ibid.* p. 79.   15   *Ibid.* p. 34.
16   *Prefaces*, p. 188.   17   *Ibid.* p. 132.
18   *Ibid.* p. 134.   19   *Ibid.* p. 135.
20   *Ibid.* pp. 137–8.
21   *The Complete Tales of Henry James*, ed. Leon Edel (Rupert Hart-Davis, London, 1962), vol. 4, pp. 147–9.
22   *Daisy Miller Etc.*, p. 31.   23   *Ibid.* p. 77.
24   *The Spoils of Poynton Etc.*, pp. 238–9.
25   *Ibid.* p. 269.   26   *Ibid.* p. 294.
27   *Ibid.* p. 286.   28   *Ibid.* p. 270.
29   *Ibid.* p. 292.   30   *Ibid.* p. 334.
31   *Ibid.* p. 288.   32   *Ibid.* p. 326.
33   *Ibid.* p. 354.   34   *Ibid.* p. 372.
35   *Ibid.* pp. 314–15.   36   *Ibid.* p. 320.

37 *The Spoils of Poynton Etc.*, p. 343.
38 *Ibid.* p. 344.   39 *Ibid.* p. 345.
40 *Ibid.* p. 348.   41 *Ibid.* p. 344.
42 *Prefaces*, p. 282.   43 *Daisy Miller Etc.*, p. 232.
44 *Ibid.* pp. 241–2.   45 *Ibid.* p. 243.
46 *Ibid.* pp. 255–6.   47 *Spoils of Poynton Etc.*, p. 244.

CHAPTER 15

1 *Prefaces*, pp. 146–7.   2 *What Maisie Knew*, p. 206.
3 Quoted by Leon Edel in *Henry James: The Untried Years* (Rupert Hart-Davis, London, 1953), p. 230.
4 *What Maisie Knew*, p. 104.   5 *Ibid.* pp. 103, 56, 45.
6 *Ibid.* pp. 163, 64.   7 *Ibid.* p. 164.
8 *Ibid.* p. 22.   9 *Ibid.* p. 14.
10 *Prefaces*, p. 143.   11 *Ibid.* p. 145.
12 *Ibid.* p. 145.   13 *Ibid.* p. 146.
14 *Ibid.* p. 146.
15 *Literary Reviews and Essays by Henry James* (Grove Press, New York, 1957), p. 293.
16 *What Maisie Knew*, p. 9.   17 *Ibid.* p. 14.
18 *Ibid.* p. 15.   19 *Ibid.* p. 18.
20 *Ibid.* p. 97.   21 *Ibid.* p. 124.
22 *Ibid.* p. 146.   23 *Ibid.* p. 124.
24 *Ibid.* p. 44.   25 *Ibid.* p. 121.
26 *Ibid.* p. 144.   27 *Ibid.* p. 302.
28 *Ibid.* p. 9.   29 *Ibid.* p. 131.
30 *Ibid.* p. 170.   31 *Ibid.* p. 125.
32 *Ibid.* p. 146.   33 *Ibid.* p. 11.
34 *Ibid.* p. 63.   35 *Ibid.* p. 83.
36 *Ibid.* p. 150.   37 *Ibid.* p. 154.
38 *Ibid.* p. 155.   39 *Ibid.* p. 176.
40 *Ibid.* p. 32.   41 *Ibid.* p. 199.
42 *Ibid.* p. 82.   43 *Ibid.* p. 34.
44 *Ibid.* p. 68.   45 *Ibid.* p. 90.
46 *Ibid.* p. 165.   47 *Ibid.* p. 313.
48 *Ibid.* p. 239.   49 *Ibid.* p. 48.
50 *Ibid.* p. 82.   51 *Ibid.* p. 105.
52 *Ibid.* p. 87.   53 *Ibid.* p. 119.
54 *Ibid.* p. 125.   55 *Ibid.* p. 133.
56 *Ibid.* p. 157.   57 *Ibid.* p. 194.
58 *Ibid.* p. 303.   59 *Ibid.* p. 296.
60 *Ibid.* p. 201.   61 *Ibid.* p. 12.
62 *Ibid.* p. 176.
63 Reprinted in *The Complex Fate* by Marius Bewley (Chatto & Windus, London, 1952), p. 131.
64 Henry James, *A Small Boy and Others* (Scribner's, New York, 1913), p. 216

65 *What Maisie Knew*, p. 25.   66 *Ibid.* p. 25.
67 *Ibid.* p. 97.   68 *Ibid.* p. 101.
69 *Ibid.* p. 82.   70 *Ibid.* p. 254.
71 *Ibid.* p. 204.   72 *Ibid.* p. 207.
73 *Ibid.* p. 207.   74 *Ibid.* p. 244.
75 *Ibid.* pp. 251–2.   76 *Ibid.* p. 313.
77 *Ibid.* p. 314.   78 *Ibid.* p. 315.
79 *Ibid.* p. 208.
80 Henry James, *The Art of the Novel*, collected in *The Future of the Novel*, ed. Leon Edel (Vintage Books, New York, 1956), p. 12.
81 Quentin Anderson, *The American Henry James* (John Calder, London, 1958), p. 268.
82 *The Awkward Age*, p. 145.   83 *Ibid.* pp. 171, 210, 275.
84 *Ibid.* p. 315.   85 *Ibid.* p. 219.
86 *Ibid.* p. 193.   87 *Ibid.* p. 131.
88 *Ibid.* p. 110.   89 *Ibid.* p. 22.
90 *Ibid.* p. 211.   91 *Ibid.* p. 342.
92 *Ibid.* p. 205.   93 *Ibid.* p. 197.
94 *Ibid.* p. 309.   95 *Ibid.* p. 440.
96 *Ibid.* p. 480.   97 *Ibid.* p. 205.
98 *Ibid.* p. 189.   99 *The Altar of the Dead Etc.*, p. 436.
100 *Ibid.* p. 466.   101 *Ibid.* p. 477.
102 *Prefaces*, p. 308.   103 *Ibid.* p. 156.
104 *The Princess Casamassima*, vol. II, p. 126.
105 Fr. Crews, *The Tragedy of Manners* (Yale University, 1957), p. 29.
106 *Roderick Hudson*, p. 24.   107 *Portrait of a Lady*, vol. I, p. 188.
108 Henry James, *The Ivory Tower* (Collins, London and Glasgow, 1917), p. 39.
109 *Ibid.* p. 57.   110 *Ibid.* p. 142.
111 *Ibid.* p. 208.   112 *Ibid.* p. 315.
113 *Ibid.* p. 331.   114 *Ibid.* p. 308.
115 *Ibid.* p. 309.

CHAPTER 16

1 *Daisy Miller Etc.*, p. 387.   2 *What Maisie Knew Etc.*, p. 374.
3 *Prefaces*, pp. 170–1.   4 *Ibid.* p. 154.
5 *What Maisie Knew Etc.*, p. 325.   6 *Ibid.* p. 325.
7 *Ibid.* pp. 328, 330.   8 *Ibid.* pp. 330, 331, 343, 362.
9 *Ibid.* p. 333.   10 *Ibid.* p. 334.
11 *Ibid.* p. 333.   12 *Ibid.* p. 345.
13 Yvor Winters, *In Defense of Reason* (Alan Swallow, Denver, 1947), p. 331.
14 *What Maisie Knew Etc.*, p. 367.   15 *Ibid.* pp. 336–7.
16 *Ibid.* p. 377.   17 *Ibid.* p. 368.
18 *Ibid.* p. 369.   19 *Ibid.* p. 342.
20 *Ibid.* p. 344.   21 *Ibid.* p. 342.

22 *What Maisie Knew Etc.*, p. 423. 23 *Ibid.* p. 343.
24 *Ibid.* p. 382. 25 *Ibid.* p. 416.
26 *Ibid.* p. 411. 27 *Ibid.* p. 424.
28 *Ibid.* p. 350. 29 *Ibid.* p. 355.
30 *Ibid.* pp. 396, 356. 31 *Ibid.* p. 442.
32 *Ibid.* p. 332. 33 *Ibid.* p. 368.
34 *Ibid.* p. 401. 35 *Prefaces*, p. 157.
36 *Ibid.* p. 155. 37 *Ibid.* p. 155.
38 *The Sacred Fount*, p. 18. 39 *Ibid.* p. 24.
40 *Ibid.* p. 64. 41 *Ibid.* p. 31.
42 *Ibid.* p. 3. 43 *Ibid.* p. 72.
44 *Ibid.* p. 142. 45 *Ibid.* p. 31.
46 *Ibid.* p. 156. 47 *Ibid.* p. 156.
48 *Ibid.* p. 31. 49 *Ibid.* pp. ii, 216, 200.
50 *Ibid.* pp. 51, 53. 51 *Ibid.* pp. 14, 41.
52 *Ibid.* pp. 44, 62, 68. 53 *Ibid.* pp. 78, 145, 203.
54 *Ibid.* p. 133. 55 *Ibid.* pp. 116, 71.
56 *Ibid.* p. 115. 57 *Ibid.* p. 83.
58 *Ibid.* p. 102. 59 *Ibid.* p. 102.
60 *Ibid.* p. 101. 61 *Ibid.* p. 19.
62 *Ibid.* p. 19. 63 *Ibid.* pp. 21, 23, 27.
64 *Ibid.* p. 100. 65 *Ibid.* p. 168.
66 *Ibid.* p. 139. 67 *Ibid.* p. 143.
68 *Ibid.* p. 25. 69 *Ibid.* p. 175.
70 *Ibid.* pp. 160, 242, 198. 71 *Ibid.* p. 204.
72 *Ibid.* p. 199. 73 *Ibid.* p. 112.
74 *Ibid.* p. 113. 75 *Ibid.* p. 137.
76 *Ibid.* p. 136. 77 *Ibid.* p. 53.
78 *Ibid.* pp. 78, 134. 79 *Ibid.* p. 80.
80 *Ibid.* p. 179. 81 *Ibid.* p. 179.
82 *Ibid.* p. 243. 83 *Ibid.* p. 246.
84 *Ibid.* p. 57. 85 *Ibid.* pp. 123, 124.
86 *Ibid.* p. 144. 87 *Ibid.* p. 144
88 *Ibid.* p. 144. 89 *Ibid.* p. 151.
90 *Ibid.* p. 55. 91 *Ibid.* p. 138.
92 *Ibid.* pp. 203, 204, 217. 93 *Ibid.* p. 228.
94 *Ibid.* p. 127. 95 *Daisy Miller Etc.*, p. 380.
96 *The Sacred Fount*, pp. 230–1. 97 *Ibid.* p. 230.
98 *Ibid.* p. 231. 99 *Ibid.* p. 121.
100 Joseph Conrad, *Notes on Life and Letters* (Dent, London, 1949), p. 17.
101 *The Sacred Fount*, p. 223. 102 *Ibid.* p. 213.
103 *Ibid.* p. 234. 104 *Ibid.* p. 71.
105 *Daisy Miller Etc*, p. 174. 106 *Ibid.* pp. 184–5.
107 *Ibid.* pp. 218–19. 108 *Ibid.* p. 217.
109 *Ibid.* pp. 193, 199.
110 From an unpublished letter, quoted by Leon Edel in his introduction to *The Sacred Fount* (Grove Press, New York, 1953), p. xxxi.
111 *The Author of Beltraffio Etc*, p. 92.

AFTERWORD

1 A. de Tocqueville, *Democracy in America* (Vintage Books, New York, 1959), vol. II, p. 82.
2 For the whole question of the relation between the individual and society as it is reflected and confronted in the American novel see Richard Chase, *The American Novel and Its Tradition* (Doubleday, New York, 1957) and A. N. Kaul, *The American Vision* (Yale University Press, 1963).
3 Thoreau, *Works*, vol. IX, p. 157.
4 Sherwood Anderson, *A Story Teller's Story*, p. 250.
5 J. D. Salinger, *Nine Stories* (Harborough, London, 1959), p. 150.
6 *Ibid.* p. 156.   7 *Ibid.* pp. 181, 186.
8 *Ibid.* p. 179.
9 Salinger, *The Catcher in the Rye* (Penguin, Harmondsworth, 1958), p. 124.
10 *Ibid.* p. 148.   11 *Ibid.* p. 176.
12 *Ibid.* p. 219.
13 Salinger, *Franny and Zooey* (Heinemann, London, 1962), p. 39.
14 *Ibid.* p. 137.   15 *Ibid.* p. 139.
16 *Ibid.* p. 139.   17 *Ibid.* p. 199.
18 *Ibid.* p. 198.   19 *The Catcher in the Rye*, p. 89.
20 *Franny and Zooey*, p. 200.   21 *Ibid.* p. 15.
22 *Ibid.* p. 191.
23 Salinger, 'Seymour: an Introduction', *New Yorker*, 6 June 1959.
24 *Ibid.*   25 *Ibid.*
26 *Ibid.*   27 *Ibid.*
28 Salinger, 'Raise High the Roof Beam, Carpenters', *New Yorker*, 19 Nov. 1955.
29 'Seymour: an Introduction.'
30 'Raise High the Roof Beam, Carpenters.'
31 *Ibid.*
32 Walker Percy, *The Moviegoer* (Popular Library, New York, 1962), p. 72.
33 Sherwood Anderson, *Horses and Men*, p. 277.
34 Sherwood Anderson, *A Story Teller's Story*, p. 231.
35 *The Moviegoer*, p. 22.
36 J. P. Sartre, *Literary Essays* (The Wisdom Library, New York, 1957), p. 36.
37 *The Moviegoer*, p. 95.   38 *Ibid.* p. 167.
39 *Ibid.* p. 202.   40 *Ibid.* p. 12.
41 *Ibid.* p. 94.   42 *Ibid.* p. 185.
43 *Ibid.* p. 61.   44 *Ibid.* p. 15.
45 *Franny and Zooey*, p. 136.   46 *The Moviegoer*, p. 15.
47 *Ibid.* p. 16.   48 *Ibid.* pp. 17–18.
49 *Ibid.* p. 68.   50 *Ibid.* p. 68.
51 *Ibid.* p. 79.   52 *Ibid.* p. 79.
53 *Ibid.* p. 51.   54 *Ibid.* p. 55.
55 *Ibid.* p. 77.   56 *Ibid.* p. 209.
57 *Ibid.* p. 208.   58 Thoreau, *Works*, vol. VIII, p. 83.
59 *A Story Teller's Story*, p. 154.   60 *The Moviegoer*, p. 213.

61 Emerson, *Works*, vol. II, p. 334.
62 F. Scott Fitzgerald, *The Great Gatsby* (Penguin Books), p. 8.
63 *Ibid.* p. 118.
64 *Ibid.* p. 188.
65 *The Crack Up*, by F. Scott Fitzgerald, ed. Edmund Wilson (New Directions, New York, 1956), p. 197.

INDEX

abstract concepts
  only have meaning if translated into
    sensory particulars (Hemingway),
    234
  suspicion of (Clemens), 151
Adams, Henry, 25, 36
adolescents, Anderson's adoption of
  their attitude to experience, 214–5,
  224
Alcott, Bronson, 10, 21
Aldrich, T. B., *Story of a Bad Boy*, 147
alienation, sense of, 343, 347, 349, 350,
  355, 356
American writers, characteristics of,
  10–15, 23, 336–8, 356–61
analysis
  suspected by the romantics, 4, 5, 9
  scorned by Carlyle, 6, 7
  never abandoned in European writ-
    ing, 10
  avoided by American writers, 10,
    358, 361; by Thoreau, 48, 59,
    Whitman, 66, Hemingway, 235,
    The Moviegoer, 354
  prelude to new synthesis, 359
Anderson, Quentin, on Henry James,
  296, 298
Anderson, Sherwood, 205–27; 12, 336,
  338, 349
  Transcendentalists and, 25, 337
  Clemens and, 126, 151
  Gertrude Stein and, 187, 188, 192,
    195, 202, 204
  Emerson and, 207
  Dial, 205; *Horses and Men*, 225;
    Poor White, 92, 217, 226; *A Story
    Teller's Story*, 185, 206, 217–19,
    223, 227; *Tar, a Midwest Child-
    hood*, 217, 224, 225; *Winesburg,
    Ohio*, 207–8, 213
animals, unselfconsciousness of, 32, 33
Arnold, Matthew, 153
art
  nourishes sympathy, 15, 334
  and nature, 23, 37, 77, 191, 345,
    357
  destroying itself (Clemens), 129
  in speculation, 310, 318, 323, 330

abnormality, if not insanity, 329; a
  sacred madness, 335
  must have organization, 357
  is inherently active, 358
Auerbach, Eric, *Mimesis*, 12

Baudelaire, C. P., 8, 10, 358
Bellow, Saul, 12, 356
  Adventures of Augie March, 187;
    Dangling Man, 1, 11
Blake, W., 2, 27, 249
Bridgman, Richard, 188
Brownson, Orestes, Transcendentalist,
  20, 22, 23

Camus, A., *L'Étranger*, 349–50
Carlyle, T., 9–10, 13, 48
  Sartor Resartus, 6–7, 9
Cash, W. J., *The Mind of the South*, 157
Cézanne, P., 195–6, 217
"charm", in description of landscapes,
  117–18
child
  angle of vision of, 7–8; in works of
    Emerson, 27, 30–5, Thoreau,
    51–2; Whitman, 84; Gertrude
    Stein, 189–91; Anderson, 205,
    James, 261, 283–4; *see also* eye,
    the naive wondering
  attitude towards, of Rousseau, 1–4,
    Wordsworth, 4–5, 21, Baudelaire,
    8, 358, American writers, 11–12,
    Alcott, 21
  as narrator, in works of Clemens,
    105, 124–5, 142, 143–54
  not made narrator by James, 261,
    280–1
child-man, (Baudelaire) 8, (Anderson)
  227
Christianity
  Alcott's test of the validity of, 21
  Emerson and, 23
cinema
  Gertrude Stein's method of writing
    compared with, 192–3
  in *The Moviegoer*, 351–2
Civil War in America, 147–8

381

Clemens, S. (Mark Twain), 104–26,
127–42, 143–54, 155–83; 10, 63, 358
Hemingway and, 187, 230, 257
Anderson and, 216
Autobiography, 127, 128, 143–4;
Huckleberry Finn, 57, 75–6,
123–6, 138, 142, 143, 148, 149, 151,
155–83, 207, 216, 255, 267, 337;
*Huckleberry Finn and Tom Sawyer
among the Indians*, 174, 175–6;
Innocents Abroad, 108–12, 131,
132; *Life on the Mississippi*, 119,
125, 160; *The Man that Corrupted
Hadleyburg*, 174; *Notebook*, 164;
Pudd'nhead Wilson, 174, 178;
Roughing it, 112–17, 132, 164;
Tom Sawyer, 122, 139–41, 155–6,
160; *Tom Sawyer Abroad*, 104–5,
155, 174, 176; *Tom Sawyer,
Detective*, 174, 178–81; *Tom
Sawyer's Conspiracy*, 174; *A
Tramp Abroad*, 117–18, 128, 136,
161–2
clothes, and civilization (Clemens),
133, 138, 158, 161
Coleridge, S. T., 27
Conrad, J., 239, 330, 334
Under Western Eyes, 333
conscience
the deformed, of corrupt civilization
(Clemens), 138, 140, 165, 166
the unexpended, of New England
(James), 263
the conscious (James), 291
consciousness
dilemma of man based on (Emerson),
32–3
filling of, with concrete detail
(Hemingway), 255
and experience (James), 297
and the artist (James), 330
Cowley, Malcolm, on Whitman, 64
culture, official, 105–6
Clemens and, 106, 129–30, 131–2,
133–4, 153, 175

death
acceptance of (Whitman), 77–9
hatred of, associated with idealization
of youth (Clemens), 144
democracy
Transcendentalist thought and, 22–3
Jacksonian, 98
clothes and (Clemens), 158–9

De Quincy, T., 57
description
is explanation (Gertrude Stein), 196,
235
is definition (Hemingway), 235
despair, vulnerability of Transcendentalists to, 24–5; of naive attitude to,
72–4, 272
detachment, art and, 40, 308
details
the whole preferred to (Rousseau), 3
movement to generalization from, by
Emerson, 28–9, 30, 35, 42, 63,
Transcendentalists, 92, 126, 236,
American writers, 336–8
reverence for, of Emerson, 37, 45,
Thoreau, 29, 87
enumeration of, by Whitman, 83,
Clemens, 115, 116, 124–5, 126,
Gertrude Stein, 204; at moments
of emotional heightening (Hemingway), 230–4, 237; to avoid
generalizing (Hemingway), 240–1
Imagists and, 92
solace of (Anderson), 92, 227, 338
over-insistence on, 178
selection of, 192; by Whitman, 70,
81–2, 356, Thoreau, 91; apparent
principle of no selection of
(Anderson), 208
mysticism of (Anderson), 213, 226
emotional mood and (Anderson),
224
material of art, 338
see also facts
Dryden, J., 126

education
Rousseau's scheme of, 1–4
Alcott's experimental, 21
Clemens on, 152
see also illiteracy
Eliot, George, 358
Eliot, T. S., 126, 224, 227
Emerson, 26–45; 21, 23, 97, 261, 336,
338–9, 355, 356
Carlyle and, 9–10, 13
Whitman and, 39, 64, 66, 70, 71, 79
Thoreau and, 46–7, 49, 50, 53, 61, 63
Clemens and, 125
Gertrude Stein and, 199, 201
Anderson and, 207, 214, 222, 223,
226
Hemingway and, 230

Hemingway, E. (*cont.*)
  Across the River and into the Trees,
    235, 237, 240–1; *Death in the After-
    noon*, 228–9, 234, 237, 244, 249,
    251; *A Farewell to Arms*, 232, 234,
    238; *For Whom the Bell Tolls*,
    232–4, 235; *The Green Hills of
    Africa*, 243, 244, 256; *In our Time*,
    250; *The Old Man and the Sea*,
    238–9; *The Snows of Kilimanjaro*,
    229, 237; *The Sun also Rises*, 239–
    40, 243, 246, 249
history
  discarded by Emerson, 9, 10, 14,
    Hemingway, 233–4, Gertrude
    Stein, 196
  Marxist view of, 245
  world of imagination and (James),
    315
Hooper, Johnson J., *Simon Suggs'
  Adventures*, 99–100
horror
  Hemingway's treatment of, 250–2
  combination with wonder, in Ameri-
    can literature, 253, 355, 356,
    361
  resulting from half-seeing by the
    innocent eye (James), 274–5
Howe, E. W., *Story of a Country Town*,
  153
Howells, William Dean, 104, 122, 127,
  136, 206
  Boy's Town, 147; *Indian Summer*,
    146–7, 148
human nature, missing from nature in
  Emerson, 38, 43, 334; Thoreau, 63
humorists
  before Clemens, 98–103
  Santayana on, 132

idealism, ascent from materialism to
  (Emerson), 28
illiteracy
  and freshness of vision, (Emerson)
    40, 44, (Thoreau) 57, (Whitman)
    66–7, 70, 84, (Clemens) 135–7
  attitude of Transcendentalists to,
    97–103
  See also vernacular
imagination
  the wondering (James), 311–12, 313
  and the physical world (James),
    314–18, 327
  the morbid (James), 328

Imagism
  pre-echoes of, in Thoreau, 62
  and Transcendentalism, 87–93
  resemblance of Anderson's mystic-
    ism of detail to, 213
Indian, the, in Thoreau, 166

James, Henry, 261–77, 278–308, 309–
  35; 339, 356, 359–60
  Gertrude Stein's imitation of, 189
  Sherwood Anderson on, 206
  Quentin Anderson on, 296, 298
  The Ambassadors, 147, 304; *The
    American*, 313; *The American
    Scene*, 263; *The Aspern Papers*,
    309, *Autobiographies*, 291; *The
    Awkward Age*, 298–303; *Daisy
    Miller*, 268, 271; *In the Cage*, 304,
    309, 310–19; *The Ivory Tower*,
    307; *Julia Bride*, 303; *The Lesson
    of the Master*, 261; *A London Life*,
    266, 267-8, 269–71, 272–5, 276–7,
    281; *The Marriages*, 275–6; *The
    Middle Years*, 335; *The Patagonia*,
    331–3; *The Princess Casamas-
    sima*, 304–5; *The Reverberator*,
    265, 271; *Roderick Hudson*, 306;
    The Sacred Fount, 276, 311,
    319–31; *The Turn of the Screw*,
    309, 316; *What Maisie Knew*,
    259, 278–98
James, William, 8, 33, 188
Jonson, Ben, 220–1
Joyce, James, 209, 231
judgement
  wonder preferred to, by romantics,
    1, 5, by narrator in *Dangling Man*,
    11, in Hemingway, 241
  education to aim at developing
    (Rousseau), 2, 3
  dignity of (James), 33, 333
Jung, C. G., 148

Keats, J., 63
knowledge
  from seeing things as though for the
    first time, 4, 53, 190, 192
  different sorts of, (Transcendent-
    alists) 21–2; (Thoreau) 48; (Huck
    Finn and Tom Sawyer) 171;
    (James) 331
  disadvantages of, (Thoreau) 47;
    (Clemens) 118, 119–21
  Maisie's, 287, 288, 294